# Justice and Compassion
in Biblical Law

# Justice and Compassion in Biblical Law

Richard H. Hiers

continuum
NEW YORK • LONDON

2009

The Continuum International Publishing Group Inc
80 Maiden Lane, New York, NY 10038

The Continuum International Publishing Group Ltd
The Tower Building, 11 York Road, London SE1 7NX

www.continuumbooks.com

Copyright © 2009 by Richard H. Hiers

All rights reserved. No part of this book may be reproduced, stored in a retrieval system, or transmitted, in any form or by any means, electronic, mechanical, photocopying, recording, or otherwise, without the written permission of the publishers.

Scripture quotations marked 'RSV' are from the Revised Standard Version of the Bible, copyright © 1946, 1952, and 1971 by the National Council of the Churches of Christ in the USA.

Unless otherwise noted, the Scripture quotations contained herein are from the New Revised Standard Version Bible, copyright © 1989 by the Division of Christian Education of the National Council of Churches of Christ in the U.S.A. Used by permission. All rights reserved.

**Library of Congress Cataloging-in-Publication Data**
A catalog record for this book is available from the Library of Congress

ISBN 9780567297891 (hardcover)
ISBN 9780567269096 (paperback)

Typeset by Newgen Imaging Systems Pvt Ltd, Chennai, India
Printed in the United States of America

And what does the Lord require of you
but to do justice,
and to love kindness
and to walk humbly with your God?

                                                  Micah 6.8

# Contents

| | |
|---|---|
| Acknowledgments | ix |
| Abbreviations | x |
| Introduction | 1 |

**Part I  Civil Law: Contracts, Torts, Inheritance, and Bequests**  7
Chapter 1  *Biblical Contract Law and Biblical Tort Law*  9
A. Biblical Contract Laws  10
B. Biblical Tort Laws and Remedies  14
C. Biblical Contract and Tort Law, and Modern Counterparts  21

Chapter 2  *Transfer of Property by Inheritance and Bequest*  25
A. Property Subject to Transfer by Inheritance or Bequest  27
B. Inheritance: Descent of Property through Intestate Succession  28
C. Wills or Bequests and Inter-vivos Gifts  51
D. Conclusions  57

**Part II  Criminal Law**  61
Chapter 3  *Biblical Trial Scenes*  63
A. Genesis 38:24-26: Tamar's Evidence  64
B. 2 Samuel 12:1-15: David as Judge and Nathan's Parable  65
C. 2 Samuel 14:1-11: A Hypothetical Case Prompts Mitigation and Alternative Sentencing  66
D. 1 Kings 3:16-28: A Maternity Suit  67
E. 1 Kings 21:1-16: A Case of Malicious Prosecution  67
F. Jeremiah 26:7-24: Defendant Testimony and Argument from Precedent  68
G. Leviticus 24:10-23: A Case of Blasphemy  69
H. Numbers 15:32-36: A Case of Possible Sabbath Violation  70
I. Susanna vv. 28-62: Cross Examination Catches the Culprits in the Courtroom  70

| | |
|---|---|
| Chapter 4 *Impartial Judgment and Equal Protection of the Laws* | 73 |
| A. Impartial Judgment | 73 |
| B. Equal Protection: Protected Classes | 75 |
| | |
| Chapter 5 *Capital Offenses* | 80 |
| A. Against Capital Punishment | 82 |
| B. Capital Offenses and Rationales for Executing Offenders | 86 |
| | |
| Chapter 6 *Due Process Protections* | 127 |
| A. Places or Cities of Refuge: Interim Protection for Offenders Awaiting Trial | 129 |
| B. "Diligent Inquiry": Investigation, Hearings, Evidence, and Cross Examination | 134 |
| C. Witnesses | 139 |
| D. The Punishment Phase: Sentencing Guidelines | 144 |
| | |
| Chapter 7 *Criminal Law in the Bible and Contemporary Application* | 153 |
| A. Modern Interpretation of Biblical Texts | 154 |
| B. The Basic Value of Human Life | 157 |
| C. The Critical Importance of Not Executing Innocent Persons | 159 |
| | |
| **Part III  Social Legislation** | 165 |
| Chapter 8 *Biblical Social Welfare Legislation* | 173 |
| A. Protections against Injustice and Mistreatment | 175 |
| B. Laws Calling for Affirmative Actions by Private Persons | 185 |
| | |
| Chapter 9 *Biblical Social Welfare Laws and Modern Social Welfare Policy* | 212 |
| | |
| Concluding Observations | 219 |
| | |
| Index of Biblical Quotations and Citations | 223 |
| Index of Names | 231 |
| Index of Subjects | 236 |

# Acknowledgments

I wish to thank the editors of the *Journal of Law and Religion, University of Detroit-Mercy Law Review,* and *Convergences* for permission to draw on articles previously published in these journals.[1] And I am grateful to the editors and publishers of *The New Oxford Annotated Bible with the Apocrypha,* Revised Standard Version,[2] and *The New Oxford Annotated Bible,* New Revised Standard Version with the Apocrypha,[3] for permission to quote from these texts. I also wish to express my gratitude to the University of Florida and the University of Oregon for providing me the use of comfortable and even elegant facilities while I was engaged in the preparation of this book.

Many former teachers, colleagues and students in the fields of biblical studies, social ethics, and law have contributed to my understanding of and reflections on the matters considered here. In particular, Melissa Aubin, Martin J. Buss, Marie A. Failinger, Duncan Ferguson, Douglas Sturm, Howard J. Vogel, and Raymond Westbrook. Some of these and others are named as authors in footnotes. I thank them all, named and un-named alike, for their guidance and encouragement.

Richard H. Hiers

---

[1] Those represented in the present book include: "Transfer of Property by Inheritance and Bequest in Biblical Law and Tradition," 10 *Journal of Law and Religion* 121 (1993–94) (hereafter *J. of L. Relig.*); "Biblical Social Welfare Legislation," 17 *J. of L. and Relig.* 49 (2002); and "The Death Penalty and Due Process in Biblical Law," 81 *University of Detroit Mercy Law Review* 781 (2004). "Justice and Compassion in Biblical Law," 1 *Convergence: Compassion: The Quest for a More Just and Loving World* (Eckerd College, 2006), pp. 75–95.

[2] Revised Standard Version of the Bible, copyright 1952 [2nd edn., 1971] by the Division of Christian Education of the National Council of the Churches of Christ in the United States of America. Citations here are to the edition, Herbert G. May and Bruce M. Metzger, ed., New York: Oxford University Press (1977), hereafter cited as *NOAB-RSV.* Quotations from the Revised Standard Version are indicated by the initials "RSV" following the corresponding biblical citations.

[3] New Revised Standard Version of the Bible, copyright 1989, Division of Christian Education of the National Council of the Churches of Christ in the United States of America. Citations here are to the 3rd edn., Michael D. Coogan, ed., New York: Oxford University Press (2001), hereafter cited as *NOAB-NRSV.* Unless otherwise indicated, quotations are from the New Revised Standard Version (NRSV).

# Abbreviations

| | |
|---|---|
| ABD | Anchor Bible Dictionary |
| ANE | James B. Pritchard, *The Ancient Near East* (Princeton Univ. Press, 1969) |
| ANE | Ancient Near East(ern) |
| ANET | James B. Pritchard, ed. *Ancient Near Eastern Texts* (Princeton Univ. Press, 1950) |
| BASOR | Bulletin of the American Schools of Oriental Research |
| BCE | Before Common Era |
| CC | Covenant Code |
| CE | Common Era |
| CH | Code of Hammurabi |
| D | Deuteronomic Code |
| DH | Deuteronomic Historian |
| H | Holiness Code |
| HBD | *Harper's Bible Dictionary* (Harper & Row, 1985) |
| IDB | *Interpreter's Dictionary of the Bible* (Abingdon, 1962) |
| JAAR | Journal of the American Academy of Religion |
| JANES | Journal of Ancient Near Eastern Studies |
| JBL | Journal of Biblical Literature |
| J. Crim.L. & Criminology | Journal of Criminal Law and Criminology |
| J. L. & Pol'y | Journal of Law and Policy |
| J. of L. & Relig. | Journal of Law and Religion |
| JNES | Journal of Near Eastern Studies |
| JSCE | Journal of the Society of Christian Ethics |
| JSOT | Journal for the Study of the Old Testament |
| NEB | *New English Bible with the Apocrypha* (Oxford Univ. Press, 1976) |
| NOAB-RSV | *The New Oxford Annotated Bible with the Apocrypha, Revised Standard Version* (Oxford Univ. Press, 1977, 1997) |

| | |
|---|---|
| *NOAB-NRSV* | *The New Oxford Annotated Bible, New Revised Standard Version with the Apocrypha* 3rd edn. (Oxford Univ. Press, 2001) |
| *N. Il. U. L. Rev.* | *Northern Illinois University Law Review* |
| NRSV | New Revised Standard Version |
| NT | New Testament |
| *NWDB* | *The New Westminster Dictionary of the Bible* (Westminster Press, 1976) |
| P | Priestly tradition |
| PC | Priestly Code |
| RD | Ritual Decalogue |
| RDC | Revised Deuteronomic Code |
| RSV | Revised Standard Version |
| SBL | Society of Biblical Literature |
| *U. Mich. L. Quad. Notes* | *University of Michigan Law Quadrangle Notes* |
| *VT* | *Vetus Testamentum* |

# Introduction

The Bible has long been a major force in the development of Western culture.[1] Yet few modern legal or biblical scholars have given more than passing attention to biblical law. In part, this lack of attention may result from the fact that much of biblical law deals with animal sacrifices, a subject commonly regarded as distasteful, misguided, irrelevant, and outmoded. Such scholars may assume that the rest of biblical law offers little worthy of their interest, either.

Proponents of Christian ethics and social ethics usually seem to be unaware of the substance of biblical law, preferring instead—if drawing on biblical insights at all—to consider only "the prophets" or the "teachings of Jesus," and possibly other New Testament sources. Modern Jewish ethicists generally view biblical law through somewhat thick Talmudic lenses and subsequent emerging tradition. Biblical laws relating to justice and compassion are rarely noticed even by Christian and Jewish interpreters and expositors. This book does not argue that Christian ethics should abandon these other biblical sources, or that Jewish ethics should ignore or bypass later interpretive authorities. Nevertheless those "doing" both Christian and Jewish ethics might well benefit from greater familiarity with the norms or standards of justice and compassion found in biblical laws relating to the interactions of persons in society. That biblical laws often express or call for compassion may be particularly surprising and significant. Likewise, secular humanists may be startled to discover how often the concerns and values implicit in biblical laws are congruent with their own convictions and social policy agendas.

This book undertakes to examine biblical laws in order to describe and consider their substance along with the concerns and values implicit in them. It is not proposed that biblical laws, without more, can be applied

---

[1] This book does not attempt to trace the influence of the Bible in the development of Anglo-American law, but does occasionally cite sources relevant to that topic.

directly to contemporary interpersonal and societal issues. It is suggested, however, that biblical laws may sometimes provide a useful frame of reference for evaluating contemporary values and practices. Biblical norms have long influenced Western civilization, and may be especially important as providing an alternative model to contemporary postmodernism's moral relativism and anomie.

This study assumes that biblical tradition—including biblical laws—developed or evolved over many centuries. The relative sequence and dating of the biblical "sources" or components considered here for the most part follows the general consensus of current biblical scholarship. Thus, the so-called Ritual Decalogue (Exod. 34.17-28) is regarded as the earliest segment of biblical law, dating possibly from the 13th century BCE. The Covenant Code (Exod. chapters 20–23) is thought to have been set down or "codified" a century or so later. The Deuteronomic Code, (here identified as Deuteronomy chapters 5 and 20–25), followed, perhaps as early as 1000 BCE. The Holiness Code (Leviticus chapters 17– or 18–26) is dated around the middle of the 7th century BCE, and was supplemented or succeeded a few decades later by what is designated here the Revised Deuteronomic Code (Deuteronomy chapters 12–19, and 26). Priestly or P tradition generally, including the so-called Priestly Code, is thought to have been formulated in the 6th or 5th centuries BCE. The Priestly Code is the term used to describe the large body of laws found in Exodus, Leviticus, and Numbers that are not attributable to earlier codes.[2]

According to biblical tradition, all laws set out in the books of Exodus, Leviticus, Numbers, and Deuteronomy were given to, and for, the people of Israel. There, "Israel" is generally understood broadly, as referring not only to the descendants of Jacob and the subsequent tribal confederation prior to the establishment of the monarchy, *c.* 1000 BCE, but also to both the Northern and Southern Kingdoms (Israel and Judah, respectively) during the divided monarchy, as well as to the Jewish people during and after the time of the Exile, and down to the close of the biblical period in the 2nd or 1st century BCE. As presented in the Bible itself, these laws were understood to have been intended for the instruction or direction of the people of Israel, not as laws for other peoples either during the biblical period or in later times. Nevertheless, these

---

[2] For more detailed discussion of biblical literature, history, and religion, see the author's book, *Trinity Guide to the Bible with the Apocrypha* (Trinity Press Int'l, 2001).

laws may contain significant insights into the human condition, understood in terms of the kinds of relationships among persons that are mutually beneficial, and that therefore constitute the community of God's people intended by its ultimate Lawgiver.

This book examines biblical law from the perspectives of both modern biblical scholarship and current jurisprudential analysis. Modern legal concepts and terminology often serve conveniently to describe much of the character and substance of biblical law.

Part I examines a number of biblical laws that could be characterized as "civil laws." For instance, as will be seen in Chapter One, several laws and narrative traditions concern or represent what we might now understand as legal contracts. Likewise, many of the laws found in Exodus chapters 21–22, would be now classified as "tort" laws. Moreover, within these chapters, most of these laws, which are often regarded as a random assortment of unrelated laws, turn out to have been organized rather carefully, almost as if under modern tort law rubrics.

Chapter Two identifies the significant distinction between "inheritance" and "bequest," a distinction familiar in modern law, but not generally used by biblical commentators. This distinction enables greater precision in describing the ways in which biblical tradition provided for transferring property from one person to another, subsequent to, or in anticipation of the transferor's death.

Part II considers what in modern times would be classified as "criminal laws." Chapter Three describes a series of trial scenes that are part of biblical tradition—though often not recognized as such. These scenes illustrate several features of biblical law that are analyzed in subsequent chapters.

Chapter Four focuses on biblical laws and traditions calling for impartial judgment. The term "equal protection of the laws" is not found in the Bible; nevertheless it serves as a useful category for describing a considerable number of biblical legal provisions that are examined in this same chapter. Several classes of protected persons are also identified in these texts.

Chapter Five presents a detailed account of biblical laws relating to capital offenses, that is, laws, which if violated, called for applying the death penalty. Here we see some interesting parallels to modern criminal law. Translators have long, and correctly, used the term "manslaughter" to describe biblical laws in regard to negligent or unintentional homicide. Other laws can be seen as instances of culpable, reckless, or intentional homicide. Most of the capital offenses involve, either explicitly or implicitly, the perpetrator's intent to commit the prohibited act. Intent is a basic element in nearly all types of modern criminal law.

Chapter Six identifies and describes a variety of biblical laws which clearly served to provide what now would be designated as "due process" protections for the accused. As will be seen, most of these provisions evidently were intended to reduce, if not eliminate, the possibility that innocent persons might be punished. These laws established procedures calculated to assure that only those who had actually committed capital crimes were to be executed, and that punishments should not exceed the seriousness of offenses committed. Chapter Seven then suggests some comparisons between biblical and modern criminal law.

Part III examines what, in modern law school curricula, would be identified as "social legislation" or "social welfare legislation." These terms may be of relatively recent origin, but rather accurately characterize the substance of such laws. Chapters Eight and Nine analyze and classify a wide range of biblical laws that may be aptly so characterized. The concluding chapter highlights certain recurrent themes and conclusions.

In this book, the principal names used to designate the deity are "God" and "YHWH." Typically, "God" translates the Hebrew name, *Elohim*, while YHWH represents a transliteration of the tetragrammaton, the Hebrew letters often found in other biblical texts as the divine name. In traditional Judaism, this name is not to be spoken. English translations usually render it as "the Lord."

One final introductory comment. Justice and compassion are sometimes regarded as antithetical or opposites. Justice may be seen as rigid, imposing certain standards or punishments without mercy or care for the well-being of those affected; and compassion can be seen as soft-hearted, if not soft-headed, sentimental, without regard for fairness or equity. In this book it is suggested that biblical concepts of justice and compassion often may be seen as different sides of the same coin. That is, a law concerned with justice, fairness, or equity may also take account of the special needs or interests of persons affected by the situation or by application of the law. For instance, as will be seen, biblical tort laws provide that wrong-doers compensate persons they have injured unintentionally. The compensation may be not only fair or just, but also compassionate, in that those injured are to be "made whole," while those who have done the injury are then free to go about their affairs without being punished or stigmatized as bad persons. Arrangements providing for the transfer of property from deceased husbands to surviving wives, sons, or daughters protect both the interest of the deceased in caring for survivors, and the interests of beneficiaries in continuing support. Criminal justice laws providing due process for the accused show compassion for those who, though innocent, might otherwise be punished for offenses committed by others, while at the same time, tend to increase the likelihood that the real perpetrators would be brought to justice. The community thereby would be spared the guilt of having shed innocent blood. Various social welfare laws clearly served to meet basic needs of persons in the community who, because they were unable to provide themselves with life's necessities, otherwise would experience serious hardship. These laws also assured that those who could afford to contribute did so fairly, and without undue hardship to themselves. All these laws functioned, and likely were intended to promote what was understood to be the well-being of the community of God's people.

Readers may well conclude that some of these arrangements were far from perfect. Yet nearly all represent some balance between justice and compassion. It will be suggested that occasionally biblical provisions may even compare favorably with certain contemporary laws and judicial practices.

# Part I

# Civil Law: Contracts, Torts, Inheritance, and Bequests

*Once when Jacob was cooking a stew, Esau came in from the field, and he was famished. Esau said to Jacob, "Let me eat some of that red stuff, for I am famished." . . . Jacob said, "First sell me your birthright." Esau said, "I am about to die; of what use is a birthright to me?" Jacob said to him, "Swear to me first." So he swore to him, and sold his birthright to Jacob.*

*Genesis 25:29-34*

*When men quarrel and one strikes the other with a stone or with his fist and the man does not die but keeps his bed, then if the man rises again and walks abroad with his staff, he that struck him shall be clear; only he shall pay for the loss of his time, and shall have him thoroughly healed.*

*Exodus 21:18-19 (RSV)*

*At the time when you end the days of your life, in the hour of death, distribute your inheritance.*

*Sirach 33:24*

Modern Western jurisprudence distinguishes between criminal and civil law. The former category relates to actions or activities which are deemed harmful to the community (or as in states like California) to "the people" generally. Criminal offenses are usually punishable by fine, imprisonment, or—if a capital offense—by execution under the authority of public officials.[1] Major civil law categories include contracts and torts.

---

[1] As to biblical criminal law, see Part II of this book.

Laws regarding transfer of property also may be classed as civil law. Chapter One examines biblical laws and narratives that represent what in modern jurisprudence, would be classified as contract laws and then turns to biblical laws governing what now would be designated as torts. Chapter Two then turns to biblical texts relating to the transfer of property by inheritance, and by making wills or bequests.

# Chapter 1

# Biblical Contract Law and Biblical Tort Law

*"But tell me, what wages am I to pay you—a drachma a day, and expenses for yourself as for my son? And besides, I will add to your wages if you both return safe and sound." So they agreed to these terms.*

*Tobit 5:14-15 (RSV)*

*When a man causes a field or vineyard to be grazed over, or lets his beast loose and it feeds in another man's field, he shall make restitution from the best in his own field and in his own vineyard.*

*Exodus 22:5 (RSV)*

Contract law concerns arrangements between persons or "parties" who seek to gain something from each other through an exchange of goods, services, or other valuables.[1] A basic feature of modern contract law is "offer" and "acceptance." To be binding, there must be a "meeting of the minds," that is, the parties must agree to the contract's terms. When one party to such an agreement fails to perform what she has agreed to do, the other party typically seeks monetary damages or some other remedy. Tort offenses, on the other hand, are those that harm individual persons or their property, whether intentionally, recklessly, or as the result of simple negligence.[2] Such harm then may be remedied by restitution or payment of damages to the persons injured or to those whose property has been damaged.

---

[1] See generally Amy Hilsman Kastely et al., *Contracting Law,* 2nd edn. (Carolina Academic Press, 2000); and the classic "hornbook," Arthur Linton Corbin, *Corbin on Contracts,* one vol. edn. (West Pub. Co., 1952), and multi-volume revised editions.

[2] See generally, W. Page Keeton, gen. ed., *Prosser and Keeton on the Law of Torts* (West Pub. Co., 1984).

## A. Biblical Contract Laws

Only a few biblical laws relate directly to contracts. All of these laws evidently were intended to protect the interests of persons likely to be affected adversely by contractual agreements. In some instances, affected persons would include parties to the agreements who were in relatively weak bargaining positions.[3] In others, the parties affected would be third persons whose interests the contracting parties might not otherwise care about.

The first 11 verses of Exodus chapter 21 relate to purchase or sales contracts. Exodus 21:1-6 sets out "the ordinances" that were to govern when someone bought a Hebrew slave. These specify that such slaves were to be freed after 6 years of service, and define the circumstances under which a slave's wife and children might, themselves, either be or become slaves, or else be freed.[4] Chapter 21:7-11 sets out those conditions or requirements that were to go into effect when a man sold his daughter as a slave. The purchaser must treat her well, and if he does not do so, she is to go free.[5]

One law that clearly has to do with debtor–creditor relations of an implicitly contractual nature emphasizes God's compassion as its basis. This is Exodus 22:25-27, which concludes:

> If ever you take your neighbor's garment in pledge, you shall restore it to him before the sun goes down; for that is his only covering, it is his mantle for his body; in what else shall he sleep? And if he cries to me, I will hear, for I am compassionate. (RSV)

The version of this law set out at Deuteronomy 24:10-13, adds a further restriction on a lender's conduct: "[Y]ou shall not go into his house to fetch his pledge" (RSV). Similarly, creditors were not to take in pledge (or as collateral) equipment that served as the basis for a debtor's livelihood:

---

[3] Modern law also generally disapproves as "unconscionable" and may not enforce "adhesion contracts," that is, contracts drafted by relatively powerful parties in circumstances that leave those in relatively weak bargaining position little choice but to "agree" to adverse terms. See Kastely et al., pp. 632–33; and Arthur Linton Corbin, *Corbin on Contracts*, multi-volume edition, revised edn., vol. 1, edited by Joseph M. Perillo (West Pub. Co., 1993), pp. 13–15.

[4] See Chapter Eight, Section B.3.b.i.

[5] See Chapter Eight, Section B.3.b.ii.

No one shall take a mill or an upper millstone in pledge, for that would be taking a life in pledge. (Deut. 24:6)

Both justice and compassion are implicit in Leviticus 19:13 and Deuteronomy 24:14-15, which require employers to pay hired servants or workers the same day they earn it.[6] This requirement may be illustrated in Jesus' Parable of the Laborers in the Vineyard (Mt. 20:1-16). In the parable, the owner of the field has his foreman pay all laborers their wages on the evening of the same day they worked (Mt. 20:8).

Compassion for needy borrowers clearly comes to expression in the law barring lenders from exacting interest from "any of my people with you who is poor" (Exod. 22:25 RSV). Another law grounded on compassion bars lending money at interest, or making a profit from selling food to a "brother [who] becomes poor, and cannot maintain himself" (Lev. 25:35-37 RSV).

Several biblical narratives describe contractual agreements. In each case, there is some "consideration," that is, something of value that one party proposes to exchange for the other's.[7] Sometimes complications arise because one party or the other engages in deceptive practices or fraud. Also one party or the other may fail to carry out contractual terms. Or the parties may have failed to agree as to specific terms. Some examples of such situations are considered in the following paragraphs.[8]

Jacob figures prominently in three of these accounts. The first is the story in Genesis 25:29-34, where Esau, faint with hunger, asks Jacob for some of the stew ("pottage") he had been boiling. Not one to miss a good business opportunity, Jacob offers to let Esau have some, but only if Esau first sells him his birthright.[9] Here the "consideration" on one side is the stew or porridge; on the other, it is the birthright. Esau agrees with an oral acceptance ("So he swore to him, and sold his birthright to Jacob."). The narrator, whose sympathies obviously are with Jacob,[10] was not troubled by the fact that Jacob obtained Esau's agreement under

---

[6] See generally, Paul Rasor, "Biblical Roots of Modern Consumer Credit Law," 10 *J. of L. & Relig.* 157 (1993–94); and Louis E. Newman, "Covenants and Contract: A Framework for the Analysis of Jewish Ethics," 9 *J. of L. & Relig.* 89 (1991).
[7] See Kastely et al., *Contract Law*, pp. 263–370; and Corbin, *Corbin on Contracts*, pp. 160–336.
[8] See also 1 Kgs 5:1-11; 2 Chron. 2:3-16; and 1 Kgs 9:10-14, describing contractual agreements between Solomon and Hiram (or Huram), King of Tyre.
[9] As to the meaning of "birthright" see Chapter Two, Section B.4.
[10] See the biblical narrator's editorial comment: "Thus Esau despised his birthright" (Gen. 25:34).

conditions that might now be considered to have involved duress.[11] On two occasions, Jacob negotiated employment contracts with his kinsman, Laban (Gen. 29:15-20; 30:25-34). Each time, however, Laban engaged in deceptive or fraudulent practices, to his own advantage (Gen. 29:21-27; 30:25-36). Apparently in those times, there was no provision for voiding contracts on the basis of fraud or misrepresentation.[12]

Another famous biblical scene also involved an oral contract. This is the story in Numbers chapters 22–24 about Balak, king of Moab, hiring Balaam, a professional prophet or execrator, to come and curse the menacing horde of Israelites who seemed about to encroach on the land of Moab.[13] Exact terms are not specified, but it is clear that Balak offered to pay Balaam a substantial fee or "honorarium" if he would undertake this task: "Let nothing hinder you from coming to me; for I will surely do you great honor, . . . and come curse this people for me" (Num. 22:17 RSV). After Balaam repeatedly blesses Israel instead of cursing them, the exasperated Balak charges Balaam, in effect, with breach of contract and refuses to pay the promised "honor" or, "honorarium" (Num. 24:10-11). Balaam replies that he never had agreed to curse Israel in the first place, so there could be no contract to breach.[14] There had been no "meeting of the minds."

Two contractual arrangements are mentioned in the Apocryphal Book of Tobit. The first of these has to do with Tobit's undertaking to hire a man to accompany his son Tobias on a journey (Tob. 5:3-15). In this instance, the parties agree to fairly specific terms. Here Tobit addresses a man named Azarias:[15]

> "But tell me, what wages am I to pay you—a drachma a day, and expenses for yourself as for my son? And besides, I will add to your wages if you both return safe and sound." So they agreed to these terms. (Tob. 5:14-15 RSV)

Later in the story, when Tobias spends the night with Raguel, another relative, it is arranged that Tobias will marry Raguel's daughter, Sarah.

---

[11] See Kastely et al. *Contract Law*, p. 552; Corbin, *Corbin on Contracts*, p. 320.
[12] See Kastely et al., *Contract Law*, pp. 571–608; Corbin, *Corbin on Contracts*, pp. 10–11, 320.
[13] For fuller discussion of this remarkable story, see the author's *Trinity Guide to the Bible*, pp. 50–51, and 293.
[14] See Num. 24:12-13: "And Balaam said to Balak, 'Did I not tell your messengers whom you sent to me, "If Balak should give me his house full of silver and gold, I would not be able to go beyond the word of YHWH, to do either good or bad of my own will; what YHWH says, that is what I will say"?'"
[15] As the story is told, Azarias is actually the angel, Raphael, in disguise.

This story has many points of interest, but the one noted here is that as part of the wedding formalities, Raguel proceeds to write a contract, to which both he and his wife, Edna, set their seals (Tob. 7:12-14 RSV). Whether this contract related directly to the wedding, or to possible dowry, or perhaps to arrangements for inheritance[16] is not indicated. It is noteworthy that both Raguel and Edna "set their seals" to the contract, indicating that not only the father, but also the mother of the bride had legal status to enter into such contractual agreements.[17] Seals are still sometimes, though rarely, applied to contracts in modern times.[18]

At least one contract is described in the New Testament. This is in Jesus' "Parable of the Laborers in the Vineyard" (Mt. 20:1-16). The parable begins:

> For the kingdom of heaven is like a landowner who went out early in the morning to hire laborers for his vineyard. After agreeing with the laborers for a denarius, he sent them into his vineyard. (Mt. 20:1-2)

As the day goes on, the owner hires more workers, but at the end of the day, pays each—including those who had worked only the last hour—a full denarius. The workers who had "borne the burden of the day and the scorching heat" complain that the others received the same pay. The owner then points out that they had agreed to these terms, and so have no grounds to complain: "Friends, I am doing you no wrong; did you not agree with me for a denarius?" (Mt. 20:13).

From these several accounts it seems likely that contractual arrangements were commonplace in the biblical period, even though biblical commentators rarely refer to these arrangements as instances of contract law.

Some of the offenses described in biblical tradition could be characterized in modern legal terms either as breach of contract violations or as "torts." Modern legal scholars, noting occasional overlap between contract and tort law, sometimes refer, humorously, to "con-torts."[19] Exodus

---

[16] See Tobit 14:12-13.
[17] See also 1 Samuel 25:14-35, describing Abigail's negotiating an agreement with David to spare the male members of her household. Here there was no formal contract, but there was a "meeting of the minds," and at the end, David granted Abigail's "petition" (1 Sam. 25:35).
[18] See Corbin, *Corbin on Contracts*, pp. 337–44.
[19] For careful discussion of the complex relation between these two categories of modern civil law, see W. Page Keeton, ed., *Prosser and Keeton on the Law of Torts* (West Pub. Co., 1984), pp. 655–76.

22:7-11 includes various instances of "breach of trust" or violation of a bailee's responsibility to care adequately for property entrusted to him by another. Some of these laws also refer to activities that in modern law would be called embezzlement or conversion. Although these laws involve elements of contract, for instance, implicit prior agreements of one kind and another, in this chapter, these laws are considered under the rubric of tort law.

## B. Biblical Tort Laws and Remedies

Biblical texts do not use the term "tort," nor do most biblical commentators.[20] Nevertheless, the term may aptly describe the substance of several biblical laws. The term "tort" probably derives from the French word, *tort*, meaning "wrong." In law, the term refers to injury to persons or damage to property. Remedies usually are in the form of restitution of that which has been taken, or compensation paid to the injured party.[21]

In Anglo American statutory and common law, torts are classified as either negligent or intentional. Intentional torts (and those resulting from reckless endangerment to others) are considered more serious than harms resulting from mere negligence.[22] Intentional tort-feasors (and those found to have committed acts of reckless endangerment) sometimes are subjected to substantial damages, typically in the form of multiple or "punitive" or "exemplary" damages, payable to the victim or, if the victim is deceased, to the victim's estate.[23] The implicit rationale for punitive damages is to discourage those who might otherwise engage in similar conduct in the future from doing so, lest others in the community be harmed. Punitive damages are sometimes considered "quasi-criminal" in that they combine both compensation for the victim and punishment for the offending tort-feasor. Modern tort law also distinguishes between tortuous conduct harmful to persons, and conduct that damages property.

---

[20] Bible dictionaries typically do not list or describe "tort" laws. Commentators sometimes refer to civil laws. See Dale Patrick, *Old Testament Law* (John Knox Press, 1985), pp. 76 and 79, identifying instances of "civil tort"; and Christopher J. H. Wright, *Old Testament Ethics for the People of God* (InterVarsity Press, 2004), pp. 283–94.

[21] See *Black's Law Dictionary*, 8th edn. (St. Paul: West Pub. Co., 2004), p. 1526, defining "tort" as "A civil wrong, other than breach of contract, for which a remedy may be obtained, usually in the form of damages." For fuller discussion, see Keeton, ed., *Prosser and Keeton*, pp. 1–7.

[22] See Keeton, ed., *Prosser and Keeton*, pp. 33–107.

[23] See *id.*, pp. 7–15.

One of the earliest biblical law codes was the Covenant Code, found in Exodus 20:1–23:33. This collection of laws contains an extended listing of criminal acts and penalties along with civil offenses and remedies (Exod. 21:12–22:27). Commentators often describe these laws as a hodgepodge, or at best as an only loosely organized assortment of miscellaneous provisions.[24] However, when modern jurisprudential concepts are applied, those laws found in Exodus 21:12 through 22:15 turn out to be clearly organized along lines that closely correspond to such concepts.

The laws set out in Exodus 21:12-32 all relate to injuries to persons, while those found in Exodus 21:33–22:15 concern injuries or damages to property. These laws can be seen to have been organized as follows:

1. Criminal law: offenses against persons. Exodus 21:12-17.
2. Civil law: tort offenses. Exodus 21:18–22:15.
   a. Injuries to persons. Exodus 21:18-32.
      i. Intentional infliction of injuries. Exodus 21:18-21, 26-27.
      ii. Negligent and reckless infliction of harm. Exodus 21:22, 28-32.
   b. Injuries to animals belonging to others through negligent or reckless conduct. Exodus 21:33-36.
      i. Leaving an open pit. Exodus 21:33-34.
      ii. One man's ox fatally injures another's. Exodus 21:35-36.
   c. Intentional and negligent conduct affecting property. Exodus 22:1-15.
      i. Theft of cattle (farm animals). Exodus 22:1, 4.[25]
      ii. Allowing animals to graze over neighbors' fields or crops. Exodus 22:5.
      iii. Allowing fire to spread and damage neighbors' crops. Exodus 22:6.
      iv. Failing to care for property in trust or bailment. Exodus 22:7-13.
      v. Property damaged or lost while borrowed. Exodus 22:14-15.

---

[24] See, for example, *The New Interpreters' Bible*, vol. I (Nashville: Abingdon Press, 1994), p. 860, commenting on the Covenant Code (Exod. 20:24–23:19): "It is a miscellaneous collection.... It is not possible to identify a coherent structure, pattern, or order for the material." Nevertheless, the article goes on to identify several categories of laws, though without mentioning either civil law or tort law. *The New Interpreters' Bible*, pp. 863–66.

[25] Exodus 22:2-3 concerns liability, if any, for killing someone who "broke in" to steal, possibly to steal cattle. These verses do not quite fit the context, and may have been added after the tort laws in Exodus 21:18–22:15 had already been in place. See below, note 40.

It is clear that these laws were not put down in random order, but on the basis of organizing principles that, to some extent, correspond to modern legal categories.[26]

The first set, Exodus 21:12-32, begins with a series of criminal laws, all but one[27] involving capital offenses.[28] These include intentional homicide (Exod. 21:12, 14), fatally striking one's father or mother (Exod. 21:15); kidnapping (Exod. 21:16); and cursing either parent (Exod. 21:17). The following verses then set out a number of tort laws, interspersed with occasional, somewhat related, criminal provisions.

Exodus 21:18-19 provides that if two men fight and one seriously injures the other who, afterwards survives, the man who caused the injury "shall pay for the loss of [the victim's] time, and shall have him thoroughly healed" (RSV).[29] These provisions evidently required payment for earnings lost while the injured man was unable to work, and for his medical expenses. The element of compassion is implicit in the fact that there is no mention of considerations such as which man started the fight, the justice of their respective arguments, or whether one acted in self-defense. This law also could have served to deter brawling, since those so involved would be on notice that they could be liable for the damages indicated if they caused serious injury to others.

The law found in Exodus 21:20-21 falls more into the category of criminal law, since it calls for punishing the offender rather than for his paying damages or making restitution. This law provides that a man is to be punished if he strikes his slave (whether male or female) and the slave dies soon afterwards. However, if the slave "survives a day or two" before dying,

---

[26] See *NOAB-RSV*, Old Testament sect., pp. 94 and 95, where the annotator correctly observes that the laws in Exod. 21:12-32 relate to "protecting human beings," while those in Exod. 21:33–22:17 deal with property. See also P. Kyle McCarter, "Exodus," in James L. Mays, Gen. ed., *Harper's Bible Commentary* (San Francisco: Harper & Row, 1988), p. 149, regarding the organizational pattern in Exodus 21:1–22:17: "The laws are grouped roughly as follows: (1) laws pertaining to slavery, requiring a seventh-year manumission of Hebrew slaves and restricting the sale of daughters (21:1-11); (2) laws of capital crimes (21:12-17), excepting unintentional homicide but including murder (21:12-14), kidnapping (21:16), and crimes against parents (21:15, 17); (3) laws pertaining to personal injuries, including injuries to slaves, inflicted by other human beings (21:18-27) and by livestock (21:28-32); (4) laws pertaining to damages to property (21:33–22:16), including livestock (21:33-36, 22:3) and real estate (22:5-6); (5) laws involving contracts (22:7-15); and (6) laws regarding the payment of the bride-price (22:16-17).

[27] The exception, Exodus 21:13, might well be categorized in modern law as relating to second degree murder. See Chapter Five, Section B.1.b.i.

[28] See Chapter Five, Section B.1.b.ii & ii.

[29] "Time and cure" are common remedies in modern admiralty or maritime law for injuries to seamen.

the man who struck him is not to be punished, the rationale being that the slave is "his money" (Exod. 21:21 RSV). This law probably was included here because it, like others in Exodus 21:18-32, concerns injuries to persons. Here there is no provision for compensating the victim's relatives.

Exodus 21:22-25 describes what is to be done in a then perhaps not-too-unusual circumstance. If rowdy men are brawling, and while doing so, injure a pregnant married woman thereby causing a miscarriage but without otherwise injuring the woman, "the man" (RSV) who caused the injury was to be fined an amount set by the woman's husband, as then determined by "the judges." Apparently these damages would be paid for the loss of the fetus or child.[30] This provision can be considered an example of tort law. But if the woman is injured or dies as a result of such injury, the criminal law, known as the "*lex talionis*" is to be applied, and the perpetrator punished accordingly.[31]

Exodus 21:26-27 governs situations where a man strikes his male or female slave, causing the loss of either an eye or a tooth. In that event, he must let the slave go free as compensation for the injury. Such compensation is in the nature of a tort remedy. Even though slaves were regarded as property (Exod. 21:20-21), slave owners or masters were not entirely free to abuse them.[32]

Laws applicable to another special situation are set out in Exodus 21:28-32. These say what is to be done when an ox fatally gores a person other than its owner. In cases where the owner of the ox was culpably negligent, guilty, in effect, of reckless endangerment, he was subject to the death penalty.[33] But there were two exceptions. Both refer to what now would be called tort actions. One exception was that the victim's family could choose to accept compensation ("ransom") instead (Exod. 21:30). Such ransom might be very substantial, possibly including punitive damages, or damages for pain and suffering of the deceased. In modern law, this provision would be seen as allowing for a civil

---

[30] This is one of two biblical texts that relate, albeit indirectly, to abortion. The only other text, which also relates only indirectly, is Ecclesiastes 6:3-5, commenting favorably on the fate of the "stillborn child."

[31] Exodus 21:23-25 is sometimes cited by proponents of capital punishment in support of more general application of the death penalty, as if its context, set out explicitly in Exod. 21:21-23, made no difference. The other two instances of the *lex talionis* found in biblical law likewise were to apply only in delimited contexts: Leviticus 24:19-30 (mayhem, or permanently disfiguring another), and Deuteronomy 19:16-21 (intentional, false, malicious testimony). See Chapter Five, Section B.1.b.ii.(a), and Chapter Six, Section D.2.

[32] See Exodus 21:1-11, discussed above and in Chapter Eight, Section B.3.

[33] See Chapter Five, Section B.1.b.ii.(b).

"wrongful death action" in tort.[34] The other exception was that if the victim was a slave, the offending ox's owner was to pay the slave's owner 30 silver shekels, evidently as compensatory damages for loss of his property (Exod. 21:32).

Exodus 21:33–22:15 lists a series of tort offenses affecting property, along with the remedial damages appropriate in each case.[35] Offenses that involve simple negligence are enumerated in Exodus 21:33-35. These laws call only for restitution or compensation in kind equivalent to the value of what was lost or destroyed. Such compensation is required if a farm animal is killed by falling into someone's open pit (Exod. 21: 33-34). In this case, the pit owner keeps the dead animal. In effect, this is a sale: the pit owner buys the dead animal for the value it had when alive. In this situation, it would be foreseeable that an animal that fell into such a pit would be killed. Foreseeable risk of harm is a basic element in modern tort law. *Quid pro quo* or equal compensation is also required if a man's cattle grazed over another's field or vineyard;[36] if a man sets a fire that accidentally spreads to a neighbor's grain field;[37] and if a farm animal is stolen or injured or dies while in the borrower's (or bailee's) possession (Exod. 22:5-6, 12, 14).

A somewhat different situation arises when one man's ox fatally injures another's ox (Exod. 21:35). Here the live ox is sold and the two men divide the proceeds of the sale, and also divide the dead animal. Arguably, this is less than full compensation for the man whose ox was killed. One could speculate that this arrangement may be in the nature of a "no fault" settlement, given the difficulty of determining which or whose ox "started it." If, however, the owner of the goring ox knew of its goring propensities, and failed to fence it in, he was to pay "ox for ox," but could keep the dead animal (Exod. 21:36). This settlement also is in the nature of a sale: the tort-feasor in effect buys the dead animal for the price of a live one. As in the case of the pit owner, there is some element of culpable negligence, because here also, it should have been foreseeable that harm would result, for an ox "that had been accustomed to gore" was likely to do so again, given opportunity.[38]

---

[34] See Keeton, ed., *Prosser and Keeton*, pp. 940–61.
[35] Excepting 22:2-3. which relates to another matter. See below, note 40.
[36] See Keeton, ed., *Prosser and Keeton*, pp. 539–41, discussing liability and "strict liability" for damage done by trespassing livestock.
[37] See *id.*, pp. 543–45.
[38] So also in modern tort law. See *id.*, pp. 542–43.

As in some types of modern tort law, where the offense (or tort) is clearly intentional, biblical tort law required the tort-feasor to pay multiple damages. Such offenses include theft, breach of trust, and embezzlement or conversion.[39] Instances of intentional torts calling for multiple damages included the following: if someone steals another's ox or sheep (Exod. 22:1, 4),[40] or if a thief allegedly steals property in a neighbor's possession (Exod. 22:7), or in cases involving "breach of trust" or property found in possession of another (Exod. 22:9). The idea of multiple damages for intentional wrong-doing is illustrated in the prophet Nathan's encounter with King David as told in 2 Samuel 12:1-6. Nathan tells David a story[41] about a rich man who had taken a poor man's pet lamb and then killed and served it up for dinner. David, as King, was also Chief Judge. Outraged, David declares that the rich man "shall restore the lamb fourfold because he did this thing and showed no pity" (2 Sam. 12:6 RSV).[42] Fourfold restitution also is exemplified in the New Testament where it is said that a man named Zacchaeus voluntarily declared: "If I have defrauded anyone of anything, I restore it fourfold" (Lk. 19:8 RSV).

Exodus 22:8-15 relates to possible or suspected embezzlement or "conversion" of property held in trust or "bailment" for another. If goods or money are stolen while entrusted to a neighbor and the thief is not found, the neighbor or bailee shall "come near before God" (RSV) in order to determine whether he has taken it (Exod. 22:8). Similarly, "If a man delivers to his neighbor an ass or an ox or a sheep or any beast to keep, and it . . . is driven away, without anyone seeing it . . ." the accused may be absolved by taking "an oath by YHWH" in order to determine "whether he has not put his hand to his neighbor's property" (RSV). A man entrusted with such farm animals must take a similar oath in order to establish his innocence if the animal died, or was injured while in his possession. The animal's owner was to "accept the oath," thereby

---

[39] On the development of modern Western tort law regarding "conversion," see *id.*, pp. 88–107.
[40] Exodus 22:2-3 says what is to be done if someone strikes, and then kills a thief "found breaking in." These verses indicate whether the person who so kills a thief is liable for homicide, a criminal offense. This law evidently was inserted between verses 1 and 4, which relate to theft, because they also refer to theft. See Chapter Five, Section B.1.b.iii. "Breaking in" here may refer entering either a house or a barn, or even possibly a farmyard, or pasture for the purpose of stealing animals of the sort referred to in verses 1 and 4.
[41] Nathan tells the story, or parable, to catch the conscience of the king: the story is really about David's murder of Uriah, and taking the murdered man's wife, Bathsheba, as his own new wife (2 Sam. 12:7-9).
[42] The Hebrew word, *rechem*, here translated as "pity" can equally well be translated as "compassion."

settling the matter (Exod. 22:10-11). But restitution was required if an animal was stolen while in the neighbor's possession (Exod. 22:12). Implicitly, the animal would not have been stolen but for the neighbor's negligence. However, if there was evidence that the farm animal had been "torn by beasts" (RSV) there was to be no need for restitution (Exod. 22:13). Also, if a borrowed or hired farm animal was injured or died while its owner was with it, restitution was not required (Exod. 22:14-15). In these cases where no restitution or compensation was called for, the reason seems to be that the person in possession of the animals at the time was presumed not to have been at fault. Interestingly, however, none of these occurrences is described in biblical tradition as "an act of God," an expression sometimes used in supposedly secular Anglo-American law with reference to unforeseeable harmful happenings or accidents.

A few tort laws are included in later biblical codes. One of these is found in the Holiness Code, and repeated twice: "He who kills a beast shall make it good" (Lev. 24:18 and 21a RSV). Here, as in several laws found in the Covenant Code, the prescribed remedy is equal compensation, whether in kind or by payment of equivalent value. This law does not distinguish between intentional and negligent killing of another's "beast."

Deuteronomy 25:1 sets out another law that may apply to civil litigation, and also, as suggested by the verses that follow (25:2-3), to criminal activity:

> Suppose two persons have a dispute and enter into litigation, and the judges decide between them, declaring one to be in the right and the other to be in the wrong.

Here, what follows is punishment, rather than restitution or some other form of compensation. This text, unlike many others relating to civil actions, refers specifically to the role of "the judges."

Anglo-American law does not provide that a person in position to do so has a duty to rescue another person from imminent harm or another person's property from likely damage. Biblical law does impose such a duty with respect to animals and other property. Deuteronomy requires a person to take affirmative action to return neighbor's stray farm animals to him, and to restore lost garments, or, inclusively, "any lost thing of your brother's which he loses and you find" (Deut. 22:1-3 RSV). Deuteronomic law also requires a person to help one's neighbor lift up his fallen ass or ox. The earlier version of this law in the Covenant Code even imposed a duty to restore an enemy's stray ox or ass, and to help him get his ass up and on its feet if the ass had foundered under its burden (Exod. 23:4-5).

Deuteronomic law also includes a safety requirement for the purpose of preventing or reducing the likelihood of foreseeable harm to persons: "When you build a new house, you shall make a parapet for your roof, that you may not bring the guilt of blood upon your house, if any one fall from it" (Deut. 22:8 RSV). It is unclear whether the parapet or railing referred here to was meant to be a temporary safeguard to prevent workmen falling during construction, or a permanent architectural safety feature.

A somewhat later law collection, known as the Priestly Code, lists various intentional torts involving inanimate property, such as "deceiving [a] neighbor in a matter of deposit or security, or through robbery" (RSV). Here the remedy is full restitution of the property in question, plus an added one-fifth (or 20 per cent) in punitive damages (Lev. 6:1-5). In addition, the perpetrator must bring a "guilt offering" to "the priest" (Lev. 6:6-7). A slightly later addition apparently was meant to provide for restitution when the person to whom the wrong had been done was no longer alive. In that case, restitution could be made to the victim's kinsman, and if there was no kinsman, to "YHWH for the priest" (Num. 5:5-10).

All of these "tort" laws and remedies evidently were meant to allocate fairly the burdens of liability. The interests of both parties enter into the equation: those who did the wrong, and those to whom it had been done. The emphasis here is upon justice. But compassion may be implicit as well, for once damages—including punitive damages—were paid, the parties could again get on with their lives. There was no provision for humiliating, ostracizing, or exiling wrong-doers who had compensated those they had injured.

## C. Biblical Contract and Tort Law, and Modern Counterparts

Biblical scholars for the most part are unfamiliar with modern Anglo-American legal concepts and categories. It is not surprising, therefore, that such concepts and categories are rarely mentioned in biblical commentaries. But it is surprising to find how closely many biblical laws approximate certain basic features of modern jurisprudence.

Biblical laws and narratives clearly indicate that in order to form a contract, both parties must agree to its terms. Typically one party (or person) will propose terms; it is then up to the other either to agree to these terms or reject them. This pattern of offer and acceptance, constituting agreement is a standard feature of modern contract law. It is illustrated in a number of biblical narratives, most notably: Jacob's offer to sell his brother, Esau, a bowl of stew in exchange for the other's birthright (Gen. 25:29-34); Jacob's and Laban's coming to terms as to labor contracts (Gen. 29:21-30; 30:25-43); Balak's hiring Balaam to curse Israel (Num. 22–24); and Tobit's hiring a companion to accompany his son Tobias on a journey (Tob. 5:14-16). Laws governing contractual arrangements evidently were intended to prevent exploitation or mistreatment of affected persons who might not otherwise be able to defend their own interests because they lacked equal bargaining position or power. Such laws related to the rights or interests of slaves (Exod. 21:1-11); debtors (Exod. 22:25-27; Deut. 24:10-13) and day laborers (Lev. 19:13; Deut. 24:14-15).

Biblical tort laws also parallel modern counterparts, both with respect to underlying concerns, values or purposes, and certain related distinctions and "elements." Such elements include a duty to care, or to avoid harming others or their property; some breach of that duty (whether intentional or negligent); and "proximate cause," that is, foreseeable harm to persons or damage to their property resulting from such breach. These elements are all present, explicitly or implicitly, in the biblical tort laws considered above. In addition, as has been seen, biblical laws set out an affirmative duty to assist others under certain circumstances. Like modern tort law, many biblical laws were intended to provide relief or compensation to persons who were injured, or whose property was damaged or destroyed as a result of other persons' conduct.

The underlying value implicit in these laws seems to have been that members of the community were entitled to bodily integrity, that is, to be free from being harmed by others; and also to be free from actions by others that resulted in loss of or damage to property. Implicitly, each member of the community had a duty of care[43] with respect to others and their property: to avoid acting in ways that foreseeably could injure others or damage their property. The dignity, worth, or value of each member of society was taken as given, even, though with significant qualifications, in the case of slaves.

Foreseeability is a basic element or feature of both biblical and modern tort law. That is, to be liable for wrongdoing, the person whose conduct resulted in harm should have been "reasonably" aware that his or her

---

[43] On "duty" in modern tort law, see Keeton, ed., *Prosser and Keeton*, pp. 356–59.

conduct could have harmful consequences of the sort that resulted.[44] Several laws relate to cases of simple negligence, where the consequences were not intended, but nevertheless could be foreseen: for instance, when someone leaves an open pit and a neighbor's ox or ass falls into it (Exod. 21:33-34), or when someone starts a fire that spreads into a neighbor's grain field (Exod. 22:6). In such cases, the law called for relief in the form of restitution or equivalent compensation. One distinctive biblical law requires those responsible for new construction to provide safety railings, in order to prevent or reduce the risk of foreseeable harm to others (Deut. 22:8).

Like modern tort law, biblical law treats reckless conduct and intentional wrongdoing more severely. Some instances of reckless endangerment can also be seen as criminal offenses.[45] Purposeful wrongdoing or intentional torts, such as theft, embezzlement, or breach of trust,[46] called for multiple or punitive damages, a common remedy for intentional torts in modern law.

Biblical scholars generally maintain that the laws found in the Covenant Code (Exod. 20:1–23:33) were set down at random, rather than in accordance with any recognizable pattern or structure based on content. However, when contemporary legal categories are used to describe the laws found in Exodus 21:12 through Exodus 22:15, it turns out that these laws appear to have been organized in a coherent structure after all.

The first block, Exodus 21:12-32, concerns injuries inflicted upon persons.[47] Some of these laws describe circumstances under which the wrongdoer would be subject to capital, or some other punishment, or might, instead, either be exonerated or required to pay damages, notably, the laws set out in Exodus 21:12-14 (homicide), and intentional or reckless conduct resulting in injuries to persons along with appropriate remedies (Exod. 21:18-25, 29-32). Two laws included here concern reckless endangerment (Exod. 21:22-25 and 21:29-31), and call for indeterminate compensation as well as possible criminal penalties. Other laws in this block call for capital punishment without mention of obviating or mitigating circumstances (Exod. 21:15-17).[48] Another set of laws requires slave owners to free slaves they have injured in certain ways.[49]

---

[44] See generally id., pp. 263–321.
[45] Also see Chapter Five, Section B.1.b.ii.
[46] See Exodus 22:1, 4, 9; Lev. 6:1–5.
[47] As noted above, Exodus 21:1-11 relate to sales contracts.
[48] As to these and other laws calling for the death penalty, see Part II of this book.
[49] See Chapter Eight, Section B.3.

The second block, Exodus 21:33 through 22:1, 4-15, consists of laws concerning theft of or damage to property. Chapter 22 verses 5 and 6 cover negligent damage to another's agricultural interests; verses 7 through 13 govern property held in "trust" or bailment; and verses 14 and 15 concern borrowed property. These laws provide for various remedies, typically in the form of restitution or cash. Persons who committed intentional torts were liable for multiple, that is, punitive damages (Exod. 22:1, 4, 7, and 9). As with the laws relating to injuries to persons, where circumstances indicated that the apparent wrongdoer was without fault, no restitution or damages payment was required (Exod. 22:8, 10-11, 13, and 15).[50]

The fact that nearly all biblical tort laws are grouped together in Exodus 21:18 through 22:15 can be regarded as a further indication that the biblical legislators or editors themselves distinguished such laws from other legal categories. In any event, recognizing these laws as tort laws should be helpful to biblical scholars when describing the substance of biblical law, and to legal scholars when undertaking to trace similarities and possible connections between ancient Near Eastern law and contemporary jurisprudence.

This series of tort laws is followed by a set of three criminal laws describing capital offenses (Exod. 22:18-20). These, along with the other criminal offenses against persons referred to in the first block (Exod. 21:12, 14-17, as well as laws involving reckless endangerment, Exod. 21:23, 29-31) are considered in Part II of this book. Those laws in the remaining portions of the Covenant Code that can be classified as social legislation (Exod. 22:21-28; 23:1-12) are examined in Part III.[51]

Before turning to these topics, attention is directed in the following chapter to another type of biblical civil law. This is the matter of transferring property by inheritance, and also doing so by testation, that is by making wills or bequests to named beneficiaries. The latter form of transfer has generally been ignored by both biblical and legal scholars.

---

[50] Exodus 22:16-17, concerning what was to be done when "a man seduces a virgin who is not betrothed" (RSV), could be read, if seen in the context of this second block, to imply that virgin daughters were regarded as property. Alternatively, this text might be seen as a displaced segment of the series of laws about injuries to persons set out in Exod. 21:12-32.

[51] The other remaining laws define various religious obligations or prohibitions: Thus Exod. 22:28-31; and 23:14-33.

## Chapter 2

# Transfer of Property by Inheritance and Bequest

*And you shall say to the people of Israel, "If a man dies, and has no son, then you shall cause his inheritance to pass to his daughter. And if he has no daughter, then you shall give his inheritance to his brothers. And if he has no brothers, then you shall give his inheritance to his father's brothers. And if his father has no brothers, then you shall give his inheritance to his kinsman that is next to him of his family, and he shall possess it. And it shall be to the people of Israel a statute and ordinance, as YHWH commanded Moses."*

Numbers 27:8-11 (RSV)

*Before she died she distributed her property to all those who were next of kin to her husband Manasseh, and to her own nearest kindred.*

Judith 16:24 (RSV)

This topic involves questions that are more complicated than one might suspect from reading typical annotations and bible dictionary articles. Commentators and annotators often have attempted to resolve such questions by making assertions grounded upon highly problematic evidence. Although many remain open, it is possible to draw some likely conclusions. This chapter does not consider texts pertaining exclusively to the "inheritance" of the land of promise by the various tribes of Israel such as Joshua 11:23; 13:1–19:51; and Ezekiel 47:13–48:29.[1] Concern

---

[1] On God's choice of certain biblical persons and their "seed" to be heirs to the land or his favor, see H. Z. Szubin and Bezalel Porten, "Testamentary Succession at Elephantine," *Bulletin of the American Schools of Oriental Research* (hereinafter *BASOR*) 252 (1983) 37. The pseudepigraphic "testaments"—The Testament of the Twelve Patriarchs, The Testament of Moses, and The Testament of Job—are not considered as testamentary documents. Other than in T. Job (see below, text accompanying note 117), there is no reference to property bequests in these "testaments." See generally, J. J. Collins, "Testaments," in

with preserving tribal inheritances is in the background of some texts that are considered; but here attention is limited to laws and traditions concerning transfer of property from persons in one generation to those of another, or, in a few instances, to other persons within the same generation in accordance with what, in modern legal terms, would be called the laws of intestate succession and bequest.[2]

This chapter begins by reviewing the kinds of property subject to transfer by inheritance or bequest. Attention then turns to texts pertaining to intestate succession—that is, the transfer of property by operation of law upon the death of the property holder without explicit provision by will or bequest as to who will inherit or take afterwards. Such transactions are referred to here as "inheritance." Certain provisions regarding levirate marriage and the Year of Jubilee are considered in this connection. The problematic nature of the so-called "birthright" is then discussed. Finally, this chapter examines a series of texts that appear to refer to bequests or deathbed wills, and also to inter-vivos gifts made by donors in anticipation of their eventual demise. Both of these latter types of transfers are characterized here as "bequests," a modern estate law term. A concluding section summarizes probable findings, and reviews a number of remaining open questions.

Three conclusions stand out in particular. The first is that biblical law and custom make a distinction between transfer of property by inheritance on the one hand, and transfer by bequest, legacy, or will on the other. This distinction is strangely absent in most scholarly discussions of relevant texts. The second conclusion is that, although relatively few scholars so recognize, there is persuasive evidence that in biblical times widows commonly inherited property upon the death of their husbands. Whether their inherited property interest was equivalent to what, in Anglo-American law would be characterized as "fee simple absolute," or some lesser possessory interest, such as usufruct or a life estate, is not so certain. The third conclusion has to do with the "birthright." That institution seems to have

---

Michael E. Stone, ed., *Jewish Writings of the Second Temple Period* (Philadelphia: Fortress Press, 1984), pp. 325–55. In such NT texts as Mt. 19:29; 25:34; Mk 10:17; Eph. 1:13-14; Col. 3:24; and 1 Pet. 1:4, "inheriting" or "inheritance" refers to receiving or entering the coming Kingdom of God or messianic age, not to inheriting property. As to such usages, see C. E. B. Cranfield, "Inherit," in Alan Richardson, ed., *A Theological Word Book of the Bible* (New York: Macmillan, 1978), pp. 112–14.

[2] This chapter does not consider biblical traditions regarding sons succeeding their fathers' office or status. On that topic, see David Daube, *Sons and Strangers* (Boston: Inst. of Jewish Law, Boston Univ. School of Law, 1984).

been a precursor or adjunct to the law or practice of intestate succession. Biblical scholars generally assume that under terms of "birthright," all first-born sons were to receive a double portion of their fathers' inheritance. The difficulty is that no biblical text so specifies. Moreover, there is little, if any, evidence that this practice was actually observed during the biblical period. It may be concluded that less is known about "birthright" than is commonly supposed.

## A. Property Subject to Transfer by Inheritance or Bequest

Virtually all kinds of property appear to have been subject to transfer by inheritance or bequest. Provision for transferring real property (land, fields, and houses) was centrally important in biblical law and tradition.[3] Wealth, generally, and certain particular forms of the same could be inherited or bequeathed, e.g., houses, fields, slaves, silver, gold, and cattle.[4] Genesis traditions tell that Abraham gave all that he had to his son, Isaac.[5] It has even been proposed that in the earliest form of levirate marriage, "the wife, being her husband's property, was passed on, like the rest of his estate, to his heir."[6] No biblical texts indicate that wives, daughters, or sisters were regarded as property subject to inheritance or bequest. However, 1 Kings 2:13-25 could be read to mean that Solomon regarded Abishag — his late father's female companion and bed-warmer, though at most, only nominally a concubine (1 Kgs 1:1-4)—as royal property reserved for the heir to the throne. It may be that in the early monarchy the king's harem was inherited by his successor.[7]

---

[3] See, e.g., Gen. 48:21-22; Lev. 25:10-34; 27:16-25; Prov. 19:14; 23:10. Raymond Westbrook has demonstrated convincingly that in biblical times, in order to acquire an inheritable estate in real property, it was necessary to pay the "full price." "Purchase of the Cave of Machpelah," 6 *Israel L. Rev.* 29–38 (1971); "The Price Factor in the Redemption of Land," *Revue International des Droits de l'Antiquite*, 3rd Ser. 32 (1985) 115–16. Westbrook cites such texts as Gen. 23:1-20 (cf. 25:9-10); 33:19; 49:29-31; and 50:13.

[4] See, e.g., Lev. 25:44-46; 2 Chron. 21:3; Prov. 19:14; Jdt. 8:7.

[5] Gen. 24:36; 25:5-6.

[6] Cyrus H. Gordon, "Fratriarchy in the Old Testament," *Journal of Biblical Literature* (hereinafter, *JBL*) 54 (1935) 230; F. Charles Fensham, "Widow, Orphan and Poor in Ancient Near Eastern Legal and Wisdom Literature," *Journal of Near Eastern Studies* (hereinafter, *JNES*) 21 (1961) 136. But see Millar Burrows, *The Basis of Israelite Marriage* (New Haven: American Oriental Society, 1939), p. 45.

[7] Roland de Vaux, *Ancient Israel: Its Life and Institutions* (New York: McGraw-Hill, 1961), pp. 115–17. Thus also the annotator, *The New Oxford Annotated Bible New Revised Standard*

## B. Inheritance: Descent of Property through Intestate Succession

The first part of this section focuses on biblical laws and traditions relating to intestate succession: that is, provisions or customs whereby on a man's death, his property would pass to other persons. As will be seen, biblical laws and traditions provided for inheritance not only by sons, but also by daughters and widows. The second part then turns to inheritance arrangements implicit in biblical law and tradition concerning "levirate marriage."

### 1. The Law of Intestate Succession

Laws may be either written or unwritten. Several written texts set out substantive provisions. Unwritten laws can be inferred by observing customs and practices as recorded in narratives and other traditions. The basic biblical law of inheritance (or "intestate succession" in modern law) is found in Numbers chapter 27. But this written law probably was supplemented by traditional practices long understood to have the force of law.[8] See, for example, Proverbs 19:14: "House and wealth are inherited from fathers, but a prudent wife is from YHWH" (RSV). As will be seen, many other texts assume that property passes by inheritance from one generation to the next.

#### a. Sons

It appears that from early times it was expected that sons would inherit their fathers' property upon the latter's demise.[9] The brief account in Joshua 17:3-6 concerning the daughters of Zelophehad clearly presumes

---

Version with the Apocrypha (hereinafter, NOAB-NRSV) (New York: Oxford Univ. Press, 1991) 427. Also, see below, note 101.

[8] Other ancient near eastern laws, known in the aggregate as "the cuneiform laws," may well have been familiar to legal/political leaders throughout the biblical period and so served as the unwritten or customary law of the land. See generally, Raymond Westbrook, "The Law of the Biblical Levirate," *Revue Internationale des Droits de l'Antiquité*, 3d Ser., 24 (1977) 85–86. It is unlikely that *all* cuneiform law was considered authoritative in Israel; but where such known laws are apparently presupposed, they may well have been applied as customary law. While the substance of Israelite law is not necessarily unique, much of it may be distinctive. See John Van Seters, "The Problem of Childlessness in Near Eastern Law and the Patriarchs of Israel," *JBL* 87 (1968) 401–08.

[9] This pattern appears in instances where the sons' mothers are already deceased or are unmentioned. In cases where widows with sons are mentioned, the *widows* evidently

that a father's property would normally pass to his sons.[10] Zelophehad had no sons; so, apparently after his death, his five daughters contended that they should be given their father's inheritance, and it was so ordered. The anecdote seems to presuppose the narrator's acquaintance with the episode described at Numbers 27:1-11, where the five daughters presented their claim to Moses,[11] who brought it to YHWH. As the story is told, YHWH then not only ruled in the daughters' favor, but also set out the following law of intestate succession for all Israel:

> And you shall say to the people of Israel, "If a man dies, and has no son, then you shall cause his inheritance to pass to his daughter. And if he has no daughter, then you shall give his inheritance to his brothers. And if he has no brothers, then you shall give his inheritance to his father's brothers. And if his father has no brothers, then you shall give his inheritance to his kinsman that is next to him of his family, and he shall possess it. And it shall be to the people of Israel a statute and ordinance, as YHWH commanded Moses." (Num. 27:8-11 RSV)[12]

That sons, if any, normally were the sole heirs (absent a surviving widow) is implied in numerous other biblical texts, for instance, Judges 11:1-2; 2 Chronicles 21:1-3; Proverbs 17:2; and Luke 12:13. But who is to be counted as "sons" for purposes of inheritance? Biblical traditions refer to sons by their fathers' concubines, their wives' maids, by slaves, and by harlots. It seems that any such sons might inherit, absent steps being taken to prevent their doing so.

---

inherited the property. See 2 Kings 4:1-7 and 8:1-6, discussed below, text preceding and accompanying notes 44 and 45.

[10] See generally, J. Weingreen, "The Case of the Daughters of Zelophehad," *Vetus Testamentum* (hereinafter, *VT*) 16 (1966) 518–22.

[11] One annotator comments, "The request of the daughters of Zelophehad was unusual in that, according to ancient law, normally women did not inherit property." *The New Oxford Annotated Bible with the Apocrypha* (hereinafter, *NOAB*) (New York: Oxford Univ. Press, 1977), pp. 200–201; *NOAB-NRSV*, p. 204. The annotator does not say what that "ancient law" was or where it is to be found. Biblical tradition contains no such law..

[12] Islamic law as set out in the *Kur'an* contained even more specific provisions. Under this law, each person or class of persons would receive a pre-determined fractional share of the estate (*fara'id*). See esp. *Suras* 4:11-14, 176; 2:180, 240; and 5:106. Such provisions assumed and limited the power of testation. See generally, David S. Powers, "On Bequests in Early Islam," *JNES* 48 (1989) 185–200. Post-biblical Judaism introduced numerous supplements to the provisions of Num. 27. See, e.g., Arnold Block and Hyman Klein, trans. & eds., *Maimonides Law of Inheritance* (London: Shapiro, Valentine & Co., 1950); Dayan I. Grunfeld, *The Jewish Law of Inheritances* (Oak Park, Mich.: Targum Press, 1987); Joseph Nissim, *Rudiments of the Jewish Law of Inheritance Upon Intestacy and Bequests*, Publications of the Society for Jewish Jurisprudence (London: Kelly & Sons, 1931); Reuven Yaron, *Gifts in Contemplation of Death in Jewish and Roman Law* (Oxford: Clarendon Press, 1960).

Genesis 30 reports that Jacob had several sons by the maids of his wives, Rachel and Leah, respectively, Bilhah and Zilpah. Rachel evidently regarded the arrangement with Bilhah as equivalent to what we might call surrogate motherhood. Thus she said to Jacob, "Here is my maid, Bilhah; go into her, that she may bear upon my knees, and even I may have children through her" (Gen. 30:3 RSV). Rachel regarded the sons subsequently born to Bilhah as her own, and she, Rachel, named them: Dan and Naphthali (Gen. 30:6, 8). Likewise, Leah named the sons Jacob had by her maid, Zilpah: Gad and Asher (Gen. 30:11-13). Rachel and Leah each gave these maids to Jacob "as a wife" (Gen. 30:4, 9). It would appear, however, that the wifely status of Bilhah and Zilpah was only nominal, and their status as maid-servants primary. Thus in Genesis 35:23-26, Bilhah and Zilpah are described simply as the maids of Rachel and Leah.[13] No tradition explicitly states that Dan, Naphthali, Gad, or Asher received an inheritance from Jacob. But these four are included among the "sons" whom Jacob "blessed" or "charged" shortly before his death (Gen. 49: 1-33). It may be inferred that they were to receive their "inheritances" along with the other brothers.[14] Genesis 48:5-6 seems to say that all of Joseph's brothers were to inherit from Jacob. Nothing here suggests that Dan, Naphthali, Gad and Asher were to be excluded. Subsequent biblical tradition reports that their descendants received "inheritances" in the form of tribal allotments (Josh. 13:24-28; 19:24-31).

The story about Sarai, Abram, Hagar, and Ishmael likewise suggests that a childless wife could "obtain children" by giving her maid to her husband "as a wife" (Gen. 16:1-3).[15] The problem for Sarai was that Hagar was not content to serve merely as a surrogate mother, but acted rather

---

[13] In Gen. 35:22, Bilhah is characterized merely as Jacob's "concubine."

[14] Thus Van Seters, "Problem of Childlessness," p. 405. Compare Code of Hammurabi, sect. 170, translated in D. Winton Thomas, *Documents from Old Testament Times* (New York: Harper & Row, 1961), p. 33, which reads:

> If a citizen, whose wife has borne him children and (also) his bondmaid has borne him children, (and) the father during his lifetime has said to the bondmaid's children, which she has borne him, 'My children'; he has added them to the children of the wife. After the father goes to his fate, the children of the wife shall divide the property of the father's house equally with the sons of the bondmaid; the son and heir, the son of the wife, shall chose a share (first) and take it.

See also Code of Hammurabi, sects. 145 and 146, which apply only when a man ("citizen") has taken a priestess as wife. Thomas, *Documents*, p. 32.

[15] Van Seters urges that unlike most other ancient Near Eastern law and custom, the biblical practice here attested was "clearly for the sake of the wife and not the husband." "Problem of Childlessness," p. 403. See also Gerhard von Rad, Genesis, *A Commentary* (Philadelphia: Westminster, 1961), p. 186. Von Rad suggests that under this arrangement the *wife* adopts the children borne by her maid. Id. at p. 289.

as a wife and mother in her own right (Gen. 16:4-6). It was Hagar, not Sarai, who would name her son Ishmael (Gen. 16:11). Ishmael is expressly described as Hagar's son (Gen. 21:9, 10, 13) as well as Abram's (Gen. 16:15-16; 21:11). As such, it seemed that he would inherit from Abraham. But Sarai (now renamed Sarah) objects and tells Abraham to send Hagar and Ishmael away, "for the son of this slave woman shall not be heir with my son Isaac" (Gen. 21:10 RSV). Abraham reluctantly obliges, and sends Hagar and Ishmael away into the wilderness (Gen. 21:11-14). We see here that if a man agreed, his wife could cause him to disinherit his son by her maid.[16]

Likewise, in Judges 11:1-2, we see that legitimate sons might, if they so desired and were able, drive off their father's son by a harlot and so cause him to be disinherited. Implicitly, Jephthah would have inherited from his father if these half-brothers had not succeeded in forcing him out.[17] Interestingly, whatever birthright may have meant,[18] it does not seem to have been a factor in the stories of either Ishmael or Jephthah, even though Ishmael was the first of Abraham's sons and Jephthah may have been the first of his father's.

---

[16] A *Harper's Bible Dictionary* commentator takes Gen. 21:10 as evidence that in biblical times "the sons of a concubine did not inherit." *Harper's Bible Dictionary* (hereinafter, *HBD*) (San Francisco: Harper & Row, 1985), p. 422. Likewise, *The New Westminster Dictionary of the Bible* (hereinafter, *NWDB*) (Philadelphia: Westminster, 1976), pp. 375–76. The point, however, is that Ishmael *would have inherited* had not Sarah insisted on, and Abraham agreed to, his banishment. Thus Van Seters, "Problem of Childlessness," p. 403, and Otto J. Baab, "Inheritance," in *The Interpreter's Dictionary of the Bible*, (hereinafter, *IDB*), vol. 2 (New York: Abingdon, 1962) p. 701. See also Gen. 25:5-6, which says that Abraham gave all he had to Isaac, but also gave gifts to the sons of his concubines, which sons, "while he was still living . . . he sent . . . away from his son Isaac, eastward to the east country." The probable implication is that Abraham sent these sons away so that they would not be around to claim a share of the inheritance he had given or bequeathed to Isaac. *The New English Bible* annotator, commenting on Gen. 21:8-21, asserts that "[a]ncient Near Eastern law stipulated that the offspring of a slave wife could either inherit with the children of the free woman or be set free." *The New English Bible with the Apocrypha*, Oxford Study Edition (hereinafter, *NEB*) (New York: Oxford Univ. Press, 1976), p. 20. The annotator does not mention which ancient Near Eastern law so provided. Possibly the annotator was thinking of the Lipit-Ishtar Law Code, sect. 25, which reads:

> If a man married a wife and she bore him children and these children are living, and a slave also bore children to her master but the father granted freedom to the slave and her children, the children of the slave shall not divide the estate with their former master.

James B. Pritchard, ed., *Ancient Near Eastern Texts* (hereinafter, *ANET*) (Princeton Univ. Press, 1950), p. 160.

[17] See Lipit-Ishtar Law Code, sect. 27, which provided that if a man's wife had not borne him children, any children borne to him by a harlot would be his heirs. *ANET*, p. 160.

[18] See Section A.4. of this Chapter.

One text, 1 Chronicles 2:34-35, suggests that a slave might serve as a surrogate father for purposes of perpetuating the family line. Having no son but only daughters, a certain Sheshan married one of them to his Egyptian slave. The son of this marriage then fathered a continuing succession of male descendants who, presumably, inherited whatever property Sheshan had to pass down to his heirs (1 Chron. 2:36-41).[19]

A few texts suggest that in the absence of other offspring, a slave might inherit, possibly as a "constructive" son, that is, a son by operation of law.[20] Thus early in the Abraham cycle, Abram complains that God has given him no offspring, with the result that a slave born in his house would be his heir (Gen. 15:3).[21] The phrasing implies that a slave born in the house of an otherwise childless father would be counted as a son. YHWH therefore assures Abram that the slave born in his house would *not* be his heir; instead, Abram's *own* son would be his heir (Gen. 15:4). The *NOAB-RSV* annotator suggests that this text may presuppose the practice attested in Nuzi, whereby "a slave could be adopted as the heir in case of childlessness."[22] Nothing is said in Genesis 15:2-4, however,

---

[19] So also Thomas and Dorothy Thompson, "Some Legal Problems in the Book of Ruth," *VT* 18 (1968) 87: "Through this marriage Sheshan himself obtained sons and heirs."

[20] Perhaps the underlying consideration in Genesis 15:3-4 was that a slave born in his master's house could be presumed to have been fathered by the master—an early version of the doctrine, *res ipsa loquitur* (The situation speaks for itself"). But see William Blackstone, *Commentaries on the Laws of England*, 9th edn. (London: W. Strahan, 1783), vol. 2, p. 12. Commenting on Genesis 15:3-4, Blackstone conjectured that the practice there attested had derived as follows:

> A man's children or nearest relations are usually about him on his death-bed, and are the earliest witnesses of his decease. They became therefore generally the next immediate occupants, till at length in process of time this frequent usage ripened into general law. And therefore also in the earliest ages, on failure of children, a man's servants born under his roof were allowed to be his heirs, being immediately on the spot when he died.

Compare Proverbs 17:2 and 29:21 which also may refer to slaves inheriting from their masters.

[21] It is not entirely clear from the context whether this slave was Eliezer of Damascus who was characterized in the preceding verse as the heir of Abram's "house." It is possible that Eliezer was an otherwise unidentified kinsman of Abram's who would have inherited under the kind of custom institutionalized in Num. 27:11. There is no mention of Eliezer in Abraham's family tree in Gen. 11:24-28; but possibly the two slaves were the same person.

[22] *NOAB-RSV*, Old Testament sect., p. 17; Von Rad suggests that Abraham may have been cognizant of such practice, noting that Nuzi texts included "several contracts, according to which in the event of childlessness slaves were adopted; their duty then was to give the testator proper burial." *Genesis*, pp. 178–79. See also Cyrus H. Gordon, "Biblical Customs and the Nuzi Tablets," in Edward F. Campbell, Jr. and David Noel Freedman, eds., *The Biblical Archaeologist Reader*, vol. 2 (Garden City: Anchor-Doubleday, 1964),

about adoption.[23] Here it seems to be enough for the slave to have been born in Abram's "house."

### b. Daughters

The law of intestate succession in Numbers 27:8 provides that if a man has no son, "his inheritance shall pass to his daughter" (RSV). Reference to "his daughter" might be read to mean that only one daughter, perhaps the older or oldest, would inherit. However, the accompanying narrative, Numbers 27:1-7, and also Joshua 17:3-6 and Numbers chapter 36, all make it clear that all five of the daughters of Zelophehad were to, and did inherit their father's property. Read in this context, Numbers 27:8 therefore probably should be understood to refer to daughter or daughters, if there were more than one.

According to Genesis 31:14-16, Rachel and Leah evidently expected to receive an inheritance from their "father's house" even though he also had sons (Gen. 31:1). Possibly daughters did inherit under Syrian law, at least if they were older than their brothers. Cyrus Gordon suggests that, pursuant to practices attested at Nuzi, Laban had adopted Jacob, and that this relationship is in the background of their property transactions and other dealings.[24] The women's complaint that their father, Laban, had been "using up the money given for us" (Gen. 31:15 RSV), could refer to their dowry,[25] which may have been in addition to their expected inheritance.[26]

Apart from these instances, there seem to be no other biblical texts reporting daughters' inheriting or expecting to inherit from their parents.[27] A few gender neutral expressions could be read to mean, in

---

pp. 22–23. Compare Code of Hammurabi, sect. 170, which provides that a man may adopt sons borne him by a bondmaid or maid servant. See above note 14.

[23] Daube suggests that traditions regarding adoption were deleted from biblical materials as part of Nehemiah's and Ezra's program of restoring family purity. Daube, *Sons*, p. 48.

[24] Gordon, "Biblical Customs," pp. 24–27. It has also been suggested that Jacob's relations with Laban and his family evidence a pattern of matrilineal descent. Nancy Jay, "Sacrifice, Descent, and the Patriarchs," *VT* 38 (1988) 59–64.

[25] See generally, Burrows, Basis, pp. 41–46.

[26] See A. M. Brown, *The Concept of Inheritance in the Old Testament*, unpublished Ph.D. dissertation, Columbia University, 1965, pp. 10–11, cited in Donald A. Leggett, *The Levirate and Goel institutions in the Old Testament: with Special Attention to the Book of Ruth* (Cherry Hill, NJ: Mack Publ. Co., 1974), p. 215 n. 21.

[27] Job 42:15 says that Job gave his daughters "inheritances along with their brothers." The likely meaning here is that he *gave* them property by bequest, not that they received these "inheritances" by intestate succession. See Section C.2. of this Chapter. It cannot be determined whether Sheshan's daughters would have inherited his property if

effect, inheritance by sons and/or daughters, but none necessarily bears that meaning.[28]

In the story of Tobit, apparently contrary to the law of intestate succession set out in Numbers 27, when Tobias' mother-in-law and father-in-law died, their daughter, Sarah, who evidently was their only child,[29] did not inherit their property. Instead, Tobias, Sarah's husband, inherited it (Tob. 14:13-14). Perhaps only unmarried daughters of sonless fathers inherited from their fathers. This conclusion accords with the further legislation concerning the daughters of Zelophehad set out in Numbers chapter 36.

Numbers 36 is concerned, in the first instance, to make sure that each of the tribes of Israel would preserve its own original inheritance as allotted in the days of Joshua. Lest inheritances be transferred from one tribe to another (Num. 36:9), the following provision was added concerning heiresses:

> [E]very daughter who possesses an inheritance in any tribe of the people of Israel shall be wife to one of the family of the tribe of her father, so that every one of the people of Israel may possess the inheritance of his fathers. (Num. 36:8 RSV)

The clear implication is that when a woman who had inherited her father's property married, the inherited property then became her husband's. Tobias's inheriting from his in-laws is only a corollary to this

---

none of them had married and had children. 1 Chron. 2:34-41. Their father saw to it that one of them did marry; the resulting line of male progeny presumably inherited. On daughters' status as heirs in other ancient Near Eastern cultures, see Zafrira Ben-Barak, "Inheritance by Daughters in the Ancient Near East," *Journal of Semitic Studies* 25 (1980) 22–33.

[28] Baab points out that the Septuagint version of the law of levirate marriage in Deuteronomy 25:6 reads "child" (*to paidion*) rather than "first son," *IDB*, vol. 2, p. 702. This change may suggest that the editor intended the text to be read so that a first-born daughter could be the deceased's heir under terms of levirate marriage, at least if there were no later-born sons. On the basis of Septuagint evidence (Deut. 25:5, 6), Westbrook concludes that "the most likely hypothesis is that until late biblical times at least, the existence of a daughter did not affect the imposition of the levirate, nor was the birth of a daughter considered fulfilment of the duty." "Law of the Biblical Levirate," p. 79. See also: Ps. 25:13 (the "children" of the righteous man shall "possess the land"); Prov. 19:14 ("House and wealth are inherited from fathers" RSV); and Prov. 23:10 ("Do not remove an ancient landmark or enter the fields of the fatherless" RSV).

[29] According to Tobit 6:10-11, Sarah was her parents' only daughter and heir. If she had had brothers, they, presumably, would have inherited under the provisions of Num. 27:8-12 and Sarah would have taken nothing.

provision, showing that if a married woman inherited from her parents, the inheritance would pass through her to her husband.[30]

The writer of Tobit evidently had some acquaintance with the provisions of Numbers chapter 36, but greatly exaggerated the latter's scope and penalties. As Tobias and the angel Raphael came near to Ecbatana, the angel, also known as "Brother Azarias," tells Tobias that as Sarah's "only eligible kinsman," he is entitled to marry her and to receive her inheritance (Tob. 6:11). It is just barely possible that there were no other men left in the whole tribe of Naphtali to which Tobias belonged,[31] but extremely unlikely, even allowing for the untimely demise of Sarah's previous seven would-be husbands who all, presumably, also had been eligible kinsmen and Naphtalites.[32] According to Numbers 36:6, the daughters of Zelophehad could marry whomever they thought best, provided the husbands came from their tribe.[33] Heiresses were not required to marry their nearest kinsman. Thus it is probably an overstatement to say that Tobias alone was entitled to marry Sarah and receive her inheritance.[34] Likewise, the angel's claim that, under the law, Sarah's father would incur the death penalty if he gave Sarah to any other man (Tob. 6:12) must be regarded as literary or dramatic hyperbole.

## c. *Widows*

Widows were not provided for in the law of intestate succession in Numbers chapter 27. As we shall see, a widow could receive her husband's property by bequest (Jdt. 8:7). But absent such bequest, might she inherit his property by operation of law? Several texts suggest that she could inherit his real property.

---

[30] Tobit 14:13. See below, note 46 and accompanying text.
[31] Tobit 1:1, 4, 5; 7:3.
[32] Possibly the narrator was thinking of levirate marriage tradition, under which the nearest surviving male kinsman had the right (or duty) to marry the sonless deceased's widow. See Section B.2. of this Chapter.
[33] More precisely, such heiresses were to marry within "the family" of their father's tribe. Westbrook suggests that this concept meant that heiresses were likely to marry relatives no more remote than cousins. See Westbrook, *Property and the Family*, pp. 22, 163–64.
[34] According to Tobit 8:20-21, Raguel, Tobias' father-in-law, promised to give Tobias half his property at the end of the wedding feast, and the rest when he (Raguel) and his wife died. This promise, under oath, could be viewed either as a will or as part of the marriage contract. See reference to a contract in Tob. 7:14. But if, under customary law, Tobias was entitled to receive his in-laws' property upon their death anyway by virtue of having been married to their only daughter, the promise merely confirmed that right.

One such text is Ruth 4:3. Here Boaz tells the late Elimelech's nearest (though nameless) kinsman that the widow, Naomi, "is selling the parcel of land which belonged to our kinsman Elimelech."[35] It is reasonable to infer that if she was selling it, title must have passed to her by operation of the law upon her husband's, Elimelech's, death,[36] unless, of course, he had bequeathed it to her.[37] Other features of the Book of Ruth likewise support the conclusion that Naomi had inherited some or all of her deceased husband's property.[38]

In cases (to be considered shortly) where a widow with a son (or sons) appears to inherit the decedent's property, it might be argued that the property was hers only as trustee, pending her son's reaching the age of majority. In Ruth, however, Naomi has no living sons and no one expects her to have any. There can be no question of Naomi's holding property as

---

[35] See also Ruth 4:5, the Hebrew text of which, translated literally, reads, "What day you buy the field from the hand of Naomi and from Ruth the Moabitess, you have bought the wife of the dead to raise up the name of the dead upon his inheritance." Translation by David Daube, *Ancient Jewish Law* (Leiden: Brill, 1981), p. 39. Cf. the King James Version. From this, it could be inferred that Ruth had inherited a portion of her father's or late husband's estate. See, however, Ruth 4:9 where Boaz says he has bought the land "from the hand of Naomi," with no mention of Ruth's ownership.

[36] Raymond Westbrook has urged that Ruth 4:3 should be understood to mean that the land had already been sold to a third party. "Redemption of Land," *Israel L. Rev.* 6 (1971) 373–75; "Price Factor," p. 126. He suggests that Elimelech or Naomi had sold the land at discount before leaving for Moab, and that in Ruth 4, it is a matter of redeeming this land from the third party. But Ruth 4:5 and 9 clearly say that the present purchase is from the hand of *Naomi*. Leggett argues persuasively against the theory that the land had already been sold. *Levirate and Goel*, pp. 218–22. So also Millar Burrows, "The Marriage of Boaz and Ruth," *JBL* 59 (1940) 446–47; de Vaux, *Ancient Israel*, pp. 166–67; and Jack S. Sasson, *Ruth: A New Translation with Philological Commentary and A Formalist-Folklorist Interpretation* (Baltimore: The Johns Hopkins Univ. Press, 1979), pp. 108–115. It appears more likely that Naomi's land was subject to redemption because her husband and their sons had died, leaving her without other means of support, than because of some possible (but unmentioned) previous sale to a third party.

[37] See Leggett, *Levirate and Goel*, p. 217; Edward F. Campbell, Jr., *Ruth: A New Translation with Introduction, Notes, and Commentary*, Anchor Bible vol. 7 (Garden City: Doubleday, 1975), p. 158. Several legal issues arise in *Ruth* 4:1-12. See Campbell, Ruth, p. 154, referring to "the ocean of ink which has been spilled over . . . unanswered questions" there. We do not attempt to solve those questions, but only to note those relating to inheritance, and to suggest some possible conclusions.

[38] So also Leggett, *Levirate and Goel*, pp. 211–18. "The announcement, made in the presence of the carefully assembled body, that Naomi was selling the property, went unchallenged; thus there can be little doubt that she was lawfully in possession of the property." *Id.* at p. 218. See also Burrows, "Marriage," p. 448: "[W]e must admit that the book of Ruth assumes the practice of inheritance by widows . . . At any rate our author assumes that his readers will not regard it as strange." Compare Sasson, *Ruth*, pp. 108–15, 117–20, 139–40. Sasson urges that although Naomi was in possession of the land and was selling it, she had not inherited it, but was holding it as Elimelech's land pending sale. When it was sold, however, she would be entitled to the proceeds.

trustee for any sons.³⁹ Therefore, she appears as owner of her late husband's property in her own right. She has had two sons, but they both predeceased her. Since the sons were grown and had survived their father, Elimelech, it is possible that at his death the sons had inherited from him.⁴⁰ Then, when her sons died, Naomi would have inherited from them,⁴¹ or at least from Chilion, since Ruth might have inherited from Mahlon. This pattern of succession is intimated in Ruth 4:9, where Boaz announces that "this day . . . I have bought from the hand of Naomi all that belonged to Elimelech *and all that belonged to Chilion and Mahlon.*" This sequence could also explain why in the Hebrew text of Ruth 4:5, Boaz tells the nearer kinsman that the field belongs to both Naomi and Ruth. Ruth would have inherited the portion that belonged to her late husband, and Naomi would have inherited the rest. Alternatively, Naomi may have inherited the whole parcel from Elimelech. The evidence could lead to either conclusion. As a convenience, we shall refer to the parcel or field as Naomi's.

It has been countered that, because Ruth "gleaned" in Boaz's field rather than Naomi's, we should conclude that Naomi no longer owned the field she was selling. Ruth 1:22, however, suggests another explanation: After many years of absence, Naomi and Ruth returned "at the beginning of the barley harvest." Very likely Naomi's field provided no harvest because no one had planted it at the beginning of the growing season.⁴² Moreover, three distinct texts (Ruth 4:3, 5, and 9) make clear that Naomi (if not also Ruth) owned the field that had belonged to the late Elimelech. The field was not the only property Naomi may have inherited from Elimelech. She also evidently had inherited the house in

---

[39] De Vaux urges that Naomi was merely acting as the guardian of her deceased son's rights. *Ancient Israel*, p. 54. But see Westbrook, "Redemption of Land," pp. 372–73.

[40] Compare Westbrook, "Law of the Biblical Levirate." Here he seems to say that Boaz redeemed *Mahlon's* land (p. 66), but later concludes that neither *Mahlon* nor Chilion ever inherited the family property (p. 77). Westbrook's theory is that either Elimelech (or Naomi, as his agent) had sold the land before moving to Moab. See also Westbrook, "The Price Factor," pp. 109–110, 126, where he suggests that the right of redemption arose only when the seller had been compelled to sell at discount because he had become poor. While Elimelech *might* have become poor and sold his land to a third party before moving to Moab, the text does not so indicate. Rather, it appears that it was the levirate law that prompted the transactions reported in Ruth ch. 4. Westbrook has carefully described the connection between levirate and redemption law. "The levirate therefore works alongside redemption. Just as the right of redemption restores to the family property that is lost (or threatened to be lost) by alienation, so the duty of the levirate restores a family to its property from which it is separated by extinction of the male line." "Redemption of Land," p. 372. The latter conditions evidently obtain in Ruth 4.

[41] Thus D. R. G. Beattie, "The Book of Ruth as Evidence for Israelite Legal Practice," *VT* 24 (1974) 254–55.

[42] So also Leggett, *Levirate and Goel*, pp. 219–20. Compare Campbell, *Ruth*, p. 157.

Bethlehem where she had lived with her husband and sons before they all went to sojourn in Moab. To be sure, no text specifically refers to Naomi's "house." But several texts suggest that after returning to Judah, Naomi resided in Bethlehem; Ruth 2:23, for instance, states that Ruth "lived with her mother-in-law" there.[43]

That widows inherited their deceased husbands' property is likewise evidenced in two different stories from the Elisha cycle. The first is 2 Kings 4:1-7, where Elisha helps a widow by causing her "cruse" or jar of oil to keep flowing until it produced enough to pay off her debts. We cannot tell whether the widow inherited her husband's debts, but she did evidently inherit and continue to live in the family house with her sons. The story in 2 Kings 8:1-6 also apparently concerns a widow with a son; her husband, who was said to be old in 2 Kings 4:8-37, is not mentioned at all in 8:1-6, which refers to *her* house and land.[44] It is reasonable to infer that her husband had died and that she had inherited his property.[45] That a widow might inherit her husband's property is also suggested in the story of Tobit. Raguel promises his son-in-law, Tobias, that he would receive the balance of his (Raguel's) property "when *my wife* and I die" (Tob. 8:20-21). The implication seems to be that if Raguel died first, his wife would inherit a life interest in the estate, which would then pass to Tobias only after her death.[46] Proverbs 15:25 suggests that widows inherited their deceased husbands' fields or land: "The Lord tears down the house of

---

[43] See also Ruth 1:22; 2:18; 3:1-3, 15-16. None of these texts suggests that Naomi and Ruth lacked a dwelling place or had to live "on the street," or that they were guests in anyone else's home. Burrows concludes that Naomi and Ruth lived in their own (or Naomi's) house. "Marriage," p. 447. Sasson assumes that they lived in Naomi's "house." *Ruth*, p. 124.

[44] 2 Kings 8:3, 5, 6.

[45] It has been suggested that Naomi and the Shunammite widow of 2 Kings 4 and 8 might have held their deceased husbands' properties as trustees or executors rather than as owners. Millar Burrows, *An Outline of Biblical Theology* (Philadelphia: Westminster Press, 1948), p. 302. There is no evidence of trusteeship or estate administration anywhere in biblical tradition, however, and it seems likely that these institutions had not yet emerged. Cuneiform laws, however, do provide for something like such trusteeship arrangements. Whether a biblical widow with a son (or sons) "inherited" property from her husband or served as "trustee" after his death by operation of law may be largely a semantic question. In either event, she apparently held many of the "sticks" of ownership, including possession and control of the property at least during her son's (or sons') minority. It is completely unclear however, when such sons attained "majority" or ownership themselves.

[46] It could be inferred instead that Raguel and his wife owned their property *jointly*; but such joint property ownership arrangements are otherwise unknown in biblical, and are rare in ancient Near Eastern tradition. But see Yochanan Muffs, *Studies in the Aramaic Legal Papyri from Elephantine* (Leiden: Brill, 1969), p. 33, n. 3.

the proud, but maintains the widow's boundaries" (Prov. 15:25).[47] Evidently a widow's property might be subjected to seizure or encroachment by predatory relatives or neighbors.[48] Micah 2:9 refers to women's houses. Read in the light of Micah 2:1-2 (condemning those who "covet fields, and seize them; and houses, and take them away"), the implication is that wicked persons sometimes preyed upon women (whether widows or daughters), unlawfully expropriating their fields and houses. It appears that Jewish women continued to inherit houses in New Testament times, and such houses continued to be preyed upon by the unscrupulous. Reportedly Jesus warned his hearers: "Beware of the scribes, who . . . devour widow's houses" (Mk 12:38-40; Lk. 20:46-47). Thus it appears that God's compassion, which called for just and compassionate treatment of the poor, orphans, and widows (Exod. 22:21-27), also came to expression in customary law or practice, whereby widows inherited their husband's property. These biblical texts, which indicate that widows inherited their husbands' real property, accord with a number of ancient Near Eastern laws and reported decisions.[49]

For example, the Code of Hammurabi, sections 171–174, provided that the bridegroom's gift to his bride would be used to support her and their children if the husband predeceased her, and that if he had not so provided for her, she was to be assigned a son's share in the deceased's estate.[50] There are no explicit biblical counterparts to these arrangements. However, it is entirely conceivable that common or "uncodified civil law" provided that a widow would inherit from her husband. Such law need not have been contrary to the law of intestate succession in Numbers chapter 27. That law may well have been meant to apply only if—as may generally have been the case—the son's mother had

---

[47] See also The Teaching of Amenope, 6:1-6, translated in Thomas, *Documents*, p. 179. The *Talmud* later assumes that a husband inherits land from his wife. Shmuel Safrai, "Sabbatical Law and Jubilee," *Encyclopedia Judaica* 14 (Jerusalem: Keter Publ. House, 1972), p. 581. Judges 17:1-4 indicates that the mother of a certain Micah, who may have been a widow, was a person of some wealth, which she may have inherited from her husband. It is not clear whether she lived in her own house, or in her son's house.

[48] Other texts also warn against moving landmarks or property markers: Deut. 19:14; Prov. 22:28, and 23:10.

[49] See, e.g., James B. Pritchard, *The Ancient Near East* (hereinafter, *ANE*) (Princeton Univ. Press, 1969), pp. 545–46; Muffs, *Studies*, pp. 33–34, n. 3; Eryl W. Davies, "Inheritance Rights and the Hebrew Levirate Marriage," *VT* 31 (1981) 138. Widows did not fare so well in post-biblical Jewish law. See Grunfeld, *Jewish Law*, pp. 10–16.

[50] Burrows, *Basis*, pp. 44–48; de Vaux, *Ancient Israel*, p. 54. As to Egyptian law c. 1100 B.C.E., see Fensham, "Widow, Orphan and the Poor," pp. 131–33; Van Seters, "Problem of Childlessness," pp. 405–06.

predeceased her husband.[51] At all events, the biblical widow's interests were at least indirectly protected under the law or practice of levirate marriage.[52]

## 2. Inheritance and Levirate Marriage

The law of levirate marriage in Deuteronomy 25:5-10 focuses attention on perpetuating a sonless deceased "brother's *name* in Israel," that is, building up a deceased "brother's house" by providing him a "son" (Deut. 25:7, 9). This law does not refer explicitly to property or inheritance; however, it is generally agreed that one of its functions was to assure retention of ancestral property within the family or clan.[53] The story of Judah and Tamar emphasizes the surviving brother's responsibility to "raise up offspring" for the deceased (Gen. 38:8), but likewise is silent on the subject of property and inheritance.[54] Westbrook argues persuasively that both Genesis 38 and Deuteronomy 25:5 nevertheless *do* relate to the inheritance of property.[55] He also observes that in both texts, the brothers to whom the law applied had lived together in an as yet undivided household.[56] Likewise, in the story of Ruth, the family property may have been, as yet, an undivided inheritance.

In the story of Ruth the property of the deceased Elimelech becomes a central topic in the negotiations between Boaz and the nearest kinsman. Scholarship is divided as to whether levirate marriage is a

---

[51] See Leggett, *Levirate and Goel*, pp. 216–17 and nn. 24 & 25. It may be more than merely coincidental that no biblical traditions report that sons or daughters inherited their father's property while his widow was still alive.

[52] Thus also Davies, "Inheritance Rights," pp. 257–68.

[53] Baruch A. Levine, *Leviticus*, JPS Torch Commentary (Philadelphia: Jewish Publication Soc., 1989), p. 254; de Vaux, *Ancient Israel*, p. 38. See particularly the Thompsons' study of "the name," in "Legal Problems," pp. 84–88.

[54] The story of Judah and Tamar does not say whether one of the twins inherited (as under the law of primogeniture) or whether both were eligible to do so. Nor is birthright mentioned here. The account of the twins' birth implies that which was born first may have been of some consequence: the midwife carefully ties a scarlet thread around the first hand to present. Deuteronomy 25:6 seems to say that only the "first son" born under levirate marriage would succeed to the name of the deceased. But it is unclear which twin was actually counted as first-born. Both sons were counted as sons of Judah (Num. 26:19-22). There are no other instances where more than one son was born under levirate marriage.

[55] He urges, for example, that Onan hoped to gain his later brother's inheritance by "marrying" Tamar, but avoiding effective intercourse with her, thus leaving no heirs to inherit in his brother's name. "Redemption of Land," pp. 374–75, n. 36; "Law of the Biblical Levirate," p. 73.

[56] Westbrook, *Property and the Family*, pp. 138, 140–41.

factor in this book; we shall assume that it is, without presuming to resolve the issue.

Naomi evidently had inherited Elimelech's land (Ruth 4:3). She had no surviving sons and was now proposing to sell the property. Elimelech's nearest kinsman (also known as the *go'el*) evidently had the opportunity, if not also obligation, to "redeem" the land "in order to restore the name of the dead to his inheritance" (Ruth 4:4-6, 10 RSV). According to Boaz, the widow of the deceased and the land were a package deal: in order to buy the land, the kinsman would have to marry the widow[57]—but Boaz did not specify *which* widow (Ruth 4:5). The next of kin seems to have acknowledged that redeeming the land and marrying "the widow" went together, but declined to exercise his option lest doing so "damage" or "impair" his own inheritance (Ruth 4:6).

Evidently the son (or sons) born to the widow of the deceased under levirate marriage would inherit the property "redeemed" by the kinsman's purchase.[58] It is unclear, however, how the nearer kinsman would have *damaged* or *impaired* his inheritance by marrying Ruth.[59] The kinsman-redeemer would have had to pay a fair price for the property; and he would have had to maintain a wife and perhaps a son. It is not clear whether he also would have been obliged to leave to the son by levirate marriage a portion of his own estate that otherwise would have passed to any other progeny he may have had. Professor David Daube insisted that any son by the prospective levirate marriage would have obtained Elimelech's patrimony, but nothing "from his physical begetter."[60] The *NOAB-RSV* annotator explains that the *go'el* backed out "because to raise up a son in the name of another would confuse the whole question of the inheritance of the estate."[61] Commenting on Deuteronomy 25:5-10, Dale Patrick suggests, "One reason the brother might not be willing to impregnate his brother's wife is that he and his children are in line for inheriting the deceased man's estate (according to Num. 27:9)".[62] But in the story of Ruth there is no suggestion that either the *go'el* or Boaz

---

[57] See generally, Leggett, *Levirate and Goel*, pp. 228–45. But see D. R. G. Beattie, "*Kethibh and Qere* in Ruth IV 5," *VT* 21 (1971) 490–94.

[58] See von Rad, *Genesis*, p. 353: "The son begotten by the brother is then considered the son and heir of the deceased man, 'that his name may not be blotted out of Israel' (Deut. 25:6)." See also Leggett, *Levirate and Goel*, pp. 247–48.

[59] "No passage in this work has produced more headaches." Daube, *Ancient Law*, pp. 40–41.

[60] *Id.*, p. 40. But see the Thompsons, "Legal Problems," p. 98; and Davies, "*Kethibh*," pp. 231, 234.

[61] *NOAB-RSV*, Old Testament sect., p. 328; cf. *NOAB-NRSV*, Hebrew Scriptures sect., p. 396.

[62] Dale Patrick, *Old Testament Law* (Atlanta: John Knox Press, 1985), p. 138.

stood to *inherit* the property.[63] Rather, title evidently had passed to Naomi, if not also to Ruth.[64] Daube's bold and ingenious proposal is that Boaz intentionally misled the nearer kinsman into believing that if he bought the property he would also be obliged to marry the widow *Naomi*![65] Daube urged that both Boaz and the *go'el* knew Naomi was too old to have children; if the nearer kinsman married her he risked dying without having heirs, thereby destroying his inheritance.[66]

Levirate marriage, if that is what we find in Ruth, entailed not only the kinsman's duty to perpetuate the name of the deceased, but also the duty to keep the deceased's property within the ancestral, patriarchal family by redeeming it, i.e., purchasing it from the widow. Otherwise, apparently, this land would remain the widow's, at least temporarily, or, if she remarried outside the family, would pass to some other

---

[63] Thus also Burrows, "Marriage," p. 446. Under terms of Numbers 27, the kinsman might be expected to have inherited the property. But the text of Ruth insists that *Naomi* owned the parcel of land. What would have happened to it if she married again? In fact, the kinsman did not inherit it because Boaz redeemed it (by purchase from Naomi) in connection with his marriage to Ruth, and, presumably, Obed eventually inherited it. Thus the kinsman was not in a position simply to assume that he and his children (if any—none are mentioned in Ruth) would inherit from Elimelech. Clearly Naomi's property interest in the parcel had priority over the kinsman's—notwithstanding the provisions of Num. 27. Exactly what the nature of her interest was, and how she had acquired it, are not, unfortunately, so certain.

[64] See above, text accompanying notes 35–43.

[65] Daube, *Ancient Law*, pp. 40–41. Compare Eryl W. Davies, "Ruth IV 5 and the Duties of the go'*el*," *VT* 33 (1983) 231–34. Davies suggests that the kinsman understood that he was to marry Naomi and, because she was past child-bearing, expected to acquire her property as his own; but then backed out on learning that the widow in question was Ruth, since she might bear a son who would claim not only the redeemed property but also a share of the *go'el*'s inheritance.

[66] Daube, *Ancient Law*, pp. 37–43. But how would those circumstances destroy the *go'el*'s inheritance? Daube's proposal assumes both that the nearer kinsman had no wife or children at the time, and that monogamy was then the standard societal norm. But it seems unlikely that the *go'el* would have had no other heirs. Compare Campbell, *Ruth*, p. 156: "[S]urely [the kinsman] is already married and has a family of his own." Westbrook notes that since Naomi was beyond the age of child-bearing, "the land purchased would pass to the redeemer's sons as part of his inheritance." "Redemption of Land," p. 374. But that would be a reason for the kinsman to *welcome* marriage with Naomi! Westbrook reads "widow of the dead" to mean Ruth, and concludes that the kinsman backed out simply because he would have had to pay money for land that would not become part of his patrimony. *Id.*, at pp. 374–75. That is, the kinsman's offspring by levirate marriage to Ruth would have inherited the property he had purchased from Naomi. This suggestion is persuasive. But that outcome would not have "destroyed" the kinsman's *inheritance* (4:6). For another ingenious theory, see Sasson, *Ruth*, pp. 136–40. Sasson suggests that as redeemer, the kinsman could have become liable to support the impoverished Naomi and Ruth's son (if any) who would ultimately inherit the parcel; moreover, under the laws of redemption in Lev. 25, the kinsman could have had to repurchase the parcel of land as often as these poor relations had occasion to sell it! Sasson denies that levirate marriage is a factor in the story of Ruth.

family.⁶⁷ Concern here is analogous to that expressed in Numbers 36 with respect to heiresses marrying outside the tribe. According to the story of Ruth, the nearest kinsman had first refusal or option both as to marrying the widow and redeeming the property. Under these circumstances, we may see another way the nearest kinsman could have "impaired" his inheritance by marrying Naomi. She was past the age of childbearing (Ruth 1:12-13); if he had no children and predeceased her, as his widow *she* could have inherited *his entire property*, or at least a life estate in it.

Another feature of levirate marriage may be seen in the Book of Ruth. The story, as told, not only evidences or legitimates extending both the duty of levirate marriage and the duty of redeeming the decedent's property to the nearest kinsman.⁶⁸ The story also, and perhaps more significantly, attests to and legitimates the practice of substituting for a widow who is beyond child-bearing years, her fertile, widowed daughter-in-law when the older widow's sons are now deceased and without heirs.⁶⁹ As Daube rightly pointed out, the first widow in line for levirate marriage in Ruth is Naomi.⁷⁰ It was, after all, Naomi who programmed Ruth's marriage to Boaz (ch. 3). As the story unfolds, Ruth is the biological mother of Obed, the son by levirate marriage, but Obed is hailed as Naomi's *go'el* (Ruth 4:15), and is presented, in effect, as the surrogate son of *Naomi* (4:17) and, therefore, implicitly, of Elimelech.⁷¹

---

⁶⁷ Thus also Beattie, "Ruth as Evidence,", pp. 251–67. Beattie concludes that widows could and did inherit their husbands' property. However, he does not see Ruth ch. 4 as instancing levirate marriage. Instead, he sees the scene as "a simple case of the second marriage to a childless widow who has inherited her husband's estate and whose children, by her second marriage, will therefore be heirs, *through her, to her first husband*." *Id.*, at p. 265, emphasis added. The kinsman backed off, Beattie suggests, because Boaz had announced his intent to marry Ruth: under these circumstances, if the kinsman redeemed the property, he would be doing so solely for the benefit of any son(s) born to Boaz and Ruth. *Id.* at p. 266.
⁶⁸ Thus Leggett, *Levirate and Goel*, p. 245. It is possible, however, that Deuteronomy 25:5-10 was meant to *limit* the obligation to the brother-in-law. Thus de Vaux, *Ancient Israel*, p. 22.
⁶⁹ Thus also E. Lipinski, "Le Mariage de Ruth," *VT* 26 (1976) 127. It should not be overlooked that the narrative also implies that the duty of the levirate includes marrying a foreign (or at least a Moabitess) widow.
⁷⁰ Daube, *Ancient Law*, p. 39. See Ruth 1:12, where Naomi speaks, albeit hypothetically, of having a husband, *presumably* a kinsman of Elimelech, and having sons whom the younger widows could marry if they waited long enough.
⁷¹ Compare Westbrook, "Law of the Biblical Levirate," p. 77, n. 43. Here he asserts that Boaz "does not raise up Elimelech's name . . . only Mahlon's." It is not clear, however, that "the dead man" (Ruth 4:5, 10) alludes to Mahlon rather than Elimelech.

## 3. Redemption, Jubilee Laws, and Inheritance

The idea that kinsmen have an obligation to "redeem" property in order to keep the inheritance in the family also appears prominently along with the laws pertaining to the Jubilee year.[72] The main legal provisions are set out in Leviticus chapter 25. Here the underlying concern is not preserving tribal inheritances, but rather preserving the land inheritances of each Israelite family or clan. To implement this policy, the Jubilee laws provided that farmland might not be sold "in perpetuity," or rather, "not beyond reclaim."[73] The theological premise is the understanding that the land ultimately belonged to YHWH, and that his people were only "strangers and guests" (Lev. 25:23).[74] Thus land, at any rate farmland, was not a commodity to be bought and sold.[75]

Under the Jubilees laws, Israelites might, in effect, lease or rent their farmland to others.[76] But they not only could, they were *obliged* to retake possession of it every fiftieth year: "In this year of jubilee each of your shall return to his property."[77] Implicitly, if the person who owned the land earlier had died, his heir or heirs would retake possession on his behalf. (It seems unlikely that the drafters of the Jubilee year law expected all property owners to live another 50 years, let alone, forever.). Although deeds for land sales were signed and witnessed, so far as we know, there was no provision for recording property transactions (compare Jer. 32:11-14); returning to the land evidently had the effect of reasserting the property owner's title to it. After so returning, presumably, the owner could "sell" or lease it again, either to the same lessee or to someone else for the next 49 years. Land "sales" or leases could be entered into at any time within the 49-year cycle, but the "price" or rent was to take into account the number of years—specifically, the number of annual crops—since the last Jubilee year (Lev. 25:15-16).

---

[72] See generally, David Daube, *Studies in Biblical Law* (New York: KTAV, 1969), pp. 43–45; Westbrook, "Jubilee Laws."

[73] See Levine, *Leviticus*, pp. 270–74. Houses within a walled city, however, could be sold in perpetuity (Lev. 25:29) unless the cities in question were "cities of the Levites" (25: 32-33). But houses within unwalled villages, like farmland, could not be sold in perpetuity (Lev. 25:21). Property not subject to sale in perpetuity supposedly would revert to its original owner in the Jubilee year.

[74] See generally, John Hart, *The Spirit of the Earth, A Theology of the Land* (Paulist Press, 1984), pp. 69–71 (translation suggested by Hart). Cf. the NRSV translation: "aliens and tenants."

[75] Westbrook, "Redemption of Land," pp. 367–68.

[76] Westbrook, "Jubilee Laws," p. 221; Levine, *Leviticus*, pp. 173, 273.

[77] Leviticus 25:13 (RSV); see also Lev. 25:10.

If a man became poor and had to "sell" (or lease) part of his property, his brother or next-of-kin was obliged to "redeem" what had been sold, evidently lest it pass out of the family in the interval before the next Jubilee year.[78] But if there was no one to redeem it, and the owner himself could not afford to buy it back in the meantime, the land would, nevertheless, revert to the owner (or, presumably, his heirs) in the year of Jubilee (Lev. 25:25-28).

Curiously, none of the redemption or Jubilee laws in Leviticus 25 refers expressly to the inheritance of land. It has often been pointed out that there is no evidence that the Jubilee year law provisions were ever carried out as such. Unlike levirate marriage, Jubilee laws do not even appear in the background of any biblical narrative except, perhaps, Ruth. But some other texts do take cognizance of the Jubilee year, and some of these explicitly relate it to the matter of inheritance.

Various laws in Leviticus 27:16-25, 28 distinguish between land a person possessed by inheritance and land one has "bought which is not a part of his possession by inheritance" (Lev. 27:22 RSV). A man may "redeem" (or repurchase) inherited land which he has vowed or pledged to Yahweh any time up to the year of Jubilee.[79] But if he failed to redeem it by the year of Jubilee, it would not revert to him, but instead would become "holy to Yahweh"[80] and "the priest"[81] would take possession of it. But if a man dedicated a field which he had bought (or leased) which was not his by inheritance, such land would not become "holy to Yahweh" in the Jubilee year. Instead, "[i]n the year of Jubilee the field shall return to him from whom it was bought, to whom the land belongs as a possession by inheritance" (Lev. 27:24 RSV). In other words, a man could not dedicate to Yahweh land that was not his by inheritance but

---

[78] Westbrook urges that the right of redemption arose only when the seller had become impoverished and sold to a third party at less than normal price. See generally, "Redemption of Land," p. 368, and "Price Factor," p. 97.

[79] A man who redeemed such land was to add a fifth of its value to the redemption price (Lev. 27:19).

[80] Leviticus 27:20 also provides that inherited land which a man has "sold" or leased to someone else, if not redeemed in the meantime, likewise would become holy to Yahweh in the Jubilee year. The Lessee's (or lease-holder's) interest would not be affected however, since the lessor (or original owner) otherwise would have retaken possession in the Jubilee year, thereby extinguishing the lessee's interest anyway.

[81] Presumably "the priest" referred to throughout Leviticus ch. 27 is the priest who happened to handle the particular case on behalf of the Jerusalem hierarchy. Similarly, modern lawyers refer, e.g., to "the magistrate" or "the judge," meaning the one who happens to hear a particular case.

belonged to someone else. Only the owner of inherited land could dedicate it to Yahweh.[82]

Numbers 36:1-4 provides another footnote to the situation of the famous daughters of Zelophehad, this time in connection with the year of Jubilee. Here we see what could have happened if Moses (or YHWH) had not provided that heiresses might marry only within their ancestral tribe. Absent such provision, the text implies, if these heiresses had married husbands from other tribes, their land would have been transferred permanently to their husbands' tribes in the year of Jubilee (Num. 36:3-4). It is unclear, however, how or why the Jubilee law as we know it from Leviticus 25 would have required that result or even been relevant to the situation.[83]

A final series of laws of inheritance relating to the Jubilee year appears in Ezekiel 46:16-18, in the somewhat curious context of "ordinances" or "laws" of the Temple revealed not to Moses, but to Ezekiel (Ezek. 44: 5–46:18). These laws concern the power of "the prince" to distribute property from inheritances—a subject strangely unrelated to Temple ordinances or laws. "The prince" may represent the King who was expected to rule Israel righteously in the ideal world after the exile or in the messianic age,[84] or may, perhaps, stand for post-exilic officials who might have been tempted to exploit their subjects.[85] These laws contain two main provisions. The first allows "the prince" to make gifts or bequests out of his own inheritance to his sons, since the sons would eventually take by inheritance anyway. But any gifts the prince gives to his servants from his inheritance are to revert to the prince (or, presumably, his heirs) in "the year of liberty" (Ezek. 46:16-17). "Gifts" here may include not only real property, but any kind of property subject to inheritance. The second provision bars the prince from taking the inheritances of others:

---

[82] Leviticus 27:28 provides that when a man has "devoted" an inherited field to Yahweh, it shall neither be sold nor be redeemed. Perhaps "devoted" property is that which has already been given to YHWH. Presumably a field so "devoted" would not be destroyed, unlike the fate of man and beast "devoted" under the old *ḥerem* tradition. See Joshua 6:17, 21; Lev. 27:29. Perhaps "the priest" would take possession of the devoted field as in the case of dedicated land released in the Jubilee year (Lev. 27:16-21).

[83] If husbands were entitled to heiresses' inheritances as suggested in the book of Tobit (Tob. 6:11 and 14:13), such inheritances would pass out of the tribe if the husbands belonged to other tribes apart from the operation of the law of the Jubilee year. See Numbers 36:3. Westbrook suggests that Num. 36:4 may have been a "mistaken gloss." Westbrook, "Jubilee Laws," p. 210. Compare Norman H. Snaith, "The Daughters of Zelophehad," *VT* 16 (1966) 127.

[84] See Ezekiel 45:7-9; cf. Isa. 11:1-9.

[85] For example, the "officials and nobles" against whom Nehemiah contended and some of the earlier post-exilic governors characterized in Nehemiah 5:1-15.

The prince shall not take any of the inheritance of the people, thrusting them out of their property; he shall give his sons their inheritance out of his own property, so that none of my people shall be dispossessed of his property. (Ezek. 46:18 RSV)

Here the peoples' inheritance appears to designate their land or real property—from which they might otherwise be "thrust out" by an unduly acquisitive prince or king. Perhaps this law was added in Ezekiel precisely because the Mosaic law contained no provision forbidding such conduct.[86]

Earlier kings and others in positions of power had not always respected the inheritances of their subjects.[87] Ezekiel (or a later editor) evidently wished to make sure that subsequent rulers, including, perhaps, early post-exilic functionaries, would know that they were not permitted to expropriate their subjects' inheritances.

## 4. The Birthright

The elusive biblical "birthright" tradition resembles intestate succession in that it seems to have affected inheritance from one generation to another by operation of law. Less is known about the biblical birthright than annotators and commentators sometimes claim. *Harper's Bible Dictionary*, for example, states flatly: "Biblical legislation . . . established the right of the firstborn to inherit a double portion of his father's possessions, i.e., twice as much as that received by each of his brothers."[88]

---

[86] See, however, the prohibition against *coveting* one's neighbor's house in Exod. 20:17 and Deut. 5:21, and that against coveting his field in the latter text. Westbrook notes that because of dating problems, we do not know "whether Ezekiel was inspired by Leviticus, or Leviticus by Ezekiel," or both by a common ideal. Westbrook, "Jubilee Laws," p. 226.

[87] 1 Kgs 21:1-16; Isa. 5:8; Mic. 2:1-2. See generally, B. Davie Napier, "Inheritance and the Problem of Adjacency: An Essay on 1 Kings 21," *Interpretation: A Journal of Bible and Theology* 30 (1976) 3–11. Weingreen argues persuasively that the Naboth story in 1 Kings 21, and also Num. 27:3-4, evidence the existence and operation of a law whereby property that otherwise would pass to heirs was confiscated by the sovereign if the owner had committed treason. "Case of the Daughters," pp. 321–22. Compare the Parable of the Wicked Tenants, Mt. 21:33-39 = Mk 12:1-8 = Lk. 20:9-15, where the tenants try to obtain the heir's "inheritance" by killing the heir.

[88] *HBD*, p. 422. Strangely, many commentators assume that Deuteronomy 21:15-17 requires that the older or oldest son receive a double share of the inheritance in circumstances where there is no question as to a loved and unloved wife. See, e.g., James Kent, *Commentaries on American Law*, 14th edn., John M. Gould, ed., (Boston: Little, Brown & Co. 1896), pp. 376–77; James G. Frazer, *Folklore in the Old Testament* (New York: Macmillan & Co., 1919), p. 430, n. 1; C. J. Mullo Weir, "Nuzi," in D. Winton Thomas, ed., *Archeology and Old Testament Study* (Oxford: Clarendon, 1967) p. 76; Richardson, ed., *Theological Word Book*, p. 83; *NWDB*, p. 376; *IDB*, vol. 2, p. 702.

The commentator cites as authority the *locus classicus*, Deuteronomy 21:15-17. But this text refers only to what must be done in the following special situation:

> If a man has two wives, the one loved and the other disliked, and they have borne him children, both the loved and the disliked, and if the first-born son is hers that is disliked, then on the day when he assigns his possessions as an inheritance to his sons, he may not treat the son of the loved as the first-born in preference to the son of the disliked, who is the first-born, but he shall acknowledge the first-born, the son of the disliked, by giving him a double portion of all that he has, for he is the first issue of his strength; and the right of the first-born is his. (RSV)

There is no biblical legislation establishing the rights of the first-born.[89] The law of intestate succession in Numbers chapter 27 is entirely silent as to any special entitlements on the part of first-born sons or daughters. To be sure, it may plausibly be *inferred* from Deuteronomy 21:15-17 that as a matter of unwritten custom or tradition at one time or another, the first-born son ordinarily received a double portion.[90] It is odd that there are no other biblical texts that illustrate or follow such a tradition.

Deuteronomy 21:16 refers to the day on which a man "assigns his possessions as an inheritance to his sons." This suggests a process very much like testation, the making of a will. What Deuteronomy 21:15-17 says, in effect, is that a man may not ignore his obligation to provide his first-born son with a double portion just because he dislikes that son's mother. Thus this law is somewhat similar in purpose to modern statutes that prevent one spouse from "writing" the other "out of" his or her will

---

[89] Nuzi evidence is ambiguous. Nashwi's will (or "tablet of adoption") provided that his adopted son, Wullu, would share his estate equally with any of Nashwi's own sons. Zike's will (or tablet of adoption) provided that a certain Shuriha-ilu would take a double share if he (Shuriha-ilu) had a son of his own. *ANET*, pp. 219–20. These texts illustrate ancient wills, but do not appear relevant as to inheritance or birthright.
The only ancient Near Eastern texts apparently providing that the oldest son take two portions of inherited land are Middle Assyrian Laws, tablet B, *ANET*, p. 185, and an old Babylonian (Mari) judicial decision, *ANE*, p. 545.

[90] Thus also Patrick, *Old Testament Law*, p. 129: "The ruling assumes the principle of primogeniture—that a man's first-born male child receives a double portion of his inheritance." But see below, note 97 and accompanying text. See generally, Eryl W. Davies, "The Meaning of *pi senayim* in Deuteronomy XX 17," *VT* 36 (1986) 341–45. Calum M. Carmichael suggests that the double portion provision in Deut. 21:15-17 may represent merely "the lawgiver's interpretation of what Jacob had done for Joseph in settling the prime inheritance upon him" in Genesis 48 and 49. "Uncovering a Major Source of Mosaic Law: the Evidence of Deuteronomy 21:15–22:5," *JBL* 101 (1984) 506–508.

by providing that the survivor may elect a "spousal share" in lieu of taking under terms of the will.[91]

The idea that the first-born son is entitled to a larger share of his father's inheritance is supported by the ancient Hittite story of Appu and his twin sons.[92] After Appu and his wife die, the twins set out to divide up the family property. The older justifies helping himself to the "sleekest cow" by arguing, "Am I not the elder? And what says the law? 'The larger portion to the eldest, the smaller to the others.'"[93] The extant portions of Hittite law codes, however, do not refer to inheritance,[94] but it may well be that the biblical birthright tradition was influenced by earlier Hittite or other ancient Near Eastern law or custom.[95]

It is remarkable, however, that no other biblical traditions indicate that the first-born son had the right to a double or even enlarged portion of the inheritance.[96] The law of intestate succession in Numbers chapter 27 makes no reference to double portions. Nevertheless, annotators typically assume or assert that the birthright Jacob purchased (or extorted) from his brother, Esau, consisted of "a double share of the inheritance."[97] The biblical account of that transaction, Genesis 25:29-34, however, gives

---

[91] Similarly, under Islamic law, a man could not disinherit his wife—or anyone else. All was spelled out. See above, note 12.

[92] Theodor H. Gaster, *The Oldest Stories in the World* (Boston: Beacon Press, 1958), pp. 159–171.

[93] *Id.* at p. 163; see also *id.* at p. 164: "The law says clearly that the eldest is to have the most."

[94] *Id.* at p. 169.

[95] The *HBD* reports that several other ancient Near Eastern cultures provided for "preferential treatment of the eldest son," but that the codes of Lipit-Ishtar and Hammurabi required that all male heirs inherit *equal* shares. *HBD*, pp. 134–35. See Lipit-Ishtar Law Code, sect. 24, *ANET*, p. 160; Code of Hammurabi, sect. 170, in Thomas, *Documents*, p. 33, quoted above, note 14. The Babylonian Theodicy, vv. 245–264, however, suggests that the first-born may have enjoyed special favor or status. Thomas, *Documents*, p. 101. See generally, Isaac Mendelsohn, "On the Preferential Status of the Eldest Son," *BASOR* 156 (1959) 38–40.

[96] Arguably, Jacob gave Joseph a double share by adopting or otherwise designating the latter's two sons as recipients of equal shares with Joseph's brothers (Gen. 48:1-6). Nothing is said here, however, about birthright or transfer of birthright. The arrangement is more in the nature of a bequest. See below, text accompanying notes 112 & 113. It may well be, however, that this scene was meant to explain how it came about that Ephraim and Manasseh enjoyed full tribal status, and provides no information as to transfer of property by inheritance or bequest. Though Joseph was Rachel's oldest son, he was not Jacob's oldest son.

[97] E.g., *NOAB-RSV*, Old Testament sect., p. 31; *NOAB-NRSV*, Hebrew Bible Sect., p. 46. Other than in the situation of Levirate marriage (Deut. 25:6), no biblical text suggests that the first-born son alone inherited when there were other sons. Frazer makes a plausible case for the idea that traces of ultimogeniture, or inheritance by the *youngest* son, can be found in biblical tradition. *Folk-Lore*, pp. 429–33. Aside from Gen. 25:29-31, however, none of the texts he discusses involve inheritance of property. In Genesis

no clue at all as to the substantive content of a birthright.[98] The story does demonstrate that whatever benefits the birthright afforded, it was considered alienable, that is, could be sold, at least between sons prior to the father's demise.[99] If we may credit the Chronicler on this point, Reuben forfeited his birthright because he had engaged in sexual relations with his father's concubine or wife, Billah.[100] Forfeiture of Reuben's birthright is not reported in Genesis traditions, however.[101] In Chronicles, the chief consequence of this forfeiture was that Reuben was "not enrolled in the genealogy according to his birthright" (1 Chron. 5:1). So we find no further evidence here as to whether birthright meant a double or enlarged inheritance.[102]

Conceivably, birthright tradition forms part of the background for the incident described in Luke 12:13: "One of the multitude said to [Jesus], 'Teacher, bid my brother divide the inheritance with me'" (RSV). The diligent *NOAB* annotator could not refrain from adding a footnote citing Deuteronomy 21:17 for the proposition that "the elder received double the younger's share."[103] There is no hint in the text, however, that the older brother was claiming a double portion. Nor is there any reference to birthright here, so we cannot be certain that it was an issue in the dispute between the brothers. Again, the birthright tradition *may* be implicated in the Parable of the Prodigal Son (Lk. 15:11-32). The younger son asked his father to give him "the share of the property" he would otherwise eventually inherit. The parable then says that the father "divided his property between them" (Lk. 15:12). Here, too, it is not

---

25:29-31, it is clearly implied that the older son normally would have enjoyed the birthright.

[98] So also von Rad, *Genesis*, p. 262, "[W]hat is to be understood by the birthright is not sufficiently clear from the narrative."

[99] Thus also *HBD*, p. 135. See generally, Reuben Ahroni, "Why Did Esau Spurn the Birthright?," *Judaism* 29 (1980) 323–31. The *NOAB* annotator inexplicably cites Gen. 25:29-34 as authority for the proposition, "In antiquity it was believed that the right of the first-born was inalienable." *NOAB*, p. 242; *NOAB-NRSV*, p. 245.

[100] 1 Chron. 5:1.

[101] See Gen. 35:22 and 49:3. The latter text reports that Jacob declared that Reuben would lose his "pre-eminence." Westbrook suggests that such pre-eminence included "the right to administer the paternal estate while still undivided, which would normally have been assigned to the first-born." Westbrook, *Property and the Family*, p. 136. Pre-eminence is also associated with birthright or the status of the first-born in Gen. 27:36-37 and 43:33. On the significance of Reuben's offense, see Judah Goldin, "The Youngest Son," *JBL* 96 (1977) 37–38. Goldin concludes that Reuben thereby intended to proclaim that he had succeeded his father, just as Absalom later did when he publicly took over his father's concubines (See 2 Sam. 16:20-22).

[102] See generally, Stanley Gervitz, "The Reprimand of Reuben," *JNES* 30 (1971) 87–98.

[103] *NOAB-RSV*, pp. 1263–64; See also *NOAB-NRSV*, New Testament sect., p. 121.

clear that the birthright tradition is involved, and there is no indication that the older brother claimed or was entitled to a double portion. The parable does suggest that a son might ask for an advance on his eventual anticipated inheritance, but whether this reflects actual practice or custom within the biblical period we cannot say; it may only be a fictive element within the parable.

In summary, the notion that the biblical birthright meant that the older or oldest son was entitled to a double portion of his father's inheritance depends entirely upon Deuteronomy 21:15-17. That text does not use the expression "birthright," nor does it require that the older son receive a double portion of the inheritance under circumstances other than the peculiar one where the father loves one wife and dislikes the other.[104] No other biblical text intimates that the first-born son was entitled to a double share of his father's inheritance.[105] Nor is there any indication that primogeniture was practiced in biblical times.[106]

## C. Wills or Bequests, and Inter-vivos Gifts

What distinguishes bequests or gifts from inheritance through intestate succession is that the former require some affirmative act by the testator or donor in order to make the gift effective. Necessarily, such act can be taken only during the lifetime of the testator or donor.

No biblical text indicates that anyone in the biblical community ever drafted and signed a will or authorized an executor to transfer property to beneficiaries upon the testator's demise. In his classic study of ancient

---

[104] Here again, it may be that biblical customary law derived from other Near Eastern cuneiform law. To what extent the latter required that the first-born son receive a double portion, however, is uncertain. See Section B.4 of this Chapter.

[105] Another aspect of birthright tradition or custom may be better attested, namely, the oldest brother's seniority and leadership status within the family. See, e.g., Gen. 43:33, 1 Chron. 26:10, 2 Chron. 21:3, and discussion of these and several other texts in Gordon, "Fratriarchy," pp. 223–31. Because we are concerned only with inheritance of property, this aspect of biblical birthright tradition is not examined further here.

[106] But see above, note 97, as to Deuteronomy 25:6. Henry Sumner Maine insisted, properly, that birthright should not be confused with primogeniture. He defined the latter as "the exclusive succession of a single son" to his father's property. *Lectures on the Early History of Institutions*, 7th edn. (1914, Port Washington, NY: Kennikat Press reprint, 1966), p. 198. Nevertheless, interpreters occasionally use the terms "primogeniture" and "birthright" interchangeably. E.g., Ahroni, "Why Did Esau Spurn," pp. 323–25. Without citing supporting evidence, de Vaux asserts, "It is probable that when land was inherited it was not shared like other property but passed to the eldest son or remained undivided." *Ancient Israel*, p. 166.

law, Henry Sumner Maine asserted that biblical Israelites or Jews had not developed the institution of testation.[107] There are no *laws* governing testamentary succession in the Bible.[108] Nevertheless, several texts do suggest that people in the biblical period occasionally did make some kind of testamentary disposition of their property. Sometimes this disposition was made shortly before the testator's death, apparently in the form of an oral deathbed will. In other instances, such gifts appear to have been made prior to the donor's imminent expectation of death. Some of these gifts, though arguably testamentary in character, could also be described as inter-vivos gifts, that is, as gratuitous transfers of property between living persons.

## 1. Gifts or Bequests in Prospect of the Testator's or Donor's Death

Deuteronomy 21:15-16 refers to "the day when [a man] assigns his possessions as an inheritance to his sons" (RSV). We may infer that this assignment was equivalent to a person's "putting his affairs in order," and more specifically, determining what property would go to which son.[109] This assignment need not necessarily have taken place in anticipation of imminent demise. It is likely that Genesis 24:36 and 25:5-6 reflect this kind of testamentary practice. In both texts it is said that Abraham gave Isaac all that he had.[110] The latter adds that Abraham also had given gifts to the sons of his concubines. Here what might be called the "bequest" is referred to as if it already had been conveyed to the beneficiaries.[111]

---

[107] Henry Sumner Maine, *Ancient Law*, 10th edn. (1920, Buffalo: Wm. S. Hein & Co. reprint, 1983), p. 209. Thus also Emanuel Rackman, "A Jewish Philosophy of Property: Rabbinic Insights on Intestate Succession," *Jewish Quarterly Review* 67 (1976) 65–89. But see Isaac Herzog, *The Main Institutions of Jewish Law*, vol. 1 (London: Socino Press, 1965), pp. 296–98. Maine, of course, would not have known the vast body of recently recovered, ancient Near Eastern materials which show that the institution of testation was well established in many of these cultures. See generally, Szubin and Porten, "Testamentary Succession," pp. 35–46.

[108] Solomon Zeitlin, "Testamentary Succession: A Study in Tannaitic Jurisprudence," in Abraham A. Neuman and Solomon Zeitlin, eds., *Seventy-Fifth Anniversary Volume* (Philadelphia: Jewish Quarterly Review, 1967), p. 574. See also the translation of Deut. 21:16 in the *NOAB-NRSV*, Hebrew Bible Sect., p. 279: ". . . on the day when he wills his possessions to his sons . . ."

[109] De Vaux suggests that 2 Samuel 17:23 and 2 Kings 20:1 refer to situations where "a father . . . gave verbal instructions about the distribution of his property." *Ancient Israel*, p. 53.

[110] Presumably this estate included, *inter al.*, the cave of Machpelah. See Westbrook, "Cave of Machpelah," cited above, note 3.

[111] See Thomas E. Atkinson, *The Law of Wills* (St. Paul: West Publishing Co., 1953), p. 7, n. 11. Atkinson observes that Sennacherib's will, executed c. 681 B.C., likewise used the

Technically, most if not all of the biblical "bequests" were inter-vivos gifts. But since most of these conveyances occurred while the donor was in advanced years and were made for the purpose of passing his property to heirs, these gifts can accordingly be said to have functioned as bequests.

We see something very like a deathbed will in Genesis 48:21-22. Here, after stating that he is about to die, Jacob tells Joseph, "I have given to you rather than to your brothers one mountain slope which I took from the hand of the Amorites with my sword and with my bow" (RSV).[112] Jacob's gift to Joseph of a double portion of his inheritance (Gen. 48:5-6) likewise appears to be a bequest made in anticipation of the testator's death.[113] Similarly, 2 Chronicles 21:2-3 reports that King Jehoshaphat gave his sons "great gifts of silver, gold, and valuable possessions, together with fortified cities in Judah," evidently just before his death.[114] Sirach 33:24 specifically commends the practice of deathbed distribution: "At the time when you end the days of your life, in the hour of death, distribute your inheritance."[115] Nearby texts caution against making earlier inter vivos gifts: e.g., "[D]o not give your property to another, in case you change your mind and must ask for it [back]" (Sir. 33:20).

A number of testamentary gifts or bequests are described in the pseudepigraphic literature.[116] Jubilees 45:14-15 says that Jacob (Israel) "gave to Joseph a double portion upon the land" (cf. Gen. 48:5-6), and gave all his books and his father's books to his son Levi, to pass on, in turn, to their sons. In the Testament of Job, that ancient worthy tells his children that he is dying, and proceeds to distribute his estate or "goods" to his seven sons, except for three magical "sashes" or phylacteries, which he gives, one each, to his three daughters (T. Job 45:1–50:3). Responding to the daughters' complaint that these were of little value, Job characterizes the sashes as "an inheritance better than that of your seven brothers" (T. Job 46:4).[117]

---

formula, "I have given" rather than "I give." *Id.*

[112] Weir quotes a Nuzi text deathbed will whereby a dying father gives a female slave to one of his sons as his wife. "Nuzi," p. 76.

[113] See Szubin and Porten, "Testamentary Succession," p. 37. But see above, note 96.

[114] Because the Chronicler reports Jehoshaphat's death and burial before stating that he gave his sons these gifts, it might be supposed that the sons received these gifts through a testamentary instrument or will (1 Chron. 21:1-3). But it is equally likely that the Chronicler merely meant to say that Jehoshaphat had given his sons these gifts prior to his death.

[115] De Vaux reads Sirach 14:13 similarly. *Ancient Israel*, p. 53.

[116] The following citations in the text are all drawn from James H. Charlesworth, ed., *The Old Testament Pseudepigrapha*, 2 vols. (New York: Doubleday, 1983, 1985).

[117] See also *Joseph and Aseneth* 29:9 (11), which tells that after reigning as king in Egypt for 48 years, Joseph "gave the diadem" to Pharoah's young son.

## 2. Inter-vivos Gifts to Eventual Heirs

Although as the biblical story is told, Job was an Edomite, not an Israelite or Jew, it is arguable that the beliefs and practices attributed to him and others in the book are more representative of biblical than of Edomite tradition.[118] Job 42:15-16 tells that Job gave inheritances to both his sons and daughters, and *then* lived 140 more years. It is unclear whether the story-teller meant to say that Job transferred all his property to his children 140 years before his death, or that he gave some property to them, retaining what he would need for his own purposes, or that he made a testamentary disposition to the effect that they would receive their inheritances after his death. The last possibility is the least likely, since it is unreasonable to suppose that the reader would expect Job's children to have survived him.[119] The former possibilities are paralleled to some extent in the Parable of the Prodigal Son (Lk. 15:11-32). There, the father gives the younger son in advance the share of the inheritance he otherwise would receive at the father's death. After this son returns from his fling at riotous living, the older brother points out that his profligate brother had "devoured" their father's property.[120] That, of course, is no problem to the prodigal's father, who eagerly welcomes him back. Yet unless at the time he advanced the prodigal his inheritance the father retained a portion of his estate for his own use, the father (and also the prodigal) would now have to live on the estate previously earmarked as the older brother's inheritance (Compare Sirach 33:20-22). Whether Job transferred all his property to his children

---

[118] See, e.g., the orthodox wisdom theology represented by Job's friends, the creation faith represented in Job 38-39, and Job's exemplification of the covenant ethic in Job 29: 11-17; 31:1-40. Dating and authorship of Job are uncertain, but its congruence with both certain biblical and cuneiform traditions is beyond doubt. See Marvin Pope, *Job*, Anchor Bible (Garden City: Doubleday, 1973), pp. XXXII–XLII.

[119] If Job had arranged to leave his property to his children upon his death, and then lived another 140 years, his children would have taken nothing unless they managed to outlive him. Job was the only biblical person since the days of the "patriarchs" (Gen. 25:7; 35:28) said to have lived as long as 140 years, let alone longer. Pope notes that the Septuagint credits Job with a total of 240 years. *Job*, pp. 353–54.

[120] "[T]his son of yours . . . has devoured your property with prostitutes." Lk. 15:30. See also Luke 15:13. Earlier wisdom traditions had warmed against such conduct. See Sirach 9:6: "Do not give yourself to harlots or you may lose your inheritance." For particularly insightful reflections on the Parable of the Prodigal Son that point to the biblical norms of justice and compassion, see Christopher D. Marshall, "Offending, Restoration, and the Law-Abiding Community: Restorative Justice in the New Testament and in the New Zealand Experience," *JSCE* 27 (2007) 3–30.

## Transfer of Property by Inheritance and Bequest 55

and then was supported by them, or retained some to provide for his own support, we cannot tell. That detail was not of interest to the narrator.

Testamentary arrangements are also noted in the story of Judith. Though her husband died unexpectedly (Jdt. 8:2-3), he "had left her gold and silver, and men and women slaves, and cattle, and fields" (Jdt. 8:7). It appears that Judith's husband had made some provision transferring his estate to her either before he was taken ill or in the interval before he died. He had other relatives (Jdt. 16:24) who otherwise, *perhaps*, would have inherited under the law of intestate succession (Num. 27:8-11).[121] Then, at the end of the story, before she died, she distributed her property to various relatives (Jdt. 16:24). Clearly her intent was to bequeath the estate to certain devisees or beneficiaries. We see here that not only men, but also women could devise property by will or bequest.

### 3. Eligible Devisees or Beneficiaries

To whom might property be willed or bequeathed? Were there any eligibility requirements? What we have called the law of intestate succession in Numbers chapter 27 evidently did not limit testators who wished to dispose of their property otherwise.[122] To be sure, sons were likely to be the sole devisees or beneficiaries. Gifts might also be given to the sons of concubines (Gen. 25:5-6). Job gave or bequeathed an inheritance not only to each of his seven sons, but also to each of his three daughters.[123] Presumably the daughters were given shares equal to those given to their brothers.[124] Proverbs 13:22 says, "A good man leaves an inheritance to his children's children" (RSV). This could have meant leaving a bequest for

---

[121] There are other instances, however, where biblical widows apparently inherited their husbands' real property notwithstanding the written law of intestate succession in Numbers chapter 27. See Section B.1.c. of this Chapter. The bequest to Judith parallels a Ugaritic oral will in which a certain Yarimanu bequeathed his entire estate—including cattle, slaves, bronze bowls, kettle and jugs, baskets, and a field—to his wife. That will, however, went on to provide that the couple's sons would be penalized if they sued their mother for the estate, but that she was to bequeath the estate to whichever son paid her respect. *ANE*, p. 546.

[122] Thus H. H. Rowley, *Job*, New Century Bible (Greenwood, S.C.: Attic Press, 1985), p. 268.

[123] An Old Babylonian text records that a woman bequeathed real property to her adopted daughter. *ANE*, pp. 543–44. Several instances of bequests to daughters are found among the 5th century B.C.E. Aramaic legal documents from Elephantine. See Szubin and Porten, "Testamentary Succession," pp. 41–44. Daughters were beneficiaries of bequests in ancient Elam, also. See Ben-Barak, "Inheritance by Daughters," pp. 31–32.

[124] So A. van Selms, *Job* (Grand Rapids: Eerdmans, 1985), p. 158. But see Zafrira Ben-Barak, "Job's Daughters and the Question of Inheritance in Israel and the Ancient Near East," SBL 1990 International. Meeting *Abstracts* 7–8: "The daughters are given

granddaughters as well as grandsons.[125] Numbers chapter 27, it will be recalled, made no provision for grandchildren. Nor did it provide for wives, but that did not prevent Judith's husband from leaving her his estate (Jdt. 8:7; 16:21). That a man might bequeath property to his widow was well-established in Ugaritic law,[126] at Nuzi,[127] and in the Code of Hammurabi (CH, sect. 150). It is not necessary to suppose that Israelites or Jews adopted such practices only in the late biblical period. The Judith story also introduces another variation on Numbers chapter 27. Before Judith died, in anticipation of her death, she distributed her estate not only to her husband's next of kin, but also to her own (Jdt. 16:24). Neither of these types of distribution was provided for in Numbers 27, which, in the first place, only governed transfer of property by intestate succession, and, second, said nothing about a widow's distributing inherited property either to her husband's relatives or to her own.[128]

Finally, one text suggests that a man might bequeath property both to a slave and to his own natural sons:

> A slave who deals wisely will rule over a son who acts shamefully, and will share the inheritance as one of the brothers. (Prov. 17:2 RSV)[129]

This is not the same situation as in Genesis 15:3-4 which suggests that a slave born in the house of a childless father might inherit his property.[130] Here, it is a matter of a good slave[131] sharing an inheritance along with his master's sons. It is likely that he would do so only if the master had so arranged by making a special bequest.

---

part of the inheritance, albeit in an inferior way." This issue evidently troubled an earlier interpreter. See above, text accompanying note 117.

[125] Grandchildren were also named as beneficiaries at Elephantine. Szubin and Porten, "Testamentary Succession," pp. 41–44. However, Proverbs 13:22 could mean only that a righteous man's wealth would be enjoyed by his intestate heirs to the third generation. Compare Ps. 37:18.

[126] See L. M. Muntingh, "The Social and Legal Status of a Free Ugaritic Female," *JNES* 26 (1967) 111, and see above, note 121.

[127] See the Thompsons, "Legal Problems," pp. 97–98.

[128] Compare the *NOAB-RSV* annotator's comment, "She distributed her property according to the Mosaic law (Num. 27:11)." *NOAB-RSV*, Apocrypha sect., p. 95; *NOAB-NRSV*, Apocrypha sect., p. 52.

[129] Compare Proverbs 29:21. There, however, the text is too uncertain to permit drawing any conclusions.

[130] See above, text accompanying notes 20–23.

[131] Proverbs 17:2 speaks of a "slave who deals wisely." In biblical wisdom writings, wisdom and goodness are closely related if not synonymous attributes.

## D. Conclusions

Previous accounts of inheritance in biblical law and tradition generally have not distinguished between inheritance by operation of law (or intestate succession) and transfer of property by bequest. The latter topic has either been ignored or subsumed under the former. Yet the distinction, common in modern law, appears valid in describing biblical law and practice.

The law of intestate succession in Numbers 27:8-11 evidently was meant to apply when the deceased had not bequeathed his property to anyone. The order of succession or descent was as follows: first the decedent's son(s), then his daughter(s), then his brothers, then his uncles, and finally, in the absence of all of the above, his family's nearest kinsman.[132] All the property would pass to the person or persons in each category; those next in order would take nothing if there was a surviving heir in the higher category. Thus, for example, a surviving daughter with no brothers would inherit everything, while the decedent's brothers would receive nothing. Various biblical texts, however, alter or supplement this pattern. As we have seen, one text suggests that a slave born in his master's house might inherit his property.[133] If the parents had no sons but an only daughter who later marries, their son-in-law might inherit everything.[134] More surprisingly, is the evidence that widows—who are not mentioned in Numbers chapter 27—might inherit their husbands' property.[135] Naomi's late husband had male relatives; yet it was she who evidently inherited his field. The widows of 2 Kings chapters 4 and 8 apparently inherited their deceased husbands' houses, even though each had a surviving son or sons. Perhaps the understanding was that the widow had a life-interest in her husband's estate, but that on her demise it would pass to their sons or others in the order of intestate succession set out in Numbers chapter 27.[136]

---

[132] It may be noted that this law makes no mention of the decedent's sisters, aunts, or nearest kinswomen.

[133] See above, text accompanying note 21.

[134] See above, text accompanying notes 29–32. It is unclear what would happen if parents had no sons, but more than one daughter and one daughter married while the others remained single.

[135] See Section B.1.c. of this Chapter.

[136] In Naomi's case, levirate marriage custom evidently provided that she might sell the inherited property to her deceased husband's nearest kinsman if that kinsman also married her—or by extension, the widow of one of her sons—in order "to restore the name of the dead to his inheritance" (Ruth 4:5 RSV). Presumably, the son born of this

Clearly bequests could be made to persons other than those identified in this law of intestate succession. That law, apparently, was not regarded as controlling with regard to bequests. Bequests could be left to widows, daughters along with sons, slaves, and possibly grandchildren. Moreover, a widow might bequeath property not only to her husband's relatives, but also to her own.[137]

Bequests were not, however, in the form of modern wills, that is, testamentary instruments or documents signed or formally "executed" by the testator, witnessed by others, and intended to become effective upon the testator's death. Instead, typically, the biblical testator, without any discernible formalities, simply gave property to the donees or devisees or stated that he had already done so. In most instances, such gifts were made when the testator or donor expected that he or she would die in the somewhat near (though not necessarily immediate) future.[138]

Though these conclusions may be reasonably likely, a number of issues remain unsettled. Possibly research into laws and customs of other ancient Near Eastern cultures may shed further light on these questions. Definitive answers may not be found, however, because the evidence is insufficient to justify final conclusions.

Instances have been seen where widows with sons apparently inherited their husbands' property.[139] At what point would such sons inherit their father's property? Was there some age of majority? Or would the widowed mother continue to hold or control the property until she died or remarried? If she remarried, would the sons then take their father's property, or would it pass to the second husband?

A somewhat similar set of questions arises with respect to sons by levirate marriage. Would such sons "inherit," that is, take possession of their nominal father's property when they reached some age of majority, or would their biological (or "surrogate") father hold it for them until his demise? When the biological father died, would the first-born son by levirate marriage inherit some of his property, thus taking away from what the father's "own" sons, if any, would have inherited; or would the first-born son by levirate marriage inherit only the redeemed property

---

marriage would not immediately inherit, i.e., take possession of the redeemed property, the day he was born. Perhaps he would do so only upon the death of his biological or surrogate father.

[137] Jdt. 16:24.
[138] See Section C.1. of this Chapter.
[139] 2 Kgs 4:1-7; 8:1-6.

that had belonged to their nominal father? If there should be more than one son by levirate marriage, would the older (or oldest) take all, or only a double portion; or would such sons share the inheritance equally?[140] What would happen if the deceased's property was redeemed and the levirate marriage was blessed with daughters, but no son?[141] Would such daughters inherit the redeemed property? Would only the first-born daughter inherit, or would all such daughters be considered heiresses, as under the laws of inheritance set out in Numbers chapters 27 and 36?

In the case of the Jubilee year laws, was it expected that the original owner himself would return to the property after 49 years, or was it understood that his heir or heirs would do so if he had died in the meantime? In case of multiple heirs, would the original property be partitioned among them, or would it be kept intact? (Or had the planners for the Jubilee year neglected to contemplate this problem?) Was it expected that the Jubilee year would be repeated every 50 years, or was it meant to be observed only once?[142] In either event, what was to be the base year from which the fiftieth would be reckoned?

Finally, as to the birthright: it is reasonable to infer from Deuteronomy 21:15-17 that at some point in the biblical period, the first-born son was entitled to receive a double portion of his father's estate, whether by inheritance or bequest, as a matter of custom. Yet a double portion entitlement is not attested by *any* other biblical text. The question remains, then, to what extent such a birthright tradition or practice actually was observed during the biblical period.

---

[140] Westbrook speculates that "all sons of the levirate union shared in the inheritance of the deceased." "Law of the Biblical Levirate," pp. 79–80. See also C. J. H. Wright, *Family*, in 2 *Anchor Bible Dictionary* 763 (Doubleday, 1992) (suggesting that other sons would be heirs to the levir's property).

[141] See above, note 28.

[142] The Jubilee year laws do not specify that the Jubilee year was to be repeated every 50 years, but refer instead to *the* year of Jubilee. Yet a cycle seems implicit in the provisions synchronizing the Jubilee year with the series of Sabbatical years in Leviticus 25:1-10, and scholars generally assume that the law intended that the cycle be repeated throughout history. Later Judaism understood that the cycles were to have been repeated. 14 *Encyclopedia Judaica* (Keter Pub., 1972), pp. 581–82.

# Part II

# Criminal Law

*It is not right to be partial to the guilty,*
*or to subvert the innocent in judgment.*

*Proverbs 18:5*

*To no man will we refuse justice.*

*Magna Carta*

Necessarily, biblical texts themselves do not distinguish between the relatively modern categories of civil and criminal law. Nevertheless, this distinction not only is useful; it is also implicit in biblical laws. Part I examined certain biblical laws that in modern times could well be considered under the civil heading, particularly, laws regarding what would now be called contracts, torts, and transfer of property by inheritance and bequest. These laws typically involve agreements between persons, requiring those who have harmed others to make compensation, and arrangements for transferring property from one person to another. Criminal laws typically define offenses against the community: actions which harm or put at risk the community or its members in ways that cannot be remedied by compensation in the form of money or replacement property. Criminal conduct generally involves the offender's intent to cause harm. The Bible includes a great many criminal laws.

Most biblical criminal laws relate to capital offenses. Accordingly, the main focus here in Part II is on capital crimes. These, and other aspects of biblical criminal law, will be considered in the five following chapters, namely, chapters Three, Four, Five, Six, and Seven.[1]

---

[1] Portions of these chapters derive from the present writer's article, "The Death Penalty and Due Process in Biblical Law," published in 81 *Univ. of Detroit Mercy L. Rev.* 781 (2004).

Chapter Three reviews a series of biblical trial scenes, most of which involve the possible application of the death penalty. These scenes also illustrate some of the due process provisions which will be examined later in Chapter Six. Chapter Four considers a number of biblical laws that call for impartial justice and, in effect, the equal protection of the laws, in the prosecution and administration of both criminal and civil matters. Chapter Five identifies the several kinds of conduct that are regarded as capital offenses in biblical law, and considers the various rationales given for applying the death penalty in cases where these offenses have been committed. Chapter Six examines the rather large number of laws that provided for certain due process protections, particularly for those accused of capital crimes. The Seventh Chapter then reflects upon on the possible relevance of some of these biblical laws in analyzing contemporary American criminal justice proceedings.

# Chapter 3

# Biblical Trial Scenes

*About three months later Judah was told, "Your daughter-in-law, Tamar, has played the whore; moreover she is pregnant as a result of whoredom." And Judah said, "Bring her out, and let her be burned." As she was being brought out, she sent word to her father-in-law, "It was the owner of these who made me pregnant." And she said, "Take note, please, whose these are, the signet and the cord and the staff."*

*Genesis 38:24-25*

*The elders said, "As we were walking in the garden alone, this woman came in with two maids, shut the garden doors, and dismissed the maids. Then a young man, who had been hidden, came to her and lay with her. We were in a corner of the garden, and when we saw this wickedness we ran to them. We saw them embracing, but we could not hold the man, for he was too strong for us, and he opened the doors and dashed out. So we seized this woman and asked her who the young man was, but she would not tell us. These things we testify."*

*Susanna, vv. 36-40 (RSV)*

Arguably, much of biblical law derives from case law decided by kings, courts or individual priests, judges, or elders.[1] A few narrative texts provide glimpses into actual cases or trials. Some of these indicate procedural features that will be considered later. Two of these scenes relate more to civil than criminal proceedings. The others involve capital offenses. Laws relating to such offenses will be examined in Chapters Five, Six, and Seven.

Nine trial scenes are reviewed in this chapter, beginning with those probably most ancient, coming down to those composed more recently.

---

[1] See generally, Hans Jochen Boecker, *Laws and the Administration of Justice in the Old Testament and the Ancient East* (Augsburg Press, 1988) (1976).

The first five trial scenes considered may date back to the 8th century BCE, if not earlier. The next two scenes found in Leviticus 24 (H) and Numbers 15 (PC) probably were set down between the 7th and the 5th centuries BCE. The story of Susanna and the Elders, which concludes this section, may have been written as late as the 2nd or 1st century BCE.

## A. Genesis 38:24-26: Tamar's Evidence

The aging patriarch Judah, on being informed that his daughter-in-law, Tamar, was pregnant long after her husband's demise, issued orders for her to be brought out and burned. In Judah's mind, evidently, Tamar's pregnancy under these circumstances presented an equivalent to what in traditional tort law might be considered another case where *res ipsa loquitur* ("the thing speaks for itself").[2]

Judah evidently assumed that Tamar had "played the harlot," that is, become a prostitute, and consequently became pregnant (Gen. 38:28 RSV). Possibly prostitution was a common law crime. There was as yet no statutory (Mosaic) law,[3] and no subsequent biblical law made prostitution as such a capital offense. In fact, Judah himself had gotten Tamar pregnant, supposing her to be a prostitute, and not recognizing her as his widowed daughter-in-law. At that time, she had prudently secured from him certain items of personal property which could serve to identify their owner: his signet, cord, and staff. Acting in her own defense, she produced these as evidence. To his credit, Judah immediately recognized and acknowledged them as his. Moreover, he commended her for undertaking to become pregnant, and admitted his own failure to provide his third son as her husband, as seems to have been expected under the customary law of levirate marriage.[4]

Here there is no mention of a formal trial before "the people" or some other form of a jury; but obviously Tamar had opportunity to speak and produce this critical evidence in a timely manner.[5] In consequence,

---

[2] See W. Page Keeton, ed., *Prosser and Keeton on the Law of Torts*, Sect. 39, 5th edn. (St. Paul: West Pub. Co., 1984).

[3] According to biblical tradition, it would be at least another generation before Moses was born. See Exodus chapter one.

[4] See generally, Donald A. Leggett, *The Levirate and the Goel Institutions in the Old Testament; with Special Attention to the Book of Ruth* (Mack Pub. Co., 1974). Also see Chapter Two, Section B.2, and Chapter Eight, Section B.2.c.

[5] Another early biblical scene (though not involving a trial) also focused on physical evidence: Genesis 44:1-17. Here Joseph had his assistant "plant" his own silver cup in his

Tamar was completely exonerated. This episode could be considered the first biblical instance of items being entered into physical evidence, though they were not, of course, labeled exhibits "A, B, and C."

## B. 2 Samuel 12:1-15: David as Judge and Nathan's Parable

As king of Israel and Judah, David was also chief judicial officer.[6] Having committed adultery with Bathsheba, and after attempting unsuccessfully to induce her husband, Uriah, to sleep with her in order to cover up the affair, David arranged for Uriah to die in battle. Subsequently, the prophet Nathan approached David in the latter's judicial capacity, and told him a story about a rich man and a poor man. Although the former had numerous flocks and herds, he took the poor man's one little pet lamb, killed and cooked it, and served it to a guest for dinner (2 Sam. 12:1-4).

> Then David's anger was greatly kindled against the man; and he said to Nathan, "As YHWH lives, the man who has done this deserves to die; and he shall restore the lamb fourfold, because he did this thing, and because he had no pity." Nathan said to David, "You are the man." (2 Sam. 12: 5-7 RSV)

King David thought that Nathan was presenting him with an actual case at law. In fact, Nathan was doing just that, but the case was that of YHWH v. David. In pronouncing judgment against "the man," David pronounced it against himself. Although the purported offense was stealing and killing a man's pet lamb, David nevertheless declared that "the man . . .

---

brother Benjamin's sack, so that he might later accuse the latter of theft. Two earlier portions of the Joseph story also involve production of fabricated or misleading physical evidence: Gen. 37:29-33, where Joseph's brothers dip his robe in animal blood in order to make their father think he had been killed; and Gen. 39:11-18, where Potiphar's wife seizes, preserves, and later produces Joseph's "garment" as evidence that he had attempted to assault her sexually. Deuteronomy 22:13-21 describes a later biblical law providing for introduction of physical evidence at trial. See Chapter Six, Section B.2.

[6] See also 2 Samuel 15:1-6, where Absalom attempts to gain supporters by proclaiming that if he were king (instead of David, his father), he would decide justly Israelites' suits brought before him for judgment. There was no "separation of powers" in those times.

deserves to die."[7] The actual sentence David pronounced called for fourfold restitution, as provided by the CC in Exodus 22:1.[8]

## C. 2 Samuel 14:1-11: A Hypothetical Case Prompts Mitigation and Alternative Sentencing

Absalom, David's ambitious, and now oldest surviving son, had arranged the murder of his older brother (2 Sam. 13:23-29), and for the past three years had taken refuge in a nearby foreign land (2 Sam. 13:34-38). David wanted to restore Absalom, but felt unable to do so. In this setting, Joab, David's army commander and friend, staged a mock trial in order to induce him to allow Absalom to return. David, however, was led to believe that this was a real case at law that called for his decision as chief judge.

An unnamed woman selected by Joab, came before David reciting the story Joab had put in her mouth: She was a widow with two sons who had quarreled, one had killed the other, and now her family demanded the death of the surviving son. She had come to the King for help, since if this other son were put to death, she and her husband would have no heir. That situation, as she put it, would both "quench" her "one remaining ember," and leave her husband "neither name nor remnant on the face of the earth" (2 Sam. 14:1-7). Specifically, she begged the King to "invoke YHWH [his] God, that the avenger of blood slay no more and [her] son not be destroyed." David then declared that her son would indeed be spared, and that "not one hair" of her son would "fall to the ground" (2 Sam. 14:11).

David soon began to suspect and then discovered that the entire proceeding had been arranged by Joab, but nevertheless decided to permit Absalom to come back to Jerusalem and live, in effect, under house arrest (2 Sam. 14:12-24). After two years, David and Absalom were, temporarily, reconciled (2 Sam. 14:28-33). We see here that the King, in his role as chief judge, might spare the life of a known murderer under certain circumstances. In the woman's case, the circumstance was the fact that—as her story was told—to kill (or allow the "avenger of blood" to kill) the offender would leave his parents with no

---

[7] Nathan implies that David had committed a capital offense; but that while YHWH would spare him, he would cause the death of David's (and Bathsheba's) new-born son.

[8] Exodus 21:37, in the Hebrew text. See Chapter One, Section B.

heir. At least in this instance, the king, as chief judge, might mitigate the death penalty otherwise prescribed in several biblical laws[9] and, in the case of Absalom, impose an alternative sentence.

## D. 1 Kings 3:16-28: A Maternity Suit

This is the famous story—whether legend or history—about the two prostitutes who each claimed to be the mother of a sole surviving infant. They came before Solomon in his judicial capacity, each testifying that the child was hers. Solomon proceeded to solve the case in the courtroom by proposing to carve the living child in two, giving half to each claimant. This horrible prospect prompted the true mother to renounce her claim in order to spare the child, thereby demonstrating that she was its mother. Solomon's proposal could be seen as an ancient instance of cross examination, albeit on the inquisitorial rather than adversarial trial model. In effect, he was asking each claimant, do you really care about this child's welfare, or do you have some other agenda? Here also we see another case where, obviously, women's testimony was admissible in court.[10] In this trial scene, which is more of a civil than criminal proceeding, there was no death penalty issue.

## E. 1 Kings 21:1-16: A Case of Malicious Prosecution

King Ahab of Israel wanted to acquire Naboth's vineyard which adjoined the royal premises, but Naboth, a good Israelite, declined to part with his ancestral inheritance. Ahab's Phoenician wife, Jezebel, then arranged to have two "base fellows" charge Naboth falsely with having cursed both God and the king. Cursing God may have been a capital offense under the law.[11] Cursing a ruler of Israel was prohibited (Exod. 22:28), but not necessarily a capital crime.[12] Under ANE common law,[13] however, treason

---

[9] See Chapter Five, Section B.1.
[10] See also Deut. 21:18-21, and 2 Sam. 14:1-11.
[11] See Exod. 22:28 and Lev. 24:15 (neither of which, however, includes a penalty clause). Leviticus 24:16 specifies the death penalty for those who "blaspheme the name" of YHWH. In Leviticus 24:10-16 and 23, the verbs translated as "blaspheming" and "cursing" are used interchangeably.
[12] Cf. 2 Samuel 16:9-14; 1 Kings 2:8-9.
[13] Similar versions of many ancient Near Eastern laws appear in more than one nation's legal tradition. Some such laws, though not part of biblical law as recorded, may underlie

was a capital offense, and if anyone was found guilty of treason, his property would go to the state instead of passing to family heirs by way of inheritance or bequest.[14] Thus, by having Naboth "framed" and executed under a charge of treason, Jezebel was able to obtain title to the property for her husband, the king, as head of state. The trial (or "kangaroo-court") took place in Jezreel, Naboth's home city, "in the presence of the people" who believed the false charges, and stoned him to death. Two witnesses testified falsely, evidently the requisite minimum number under common law to sustain a capital charge.[15]

## F. Jeremiah 26:7-24: Defendant Testimony and Argument from Precedent

In Jeremiah's famous "Temple sermon" (Jer. ch. 7) this prophet declared that his contemporary countrymen who violated YHWH's requirements of justice and mercy would not be spared divine judgment even were they to take refuge in YHWH's "house," that is, the Jerusalem Temple. Jeremiah declared that YHWH had destroyed his "place" at Shiloh centuries earlier; and that YHWH would now "pour out" his anger and wrath on "this place"—the Jerusalem Temple. Chapter 26 reports an abbreviated version of this same episode, and then describes the reactions of various priests and other prophets: "This man deserves the sentence of death because he has prophesied against this city . . ." (Jer. 26:11). In effect, Jeremiah was charged with sedition or treason.[16]

A trial of some sort then was held before "all the princes and all the people." Speaking in his own defense, Jeremiah—like a later Socrates—

---

certain narratives. On ANE common law, see generally, Raymond Westbrook, *Studies in Biblical and Cuneiform Law*, Cahiers de la *Revue Biblique* no. 26 (Paris: J. Gabalda, 1988). For comparison of relevant biblical and ANE laws in convenient, modern translation, see Edwin M. Good, "Capital Punishment and Its Alternatives in Ancient Near Eastern Law," 19 *Stanford Law Rev.* 947 (1967), pp. 947–77, and Victor H. Matthews & Don C. Benjamin, *Old Testament Parallels: Laws and Stories from the Ancient Near East* (New York/Mahwah, NJ: Paulist Press, 1997), pp. 83–123.

[14] See J. Weingreen, "The Case of the Daughters of Zelophehad," 16 *VT* 521–22 (1966), and Raymond Westbrook, Property and the Family in Biblical Law, *JSOT* Supp. Series no. 11 (JSOT Press, Sheffield, 1990), pp. 123–24.

[15] Biblical *laws* specifying a minimum of two witnesses probably were written later than the time of Ahab. See Deut. 17:6; 19:15; Num. 35:30. See Chapter Six, Section C.1.

[16] See Baruch A. Levine, "Capital Punishment," in Morton Smith and R. Joseph Hoffmann, eds., *What the Bible Really Says* (Buffalo: Prometheus Books, 1989), pp. 23–24. Levine concludes that during the period of the monarchy, sedition was a capital offense. *Id.* at p. 24. See also Good, "Capital Punishment" (cited above in note 13), pp. 966–67, citing other possible biblical instances of execution for treason.

urged the court, "Do with me as seems good and right to you;" but reminded them that it was YHWH who had sent him "to prophesy against this house and this city" (Jer. 26:12-15). The "princes and all the people" reportedly found this argument persuasive, and declared, "This man does not deserve the sentence of death for he has spoken to us in the name of YHWH our God" (Jer. 26:16). In addition, "some elders of the land" then cited precedent in the prior case when the prophet, Micah, had declared that YHWH would destroy his "house" at Shiloh for similar reasons, but was not put to death.[17] Jeremiah's life was then spared. Here we can see a "court" swayed by persuasive argument based on policy considerations—in effect, that prophets speaking on YHWH's behalf should be accorded "free speech." In addition, we see clearly the importance of precedent or prior case law—a basic feature of modern-day jurisprudence which values precedent, among other reasons, so that persons may govern their conduct to accord with established law, and so that courts will not have to rework their policy analyses each time they confront a new case.

## G. Leviticus 24:10-23: A Case of Blasphemy

A man of mixed (Egyptian-Israelite) parentage, while arguing (if not fighting) with another man, "blasphemed the Name in a curse" (Lev. 24: 10-11).[18] Because there was no specific precedent or statutory law on point, the offender was placed in custody pending further authoritative instructions. In this story, custody was intended to secure the prisoner pending further legal procedures (Lev. 24:12). YHWH then instructed Moses to order the death penalty. A new procedure is indicted here: all who had heard the man cursing or blaspheming were called on to "lay their hands upon his head," thereby in effect testifying against him.[19] Again, as the case is reported, multiple witnesses so testified as was then required by statutory law in capital cases.[20] The law of the case is

---

[17] Jeremiah 26:17-19, 24. Another prior case also is cited in the account: that of a prophet named Uriah who was put to death for making a similar proclamation. Jer. 26:20-23. Possibly the "court" was confronted with two conflicting lines of precedent and chose to go with that of the Micah case. Alternatively, some interpreters suggest that the reported Uriah case may have been merely a fictitious addition to the story later intended to dramatize the perilous nature of Jeremiah's prophetic career.

[18] See Chapter Five, Section B.1.d.i.(c).

[19] Lev. 24:14. See also Susanna v. 34.

[20] See Chapter Six, Section C.1.

articulated in terms clearly intended to be binding precedent in the future:

> He who blasphemes the Name of YHWH shall be put to death; all the congregation shall stone him; the sojourner as well as the native, when he blasphemes the Name, shall be put to death. (Lev. 24:16 RSV)

Here, clearly, case law was understood to supplement statutory authority.[21] The story concludes in v. 23, reporting that "the people of Israel" stoned the blasphemer to death.

## H. Numbers 15:32-36: A Case of Possible Sabbath Violation

Here another episode or story contributes to the growth of the law. A man was found gathering sticks on the sabbath day. According to Exodus 35:2, which, like Numbers 15, probably represents the PC or P tradition, anyone who "worked" on the sabbath was to be put to death. But what sort of activity on the sabbath constituted "work"? As in the previous instance, absent statutory law or decisional precedent on point, the accused was "put . . . in custody, because it was not clear what should be done to him" (Num. 15:34). Again, as the story is told, YHWH then informed Moses that the offense in question was capital and that the offender should be executed. In both instances, the accused might have objected that new law was being applied against them *ex post facto*, or retroactively. Here the accused had no expressed notice that the act of gathering sticks would constitute a capital offense. Although the law or rule of the case is not spelled out, those similarly situated afterwards would, presumably, know better than to gather sticks on the sabbath.

## I. Susanna vv. 28-62: Cross Examination Catches the Culprits in the Courtroom

Court was held regularly at Joakim's house, he being a wealthy and honored member of the Jewish community.[22] Two elders, recently

---

[21] Although the incident is reported as part of the Holiness Code, it may reflect Priestly editing.

[22] The story of Susanna may belong more in the category of fiction than history. Nevertheless, it probably portrays accurately various late-biblical legal traditions and practices.

appointed as judges, frequently presided over trials at Joakim's house. These two elders/judges independently became infatuated with Joakim's beautiful wife, Susanna. Discovering their common lust, they conspired to coerce her into having sexual intercourse with them: "[G]ive your consent, and lie with us. If you refuse, we will testify against you that a young man was with you" (vv. 20-21). Susanna refused, though knowing that these judges' false testimony could lead to her death.[23] They then charged her with adultery. Trial took place at Joakim's house before "the people." Susanna was summoned to appear, and with her came her parents, children, and other family members. The two elders/judges stood up, laid their hands on Susanna's head,[24] and recited their false testimony. It is not clear whether she was not allowed to speak on her own behalf, or whether she chose not to do so. The "assembly," acting as jury, believed the elders' testimony, and "condemned her to death" (v. 41).

Young Daniel, inspired by God, now appeared as Susanna's advocate or defense counsel, and called for further proceedings:

> Taking his stand in the midst of them, he said, "Are you such fools, you sons of Israel? Have you condemned a daughter of Israel without examination and without learning the facts? Return to the place of judgment. For these men have borne false witness against her." (vv. 48-49 RSV)

Earlier laws provided, in some instances, for examination or inquiry into "the facts," but what follows is the first explicit instance of cross-examination by counsel in courtroom proceedings.[25] First, Daniel orders the two adverse witnesses (the two elders/judges) separated or sequestered during examination. After preliminary "badgering," Daniel elicits conflicting testimony from each as to the exact site of the alleged adulterous affair. Daniel then charges them both with bearing false witness, after which the assembly found them guilty and put them to death "in accordance with the law of Moses"[26] (vv. 60-62). The story illustrates

---

[23] See Lev. 20:10; Deut. 22:22.
[24] Cf. Lev. 24:14.
[25] The court evidently consisted of both "all the people" and other "elders" (Susanna v. 50). It is unclear who these other "elders" were. No "elders" other than the two malicious judges are mentioned in the first phase of the trial. Whether there was a presiding judge at either phase of the trial is not indicated. Daniel's appearance here as defense counsel evidently was pro bono, not for fee.
[26] It might be asked how Daniel and the assembly knew that *both* were lying, since, on the record evidence, either one of them might have been telling the truth, while the other had lied.

application of the law governing penalties for false malicious witnesses (Deut. 19:16-21). It also, again, illustrates the law requiring a minimum of two adverse witnesses to sustain a charge alleging capital crimes.[27] Implicitly, in both the story and the related witness laws, the accused is presumed innocent until proven guilty. As the story is told, "the whole assembly" found in Susanna's favor (v. 60), in effect, reaching a unanimous verdict. The concluding clause in v. 62 underscores the result of the proceedings: "Thus innocent blood was spared that day."[28]

---

[27] See Six, Section C.1.
[28] As will be seen in Chapter Six, much of biblical law functioned, and no doubt was intended to prevent the execution of innocent persons. Lest innocent persons be put to death was a core biblical concern.

# Chapter 4

# Impartial Judgment and Equal Protection of the Laws

*I charged your judges at that time: "Give the members of your community a fair hearing, and judge rightly between one person and another, whether citizen or resident alien. You must not be partial in judging: hear out small and the great alike; you shall not be intimidated by anyone, for the judgment is God's."*
Deuteronomy 1:16-17

*No State shall . . . deny to any person within its jurisdiction the equal protection of the laws.*
U.S. CONST. AMEND. XIV Sect. 1

The concepts "impartial judgment" and "equal protection of the laws" are closely related. Presumably, an impartial judge would not be influenced by the status of persons coming before her.[1] Perhaps it is a matter of emphasis. At any rate, a number of biblical texts call on judges to be impartial in their judgment; while several other texts identify particular classes of persons who are to be treated equally. Some of these laws might also have been meant to apply in civil cases; but generally they appear to have referred to criminal proceedings. Laws calling for impartial judgment are considered first.

## A. Impartial Judgment

A variety of biblical laws and other biblical texts emphasize that judges (or others who decide cases) must do so impartially: that judges should be no respecters of persons; i.e., that the law should apply regardless of

---

[1] In passing, it may be noted that the first judge said actually to sit judging cases in a judicial capacity in the Book of Judges was Deborah. See Judges 4:4-5. She was also the only woman reported to have so served.

the status of the parties before the court.² Perhaps the broadest statement is in the RDC's admonition at the investiture of new (secular) judges:

> You shall not pervert justice; you shall not show partiality; and you shall not take a bribe . . . Justice and only justice shall you follow . . . (Deut. 16:18-20 RSV)³

Several wisdom texts likewise emphasize the importance of judging impartially the righteous or innocent, on one hand, and the wicked on the other.⁴ In this connection, the CC warns particularly against putting to death innocent and righteous persons: "Keep far from a false charge, and do not kill the innocent and those in the right, for I will not acquit the guilty" (Exod. 23:7).⁵ The implication seems to be that if there was any serious question as to the truth of adverse evidence in a capital case, the accused should be spared execution; moreover, that YHWH himself would attend to the just fate of the real offender, whether the accused or some other person. At any rate, here, and elsewhere thematically in

---

[2] See Dale S. Recinella, *The Biblical Truth about America's Death Penalty* (Boston: Northeastern Univ. Press, 2004), pp. 228–305, contrasting biblical laws against preferential treatment of privileged classes with patterns and instances in various U.S. jurisdictions.

[3] See also Deut. 1:16-17, quoted at the beginning of this chapter. Deuteronomy 16:18-20 may have been part of the RDC, or it may have been added subsequently. With the closing of rural cult shrines pursuant to the requirement that YHWH might be worshiped only at the Jerusalem Temple, local priests who had, it seems likely, functioned as judges, evidently were replaced by local, secular judges.

[4] See, e.g., Prov. 18:5 (RSV): "It is not good to be partial to a wicked man, or to deprive a righteous man of justice." See also Prov. 17:15; 24:23-25, and Sir. 4:9 and 42:1-2. See generally, T. B. Maston, *Biblical Ethics* (Mercer Univ. Press, 1982), pp. 94–95.

[5] On this same point, see Gen. 18:22-33. Here is told the ancient story of Abraham's bargaining with YHWH over the fate of Sodom.

Because of that city's reported wickedness, YHWH is thinking about destroying it and all its people, but first consults with Abraham. Abraham then raises the crucial question, whether it is right for YHWH to "destroy the righteous with the wicked." (Gen. 18:23 RSV). "Far be it from [God] to do such a thing, to slay the righteous with the wicked, so that the righteous fare as the wicked . . . Shall not the Judge of all the earth do right?," Abraham asks (Gen. 18:25 RSV). At first YHWH agrees to spare the city if fifty righteous persons can be found; and at the end, following negotiations with Abraham, YHWH agrees to spare the city if even ten such persons could be found. Gen. 18:32 (Compare Jer. 5:1 and Ezek. 22:30, where just one righteous person would be enough to cause God to spare the people of Jerusalem and the land of Judah). The story does not condemn capital punishment as such; but it does expressly challenge the propriety of punishing the innocent along with the guilty. As will be seen, many biblical laws were intended to assure that only those who had actually committed capital crimes would be subjected to the death penalty. See Chapter Six.

Biblical law, it is critically important to protect the lives of the innocent accused.

This broadly phrased mandate is applied in many other laws to particular categories of persons. In effect, persons in these categories or classes were to be entitled to what in modern jurisprudence is called the equal protection of the laws. Such protection was to be accorded not simply because YHWH/God so demanded, but, more fundamentally, because YHWH/God, himself, "executes justice" in this manner:

> For YHWH your God is God of gods and Lord of lords, the great, the mighty, and the terrible God who is not partial and takes no bribe. He executes justice for the fatherless and the widow, and loves the sojourner, giving him food and clothing. (Deut. 10:17-18 RSV)

## B. Equal Protection: Protected Classes

The principle of impartial judgment is most consistently articulated in connection with cases involving the poor and sojourners or resident aliens. Implicitly, the principle was that the laws should apply equally to all distinguishable classes of persons. Thus it seems appropriate to designate this principle as according "the equal protection of the laws." Impartial judgment or equal protection, however, seems to have been applied less consistently in regard to gender-based discrimination, and only to a limited extent with respect to slaves.[6]

### 1. The Poor

The Covenant Code cautions those who judge suits—who may be either elders or officials of some sort—to be impartial in judging the poor, neither favoring nor disfavoring their cause, and to decide on the facts, rather than with respect to persons or corrupt influence:

---

[6] As to the principle of equality in biblical and Jewish law, see generally Ze'ev W. Falk, *Law and Religion: The Jewish Experience* (Jerusalem: Mesharim, 1981), pp. 90–103, and Ze'ev W. Falk, *Religious Law and Ethics: Studies in Biblical and Rabbinical Theonomy* (Jerusalem: Mesharim, 1991), pp. 32–35. See also Pamela Barmash, *Homicide in the Biblical World* (Cambridge Univ. Press, 2005), p. 175, as to the *lex talionis* or principle of equivalent *punishment*: "Lex talionis makes rich and poor equal in biblical law. More than that, status, with the exception of the slave is simply not a factor in biblical law." The lex talionis is considered in Chapter Six, Section D.2.

> [N]or shall you be partial to a poor man in his suit.
>
> [. . .]
>
> You shall not pervert the justice due to your poor in his suit. Keep far from a false charge, and do not slay the innocent and righteous, for I will not acquit the wicked. And you shall take no bribe, for a bribe blinds the officials, and subverts the cause of those who are in the right. (Exod. 23:3, 6-8 RSV)

The Holiness Code likewise admonishes those who will decide such cases:

> You shall do no injustice in judgment; you shall not be partial to the poor or defer to the great, but in righteousness shall you judge your neighbor. (Lev. 19:15 RSV)

Some of the classical prophets emphasized this concern, pronouncing YHWH's judgment against the wealthy and powerful who had oppressed or failed to protect the rights or interests of the poor.[7]

### 2. Sojourners or Resident Aliens

The principle of equal or impartial justice is applied broadly to *gerim*, that is, sojourners or persons of foreign origin living in Israel. Several such texts appear in H. Thus, for instance, Leviticus 19:33-34 (RSV):

> When a stranger sojourns with you in your land, you shall not do him wrong. The stranger who sojourns with you shall be to you as the native among you, and you shall love him as yourself; for you were strangers in the land of Egypt: I am YHWH your God.

Likewise, in Leviticus 24:22 (RSV): "You shall have one law for the sojourner and one for the native; for I am YHWH your God."[8]

---

[7] See, e.g., Amos 2:6-7; 4:1; 5:11-12; 8:4-6; Isa. 1:16-17, 23; 3:14-15; Jer. 5:28-29. See also Prov. 29:7 (RSV): "A righteous man knows the rights of the poor; a wicked man does not understand such knowledge"; and Prov. 29:14 (RSV): "If a king judges the poor with equity, his throne will be established for ever." Cf. Jer. 22:16 (commending King Josiah for having "judged the cause of the poor and needy").

[8] It is not clear from the context whether this equal treatment requirement was intended as a general principle applicable in connection with all laws, or whether it was

Equal protection also meant equal liability under the law. Aliens who sacrificed their children to Molech would have been subject to the same death penalty that applied to Israelites who did so (Lev. 20:2). Likewise, resident aliens who "blaspheme the name" would be just as accountable as native-born Israelites (Lev. 24:16).[9] Implicitly the *lex talionis* was grounded in and gave expression to the idea of equality or impartial justice: *any* person who injured another, or took another's life, was to experience the same kind of deprivation in return.[10]

Two provisions of the PC also apply specifically to both sojourners and native-born. As read in its immediate context, the equal protection provision of Numbers 15:14 seems to have applied only to the matter of presenting offerings by fire or burnt offerings:

All who are native shall do these things in this way, in offering an offering by fire, a pleasing odor to YHWH. And if a stranger is sojourning with you, or any one is among you throughout your generations, and he wishes to offer an offering by fire, a pleasing odor to YHWH, he shall do as you do.[11]

However, as the text continues, this principle evidently was generalized so as to apply to all types of laws:

For the assembly, there shall be one statute for you and for the stranger who sojourns with you, a perpetual statute throughout your generations; as you are, so shall the sojourner be before YHWH. One law and one ordinance shall be for you and for the stranger who sojourns with you. (Num. 15:15-16 RSV)[12]

Unlike earlier provisions as to cities of refuge[13] which are silent on this point, the PC explicitly provides that strangers and sojourners, as well as Israelites, might seek protection in such cities (Num. 35:15).

---

meant to apply only to those laws set out in the verses immediately preceding (Lev. 24:10-21).

[9] See Chapter Five, Section B.1.d.i.(c). See also Lev. 18:26-30, calling for both natives and sojourning strangers to keep YHWH's "ordinances and statutes" and to keep from doing any of the enumerated "abominations."

[10] See Falk, *Law and Religion* (cited above in note 6), p. 96. As to the *lex talionis*, see Chapter Six, Section D.2.

[11] Num. 15:13-14 (RSV).

[12] Compare Exodus 12:43-49, which says in effect that only *circumcised* alien sojourners might partake of the Passover meal. See Falk, *Law and Religion* (cited above in note 6), pp. 23–24.

[13] See Chapter Six, Section A.

### 3. Women

Equal protection provisions are somewhat ambiguous with respect to gender. As has been seen in Chapter Two, it appears that widows could inherit property from their pre-deceased husbands; however daughters could inherit only in special circumstances. Some laws clearly applied equally. Striking or cursing either father or mother was a capital crime (Exod. 21:15, 17; Lev. 20:9), as was failing to obey "the voice" of either parent (Deut. 21:18-19). Male and female slaves were both covered under the law against fatal battery by their owners (Exod. 21:20-21). A man who, in certain circumstances, negligently caused the death of a married, pregnant woman was to be put to death according to what seems to be the earliest version of the *lex talionis* (Exod. 21:22-25). Men and women, as well as sons and daughters, were protected under the Covenant Code's provisions regarding oxen that gored people to death (Exod. 21:28-31).

A few laws specified that men and women were equally liable for certain offenses. Both men and women were subject to capital punishment for "buggery" (Lev. 20:15-16), and also for allotheism, or the worship of other gods (Deut. 17:2-5). Likewise both men and women incurred the death penalty for adultery (Deut. 22:22-27; Lev. 20:10). And, although the Covenant Code applied the death penalty only to sorceresses (Exod. 22:18), the Holiness Code extended that form of punishment to both male and female mediums and wizards (Lev. 20:27).

On the other hand, while a new bride might be executed if her parents failed to produce adequate evidence of her virginity, her accusing husband would only be subject to whipping and fine if his suspicions were proven false (Deut. 22:13-21).[14] Perhaps the accusing husband would have been subject to the death penalty if it was shown that he had *maliciously* offered false testimony against his bride (Deut. 19:16-21), another version of the *lex talionis*.[15] There are no laws providing for punishment, let alone capital punishment, in the case of new husbands who are later found to have "sown their wild oats" before marriage.

---

[14] See Chapter Five, Section B.1.c.ii.(b). Compare the absence of any penalty or punishment for the suspicious husband whose wife might be vindicated after undergoing trial by ordeal in the form of the "cereal offering of jealousy" (Num. 5:11-31).

[15] See Chapter VI.D.2. However, the "tokens of virginity" law of Deuteronomy 22:13-21 seems to presume good faith suspicion on the part of the accusing husband.

## 4. Slaves

Clearly the concept of equal protection did not extend to the status of slaves *vis a vis* free persons. Exodus 21:20 provided that a man who fatally struck his male or female slave with a rod would be punished, but not, it seems, subjected to the death penalty.[16] Moreover, if the slave survived a day or two, the owner would not be punished at all, "for the slave" was "his money" (Exod. 21:21). None of the other homicide laws exempted perpetrators from penalties if their victims did not die immediately. Similarly, the CC's law providing the death penalty for owners of oxen that gored persons to death did not apply if the goring victim was a slave. In that case, the ox's owner would only be required to pay the slave's owner 30 shekels of silver, evidently the going market price for a slave (Exod. 21:32). It may or may not be significant that these laws providing unequal protection for slaves, all found in the CC, were not repeated in the later law codes. Perhaps these laws were still considered to be in effect. Or perhaps it may have been understood that they had been abandoned or repealed *sub silentio*.

---

[16] Compare Exodus 21:12-14, regarding free persons. But see Levine, "Capital Punishment" (cited in Chapter Three, note 16), pp. 13–14. Westbrook, *Studies* (cited in Chapter Three, note 13), pp. 89–100, on the basis of other ANE laws, proposes that the death penalty was meant to apply in this circumstance.

Chapter 5

# Capital Offenses

*You shall not kill.*
                                  Exodus 20:13; Deuteronomy 5:17 (RSV)

*You shall not murder.*
                                  Exodus 20:13; Deuteronomy 5:17 (NRSV)

Modern opponents and proponents of capital punishment, alike, often turn to "the Bible" in order to support their respective viewpoints. Those with either secular or religious "liberal" (or humane) concerns tend to emphasize certain biblical texts that can be read to oppose the death penalty, while "conservatives," especially religious conservatives, often advocate capital punishment, citing other biblical texts as authority.[1] Biblical texts occasionally are even cited as authority in judicial opinions.[2] This chapter does not undertake to resolve ongoing debates as to the propriety or effectiveness of capital punishment.[3] The purpose here, rather, is to achieve a more complete and accurate understanding of

---

[1] See, e.g., Glen H. Stassen, "Biblical Teaching on Capital Punishment," and Jacob J. Vellenga, "Is Capital Punishment Wrong?," in Glen H. Stassen, ed., *Capital Punishment: A Reader* (Cleveland: Pilgrim Press, 1998), pp. 119–136. Both articles are republished in Daniel K. Judd, *Taking Sides: Clashing Views on Controversial Issues in Religion* (Guilford, CT: McGraw-Hill/Dushkin, 2003), pp. 186–201. Citations below are to the 1998 publication. See generally James J. Megivern, *The Death Penalty: An Historical and Theological Survey* (New York/Mahwah, NJ: Paulist Press, 1997), pp. 9–19, noting certain problematic aspects of biblical interpretation, and critiquing several contemporary treatments of biblical passages as proof-texts favoring capital punishment. The fact that states such as Texas and Florida which carry out the greatest number of executions are located in what once was designated "the Bible Belt," or Southern United States, may not be entirely coincidental. See Chapter Seven, notes 33 and 74. And see Recinella, *The Biblical Truth* (cited in Chapter Four, note 2), pp. 6–16.

[2] See a collection of such citations by Michael Medina, "The Bible Annotated: Use of the Bible in Reported American Decisions," 12 N. Il. U. L. Rev. 187, 189–91, 195, 198–99, 202, 214, 216–18, 221, 226, 247 (1991).

[3] Several law journal symposia on death penalty issues have been published in recent years. See, e.g., 53 *DePaul L. Rev.* No. 4 (2004); 33 *U. New Mex. L. Rev.* No. 2 (2003); 86 *Judicature*

biblical perspectives and concerns in regard to the death penalty, in contrast to understandings that rely primarily upon a few selected prooftexts or slanted interpretations.

When relevant biblical laws and texts are understood both for what they actually say and in their respective historical contexts, it can be seen that biblical perspectives are more complicated than either modern proponents or opponents of the death penalty usually recognize. Moreover, it will become evident that biblical laws provided a rather remarkable array of due process protections for persons accused of capital offenses. These due process provisions appear especially in some of the later biblical law codes. Biblical texts relating to due process protection have largely been ignored by both biblical and legal scholars.[4] This topic will be considered in Chapter Six.

The first part of this chapter reviews those biblical texts that have been (or could plausibly be) read as repudiating or opposing capital punishment. The next, and more extensive part discusses the many legal texts that explicitly call for, or illustrate application of the death penalty. Various rationales for capital punishment indicated in several texts setting out capital offenses also are considered here.

---

No. 2 (2002); 81 *Oregon L. Rev.* No. 1 (2002); 29 *Hofstra L. Rev.* No. 4 (2001); and 33 *Conn. L. Rev.* No. 3 (2001).
See also Jonathan Alter, "The Death Penalty on Trial," *Newsweek*, June 12, 2000, pp. 24–34; Hugo Adam Bedau and Michael L. Radelet, "Miscarriages of Justice in Potentially Capital Cases," 40 *Stan. L. Rev.* 21 (1987); Donald A. Cabana, *Death at Midnight: The Confession of an Executioner* (Boston: Northeastern Univ. Press, 1996); Frank O. Carrington, *Neither Cruel Nor Unusual: The Case for Capital Punishment* (New Rochelle, NY: Arlington House, 1978); Thomas Draper, ed., *Capital Punishment* (New York: H. W. Wilson Co., 1985); Samuel R. Gross, "Lost Lives: Miscarriages of Justice in Capital Cases," 42 *U. Mich L. Quad. Notes* 82–94 (1999); Ernest van den Haag & John P. Conrad, *The Death Penalty A Debate* (New York/London: Plenum Press, 1983); Kenneth C. Haas & James A. Inciard, eds., *Challenging Capital Punishment: Legal and Social Science Approaches* (Newbury Park: Sage, 1988); Michael L. Radelet, ed., *Facing the Death Penalty: Essays on a Cruel and Unusual Punishment* (Philadelphia: Temple Univ. Press, 1989); Michael L. Radelet, Hugo Adam Bedau, and Constance E. Putnam, *In Spite of Innocence* (Boston: Northeastern Univ. Press, 1992); Gregory D. Russell, *The Death Penalty and Racial Bias: Overcoming Supreme Court Assumptions* (Westport, CT: Greenwood Press, 1994); Glen H. Stassen, ed., *Capital Punishment: A Reader* (Cleveland: Pilgrim Press, 1998); Lloyd Steffen, *Executing Justice: The Moral Meaning of the Death Penalty* (Cleveland: Pilgrim Press, 1998); and articles in *Phi Kappa Phi Forum* 82, 1 (Winter, 2002), 19–27. Many such studies, of course, evaluate the effectiveness or propriety of capital punishment without reference to biblical texts or norms.

[4] But see Steven A. West, "Scripture Can Advocate Capital Punishment," 12 *Christian Legal Soc. Quarterly* 9, 11-12 (no. 3, 1991), describing certain biblical provisions as "due process" protections. See also Good, "Capital Punishment" (cited in Chapter Three, note 13), pp. 972–74 (1967). Good discusses certain "procedural requirements in capital cases" found in Ancient Near Eastern (ANE), including biblical, law, though not in terms of "due process" procedures or protections.

Narrative traditions and other biblical writings often presuppose or apply various laws relating to the death penalty. Such writings also are examined here with a view to their likely dating and historical setting. Proceeding in this manner makes it possible to trace certain developments or changes in law within the biblical period. It will be seen that some laws appear to have been modified or qualified in the course of time, and that new laws evidently were added while others, if not repealed or abandoned, were no longer included in later codes or instanced in later narrative traditions.

## A. Against Capital Punishment

Several texts have been interpreted to mean that people—at any rate, the people of Israel—should never kill other people under any circumstances. Those who harm others should be forgiven, and even murderers should be permitted to live, whether banished or as fugitives in exile. At any rate, retribution, if called for, should be left to the Almighty.

At the outset, it is to be observed that reading or translating biblical language necessarily often involves some degree of interpretation. The old Episcopal *Book of Common Prayer*, for instance, rendered the Decalogue's Sixth Commandment narrowly: "Thou shalt do no murder."[5] On the other hand, the more literal, modern Revised Standard Version translates the same text without qualification, "You shall not kill." Some interpreters have urged that this "commandment" was intended or understood to prohibit capital punishment.[6] Perhaps it was;

---

[5] *The Book of Common Prayer*, p. 69 (New York: Harper & Bros, 1944) (1928). See also the New Revised Standard Version, Exod. 20:13 and Deut. 5:17: "You shall not murder"; the New English Bible (same verses): "You shall not commit murder"; and the Revised English Bible (same verses): "Do not commit murder."

[6] See, e.g., Ramsey Clark, *Crime in America: Observations on Its Nature, Causes, Prevention, and Control* (New York: Pocket Books, 1970), pp. 314–15, and Millard Lind, *The Sound of Sheer Silence and the Killing State* (Telford, PA: Cascadia Publishing House, 2004), pp. 52–53, implying that the Sixth Commandment can be so read; See also Gerald J. Blidstein, "*Capital Punishment*: The Classic Jewish Discussion" in Stassen, ed., *Capital Punishment* (cited above in note 3), pp. 107–17, observing that in Hebrew and in Rabbinic interpretation, the verb "to kill" (*razach*) used in the Sixth Commandment does not distinguish between justifiable homicide and murder. Compare Walter Harrelson, *The Ten Commandments and Human Rights* (Philadelphia: Fortress Press, 1980), p. 108: "There can be no question . . . of our Sixth Commandment's having the initial meaning that human life is never, under any circumstances, to be taken by another human being or by the appointed authorities in Israel." And see extensive discussion by Lloyd R. Bailey, *Capital Punishment: What the Bible Says* (Nashville: Abingdon Press, 1987), pp. 44–48, proposing

however, it is not certain which translation more closely represents the original "legislative intent."

Various texts suggest that it was understood that offenders might or should be spared alive. Cain, the first murderer, was not sentenced to death. Rather, he was condemned to be "a fugitive and a wanderer on the earth" (Gen. 4:14).[7] Moreover, as the story is told, YHWH "marked" Cain[8] in some visible manner to protect him from any would-be, self-help avengers (Gen. 4:15).[9] The author of Proverbs 28:17 advised that anyone who was "burdened with the blood of another" should be allowed (or condemned) to "be a fugitive until death." In effect, these texts suggest that murderers were to receive a life sentence as fugitives or exiles.[10] As his story continues, Cain had a wife and children, and "built a city" (Gen. 4:17). It may be inferred from his descendant Lamech's braggadocio, that afterwards someone did kill Cain, and that YHWH then made good on his warning of seven-fold vengeance against Cain's killer.[11] A story found in 2 Samuel 14:1-11 shows that during the time of the monarchy, a king might spare the life of a murderer if, as a mitigating factor, his execution would leave his parents without any heir, and a sequel to this scene shows that a murderer might be allowed to live indefinitely under house arrest.[12]

Frequently biblical prophets called on their contemporaries to turn from their transgressions in order that God might spare, rather than destroy them. Thus for example, Amos 5:14-15:

---

that the Sixth Commandment "forbids premeditated, malicious violence," but does not bar execution for capital offenses.

[7] See discussion by Recinella, *Biblical Truth* (cited in Chapter Four, note 2), pp. 41–46. As to various critical issues presented in the story of Can and Abel, see Barmash, *Homicide* (cited in Chapter Four, note 6), pp. 12–19.

[8] The nature of this "mark" is not indicated; but clearly it was intended to protect Cain, and was not part of his punishment. Compare Nathaniel Hawthorne's *The Scarlet Letter*.

[9] See Julian H. Wright, Jr., "Pardon in the Hebrew Bible and Modern Law," 3 *Regents U. L. Rev.* 1, 16 (1993): "The first act of 'executive clemency' in the Hebrew Bible occurs in Genesis when God commutes the sentence given to the first murderer, Cain." In the story as told, however, there was no death sentence to "commute." Likewise, Stassen overstates his point when he comments that the Torah (or Biblical law) "*forbids* the death penalty for the prototype of all murderers, Cain who killed his brother Abel . . ." Stassen, "Biblical Teaching" (cited above in note 1), p. 120. Stassen correctly points out that Cain as well as Moses and David were not subjected to the death penalty for murders they committed. *Id.* Other biblical figures likewise spared could be mentioned as well, such as Absalom and Solomon.

[10] Thus, e.g., Gardner C. Hanks, *Against the Death Penalty: Christian and Secular Arguments Against Capital Punishment* (Scottdale, PA: Herald Press, 1997), p. 26.

[11] Gen. 4:23-24; cf. Gen. 4:15.

[12] See Chapter Three, Section C.

> Seek good, and not evil, that you may live; and so YHWH, the God of hosts, will be with you, just as you have said, Hate evil, and love good, and establish justice in the gate; it may be that YHWH, the God of hosts, will be gracious to the remnant of Joseph.[13]

Several biblical texts urge that people were not to seek or execute vengeance against others. The Apostle Paul construed earlier biblical tradition in his classic admonition:

> Beloved, never avenge yourselves, but leave room for the wrath of God; for it is written, "Vengeance is mine, I will repay, says the Lord." (Rom. 12:19)[14]

This text does not authorize humans to act as avenging agents of the Almighty; on the contrary, any and all vengeance is to be left to God. The biblical text Paul apparently had in mind was Deuteronomy 32:35: "Vengeance is mine and recompense . . ."[15] Other biblical texts likewise characterize vengeance as a proper basis for God's or YHWH's actions against the unrighteous or ungodly,[16] implying, arguably, that humans—at any rate, God's people—should refrain from taking vengeance themselves.

More typically, biblical texts refer to God or YHWH as the Judge who, in times past, justly punished the wicked for their depravity, and could be expected to do so again in or at the end of history. Classic stories of such past actions include the flood saga (Genesis 6–9);[17] the Sodom and Gomorrah narrative (Gen. 18:16–19:25); and the Deuteronomic Historian's commentary on the demise of the kingdom of Israel.[18] It was also believed that YHWH or God judged and would judge nations and individuals in the future as well.[19]

---

[13] See also, e.g., Jer. 4:1-4; Ezek. 18:21-32 and Amos 5:6-7.
[14] See also Heb. 10:30.
[15] See also Prov. 20:22: "Do not say, 'I will repay evil'; wait for YHWH and he will help you." And see Sir. 28:1 (RSV), "He that takes vengeance will suffer vengeance from the Lord." Also see Lev. 19:18: "You shall not take vengeance . . . against any of your people."
[16] See, e.g., Lev. 26:25; Mic. 5:15; Sir. 39:28-31.
[17] See esp. Gen. 6:5 (RSV): "YHWH saw that the wickedness of man was great in the earth, and that every imagination of the thoughts of his heart was only evil continually."
[18] 2 Kgs 17:1-20.
[19] See, e.g., Exod. 22:21-24 (individuals); Exod.. 34:6-7 (individuals); 2 Sam. 12:7-12 (Nathan's pronouncement against King David); Mic. 4:1-4 (nations); Jer. 2:33-35 (unrighteous individuals); Ezek. 7:1-27 (the nation Judah). See also Pss. 9:7-8; 10:15-18; 96:10-13; Prov. 22:22-23; Sir. 16:6-14; 35:12-20.

Some biblical texts imply that divine justice is self-executing without explicit reference to God as Judge. Such texts declare that in this life the righteous are rewarded, typically with longevity and wealth, while the wicked either are cut off in the midst of their sinning, or otherwise come to grief.[20] Somewhat later, perhaps, the author of Wisdom of Solomon urged that the righteous would be vindicated and the wicked punished in the next life if not this one.[21] Texts which maintain that God judges or will judge those who do wrong could be read to mean that his people should refrain from condemning others—how much more from administering the death penalty—and should leave it to God to execute vengeance or retribution upon those so deserving. Moreover, according to Ezekiel, God preferred that offenders change their ways rather than perish:

> But if a wicked man turns away from all his sins which he has committed and keeps all my statutes and does what is lawful and right, he shall surely live; he shall not die. None of the transgressions which he has committed shall be remembered against him, for the righteousness which he has done he shall live. Have I any pleasure in the death of the wicked, . . . and not rather that he should turn from his way and live? (Ezek. 18:21-23 RSV)[22]

In this vein, Sirach 27:30–28:7 commended forgiveness and mercy, and renunciation of enmity, anger and wrath. In the New Testament, Jesus called on his hearers to refrain from judging others (Mt. 7:1-2; Lk. 6:37), and to forgive others' offenses (Mt. 6:14-15; 18:35; Mk 11:25-26). He warned that it was not enough to keep the Sixth Commandment, "You shall not kill." People should also refrain from being angry with or insulting others (Mt. 5:21-22). In the story of the woman who had been

---

[20] See, e.g., Ps. 37; Prov. 2:20-22; 10:3-4, 7, 30; 11:17-19; 12:7, 21.

[21] Wisdom of Solomon 1:16–5:23; See also Dan. 12:1-3. Similar hopes and expectations are expressed in 2 Esdras and many New Testament writings.

[22] See also Ezek. 18:27-28, 31-32; and 33:11-16, where Ezekiel says much the same as in the quotation above in the text. Stassen urges that in practice, even during biblical times, the death penalty was gradually if not progressively abandoned: "One almost never hears of it in the Prophets and the Writings . . .," Stassen, "Biblical Teaching" (cited above in note 1), p. 127. On the other hand, Vellenga insists that the prophets "were opposed to laws being flouted and criminals not being punished." Vellenga, "Is Capital Punishment Wrong?" (cited above in note 1), p. 133. To substantiate this claim, Vellenga quotes Isaiah 59:14-18. *Id.* This text accords with others, affirming that vengeance is *YHWH's*. See above, notes 14–16 and accompanying text. But the Isaiah text does not, in its terms, refer to, much less, endorse capital punishment by human agency.

"caught" in adultery,[23] Jesus seems to countermand or over-rule the "law of Moses."[24] Under that law, adultery was a capital offense; both the adulterer and adulteress were to be executed. According to John 8:5, Mosaic law required that the woman be stoned to death.[25] But Jesus' response was, "Let him who is without sin among you be the first to throw a stone at her" (Jn 8:7 RSV). Jesus did not pronounce the woman forgiven, but stated that he did not condemn her, admonishing her not to "sin again."[26] Would Jesus have said the same to a person convicted of murder? There is no New Testament case on point.[27]

From these texts, it certainly can be argued that at least some biblical figures or writers opposed capital punishment. Judgment should be left to God, who preferred that offenders be permitted to live, so that they might turn around or repent; or at any rate live out their lives as exiles or fugitives. On the other hand, a great many texts rather clearly authorized and ordained capital punishment for a wide range of offenses.

## B. Capital Offenses and Rationales for Executing Offenders

Although many biblical texts and traditions commonly cited by death penalty proponents do not, in fact, advocate or illustrate capital punishment,[28]

---

[23] Jn 8:1-11, according to some manuscripts. See also Mt. 1:18-19, discussed below in note 153
[24] Probable reference is to Lev. 20:10 and Deut. 22:22.
[25] Stoning is specified in Deut. 22:23-24 in a somewhat different context, but not in Lev. 20:10 or Deut. 22:22. In the Johannine story, nothing is said about punishing the *adulterer*.
[26] See generally, Hanks (cited above in note 10), p. 41; Levine, "Capital Punishment" (cited in Chapter Three, note 16), p. 29.
[27] Barabbas, who, according to two gospel accounts had committed murder, was spared execution under *Roman* law: Mk 15:6-15; Lk. 23:18-25. See generally Edward McG. Gaffney, Jr., "Scripture Does Not Advocate Capital Punishment," 12 *Christian Legal Soc. Quarterly* 9 (n. 3, Fall 1991) (arguing in effect that New Testament texts qualify if not overrule Old Testament capital laws). But see Bailey, *Capital Punishment* (cited above in note 6), pp. 47–83, urging that the New Testament in no way repudiates or delimits biblical laws requiring capital punishment. Some Christian commentators also oppose the death penalty as applied in the United States on the basis of their understandings of faith and ethics, without direct reference to biblical texts. See, e.g., Timothy W. Floyd, "What's Going On?: Christian Ethics and the Modern American Death Penalty," 32 *Texas Tech. L. Rev.* 931 (2001).
[28] See, e.g., comments by death penalty advocates quoted in Irene Merker Rosenberg and Yale L. Rosenberg, "Lone Star Liberal Musings on 'Eye for Eye' and the Death Penalty," 1998 *Utah L. Rev.* 505, 539 (1998); Vellenga (cited above in note 22); and Megivern on use of Gen. 9:5-6, quoted below in note 129. For further discussion of uses and misuses of biblical texts in capital trials in the United States, see Gary T. Simson & Stephen P. Garvey, "Knockin' on Heaven's Door: Rethinking the Role of Religion in Death Penalty Cases," 86 *Cornell L. Rev.* 1090, 1091, 1109–25 (2001).

a great many biblical laws do enumerate capital offenses.[29] Additionally, various narratives, including a few trial scenes, report executions with evident approval. The types of offenses subject to the death penalty will be described first. Explicit biblical theories or rationales for capital punishment will then be considered. As will be seen, many biblical laws calling for capital punishment are grounded upon conviction that all human lives are of great value.

## 1. Capital Offenses in Biblical Laws and Narratives

Modern scholars generally agree that biblical law was codified in several stages during the long history of Israel, Judah, and the Jewish people, between c. 1200 and 400 BCE. Capital offenses found in each code will be identified and described beginning with the earliest and coming down to more recent codes.[30] This procedure makes it possible to trace several developments in the law.[31] Generally capital laws set out in a given

---

[29] See Elie Spitz, "The Jewish Tradition and Capital Punishment" in Elliot N. Dorff and Louis E. Newman, eds., *Contemporary Jewish Ethics and Morality: A Reader* (New York: Oxford Univ. Press, 1995), p. 344: "Capital punishment was not an ethical problem in the Bible. Indeed, it was a commanded punishment for a whole range of offenses, from witchcraft to striking a parent to murder." And see Gardner C. Hanks, *Capital Punishment and the Bible* (Scottsdale, PA: Herald Press, 2002), pp. 53–54, listing numerous biblical capital offenses. On the other hand, early and subsequent rabbinic tradition interpreted such texts so as to make it difficult if not impossible to justify capital punishment. See, e.g., Haim Heymann Cohn, *Human Rights in Jewish Law* (New York: KTAV, 1984), p. 217; Aaron Kirschenbaum, "The Role of Punishment in *Jewish Criminal Law*: A Chapter in Rabbinic Penological Thought," in Martin P. Golding, ed., *Jewish Law and Legal Theory* (New York: New York Univ. Press, 1993), pp. 451–474; and Irene Merkel Rosenberg and Yale L. Rosenberg, "The Legacy of the Stubborn and Rebellious Son," 74 *Mich. L. Rev.*, 1163–65 (1976). For an alternative perspective on rabbinic death penalty jurisprudence, see Beth A. Berkowitz, *Execution and Invention: Death Penalty Discourse in early Rabbinic and Christian Cultures* (Oxford Univ. Press, 2006), proposing that the rabbis' concern was to advance their own status and authority by depicting an imaginary world where they could impose the death penalty on those who failed to accept their interpretations of the Torah.

[30] See generally Roland de Vaux, *Ancient Israel: Its Life and Institutions* (New York: McGraw Hill, 1961), p. 158 (listing categories of capital offenses).

[31] See in this connection, Raymond Westbrook's observation at the conclusion of his magisterial study of Biblical and Ancient Near Eastern law:

[B]iblical law is neither a mass of internal contradictions nor a monolith, but reflects a single, coherent common law, upon which different opinions were expressed. These opinions coincide, not surprisingly, with the major sources identified by modern biblical criticism.

Raymond Westbrook, *Studies in Biblical and Cuneiform Law*, Cahiers de la *Revue Biblique* no. 26 (Paris: J. Gabalda, 1988), p. 135. As to connections between biblical and other ANE capital laws, see Raymond Westbrook, "A Matter of Life and Death," *JANES* 25 (1997), 61–70. Compare studies that simply describe or list capital laws without

code share significant features or concerns. For this reason, each code's capital laws will be considered together. Similar laws, modifications, and new laws found in subsequent codes will then be examined. For purposes of this study, biblical law codes are understood to have been set down in the following sequence: first the Ritual Decalogue (RD), then the Covenant Code (CC), followed by the Deuteronomic Code (D), the Holiness Code (H), the Revised Deuteronomic Code (RDC), and finally, the Priestly Code or laws (PC).[32] New offenses are added in each of the later codes, while most of those promulgated earlier are omitted (though never formally repealed) or modified.[33] Other biblical writings, particularly narratives, occasionally illustrate codified laws.[34] In some instances, statutory penalties may have been mitigated in practice.

### a. The "Ritual Decalogue": Exodus 34:17-28

The earliest identified code, the "Ritual Decalogue" (RD), found in Exodus 34:17-28,[35] may date from as early as the 13th century BCE.

---

attempting to note connections or developments. See, e.g., Robert M. Bohm, *Deathquest: An Introduction to the Theory and Practice of Capital punishment in the United States* (Cincinnati: Anderson, 1999), pp. 177–80; Mark Costanzo, *Just Revenge: Costs & Consequences of the Death Penalty* (New York: St. Martin's Press, 1997), p. 130; Hanks, cited above in note 29; and Vernon W. Redekop, *A Life for Life? The Death Penalty on Trial* (Scottdale, PA: Herald Press, 1990), pp. 25–27.

[32] See above, Introduction to this book. As to various law codes, see generally, David Daube, *Studies in Biblical Law* (New York: KTAV, 1969), pp. 74–101; and the classic, Julius Wellhausen, *Prolegomena to the History of Ancient Israel* [1878] (New York: Meridian, 1957). Modern scholars diverge as to the dating, characteristics, and even the existence of biblical law codes. The system of codes identified in this book provides a convenient framework for classifying and analyzing biblical law, but must be considered tentative.

[33] Albrecht Alt, some decades ago, proposed that "apodictic" laws (typically beginning "Thou shalt . . ." or "Thou shalt not . . .") should be distinguished from "casuistic" laws (formulated, e.g., "When a man . . ." or "Whoever . . ."). See Albrecht Alt, "The Origins of Israelite Law" [1934], reprinted in Albrecht Alt, *Essays on Old Testament History and Religion* (Garden City: Doubleday/Anchor, 1968), pp. 101–71. Alt urged that only laws set out in the apodictic format should be considered genuinely Israelite, and that the casuistic laws were borrowed or adapted from Canaanite or other Ancient Near Eastern sources. Alt's thesis has been accepted by many, but criticized by other scholars. See, e.g., Theophile James Meek, *Hebrew Origins* (Harper & Row, 1960), pp. 72–81. For purposes of this study, all biblical laws, whatever their possible or putative ANE parallels or origins, are assumed to represent concerns of the Israelite communities that drafted or selected, and then perhaps modified them for inclusion in their collections of statutory law.

[34] One modern scholar has suggested that, conversely, most or all biblical laws were developed relatively late in the biblical period, in response to situations described in earlier biblical narratives. See Calum M. Carmichael, *Laws and Narratives in the Bible* (Ithaca: Cornell Univ. Press, 1985) pp. 210–24, and *Biblical Laws of Talion* (Oxford Centre for Postgraduate Hebrew Studies, 1986) pp. 21–39.

[35] See generally, Klaus Koch, *The Growth of the Biblical Tradition: The Form-Critical Method* (New York: Scribner's, 1969), pp. 48–51.

This code enumerates a series of prohibitions, several of which are repeated in later codes which in some instances provide that violators are to be executed. The RD itself, however, includes no mention of capital punishment or any other penalties. It may have been understood that those who committed these offenses would be subject either to divine retribution or to retaliation at the hands of victims' relatives.

### b. The Covenant Code: Exodus chapters 20–23

Nearly as early, perhaps, was the Covenant Code or Book of the Covenant, an extensive codification of Israelite law, found in Exodus 20–23.[36] It begins with the Decalogue or "Ten Commandments," Exodus 20:2-17, which may have been recorded earlier.[37] Like the Ritual Decalogue, the Decalogue itself includes no penalty provisions. Several capital offenses are set out elsewhere in the CC, however, notably in Exodus chapters 21 and 22.

#### i. Exodus 21:12-14: homicide, premeditated and otherwise

The first capital offense mentioned in the CC is homicide (Exod. 21: 12-14): "Whoever strikes a man so that he dies shall be put to death." This law goes on, however, to distinguish between premeditated murder, when "a man willfully attacks another to kill him treacherously,"[38] and unpremeditated, though apparently intentional homicide, when the offender "did not lie in wait for [the victim], but God let him fall into his hands." Some interpreters read this language to mean negligent or accidental homicide.[39] That category appears later in Deuteronomy 19:4-10 and

---

[36] See generally, Anthony Phillips, *Ancient Israel's Criminal Law* (New York: Schocken, 1970), pp. 158–61.

[37] Another version of the Decalogue is to be found in Deut. 5:6-21. It need not be determined here whether the Decalogue was codified prior to or apart from the larger codes with which it is now associated. On the Decalogue, see generally, Ben-Zion Segal & Gershon Levi, eds., *The Ten Commandments in History and Tradition* (Jerusalem: The Magnes Press, Hebrew Univ., 1990); Walter Harrelson, *The Ten Commandments and Human Rights* (Philadelphia: Fortress Press, 1980); and Koch, *Growth* (cited above in note 35), pp. 44–51.

[38] We see here the equivalent of "malice aforethought," an element of first degree murder in modern criminal law. See Wayne R. LaFave, *Criminal Law*, 3rd edn. (St. Paul: West Group, 2000), pp. 653–55, 692–98. As to counterparts in Ancient Near Eastern (ANE) or cuneiform law, see Good, "Capital Punishment" (cited in Chapter Three, note 13), pp. 951–53, and Westbrook, *Studies* (cited above in note 31), pp. 47–49.

[39] See, e.g., George E. Mendenhall, *Law and Covenant in Israel and the Ancient Near East* (Pittsburgh: Biblical Colloquium, 1955), p. 16. In modern criminal jurisprudence, this

Numbers 35:9-15, but is not indicated here.[40] This language seems to refer to a chance encounter with an enemy, rather than to a fatal attack prompted by sudden "heat of passion."[41] The opportunistic or chance homicide perpetrator is seen as a less serious offender; he may flee to a designated sanctuary, presumably to escape self-help revenge at the hands of the victim's friends and relatives, and there await further proceedings.[42] The willful or premeditated murderer, on the other hand, was to suffer the death penalty (Exod. 21:14).

*ii. Negligent homicide*

Conduct or inaction unintentionally resulting in loss of human life was subject to the death penalty in two particular circumstances. Arguably both situations involve culpable negligence. At any rate, both call in effect for strict liability when the offender's conduct violates the terms of the respective statutes. These situations have already been considered in Chapter One as illustrations of biblical tort law. They also can be seen as involving aspects of criminal law.

### (a) Exodus 21:22-25: a married, pregnant woman harmed by brawling males

One kind of situation would arise if a married, pregnant woman suffered miscarriage and died after being struck by one of two (or more) brawling males. The man responsible for the fatal injury was to be put to death: "[Y]ou shall give life for life . . . " (Exod. 21:22-23).[43] This provision is the

---

offense could be regarded as second degree murder. See LaFave, *Criminal Law* (cited above in note 38), pp. 698–99.

[40] Carmichael, following Daube, attributes to the Exodus law what he calls a "more profound religious view of accidental homicide": "[T]he visible agents of a killing—hand, axe, stone—are equally directed by the ultimate mover, and the matter is fundamentally equated with accident in which no human cause is discerned at all." Calum M. Carmichael, *The Laws of Deuteronomy* (Ithaca: Cornell Univ. Press, 1974), p. 113. See also Falk, *Religious Law* (cited in Chapter Four, note 6), p. 58: "The responsibility for killing another human being could not extend to cases which were actually acts of God, i.e., where God had 'let the victim fall into the hand of the person who caused the death.'" Modern jurisprudence characterizes as "acts of God" only those accidents that involve no human agency, or at any rate no foreseeability or duty of care. It is not at all clear that Exod. 21:12-14 refers to *accidental* homicide. See Sections B.1.e.i. and B.1.f.ii. of this chapter.

[41] In modern criminal jurisprudence, such homicide is generally classified as voluntary manslaughter. See LaFave, *Criminal Law* (cited above in note 38), pp. 703–17.

[42] Exod. 21:13. See Chapter Six, Section A.

[43] In the Code of Hammurabi, HC 209, 210, under these circumstances, the *daughter* of the person who caused the fatal injury was to be put to death. In the biblical law, there is no

earliest instance of the commonly so-called biblical "*lex talionis*," or law of retribution in kind.[44] If the woman died, even though the responsible male did not intend her death, he is held strictly liable for the consequences of his conduct. This law implies an irrebuttable presumption that such conduct was reckless or otherwise culpable.[45] Under its terms, if the pregnant woman is permanently injured, but does not die, the man responsible for the injury is to have the same kind of injury inflicted upon him: "eye for eye, tooth for tooth . . . " In such cases, the death penalty is not to apply. If the woman survives and is not permanently impaired, the brawling male responsible for the miscarriage is subject to civil liability in the form of a fine, rather than to the *lex talionis*. In its terms, this law does not apply if the victim was pregnant but unmarried, or married but not pregnant.

**(b) Exodus 21:28-32: Failure to confine a goring ox with a bad history**

The other circumstance involves death at the horns of another's goring ox (Exod. 21:28-32). An ox that gores a man, woman, or child to death is to be killed.[46] Moreover, the ox's owner must be put to death "if the ox has been accustomed to gore in the past, and [the] owner has been warned, but has not kept it in" (Exod. 21:29 RSV). Here the death penalty is applied because the owner knowingly failed to take appropriate measures to prevent foreseeable risk of fatal harm. Evidently the owner would not be subject to the death penalty if he knew of the ox's goring proclivity, *unless* he also had been *warned*.[47] However, this law allows two exceptions. One is that, at the option of the victim's relatives or representatives, the culpable owner may be required to pay compensation instead of being put to death.[48] In that case, however, he must pay

---

mention of the offender's daughter, and it may be assumed—though it is not specifically stated—that the offender himself was the person subject to the death penalty.

[44] See Chapter Six, Section D.2. For other ANE parallels, see Good, "Capital Punishment" (cited in Chapter Three, note 13), pp. 953–54.

[45] The implicit rationale is that risk of harm was foreseeable: the man should have known better than to take part in brawling in the vicinity of a pregnant woman. See Levine, "Capital Punishment," (cited in Chapter Three, note 16), pp. 14 (referring to "the gross negligence and indifference to human life exhibited by the fighting men").

[46] The ox is to be stoned to death, but its flesh is not to be eaten. As to various rationales for these procedures see Westbrook, *Studies* (cited above in note 31), pp. 83–88, and Theodor H. Gaster, *Myth, Legend and Custom in the Old Testament* (Glouster, MA: Peter Smith, 1981), vol. 1, pp. 243–50.

[47] The text does not indicate whether such warning was to have been given officially, e.g. by one of the local elders, or by any person in the community.

[48] Exod. 21:30-31. As to Canaanite and Babylonian parallels and influence, see Meek, *Hebrew Origins* (cited above in note 33), pp. 70–71, and Westbrook, *Studies* (cited above

"whatever is laid upon him" for the "redemption of his life" (Exod. 21:30). In modern terms, the victim's relatives may seek damages in tort rather than the offender's death at the hands of the criminal justice system.[49] The other exception obtained only if the gore victim is a slave (whether male or female). In that case, the ox's owner is to pay the slave's master 30 silver shekels in damages.[50]

### iii. Exodus 22:2-3: killing the night-time intruder

Homicide or killing a man in one other special circumstance also may have been considered a capital crime. When a property owner strikes a *burglar* (understood, as at common law, to mean a thief or robber who enters the premises at night)[51] and the burglar dies, "there shall be no blood guilt" (Exod. 22:2 RSV). The fact that it was night-time excuses the killing.[52] However, "if the sun has risen upon" the intruder, "there shall be blood guilt for him" (Exod. 22:3 RSV). Here even the life of the burglar is understood to be valued. Whether the property owner who killed the daylight intruder would then be subject to the death penalty is not explicitly stated. Perhaps a fine or compensatory damages could be paid, or a sacrificial offering presented instead. The fact that no specific penalty was prescribed *could* mean that the judges or court might exercise discretion.[53]

---

in note 31), pp. 57–61.

[49] It could have been presumed that negligent tort-feasors generally would rather pay substantial damages than be executed. See Prov. 13:8a (RSV): "The ransom of a man's life is his wealth." As to ransom as an option to killing the murderer in cuneiform law, see Westbrook, *Studies* (cited above in note 31), pp. 49–55.

[50] Exod. 21:32. Compare Exod. 21:20: If a man strikes his slave (male or female) with a rod, and the slave dies subsequently as a result, the slave owner is to be "*punished*," but evidently not subjected to the death penalty. But see Levine, "Capital Punishment" (cited in Chapter Three, note 16), pp. 13–14, contending that Exod. 21:20 meant that the slave's master would be subject to the death penalty if the slave died immediately.

[51] See Wayne R. LaFave and Austin W. Scott, Jr., *Handbook on Criminal Law* (St. Paul: West Publishing Co., 1972), pp. 713–14. For ANE parallels, see Westbrook, "Matter" (cited above in note 31), p. 62.

[52] The rationale may have been either that the nocturnal robber's crime was more serious, since the sleeping householder would be vulnerable to assault; or that the property owner, unable to see clearly whether the intruder was armed, would be entitled to act in self-defense. See Falk, *Law and Religion* (cited in Chapter Four, note 6), pp. 124–25; also his *Religious Law* (cited in Chapter Four, note 6), p. 60: "The justification for killing a thief who was caught while breaking in at night is based on the right of self-defense, but also on the probability of violence against the owner of the home." Surprisingly, perhaps, no biblical law explicitly provides for the "self-defense defense" in cases of homicide or other violent offenses. The availability of this legal defense may or may not have been presumed in ancient Israelite or Near Eastern common law.

[53] Cf. Deut. 25:1-3; Ezra 7:25-26. Compare Levine, "Capital Punishment" (cited in Chapter Three, note 16), p. 15: "It is doubtful whether this law actually mandates the

### iv. Exodus 21:15, 17: striking and cursing parents

Two laws make offenses against parents capital crimes: either striking or cursing one's father or one's mother (Exod. 21:15, 17).[54] Both implicitly involve violations of the Fifth Commandment, "Honor your father and your mother" (Exod. 20:12). Such violation may have been thought so extreme as to imperil Israelite society.[55] The prohibition against striking parents would, of course, function to protect them from physical harm. Cursing parents would show disrespect and could have been thought likely to cause them both emotional and physical harm. The verb translated to "curse" might also mean to "degrade" or "shame."[56] Neither law mentions any age limitation that might excuse a youthful offender.

### v. Exodus 21:16: kidnapping

This law includes certain particular elements: "Whoever steals a man, whether he sells him or is found in possession of him, shall be put to death" (RSV). Here "man" (Heb. *'ish*) could have been understood to include any person, whether man, woman, or child, and may therefore better be translated as "person" instead.[57] Implicitly, kidnapping was a way of obtaining slaves who could then be sold or kept as such.[58] This law makes no distinction between kidnapping Israelites or foreigners, or between selling them to other Israelites or to foreign buyers outside the community.[59] In its terms, the death penalty would not apply if the person stolen had later been given away or set free.

### vi. Exodus 22:18-20: other capital offenses

Exodus 22:18-20 lists three additional capital crimes. It is unclear why these three are separated from the other capital offenses found earlier in

---

death penalty. More likely, the case could be disposed of in less severe ways."

[54] As to cursing parents, see also Lev. 20:9, considered in Section B.1.d.ii(a) of this chapter.

[55] Exodus 20:12 implies that failure to observe the Fifth Commandment could shorten Israel's tenure in the promised land.

[56] See Levine, "Capital Punishment" (cited in Chapter Three, note 16), p. 13. As to possible tangible harm resulting from cursing, see below, note 93.

[57] The New Revised Standard Version so translates this text. *Compare* Good, "Capital Punishment" (cited in Chapter Three, note 13), p. 953 ("... 'ish ... can only mean male").

[58] Cf. Deuteronomy 24:7 (making it a capital offense to steal a fellow Israelite and either treat him as a slave or sell him).

[59] Compare Phillips, *Criminal Law* (cited above in note 36), pp. 130–31. Phillips finds these distinctions implicit in the text.

the Covenant Code. Possibly the several laws providing for restitution (damages, including multiple damages) in cases of stolen or damaged property found in Exodus 22:1, 4, 5-17 were inserted into an earlier compilation of capital offenses. Textual problems at the beginning of Exodus chapter 22 suggest that some material may have been added or interpolated here. The three are as follows.

### (a) Exodus 22:18: sorcery

The first of these laws states, without further elaboration, "You shall not permit a sorceress to live" (Exod. 22:18 RSV). According to the account in 1 Samuel 28:3-25, King Saul had attempted to *deport* all mediums and wizards, and any who remained did so at peril of his or her life (1 Sam. 28:3, 9). This story, which seems to reflect favorably on the female medium (or "witch") at Endor, suggests that at least in Saul's time, a sorceress might nevertheless live—provided she either left the country or discontinued publicly practicing her art. At any rate, the story instances an occasion when the severity of the Exodus 22:18 provision was mitigated in practice.

### (b) Exodus 22:19: "buggery" or "bestiality"

Exodus 22:19 makes what was known in earlier Anglo-American law as one form of "buggery" a capital crime: "Whoever lies with an animal shall be put to death." The term "whoever" appears to mean either male or female.[60] Here there is no provision for the death of the "beast." Sodomy is not mentioned in the CC. No reports of either buggery or its punishment are to be found anywhere in biblical tradition.

### (c) Exodus 22:20: sacrificing to other gods

Several later biblical laws make allotheism, or the worship of other gods, a capital offense. Possibly the last capital crime listed in the CC is that of *sacrificing* to any god other than YHWH. Those who do so "shall be utterly destroyed" (Exod. 22:20 RSV). This may mean, as in Exodus 22:21-24, that YHWH himself would destroy such persons;[61] but more likely, as in

---

[60] Cf. Lev. 20:15-16, considered in Section B.1.d.ii.(a) of this chapter. Good, "Capital Punishment" (cited in Chapter Three, note 13), pp. 960–61, identifies provisions in the Hittite Code that make male intercourse with certain beasts a capital offense.

[61] According to Exodus 22:21-24, which follow, YHWH or God says that *he* will kill any Israelite who afflicts widows or orphans, and also, perhaps, any who wrong or oppress strangers. It is not said, explicitly, that Israelites or their agents should execute such allotheists.

Exodus 22:18 and 19, the meaning is that the Israelite community or its representatives were to apply the death penalty.[62]

### c. The Deuteronomic Code: Deuteronomy 5, 20–25

This collection of laws was early recognized as (and thus named) the "second" law code. It includes a few laws found in the CC and adds many more. Initially, it may have been written down between 1100 and 1000 BCE.[63] Several provisions, particularly those calling for sacrificial worship in only one place (viz., Jerusalem) and various accommodations to that requirement probably were added more recently, perhaps in the latter part of the 7th century BCE. In this book, the symbol "D" is used to designate what may have been the earlier, if not original version of the Deuteronomic Code. Laws found in Deuteronomy chapters 12–19, and 26 generally relate to centralization of sacrificial worship in Jerusalem. In this study, these chapters are referred to as the Revised Deuteronomic Code or "RDC." Capital laws found in the RDC will be considered below in Section B.1.e. of this chapter.

*i. Held-over capital legislation: kidnapping, abduction or "man-stealing": Deuteronomy 24:7*

Surprisingly, perhaps, only one of the several capital offenses defined in the CC is repeated in D: that concerned with kidnapping. All the other capital offenses found in D appear there for the first time.[64] It may well be asked whether the other capital offenses set out in the CC but omitted from D were still thought to apply, or whether their absence from D meant that they had been forgotten, abandoned, or at least tacitly repealed.

Deuteronomy 24:7, the Deuteronomic law making kidnapping a capital offense, is drafted more narrowly and precisely than its early

---

[62] That understanding is implicit in certain early biblical narrative traditions. See, e.g., Exod. 32:25-28 (pursuant to the "golden calf" episode); Num. 25:1-17 (the somewhat incoherent story of Israelite sacrifice to Moabite gods and/or the "Baal of Peor"); and 1 Kgs 18:40 (following Elijah's contest at Mt. Carmel).

[63] Absence of any allusion to the monarchy suggests dating prior to the time of Saul and David. Some interpreters suggest a more recent date, for instance in the 8th or 7th century BCE. This question need not be decided for present purposes.

[64] Deuteronomy 19:4-13 (in regard to manslaughter, murder and cities of refuge) will be considered in Section B.1.e.i. of this chapter in connection with laws set out in the RDC. See also Chapter Six, Section A.3.

counterpart in the CC, Exodus 21:16. Under the Deuteronomic version, the death penalty applies only if the person kidnapped (or stolen) is a fellow-Israelite. Moreover, it is not enough if the person kidnapped is found in the kidnaper's possession, as in Exodus 21:16. In order to warrant execution, the kidnaper must have treated his victim as a slave or as merchandise.[65] Both versions of the law make it a capital offense if the kidnaper *sells* the abducted person. In that case, implicitly, the person would have been sold as a slave.

*ii. New capital offenses in the Deuteronomic Code*

The four new capital laws found in D all relate to the horizontal dimension of the covenant: that is, to interactions between or among persons who were members of the Israelite community. One concerns parent–child relations. The other three have to do with adultery.

### (a) Ungovernable sons: Deuteronomy 21:18-21
This law reads as follows:

> If a man has a stubborn and rebellious son, who will not obey the voice of his father or the voice of his mother, and, though they chastise him, will not give heed to them, then his father and his mother shall take hold of him and bring him out to the elders of his city at the gate of the place where he lives. (RSV)[66]

According to Deuteronomy 21:20, the parents then were to recite the following allegations: "This, our son is stubborn and rebellious; he will not obey our voice; he is a glutton and a drunkard" (RSV).[67] Perhaps it was expected that the elders would inquire further before proceeding to

---

[65] See Phillips, *Criminal Law* (cited above in note 36), pp. 131–32. Phillips refers to somewhat similar laws in the Code of Hammurabi and the Hittite Law Code. Id., p. 132.

[66] Deuteronomy 21:18-19. Elders function as judges in other biblical cases at trial. See, e.g., Deut. 22:13-21; Josh. 20:4; Jer. 26:7-19; and *Susanna*, v. 50.

[67] Gluttony and dipsomania may have been considered typical behavioral characteristics of "stubborn and rebellious sons." However, these conditions, without more, were not prohibited in any biblical law, much less criminalized as capital offenses. Compare Judd, *Taking Sides* (cited above in note 1), p. 185 (erroneously asserting that "gluttony and excessive drinking" were capital offenses as such). Note that both the mother and father were to bring their son before the elders and both were to prefer charges. See generally, Carolyn Pressler, *The View of Women Found in the Deuteronomic Family Laws* (Berlin: Walter de Gruyter, 1993), pp. 17–20.

carry out the death penalty; but there is no mention of such inquiry in this context. Possibly the offender would be put to death only if the elders believed the parents' testimony.[68] This law could be seen as an extension of, or at least related to, the provisions in the CC making it a capital offense to strike or curse one's parents (Exod. 21:15, 17). It might be noted that in its terms, this law applies only to sons, not to daughters. Possibly Israelite daughters were expected to be more amenable to the exercise of parental authority.[69] Falk suggests that the harsh nature of the punishment provided here was intended to prevent such a son "from attacking his parents" and to deter others from engaging in stubborn and rebellious conduct.[70] Again there are no reported cases when this law was carried out. Perhaps its being "on the books" had some deterrent effect.

### (b) Adultery: Deuteronomy 22:13-27

A series of three new capital laws relate to sexual offenses or allegations of such offenses involving women who were either married or betrothed. These are grouped together in Deuteronomy 22:13-27. Adultery was prohibited under the "Seventh Commandment" of the Decalogue (Exod. 20:14; Deut. 5:18). But neither adultery nor any other sexual activity—aside from buggery—had been criminalized, much less subject to capital punishment in the CC. Both D and the later Holiness Code (H) treat adultery as a capital offense.[71]

*Deuteronomy 22:13-21: alleged prenuptial promiscuity.* This law sets out procedures to be followed when a newly married husband charges his bride with having engaged in sexual intercourse prior to their marriage.

---

[68] Some sort of proceeding is implicit here. See Falk, *Law and Religion* (cited in Chapter Four, note 6), p. 80: "The [father of a rebellious son] is asked to submit his grievance to a judicial tribunal rather than to exercise his *ius vitae necisque* and the *patria potestas*." Compare Levine, "Capital Punishment" (cited in Chapter Three, note 16), p. 18: "If all efforts at disciplining him fail, the elders are to condemn such a son to death." However, there is no indication in the biblical text that mediation or discipline were contemplated as alternative or preliminary measures.

[69] See Sir. 7:23-25; 22:3-5; 26:10-12; and 42:9-11 (noting parental problems with daughters, but not indicating recourse to capital punishment).

[70] Falk, *Religious Law* (cited in Chapter Four, note 6), p. 60.

[71] Phillips states that prior to "the Deuteronomic legislation" an adulterous wife was not subject to punishment, but her adulterous lover could be "tried, convicted, and executed for the crime of adultery." *Criminal Law* (cited above in note 36), p. 110. That may have been the case, but it is not clear that the evidence cited (Deut. 7:3-4) warrants so concluding. Phillips suggests that the Deuteronomic Reform made women "equal members of the covenant community" and thus equally liable under the law. *Id.* See Chapter Four, Section B.3. As to adultery in the Holiness Code, see below, text accompanying notes 94 and 95. Good, "Capital Punishment" (cited in Chapter Three, note 13), pp. 957–58, discusses ANE parallels.

If, after evidentiary examination, the woman is found guilty as charged, she is to be put to death. However, if the evidence does not support the allegation, the husband who has falsely charged her is to be punished both by whipping and a 100-shekel fine.[72]

*Deuteronomy 22:22: adultery with a married woman.* Here adultery is made a capital offense when "a man is caught lying with the wife of another man." Adultery was not identified as a capital offense under the CC. In this D law, both "the man who lay with the woman" and the woman are to be put to death.[73] In its terms, this law applies whether the male adulterer was married or single. The law is silent as to what must be done if a married man is found lying with a single woman. No other biblical law addresses the latter situation either.

*Deuteronomy 22:23-27: intercourse with a betrothed virgin.* This law applies when a man "meets" a virgin who is betrothed (presumably to another man) and lies with her. No due process procedures are specified. However, certain presumptions were to apply. If the meeting (or assignation) occurred in town, both the man and the woman were to be put to death: the woman "because she did not cry for help" (Deut. 22:24). It appears to have been presumed both that if the woman had been sexually assaulted or raped in a town or city, she would have been able to cry for help, and that someone would have heard her cry and either then came to rescue her or later appeared to testify. Perhaps, if someone did hear the cry and render assistance or later testify on her behalf, it would be a different case and the woman would be spared. But absent such third-person rescue or testimony, the irrebuttable presumption appears to be that she had consented to the liaison.

A different presumption operated if a man meets, seizes, and lies with a betrothed young woman "in the open country" (Deut. 22:25). In that circumstance, the man is to be executed, but nothing shall be done to the young woman for she "has not committed an offense punishable by death"

---

[72] See generally, Pressler, *View of Women* (cited above in note 67), pp. 22–31. Pressler suggests that the text also indicates that a slandered woman's parents could bring charges against the husband for defamation and receive monetary damages. As to evidentiary procedures, see Chapter Six, Section B.

[73] This law, obviously, was not applied in the case of King David. David was condemned for marrying Bathsheba after murdering her husband, but not for his previous adultery with her. 2 Sam. 12:9. Nor was he condemned for earlier taking Paltiel's wife, Michal, Saul's daughter. 2 Sam. 3:12-16. In regard to the complex character of biblical and ANE law and practice as to punishment for adultery, see Raymond Westbrook, "Adultery in Ancient Near Eastern Law," *Revue Biblique* 97 (1990) 542–580.

(Deut. 22:26a-b).⁷⁴ This law is based by analogy on the "case of a man attacking and murdering his neighbor" (Deut. 22:26c RSV).⁷⁵ Here the irrebuttable presumption is that if the encounter occurred in open country, the woman had not consented, had cried out for help, but no one was there to hear, and so she was to be deemed innocent. How it was to be determined whether the man had "seized" her, that is, taken her by force is not specified.⁷⁶ Evidently the woman's own testimony would be credited.

### d. The Holiness Code: Leviticus chapters 18–26

Biblical scholars do not agree entirely as to the exact scope of the Holiness Code or "H."⁷⁷ For present purposes, it is considered to comprise Leviticus chapters 18–26.⁷⁸ The Holiness Code appears to have been set down after the original portion of the Deuteronomic Code, but prior to the Deuteronomic Reform and the composition of the chapters in Deuteronomy that reflect the innovations introduced by it.⁷⁹ Several of the capital laws found in H repeat, extend, modify, or qualify earlier legislation, while others define new capital offenses. As in the case of the earlier codes, a few H laws refer primarily to the "vertical" relationship of Israel or individual Israelites with YHWH. Most, however, concern relations between or among persons (or in a few instances, persons and animals).

### i. Laws relating to God or religious practices: the vertical dimension

The Holiness Code contains no provisions applying the death penalty to the worship of other gods. This absence could mean that, at the time H was codified such worship was no longer considered a capital offense.

---

⁷⁴ T. J. Meek points to somewhat similar presumptions in the Hittite Code, sect. 191: "If a man seizes a woman in the mountains, since it is the man's wrong, he shall be put to death. But if he seizes her in the house, since it is the woman's fault, the woman shall be put to death. If the husband finds them and then kills them, he is not to be punished." *Hebrew Origins* (cited above in note 33), p. 62.

⁷⁵ In such a case where there are no witnesses, and one person was dead, the other— evidently according to otherwise unreported biblical or ancient near eastern common law—would be presumed to have murdered the deceased.

⁷⁶ Deut. 22:25; cf. Deut. 22:23, where there is no mention of the man's *seizing* the woman.

⁷⁷ As to H, see generally Gerhard von Rad, *Studies in Deuteronomy* (London: SCM Press, 1953), pp. 25–36.

⁷⁸ Scholars sometimes include Leviticus chapter 17 as well. As to the present topic, however, the question is moot, since chapter 17 includes no laws sanctioned by capital punishment.

⁷⁹ See Section B.1.e. of this chapter. The Holiness Code does not call for or presuppose sacrificial worship in only one place. See favorable references to plural "sanctuaries" in Lev. 21:23 and 26:31. However, H includes some expressions that suggest possible later editing under Priestly auspices.

Possibly the several new capital laws against allotheism subsequently set out in Deuteronomy chapters 13, 17, and 18 reflect renewed concern on the part of the Deuteronomic reformers about such worship.[80] Alternatively, the earlier capital law against sacrificing to other gods (Exod. 22:20) may have been considered still in effect. Three H laws concern religious practices: one extends and modifies prior law; two others are new.

### (a) Leviticus 20:6, 27: mediums or wizards

The Covenant Code had called for the death of any sorceress (Exod. 22:18). The Holiness Code extends the death penalty to male as well as female practitioners of the occult arts: "A man or a woman who is a medium or a wizard shall be put to death" (Lev. 20:27).[81] Moreover, H makes it unlawful to "turn to" or consult mediums or wizards, but does not prescribe the death penalty for such consultation (Lev. 19:31; 20:6). The latter text warns that YHWH would set his face against any who consulted mediums or wizards, and "cut them off from among" their people. In other words, the administration of any penalty for these offenses would be left to YHWH.

### (b) Leviticus 20:1-5: offering children to Molech

This new law prohibited Israelites from offering or giving their children to Molech. Molech, according to 1 Kings 11:7, was the god worshiped by Ammonites, a neighboring people. Leviticus 18:21 prohibits the practice of offering or devoting children by fire to Molech; and Leviticus 20:1-5 apparently makes doing so a capital crime. Such offerings would constitute apostasy and allotheism, by acknowledging and honoring Molech as a god. They also would violate the covenant's horizontal dimension, by causing the death of Israelite children.[82] Leviticus 20:1-5, however, seems to acknowledge or recognize the possibility of noncompliance with its capital penalty requirement:

---

[80] In this book, the term "Deuteronomic reformers" designates those supposed to have been responsible for much if not all of the legislation found in Deuteronomy, chapters 12–19 and 26. See Section B.1.e.ii.(a) of this chapter.

[81] But see Lev. 19:26b, which, though banning augury or witchcraft, provides no penalty. See also Deut. 18:10-14, which seems to call for banishment, though not execution, of "any one who practices divination, a soothsayer, or an augur, or a sorcerer, or a charmer, or a medium, or a wizard, or a necromancer" (RSV). These practitioners were not necessarily allotheists. Perhaps the Deuteronomic reformers were more tolerant of such practices than those who had established the death penalty for sorcerers, mediums, and wizards in the CC and H.

[82] Deuteronomy 12:29-31 and 18:10, both part of the RDC, also warn against such practices.

But if the people of the land do at all hide their eyes from that man, when he gives one of his children to Molech, and do not put him to death, then I will set my face against that man and against his family, and will cut them off from among their people, him and all who follow him in playing the harlot after Molech. (RSV)

This "but if" provision evidently meant that if Israelites failed to put such Molech worshipers to death, YHWH himself would banish them.[83] Alternately, "cut them off from among their people" could have meant that YHWH himself would cause them to die. Either way, the provision suggests that the drafters recognized their contemporaries' hesitancy to apply the death penalty in such cases.

### (c) Leviticus 24:10-16: blaspheming "the Name"

This new law criminalizes blasphemy or blaspheming "the Name" of YHWH.[84] Unlike most of the laws traditionally attributed to Moses, this one derives from a reported "case" rather than from YHWH's purported pronouncements upon Mts. Sinai or Horeb. A man, whose mother was Israelite and father Egyptian, while quarreling with an Israelite, had "blasphemed the Name, and cursed" (Lev. 24:10-11 RSV). The substance of the "blasphemy" is not indicated; but probably involved some inappropriate, possibly derogatory use of the divine name. The blasphemer was then brought before Moses, who, however, did not yet know what should be done since there was no previous statute on point. "So they put him in custody, till the will of YHWH should be declared to them" (Lev. 24:12 RSV).[85] Subsequently, as the story is told, YHWH instructs Moses to order the blasphemer executed.[86] The resulting rule or law of the case is stated in Leviticus 24:16:

He who blasphemes the name of YHWH shall be put to death; all the congregation shall stone him; the sojourner as well as the native, when he blasphemes the Name, shall be put to death. (RSV)

---

[83] Cf. Gen. 4:12. Deuteronomy 18:10 also may have meant that Molech worshipers ("anyone who makes a son or daughter pass through fire") were to be banished or exiled.

[84] Cf. Exod. 22:28a: "You shall not revile God." No penalty for doing so is indicated in the CC.

[85] This text and Numbers 15:34 are the only explicit references in the Old Testament or Hebrew Scriptures to arrest and custody pending trial or sentencing. As to cities of refuge where offenders might seek refuge pending trial, see Chapter Six, Section A.

[86] It is not said whether this instruction was derived from or conveyed through the ephod or "lot" or received through some other medium.

Although blasphemy is not mentioned as a capital offense in earlier law codes, it may have been so treated in previous Israelite common or case law. If so, the point of this episode might have been to make clear that the law applied to resident aliens as well as to native-born Israelites, or as in the reported case, to persons of mixed nationality who blasphemed.

### ii. Laws affecting the community: the horizontal dimension

Several earlier laws concerning relations within the community are repeated in H, generally with some variations or modifications. Also, a number of new laws with this focus appear for the first time in H. Several of the laws concern illicit or improper sexual activity.

### (a) Modifications or variations on earlier laws

Over time, older laws become modified, whether by new case law or interpretive "construction" as to their meaning and scope, or through new "legislative" enactments. The H laws described in this subsection present relatively slight variations on earlier "statutes."

*Leviticus 24:17, 21b: homicide.* Here as in the CC (Exod. 21:12), a person who commits homicide is subject to the death penalty: "He who kills a man shall be put to death" (RSV). Unlike the CC, however, these H texts do not distinguish between accidental or negligent, and intentional homicide.[87] Moreover, H contains no provision for cities of refuge where those who have killed other persons may seek sanctuary pending further proceedings.[88] If H is properly dated prior to the Deuteronomic Reform, this omission may be accounted for on the theory that, prior to this reform, persons seeking refuge as "manslayers" could find sanctuary at any of the numerous local religious shrines then scattered throughout Israel. Closing or destroying those shrines was a core feature of the Deuteronomic Reform.

The fact that the homicide law is repeated twice (as is the law regarding killing "an animal" or "a beast," Leviticus 24:17, 21a), suggests possible scribal error in copying. Or it may be that one version was originally part of the *lex talionis* at Leviticus 24:19-20. These verses, for the first time, extend that *lex* from its narrow context in Exodus 21:22-25 so as to apply to mayhem or permanent disfigurement generally.[89] In addition, as in

---

[87] Cf. Exod. 21:13-14 and Deut. 19:4-13.
[88] See Chapter Six, Section A.
[89] At common law, mayhem originally referred to the kinds of disfigurement or disablement that would adversely affect the victim's ability to fight. In American statutory law,

Exodus 21:23, the laws set out in Leviticus 24:17 and 21b require taking "life for life," that is, execution of the one who has killed another person.[90]

*Leviticus 20:9: cursing father or mother.* Like D, H does not include any laws making it a capital offense for a person to strike his parents.[91] Leviticus 20:9, however, like Exodus 21:17, makes it a capital crime to *curse* one's father or mother, another offense not included in D. The only addition to the earlier provision is in Leviticus 20:9b (RSV): "[H]e has cursed his father or his mother, [therefore] his blood is upon him[self]." Thus it is said that those who have cursed a parent are responsible for their own death.[92] Perhaps this added statement was intended to ease the conscience of those who might otherwise feel hesitant to apply the death penalty in this setting.[93]

*Leviticus 20:10: adultery.* The version of the Decalogue found in the Covenant Code (Exod. 20:14) prohibits adultery, but does not provide any penalty for its commission.[94] But here, H, like D,[95] treats adultery as a capital offense. Neither the D nor the H version of the law defines or penalizes adultery in a case where a married man has sexual intercourse with an unmarried woman.

*Leviticus 20:15-16: buggery with an animal or a beast.* The CC had provided that anyone who lay sexually with a beast would be put to death (Exod. 22:19). The H version specifies that the anti-buggery law is gender inclusive: it applies both to men and to women. The provision as to women, however, contains an additional element: "*If a woman approaches any beast and* lies with it . . . " (Lev. 20:16 RSV). Conceivably, this provision was intended to excuse a woman in the unlikely event that she was approached by a beast, that is, victimized by the animal.[96] At least she could have so contended as a defense under this H revision.

---

mayhem generally means any kind of dismemberment or permanent disfigurement. See LaFave, *Criminal Law* (cited above in note 38), pp. 749–50.

[90] As to the three biblical versions of the *lex talionis*, see Chapter Six, Section D.2.

[91] Cf. Exod. 21:15.

[92] The expression, "his blood is upon him," places responsibility for adverse consequences on those who have committed capital offenses. See, e.g., Lev. 20:11, 12, 13, 16, & 27.

[93] Several biblical texts suggest that cursing was expected to operate *ex opere operato* (or automatically) with tangible, deleterious consequences. See, e.g., the Balaam–Balak story in Num. 22–24 and the recitation of curses in Deut. 27:13-26. Cf. Ps. 109:17-19. Thus cursing parents could have been understood to cause them tangible or physical harm. See Good, "Capital Punishment" (cited in Chapter Three, note 13), p. 956.

[94] So likewise the version in Deut. 5:18.

[95] See Deut. 22:22.

[96] Such circumstances may have been imagined in ancient folklore; but there are no biblical examples.

*Leviticus 19:20-22: sexual intercourse with a betrothed female slave.* This law modifies or limits the scope of the D provisions that made it a capital offense for a man to have sexual intercourse with another man's betrothed, virgin "wife" inside city limits (Deut. 22:23-24). This H law carves out an exception when the betrothed woman is a slave who has not yet been ransomed or given her freedom. In this situation, neither is to be put to death. The woman is excused "because she was not free" (RSV), a rationale somewhat similar to the D presumption of innocence on the part of a betrothed virgin when the sexual encounter occurred in the countryside (Deut. 22:25-27).[97] The H provision does not excuse the male; he is guilty of sin (Lev. 19:22). However, he can absolve himself of that sin by offering a prescribed guilt offering, administered by "the priest," in order that his sin will be forgiven (Lev. 19:21-22).[98]

### (b) New capital laws

The new capital laws regarding community interactions first articulated in H all define illicit sexual conduct. One series condemns various types of incest. Homosexual intercourse is prohibited for the first (and only) time. And another new law provides for the execution of priests' daughters who engage in prostitution.

*Leviticus 20:11-12, 14: incest.* Twelve different categories of incestuous sexual liaisons are prohibited in Leviticus 18:6-18.[99] Generally, it seems, these prohibitions were meant to apply in regard to both marriage and extra-marital sexual intercourse. Some, but not all of Leviticus Eighteen's proscribed categories were made subject to capital punishment under the provisions of Leviticus chapter 20.[100]

Only three categories are subject to the death penalty under Leviticus 20. *First*, sexual relations between a son and his father's wife (Lev. 20:11). This apparently would include intercourse with either the son's own

---

[97] Leviticus 19:20-22 does not distinguish between urban and rural settings.

[98] For alternative interpretations of this law, see Westbrook, *Studies* (cited above in note 31), pp. 101–09.

[99] None of the offenses proscribed in Leviticus 18 includes punishment directives or sentencing guidelines. There it may have been understood that YHWH himself would punish the offenders.

[100] On biblical incest laws, see generally David Daube, *Studies in Biblical Law* (cited above in note 32), pp. 77–82. Categories prohibited in Leviticus 18 but *not* subject to the death penalty under chapter 20 include the following relationships: brother–sister (18:9, 11; see also 20:17; cf. 2 Sam. 13:1-14); grandfather–granddaughter (18:10); nephew–aunt (18:13-14; see also 20:19); brother–brother's wife (18:16; see also 20:21); husband–wife's granddaughter (18:17); and husband–wife's sister (18:18).

mother, or with his father's other wife or wives.[101] *Second*, intercourse between a man and his daughter-in-law (Lev. 20:12). And *third*, a man's "taking" both a woman and her mother (Lev. 20:14).[102] All sexual partners in these incest categories were to be put to death.[103]

*Leviticus 20:13: homosexual intercourse.* Such intercourse was not mentioned in any other law code. Here it is characterized as an "abomination" or morally repugnant, and listed with other capital sexual offenses:[104] "If a man lies with a male as with a woman, both of them have committed an abomination; they shall be put to death."[105] No biblical traditions explain why homosexual conduct was disapproved or sanctioned by the death penalty for the first time in H. Such conduct may, of course, have been criminalized in earlier Israelite or ANE common law. Homosexual conduct is neither condemned nor even mentioned again in the later RDC or PC. Homosexual *assault* or *rape* was clearly disapproved in the old story of the angels' visit to Sodom (Gen. 19:4-11).[106] Neither this, nor any other biblical law or narrative, concerns lesbian or female homosexual relations.

*Leviticus 21:9: a priest's daughter who "plays the harlot."* Chapters 21 and 22 detail numerous directions as to the conduct and responsibilities of priests. Priestly purity and ritual procedures are emphasized for the first

---

[101] See also Amos 2:7b. According to Gen. 35:22 and 49:3-4, Jacob's son, Reuben, lay with Bilhah, Jacob's concubine (described also as Jacob's wife in Gen. 30:4), but was not punished for so doing. At that time, Mosaic law would not yet have been in effect. But see also 2 Sam. 16:21-22 (David's son, Absalom so acts with impunity). Neither Leviticus 18 nor 20 prohibit sexual intercourse between a man and his daughter or between a man and his niece.

[102] A man's having sexual intercourse with his mother-in-law is not specifically forbidden in chapter 18, but this meaning is implicit in Leviticus 20:14. See also Deut. 27:23.

[103] Leviticus 20:17, and 19-21 address four types of incest noted also in Leviticus 18, but mandate or anticipate noncapital forms of punishment: brother–sister; nephew–aunt, nephew–uncle's wife; and brother–brother's wife liaisons. Those engaged in the latter two modes of incest, it is said, will be (or will die) childless (Lev. 20:20-21). Curiously, one late tradition purports to *require* certain classes of relatives to marry. See Tob. 6:12, according to which a father must give his daughter to her only eligible kinsman-suitor on pain of death. Reference to the death penalty here is probably only a literary fiction intended to heighten the drama. There is no such biblical law or ANE legal equivalent to this requirement. As to incest in other ANE laws, see Good, "Capital Punishment" (cited in Chapter Three, note 13), pp. 959–60.

[104] Leviticus 20:1-16 lists a series of capital offenses; those enumerated in vv. 10-16 all pertain to sexual activities.

[105] A number of early texts could be read to suggest that David and Jonathan enjoyed with impunity a relationship that extended beyond conventional male bonding: 1 Sam. 18:1, 3; 19:1; 20:17, 30, 41; 2 Sam. 1:26. But see Good, "Capital Punishment" (cited in Chapter Three, note 13), p. 960 and *id.* n. 62 (concluding otherwise).

[106] See also Judges 19:22-30. In the New Testament, Paul comments unfavorably on both lesbian and male homosexual passion and acts (Rom. 1:26-27).

time in H, though not to the same extent as in the later PC. Here, as in the PC, it is understood that priests must be descendants of Aaron,[107] and must remain "holy" (*qadosh* or *qadash* [Lev. 21:6, 7]) or separate from "unclean" persons or things. Thus, priests might not marry harlots or divorced women (Lev. 21:7).[108] A priest's daughter who "plays the harlot" (probably meaning, having consensual sexual intercourse with anyone other than her husband) "profanes" both herself and her father, and is, therefore, to be put to death.

### e. *The Revised Deuteronomic Code (RDC): Deuteronomy chapters 12–19 and 26*

At some period in the late 8th or 7th centuries BCE, possibly during the long, corrupt, and apostate reign of King Manasseh, a major reform movement became active in Judah. The reformers were no doubt aware of the fate of the Northern Kingdom, Israel, which had been over-run by Assyria in 722 BCE. Various prophets had interpreted that catastrophe prospectively or contemporaneously as YHWH's judgment against Israel for its chronic pattern of turning away from YHWH to the worship of other gods, and the numerous injustices consequent upon its failure to keep his commandments.[109] The Deuteronomic historians so understood such matters in retrospect.[110] The Deuteronomic reformers, understandably, were concerned that the peoples' persistent pattern of apostasy—turning from YHWH and to the worship of other gods—would likely bring divinely ordained catastrophic judgment upon the Southern Kingdom, Judah, as well. The major literary or statutory product of—if not inspiration for—the Deuteronomic Reform was the new collection of laws found in Deuteronomy chapters 12–19 and 26, characterized in this book as the Revised Deuteronomic Code (RDC).

The key feature of the Deuteronomic reform was the requirement that now YHWH might be worshiped with sacrifices, tithes, and other offerings *only in the one place* [implicitly, Jerusalem], and that the many cult shrines where in previous years, decades and centuries, YHWH had been worshiped—along with indigenous Canaanite deities—must be closed

---

[107] Unlike the PC, however, H does not distinguish between priests and Levites.
[108] It may have been assumed, but is not explicitly stated that priests themselves were to refrain from having sexual intercourse with harlots.
[109] See, e.g., Hos. 4:1–10:15; Amos 2:6–9:8b.
[110] See 2 Kgs 17:1-18.

down and destroyed. The reformers' intent, evidently, was to discourage the continuing love affair of the people of Judah with such deities, lest YHWH bring disaster upon that nation in the same way that he had done to Israel nearly a century earlier. These provisions, along with a series of related accommodations to the closing of the cult shrines, are set out in Deuteronomy 12–19. These chapters may also include other or earlier laws, some deriving, perhaps, from D, the earlier or original Deuteronomic Code. For purposes of this study, Deuteronomy 12–19 is considered as a separate Code, labeled, as a convenience, the Revised Deuteronomic Code, or RDC.

*i. An old law amended: Deuteronomy 19:4-13—homicide*

The RDC includes only one capital law somewhat similar to an earlier provision: this is a law distinguishing between separate categories of homicide and adding certain arrangements for the protection of the accused.

This Code contains an extensive section governing arrangements for dealing first with "the manslayer" and then with intentional murder (Deut. 19:4-13). The CC did not refer to manslaughter or accidental homicide.[111] Instead, it provided that a man who fatally struck another, but without plotting to do so in advance might flee to a "place" or sanctuary of some sort (Exod. 21:13), perhaps one of the many old rural and urban cult shrines functioning prior to the Deuteronomic Reform. In some modern jurisdictions, this kind of offense might be classified as second degree murder.[112] The RDC specifically defines manslaughter, namely, as an offense when "any one kills his neighbor unintentionally without having been at enmity with him in the past" (Deut. 19:4 RSV). This definition is followed immediately by the example:

... as when a man goes into the forest with his neighbor to cut wood, and his hand swings the axe to cut down a tree, and the head slips from the handle and strikes his neighbor so that he dies. (Deut. 19:5 RSV)

---

[111] The CC did address two narrowly defined instances of culpable or recklessly negligent homicide: (a) where a married pregnant woman dies from injury caused by brawling males that resulted in a miscarriage (Exodus 21:22-23), and (b) where an ox fatally gores someone after its owner had notice of its proclivity to gore but failed to provide adequate fencing (Exod. 21:28-32). See Section B.1.b.ii of this chapter. The CC also distinguished between premeditated murder and cases where "God let [the victim] fall into [the offender's] hands." See Section B.1.b.i of this chapter.

[112] See LaFave, *Criminal Law* (cited above in note 38), p. 698.

The accidental or negligent manslayer may flee to one of several cities of refuge and there obtain protection,

> ... lest the avenger of blood in hot anger pursue [him] and overtake him ... and wound him mortally, though the man did not deserve to die, since he was not at enmity with his neighbor in time past. (Deut. 19:6)[113]

The manslayer was to be protected not only for his own benefit, but also to prevent "the guilt of bloodshed" from coming upon the community as a whole. Such guilt would result if "innocent blood" was "shed"—i.e., by the execution of a merely negligent manslayer (Deut. 19:10).

The Deuteronomic definition of intentional homicide likewise is more exact than its earlier counterpart, particularly with regard to the elements of subjective intent and planning: "But if any man hates his neighbor, and lies in wait for him,[114] and attacks him, and wounds him mortally so that he dies ..." (Deut. 19:11 RSV), the murderer was to be executed. As read, Exodus 21:14 could include *attempted* murder. The Deuteronomic version specifies that in order for the offender to be liable, the intended victim must have died as a result of the premeditated assault.

*ii. New capital laws*

Several new capital laws found in the RDC are directed against worshiping or inciting others to worship alien deities. Two other new laws criminalize as capital offenses certain types of conduct that would disrupt important structural aspects of community existence. Both of these community laws relate directly to the judicial system.

### (a) False prophecy, apostasy, and inciting to allotheism

Five of the seven new capital laws found in the RDC are directed against worship of other gods (allotheism) and/or false prophecy. These are all found between chapters 12 and 18, and may well reflect the Deuteronomic Reform's concern with the persistent tendency of Judahites (if not also earlier Israelites) to "go after," that is, turn to and serve such

---

[113] As to cities of refuge, see Chapter Six, Section A.
[114] Cf. Exod. 21:13-14, where lying in wait is only by implication an element in the definition of premeditated murder.

other deities.[115] At any rate, these new laws, unlike Exodus 22:20, make clear that the community is responsible for the punishment of such offenders. Moreover, while Exodus 22:20 provided only that any who *sacrificed* to other gods would be destroyed, these new laws apply to any kind of worship or incitement to worship or serve such deities. Nevertheless, each of the new provisions is somewhat narrowly tailored.

*Deuteronomy 13:1-5: incitement to allotheism—prophets and dreamers of dreams.* This law focuses on "prophets" or "dreamers of dreams"[116] who attempt to authenticate their credibility by performing or foretelling certain "signs" or "wonders." If the signs or wonders "come to pass," that is, occur, *and* if such prophets or dreamers call on others to "go after" and serve other gods, those prophets or dreamers are to be put to death. Nothing is said as to prophets or dreamers of dreams who give signs or wonders that do *not* come to pass. Perhaps such persons would have been considered thereby sufficiently discredited and therefore less dangerous, and possibly tolerated as mere eccentrics.[117]

*Deuteronomy 13:6-11: secret incitement to allotheism—family and friends.* Secret incitement by immediate family members or dear friends to worship other gods was evidently considered a very serious threat to the community's relationship with YHWH:

> If your brother, the son of your mother, or your own son, or your daughter, or the wife of your bosom, or your friend who is as your own soul, entices you secretly, saying, "Let us go and serve other gods," . . . you shall not yield to him or listen to him, nor shall your eye pity him, nor shall you spare him, nor shall you conceal him; but you shall kill him . . . (Deut. 13:6-9a RSV)

In the biblical perspective generally, and especially in the view of Deuteronomic tradition, constant fidelity to YHWH was a matter of life and death for the whole community. YHWH had brought Israel "out of the land of Egypt, out of the house of bondage" (Deut. 13:10 RSV). So long as his people remained faithful to him, YHWH would continue to shower his blessings upon them (Deut. 28:1-14); but the consequences

---

[115] See generally, Calum M. Carmichael, *The Laws of Deuteronomy* (Ithaca: Cornell Univ. Press, 1974), pp. 70–77.
[116] These categories could have included primitive fortune tellers or astrologers.
[117] Compare 1 Sam. 21:10-15.

of apostasy—turning from YHWH and his law—would be utterly catastrophic (Deut. 28:15-68). There are no recorded biblical instances where this deadly serious law was carried out.

In its terms, this law does not provide for punishing persons outside the circle of intimate family members or friends who promote allotheism. Perhaps such outsiders were thought less dangerous because they were less likely to succeed with their enticements. Or it may already have been understood that such other persons were to be executed; in that case, the purpose of Deuteronomy 13:6-11 would have been to ensure that no one, not even family members or dearest friends, would be exempt from its penalties. Interestingly, this law does not provide for punishing any such persons who might *publicly* incite or encourage friends or relations to idolatry or allotheism. Possibly open encouragement was considered tolerable because it could be corrected or countered by others.

*Deuteronomy 13:12-18: inciting cities to allotheism.* Here it is said that if "certain base fellows" from among the Israelites succeed in "drawing away" (RSV) the inhabitants of an Israelite (or Judahite) city from YHWH and in enticing them to "go and serve other gods" (RSV), all the inhabitants of that city are to be destroyed, along with their cattle.[118] Again, this law may reflect the ideology of the Deuteronomic Reformers, which is expressed also in the *herem* tradition.[119] The explicit rationale for this drastic action was to assuage the ferocity of YHWH's anger, which otherwise would be inflicted upon all Israel, and thereby to induce him to show them mercy and compassion (Deut. 13:17). The law is somewhat narrowly crafted in that it applies only if those who incited Israelite towns to

---

[118] Perhaps it was understood that the apostates had ritually contaminated their cattle by offering some to alien deities. Because the laws included in the RDC are all attributed to Moses (or YHWH's giving the laws to him in the era of Israel's sojourn in the wilderness) they are phrased as if intended for all Israel, not just for Judah in the period following the Assyrian conquest of Israel. After the demise of Israel, the Northern Kingdom, Judah, the surviving Southern Kingdom is often identified in biblical terms as "Israel" and its people as "Israelites."

[119] The *herem* was the practice of destroying (or otherwise consecrating to YHWH) persons defeated in war, and sometimes their livestock and other property. See de Vaux (cited above in note 30), pp. 260–63. In Deuteronomic editing of early tradition following the Deuteronomic Reform, this archaic practice apparently was reemphasized in order to underscore the critical importance of remaining faithful to YHWH and avoiding worship of other gods. Because the *herem* supposedly was practiced against enemies defeated in battles during the conquest of Canaan, it is not considered as a form of capital punishment in this book. But see Good, "Capital Punishment" (cited in Chapter Three, note 13), pp. 971–72, noting texts where the *herem* may have been applied against Israelites who failed to observe the practice.

commit apostasy were themselves Israelites.[120] Moreover, it may be that the *herem* was supposed to apply only if *all* "the inhabitants of the city" had turned to other gods (Deut. 13:13).

*Deuteronomy 17:2-7: allotheism generally.* This law made it a capital offense for a man or woman in any Israelite town to go, serve, and worship other gods or celestial beings.[121] Implicitly, this law against allotheism would apply to Israelites and foreigners alike; but not, in its terms, to persons living in rural areas. As will be noted, certain due process protections for the accused are provided in Deuteronomy 17:4-6: diligent inquiry as to the facts[122] and corroborating testimony by one or two additional witnesses.[123]

*Deuteronomy 18:20: allotheistic and presumptive, false prophets.* Two types of prophets are made subject to the death penalty under this law. Any prophet who "speaks in the name of other gods . . . shall die." The law also assigns the same fate to any prophet "who presumes to speak . . . a word" in the name of YHWH which YHWH had "not commanded him to speak." Whether or not such a prophet had been so commanded was to be determined by observing whether the "word" that had been spoken came to pass, i.e., came true (Deut. 18:21-22). Thus even a prophet who thought he was speaking on YHWH's behalf might be put to death.[124] This provision does not appear to take into consideration the possibility that YHWH might change his mind, as is suggested in Amos chapter 5 or illustrated in the Jonah story (Jon. 3:10). There is no evidence that this law was ever enforced.

## (b) Offenses against the community: protecting the innocent and upholding judicial integrity

Two of the new Deuteronomic laws refer to judicial proceedings. One provides penalties for malicious false testimony. The other sanctions refusal or failure to abide by the court's decision. Both may have been part of the RDC; or they may have been laws originally included in D, but

---

[120] Such appears to be the meaning of the expression, persons "who have come out among you."

[121] Compare Exod. 22:20; see Section B.1.b.vi(c) of this chapter. The Deuteronomic law specifically prohibited worshiping "the sun or the moon or any of the host of heaven." (Deut. 17:3 RSV).

[122] See Chapter Six, Section B.

[123] See Chapter Six, Section C.1.

[124] This law does not conflict with Deuteronomy 13:1-5. In that law, a prophet whose signs or wonders came to pass would be put to death only if he called upon people to worship and serve *other* gods.

now relocated in Deuteronomy chapters 12–19 among the laws emanating from the Deuteronomic Reform.

*Deuteronomy 19:16-21: malicious, false witnesses.* This law, based on, or further applying the *lex talionis*, calls for the death penalty when a malicious witness is found to have accused his brother (or fellow citizen) falsely of a capital offense: "[Y]ou shall do to him as he had meant to do to his brother" (Deut. 19:19). The language here may have been understood to be gender inclusive. This law is illustrated in the story of *Susanna and the Elders*, where two elders are put to death after they were found to have accused Susanna maliciously and falsely of adultery.[125] The apparent purpose of this law was to uphold the integrity of the judicial process and also to protect innocent persons from harm. This law evidently presumes that the innocent were understood to have a *right* to be free from abuse of judicial process by malicious persons.

*Deuteronomy 17:8-12: refusal to accept the court's ruling.* Under this law, it was a capital offense to refuse to accept a court's verdict—at any rate in difficult cases that have been decided by the presiding Levitical priest and/or "the judge who is in office" at the Jerusalem Temple:

> The man who acts presumptuously, by not obeying the priest who stands to minister there before YHWH your God, or the judge, that man shall die. (Deut. 17:12)

As here written, this law clearly reflects the Deuteronomic Reform, which centralized worship in the Jerusalem Temple. The priest or judge in Jerusalem functioned, in effect, as supreme court. To ignore or disobey its orders would constitute anarchy, if not also apostasy and treason. Here we see a severe penalty for what would be equivalent in modern jurisprudence to contempt of court.

### f. The Priestly Code or Priestly Legislation

This is the latest of the biblical law codes. Priestly laws may or may not have been promulgated in a single code. Perhaps it would be more accurate to

---

[125] Susanna vv. 52-62. The situation set out in Deuteronomy 22:13-21 may be distinguishable. There the husband whose allegation against his new bride is found false evidently is presumed to have made "the shameful charges against her" (Deut. 22:17 RSV) mistakenly, but without malice. For further analysis of the *lex talionis* in Deut. 19:16-21, see Chapter Six, Section D.2. As to ANE parallels to the biblical law against perjury, see Good, "Capital Punishment" (cited in Chapter Three, note 13), p. 968.

refer to priestly *legislation*.¹²⁶ Priestly laws are found in portions of Exodus, Leviticus, and Numbers, and are generally thought to have been written down between 450 and 400 BCE. By then, the kingdoms of Israel and Judah both had been over-run by other nations, and the Jewish people along with their former homelands were now encompassed within the Persian empire. The Jerusalem Temple, the sabbath, and various other holy days or festivals[127] were Judaism's main religious institutions. After the Deuteronomic Reform, sacrifices could be offered to God or YHWH only at the Jerusalem temple. Such sacrifices were now presented by priests, rather than by lay individuals.

The PC is thought to have been composed and promulgated under the auspices of the Jerusalem priesthood, and probably embodies earlier as well as more recent laws. Most of these laws had to do with sacrificial offerings, how they were to be presented, and the duties and prerogatives of priests. Priests were now differentiated from Levites. The latter—notwithstanding provisions of the Deuteronomic Reform guaranteeing them equal standing with the Jerusalem priesthood[128]—were now relegated to the status of lower ranking Temple functionaries or *assistants* to the priests. Some of the new capital laws found in the PC were intended to legitimate the superior status of priests and keep Levites and others in their place. Others dealt with sabbath violations. Case law narratives purporting to date from early times were recorded in P traditions to illustrate such laws.

In contrast to D, the PC, as such, contains no provisions calling for the execution of those who worshiped other gods. Moreover, the PC includes only one law or set of capital laws pertaining to offenses proscribed by earlier laws.[129]

---

[126] See generally, Phillips, *Criminal Law* (cited above in note 36), pp. 183–89.
[127] See Theodor H. Gaster, *Festivals of the Jewish Year* (New York: Morrow Quill, 1978).
[128] See Deut. 18:1-8.
[129] See the law or laws regarding manslaughter and murder, Numbers 35:6-34, discussed in Section B.1.f.ii. of this chapter. But see the P account of God's warning to Noah, the forefather of all later humankind: "For your lifeblood I will surely require a reckoning; of every beast I will require it and of man; of every man's brother I will require the life of man. Whoever sheds the blood of man, by man shall his blood be shed; for God made man in his own image" (Gen. 9:5-6). This sometimes so-called "natural" or "divine" law evidently was thought to apply to all humankind, not only to Israel.

On Genesis 9:5-6, see generally Megivern, *Death Penalty* (cited above in note 1), pp. 14–16. Megivern writes, "In the history of Christian theological legitimization of the death penalty, Genesis 9:6 has probably been cited more frequently than any other text as basic proof of the propriety of humans executing fellow human malefactors." He points out several problems with taking this text as justification for latter-day application of the death penalty, including its failure to distinguish between negligent and intentional homicide. He further observes: "Those who appeal to [Genesis 9] as their authority for blanket

### i. Religious practices

Most of the new capital laws found in the PC relate to religious institutions. Two or three had to do with protecting or preserving the exclusive pre-eminence of the Jerusalem priests and their proto-typical predecessors who, according to Priestly tradition, enjoyed similar status when officiating at the tabernacle or tent of meeting in ancient times.

### (a) Protecting priestly prerogatives

Although the text of Numbers 3:38 is phrased as narrative rather than law, its import is unmistakable:

> And those to encamp before the tabernacle on the east, before the tent of meeting toward the sunrise, were Moses and Aaron and his sons, having charge of the rites within the sanctuary, whatever had to be done for the people of Israel; and anyone else who came near was to be put to death. (RSV)

According to P law, only priests ("Aaron" and his male descendants) were to enjoy the privileges and perquisites associated with performing the sacred ceremonies in the central sanctuary. Others who ventured to "come near" were to be put to death.[130]

The Priestly story as to the fates of the Levites, Korah, Abiram, and On, along with their supporters, found in Numbers, chapter 16, illustrates the point that Levites were supposed to be content with their subordinate status in the priestly hierarchy. According to Numbers 18:1-7, YHWH told *Aaron*—the forefather of all priests, according to P tradition—that the tribe of Levi, that is, all Levites, should minister to him and his sons, but must keep their distance from the "vessels of the sanctuary," "the altar and all that is within the veil." Levites or any others besides priests who ventured to "come near" were to be put to death.[131]

---

approval of the death penalty invariably narrow its application without further ado to the single [category] of first-degree murder. This kind of arbitrary restriction, devoid of any textual basis, is a good example of why such proof-texting has been thoroughly discredited." *Id.*, p. 15. Another commentator urges that Genesis 9:6 should be read merely as a descriptive "proverb," rather than as a law authorizing capital punishment. Lind, *Killing State* (cited above in note 6), p. 44.

[130] See also Num. 1:51; 3:10; 18:7, and other texts relating to priestly practices discussed by Good, "Capital Punishment," (cited in Chapter Three, note 13, pp. 968–69.

[131] See also Num. 18:21-22 which warns that any Israelites other than priests or Levites who came near the tent of meeting must die. In P tradition, the tent of meeting or tabernacle was understood as the ancient prototype for the later Jerusalem Temple where priests officiated after it was rebuilt in 515 BCE.

## (b) Sabbath violations

That Israelites and their farm animals should do no work on the sabbath had been specified in three earlier codes,[132] but none of these codes had made noncompliance a criminal offense. Under the PC, however, working on the sabbath became not only criminal, but a capital offense.[133] What kinds of activities constituted work still remained to be defined.[134] A story in Numbers 15:32-36, probably part of the P narrative, addresses that matter. A man had been caught "gathering sticks on the sabbath day." "Because it had not been made plain what should be done to him" (RSV),[135] the man was put "in custody," pending further disclosure of divine intent (Num. 15:34). Whereupon, as the story goes, YHWH told Moses that the man was to be put to death by stoning at the hands of "the whole congregation" or community, which, accordingly, proceeded to "stone him to death with stones" as directed in Numbers 15:35-36.

### ii. Community inter-relations: manslaughter and murder

The only capital law in the PC concerned with relations between or among members of the community is that dealing with manslaughter (or unintentional homicide) and murder, found in Numbers 35:6-34. The earlier version of this law in the RDC, Deuteronomy 19:4-13, has been considered previously.[136] Several aspects of this law will be examined later, for instance, due process arrangements and, particularly, cities of refuge. Three points stand out with respect to the definition of capital offenses in Numbers 35.

In the first place, this PC law provides a much more detailed inventory of indicia for intentional homicide or murder. The type of weapon used was considered dispositive: if one person fatally struck another "with an instrument of iron," or with a stone or wooden weapon of lethal weight or proportions ("by which a man may die" RSV), the crime was murder,

---

[132] RD: Exod. 34:21; CC: Exod. 20:8-11; 23:12; D: Deut. 5:12-15.
[133] Exod. 31:12-17; 35:2-3.
[134] That issue is considered later both in the New Testament and Talmud, especially the latter's tractate *Shabbath*. See, e.g., Mk 2:23–3:6; Lk. 6:1-11; and *The Talmud, Shabbath* I & II, tr. H. Freedman (London: Soncino Press, 1938). See, e.g, *Shabbath* 11a-b (I: 41-45); 12a-b (I: 45-50); 365-37a (I: 169-73).
[135] According to Exodus 35:3, a PC provision, *kindling a fire* on the sabbath was prohibited; but there was no specific prohibition against gathering sticks preliminary to doing so.
[136] See Section B.1.e.i. of this chapter.

and the killer was to be put to death (Num. 35:16-18). Use of such weapons raised an irrebuttable presumption of intent to kill.[137]

Intent as well as *modus operandi* were critical in other circumstances:

> If [one person] stabbed [another] from hatred, or hurled [something] at him, lying in wait, so that he died, or in enmity struck him with his hand, so that he died, then he who struck the blow shall be put to death; he is a murderer. (Num. 35:20-21 RSV)

Additionally, this law gives a somewhat different set of illustrations as to actions deemed to constitute manslaughter or unintentional homicide:

> But if he stabbed him suddenly without enmity, or hurled anything on him without lying in wait, or used a stone, by which a man may die, and without seeing him cast it upon him, so that he died, though he was not his enemy, and did not seek his harm . . .[the offense may be deemed manslaughter] (Num. 35:22-23 RSV)[138]

This text does not make clear under what circumstances one person might stab another "suddenly without enmity."[139] Here, as in Exodus 21:12-13, an impromptu, rather than premeditated act is considered less serious than a fatal, willful or intentional attack. Perhaps the act might have been provoked by a sudden argument or insult, and carried out on the spur of the moment or in "heat of passion."[140] The hurled stone example clearly illustrates accidental (if reckless) conduct.[141] Such types of homicide evidently were considered less serious (or more excusable), and therefore not subject to the death penalty.

---

[137] See Falk, *Law and Religion* (cited in Chapter Four, note 6), p. 124. In effect, a person who struck another with such weapons would be strictly liable and subject to execution if the battery victim subsequently died. It is not clear whether such weapons might constitute sufficient circumstantial evidence to convict, or whether, in addition, it would have been necessary for two or more witnesses to have observed the fatal attack. See Chapter Six, Section C.1. In modern American jurisprudence, use of deadly weapons such as iron bars, baseball bats, bricks, or stones is considered evidence of intent to kill. See Lafave, *Criminal Law* (cited above in note 38), pp. 661–63.

[138] Compare Deut. 19:5.

[139] Under Exodus 21:12-13, a man who fatally struck another might avoid the death penalty "if he did not lie in wait for [the victim], but God let him fall into his hand."

[140] See LaFave on common law manslaughter and second degree murder, *Criminal Law* (cited above in note 38), pp. 698–99, 703–17.

[141] Compare the flying axe head example in Deut. 19:4-5.

Finally, the Numbers law adds a new, though somewhat odd, provision. If a "manslayer" who has found sanctuary in a city of refuge and has been judged innocent as to intentional homicide subsequently ventures beyond that city's boundaries any time before the death of the high priest then in office,[142] he may be killed by the victim's "avenger of blood" (Num. 35:26-28).[143] But if the manslayer remains in the city of refuge until the high priest's death, he is then free to return to his home fully protected by law (Num. 35:28).[144] The text does not explain why a person found innocent of murder must nevertheless be compelled to live confined in a city of refuge afterwards, and risk execution by his victim's "avenger" if he leaves that city; nor is it explained why the death of the high priest triggers his release from such constraint. Possibly this arrangement was intended to appease victims' friends or relatives who might still harbor desire for vigilante or self-help justice notwithstanding the verdict of innocence, while keeping adjudged manslayers safe from such would-be avengers through protective detention. By the time of the high priests' death, perhaps avengers' rage would have abated. Or the high priest's death might have been regarded as a divine signal that the manslayer had served enough time.[145]

### g. *Capital laws continuing in effect, repealed, or abandoned?*

As has been seen, capital offenses are to be found in each of the main law codes. But how were these codes understood in relation to one another? Was each code intended to include only those capital laws thought to be in effect at the time it was promulgated? In that case, capital offenses articulated in earlier codes, but not included in the new ones would have

---

[142] Presumably the high priest would be in office in Jerusalem.

[143] As to the Numbers text regarding cities of refuge, see Chapter Six, Section A.5.

[144] Implicitly, if "the avenger of blood" were to kill him in these circumstances, the avenger would be "guilty of blood" (Num. 35:27), and therefore subject to punishment, presumably the death penalty. It is not clear whether Numbers 35:32 means that the manslayer must pay ransom after the death of the high priest in order to be free to leave, or simply that he could not obtain his freedom by paying ransom until the high priest had died. The latter meaning may be more likely.

[145] Westbrook suggests another possibility: that here the term "high priest" referred to the priest or chief priest in whichever cities the homicide occurred, and that such priest would have been ritually polluted if the manslayer returned during his lifetime. Westbrook, *Studies* (cited above in note 31), p. 81. It is not apparent, however, what priests would be doing in cities other than Jerusalem a century or more after the Deuteronomic Reform, why such priests would be designated as "the high priest," or why the manslayer's return would not ritually pollute any successor local priest.

been effectively repealed or considered no longer operative. Or were provisions in the later codes meant to supplement those set down in earlier codes? Since all the first four, and possibly the first five books of the Bible were preserved and edited under priestly auspices, it would not be surprising if the P editors understood that capital laws contained in the earlier codes remained in effect, along with those added in the PC. On the other hand, the P editors evidently were interested in preserving old traditions, and might have included earlier laws simply out of respect for their antiquity, without intending them to remain binding in actual practice. Likewise, we cannot be certain regarding the extent to which the later codes were meant to replace, or only to supplement laws and codes promulgated or operative in still earlier times. Some laws may indeed have fallen into disuse, or otherwise been effectively repealed. At all events, it may be instructive to conclude this discussion of capital offenses by tracking particular laws as they appear in, or were omitted from, subsequent codes.

Comparison of the capital laws found in each of the codes indicates that in many instances the new laws were intended to amend or replace earlier provisions. Surprisingly few capital laws detailed in one code are repeated in later codes. Arguably, such laws could, in effect, have been considered abandoned. On the other hand, each code includes some number of new capital laws. Consequently, it cannot accurately be said that the concept of capital punishment as such was abandoned in biblical times. Several newer laws, however, do appear to mitigate the severity of earlier provisions.

Of all the capital offenses, only one, murder, appears in as many as three codes: the CC (Exod. 21:12-14); the RDC (Deut. 19:4-13); and the PC (Num. 35:6-34). In each instance, these laws undertake to distinguish between murder and some less serious type of homicide.[146] Each of the later versions modifies or adds to the earlier formulation(s). For instance, both Deuteronomy 19:4-13 and Numbers 35:6-34 distinguish between intentional murder and manslaughter, and make clear that the latter is not a capital offense.[147] It appears likely that these later versions were intended to amend or supersede earlier laws that did not make this distinction.

Only five other capital laws are found in as many as two codes. One is the provision against kidnapping in CC (Exod. 21:16) and

---

[146] Compare Lev. 24:17, 21 in H, which does not distinguish murder from manslaughter, but simply makes it a capital offense if a person "kills a man."

[147] See Sections B.1.b.i., and B.1.f.ii. of this chapter.

D (Deut. 24:7). The later, Deuteronomic law provides for capital punishment only if the kidnapped victim was an Israelite, and if the kidnaper has treated his victim as a slave or sold him. Here again, the later version evidently qualifies the earlier.[148] Another is the offense of cursing either parent, found in the CC (Exod. 21:17) and H (Lev. 20:9), both stated in similar terms.[149] The third is the prohibition against "buggery" or sexual intercourse with an animal. This is stated tersely in the CC (Exod. 22:19) and then restated in H, in somewhat qualified terms (Lev. 20:15-16).[150] The fourth is adultery with a married woman, found in both D (Deut. 22:22) and H (Lev. 20:10). Finally, both the CC (Exod. 22:20) and the RDC (Deut. 17:2-7) include provisions making, respectively, offering sacrifices to, and worship and serving other gods capital offenses. Kidnapping is not mentioned in H, RDC, or PC; and neither the laws against cursing parents nor those against buggery with beasts are repeated in D, RDC, or the PC. Adultery is not included in the two latest codes, RDC and PC. However, the relatively late stories of Susanna[151] and "the woman caught in adultery" (Jn 8:3-11) suggest that adultery may have continued to be regarded as a capital offense in the late biblical period.

Three other laws found in early codes appear to have been complemented or qualified in later codes. The Covenant Code condemns sorceresses to death (Exod. 22:18). Later, H provides for the execution of mediums or wizards, whether male or female (Lev. 20:27). Evidently these laws were not always enforced in practice.[152] Nothing is said about sorceresses, mediums, or wizards in D, or in the later RDC, or the PC. The Covenant Code made it a capital offense to offer sacrifice to other gods (Exod. 22:20). Similarly, but more broadly, the RDC prescribed the death penalty for individuals who worshiped or served other gods (Deut. 17:2-7); this law would apply whether or not such worshipers offered sacrifices. Such laws are not to be found in D or H, and were not repeated in the PC. Finally, D made it a capital offense for a man to have sexual intercourse with a woman betrothed to another man within city limits

---

[148] See Sections B.1.b.v. and B.1.c.i. of this chapter.
[149] Compare Prov. 20:20, which may or may not imply that the offender will be subject to capital punishment: "If one curses his father or his mother his lamp will be put out in utter darkness." This text could be read to mean that those who curse their parents need not be put to death, but would instead experience some form of divine retribution.
[150] See Sections B.1.vii.(b) and B.1.d.ii.(a) of this chapter.
[151] See Susanna, v. 41, and Chapter Three, Section I.
[152] See 1 Sam. 28:3-25 (Saul had *deported* other wizards and mediums and consulted the medium at Endor). See also Ezek. 13:17-23, which seems to say that YHWH would punish female occult practitioners.

(Deut. 22:23-27). Here both the man and the woman were to be put to death.[153] The Holiness Code subsequently added an exception in the case of a betrothed woman who was a slave. In that circumstance, neither the woman nor the man would be subject to the death penalty (Lev. 19:20-22). This H law evidently presupposes that the provisions of Deuteronomy 22:23-27 were otherwise still operative.

All other capital offenses are found only once: in one code or another. This fact, as such, does not tell us whether such laws were still considered to apply in later times. Some appear to have been abandoned or mitigated. Others may have remained in effect.

The following capital offenses articulated in CC are not repeated in any later codes: children striking either parent (Exod. 21:15); wrestling males inadvertently causing the death of a pregnant woman (Exod. 21:22-25); and failure to restrain an ox previously known to gore that then kills someone (Exod. 21:28-32).[154] From Proverbs 19:26, it appears that a son who struck (or "did violence") to his father in later times, though causing "shame and reproach," would not be put to death. Possibly these laws, unique to the CC, fell into abeyance or were otherwise mitigated in practice.

The Deuteronomic Code mandates the death penalty for two categories of offenders not mentioned in any other code: the ungovernable son (Deut. 21:18-21); and the new bride whose husband accuses her of lacking "tokens of virginity" when such "tokens" are not subsequently produced (Deut. 22:13-21).[155] Proverbs 19:26 suggests that ungovernable sons may not have been executed in later times. The laws and underlying presumptions of guilt concerning tokens of virginity (Deut. 22:13-21) and adultery with betrothed virgins in cities (Deut. 22:23-24) readily could have proven impractical as well as morally objectionable. From the facts that no biblical narratives report instances when these laws were enforced, and the absence of such laws in the later codes, it might be concluded that these laws had been abandoned or tacitly repealed.

Five new and unique types of capital offenses appear only in H. One concerns the practice of giving (or sacrificing) children to Molech

---

[153] See Section B.1.c.ii.(b) of this chapter, describing different presumptions depending on whether the encounter occurs in urban or rural areas. The Gospel of Matthew's account of Joseph's reaction upon discovering that Mary, his betrothed, was pregnant, could suggest that by late biblical times, this kind of offense was no longer considered capital: "... Joseph, being a just man and unwilling to *put her to shame*, resolved to divorce her quietly" (Mt. 1:18-19 (RSV), emphasis supplied).

[154] See Sections B.1.b.ii, and B.1.b.iv of this chapter.

[155] See Sections B.1.c.ii.(a) and (b) of this chapter, and Chapter Six, Section B.2.

(Lev. 20:1-5). Several types of incestuous relationships are condemned (Lev. 20:11-12, 14). Males who engage in homosexual intercourse are to be put to death (Lev. 20:13). A priest's daughter who practices harlotry is to be executed (Lev. 21:9).[156] Finally, blaspheming "the Name" is made punishable by death (Lev. 24:10-23). Again, there are no subsequent biblical cases of execution for these offenses. The fact such laws are not found in the RDC or the PC may or may not mean that they were abandoned in later times.

The Revised Deuteronomic Code promulgates six unique capital laws. Three of these laws concern enticing Israelites to worship other gods (Deut. 13:1-5, 6-11, and 12-18). Another concerns false prophets and prophets who prophesy in the name of other gods (Deut. 18:20-22). The fifth makes "presumptuous" refusal to obey a court order a capital offense (Deut. 17:12). And the sixth prescribes the death penalty for any malicious witness who offers false testimony in a capital case (Deut. 19:16-21).

Enticing others to commit apostasy and allotheism can be seen as extensions of the capital offense of sacrificing to other gods (Exod. 22:20; Deut. 17:2-7). Concern about false prophets also was expressed by Jeremiah and Ezekiel[157] whose early careers may have been contemporary with the Deuteronomic Reform. Earlier biblical tradition also reported favorably the execution of prophets (and priests) who served and advocated worship of other gods.[158] On the other hand, there was no biblical precedent for killing YHWH prophets who prophesied falsely. Their fate was to be left to YHWH's judgment.[159] The provision governing prophets prophesying on behalf of other gods may have put prior common law into statutory form. The law regarding failure to obey court orders also may have derived from earlier practice or case law. If the late biblical story of Susanna is taken as evidence, the provision as to malicious, false witnesses remained in effect throughout the remainder

---

[156] It is not certain whether this provision was meant to apply only if the woman became a professional prostitute; or whether it might also apply if, while unmarried, she had sexual intercourse with a male. Compare Genesis 38:24 where, in an early tradition, a widow who became pregnant after her husband's death was accused of harlotry, here assumed to have been a capital offense. But see Westbrook, "Adultery" (cited above in note 73), p. 572, suggesting that the widow's father-in-law, Judah, representing his minor son to whom she was tacitly betrothed under the law or practice of levirate marriage, accused her of *adultery*. As to levirate marriage, see Chapter Eight, Section B.2.c.

[157] See, e.g., Jer. 23:9-40; Ezek. 13:1-16.

[158] 1 Kgs 18:40. See also the fate of the priests of the bogus god, Bel, in the late biblical story of Bel and the Dragon. Here, however, the Persian monarch executes the priests in accordance with his own authority (vv. 8, 21-22), not under Israelite law.

[159] See, e.g., Mic. 3:5-8; Jer. 28:12-17.

of the biblical period.[160] None of these six new RDC laws is repeated in the PC.

As noted, homicide is the only earlier capital offense included in the PC.[161] The new capital laws found in the PC concerned working on the sabbath (Exod. 35:2-3; Num. 15:32-36); Levites encroaching on the prerogatives of priests (Num. 3:38; 16:1-49); and all other persons except priests coming too close to the tabernacle's (or Jerusalem Temple's) sacred precincts (Num. 18:7, 22).

So it remains unclear whether earlier capital laws omitted from later codes were thought no longer in effect, or whether, from the standpoint of later biblical jurisprudence, all capital laws were thought to remain operative. In several instances, the later laws seem to have been meant to modify or qualify earlier ones. But in other instances, the later laws seem to presuppose that earlier ones remained in effect. If at any particular time only the capital offenses contained in the latest code were applicable, less than a dozen such offenses then would have been "on the books." But if the capital offenses contained in the codes were cumulative, that is, retained and added to by the promulgation of each new code, the total such offenses would have come to nearly 50 as of the final compilation of the laws found in Exodus through Deuteronomy.

## 2. Rationales: Why Capital Punishment?

Most of the texts that offer a rationale or justification for capital punishment are to be found in D and the RDC. The CC provides no rationale or explanation whatsoever. The Holiness Code does so only once; and the PC likewise presents such justification in only one instance. Taken together, the laws embodied in these codes articulate three distinct rationales or purposes: (1) vindicating the image of God inherent in human life; (2) purifying the community or the land by disabling or removing offenders; and (3) deterring others from committing like offenses.

### a. *Vindicating the image of God*

The epilogue to the flood narrative suggests a distinctive rationale for the death penalty in homicide cases. After the flood was over, God tells Noah:

---
[160] See Susanna vv. 61-62.
[161] See Section B.1.f.ii. of this chapter.

For your lifeblood I will surely require a reckoning; of every beast I will require it and of man; of every man's brother I will require the life of man. Whoever sheds the blood of man, by man shall his blood be shed; for God made man in his own image. (Gen. 9:5-6 RSV)

Here the rationale is, in effect, that because a human being is in some sense in God's image, as well as made by God, to kill a human is an act of sacrilege, an act so heinous that any one (even a beast) who fails to respect that image deserves to die.[162] Implicitly, also, this rationale suggests that every man is a "brother" of every other man and should therefore respect the other's life.[163] Genesis 9:5-6 does not specifically distinguish between manslaughter and murder.[164] It would be tempting to read "intentionally" before "sheds" or "innocent" before "blood of man," so as to reconcile this text with the distinction elaborated in Numbers 35:9-34. Such distinction *may* have been intended in Genesis 9, which quite possibly, like Numbers 35, represents P narrative. On the other hand, if Genesis 9 represents more ancient tradition,[165] it could be that the distinction between manslaughter and murder made in Deuteronomy 19:4-13 and Numbers 35:9-34 was meant to delimit the broad scope of Genesis 9:5-6 (and also, perhaps that of Lev. 24:17, 21b) in the same way that a similar distinction set out in Exodus 21:13-14 qualifies Exodus 21:12 which reads "Whoever strikes a man so that he dies shall be put to death."

### b. *Purging the land and Israel of guilt and evil*

The Priestly Code provides a somewhat different justification for the death penalty. Numbers 35:31-32 declares that neither a murderer nor a

---

[162] Thus Igor Primovatz, *Justifying Legal Punishment* (Atlantic Highlands, NJ: Humanities Press Int'l, 1989), p. 158. See Norman P. Dake, "Who Deserves to Live? Who Deserves to Die? Reflections on Capital Punishment," in Stassen, ed., *Capital Punishment* (cited above in note 3), p. 162. See also above, note 129.

[163] Compare the Cain/Abel story in Genesis 4:1-16. And see generally, Megivern, *The Death Penalty* (cited above in note 1), pp. 14–16. Conversely, both the "image of God" and "every man a brother" rationales could equally justify refusal to execute persons who have committed homicide. See Aaron M. Schreiber, *Jewish Law and Decision-Making: A Study Through Time* (Temple Univ. Press, 1979), p. 42: "Does this supply the reason for the extremely severe punishment provided for murder? Could it, on the other hand, be utilized to protect the accused, who was also created in God's image?" See also Blidstein, "Capital Punishment" (cited above in note 6), p. 113.

[164] So also Lev. 24:17, 21b.

[165] Thus Joseph Blenkinsopp, *Wisdom and Law in the Old Testament: The Ordering of Life in Israel and Early Judaism*, rev. edn. (Oxford Univ. Press, 1995), pp. 92–93.

manslayer sheltered in a city of refuge may be ransomed. Prior to this law, perhaps, ransom was allowed: by paying ransom, murderers might spare their lives, and manslayers (those who have fled to a city of refuge) might "return to dwell in the land before the death of the high priest."[166] Such ransom no longer would be allowed:

> You shall not thus pollute the land in which you live; for blood pollutes the land, and no expiation can be made for the land, for the blood that is shed in it, except by the blood of him who shed it. You shall not defile the land in which you live, in the midst of which I dwell; for I YHWH dwell in the midst of the people of Israel. (Num. 35:33-34 RSV)

Here the ultimate rationale for executing (or allowing the avenger of blood to execute) a murderer is to prevent pollution of the land, which in turn would be an affront to YHWH.[167] Since the only expiation for shedding (innocent) blood is the blood of the murderer, the murderer's blood must be shed. It is unclear how this rationale relates to the requirement that the manslayer remain confined within his city of refuge until the death of the high priest.[168]

A somewhat similar theory for applying the death penalty in a murder case is indicated in Deuteronomy 19:13 (RSV): "You shall purge the guilt of innocent blood[169] from Israel so that it may be well with you." Again we see here, implicitly, the idea that shedding innocent blood pollutes the land, which can then be purified only by shedding the blood of the murderer. The one, so to speak, counter-acts the other. Deuteronomy 21:1-9 casts some additional light on this matter. This text sets out what is to be done if a person has been murdered in open country, but the murderer cannot be identified.[170] The elders of the nearest city are to

---

[166] Num. 35:31-32.
[167] Compare Deut. 23:12-14, discussed in Section B.1.f.ii of this chapter.
[168] See Num. 35:31-32. Possibly this requirement reflects an underlying belief that manslayers must make expiation for the blood they have shed, even though they did not intend to kill their victims. In such cases, somehow, keeping manslayers in custody would be enough to prevent pollution of the land. We see here a mitigation of the unqualified requirement of Gen. 9:6, "Whoever sheds the blood of man, by man shall his blood be shed; for God made man in his own image." There, no distinction is made between manslayer and murderer; both were to be put to death. As to Gen. 9:5-6, see Megivern's comment, quoted above in note 129.
[169] Alternate translation: "the blood of the innocent." See generally, Barmash, *Homicide*, above Chapter Four, n.6, pp. 84–115, examining biblical and ancient Near Eastern traditions indicating that blood, particularly when shed in a homicide, polluted the land.
[170] Strangely, there is no corresponding provision in case the murder took place within a city. Perhaps it was assumed that in cities, murderers always would be found out.

perform a ceremony involving breaking the neck of a young heifer in a particular kind of setting, and then reciting a statement asking YHWH to forgive "the guilt of innocent blood" that otherwise would be imputed to the people of Israel (Deut. 21:7-8). This ceremony would thereby "purge the guilt of innocent blood" from Israel's midst (Deut. 21:9). One way or the other, Israel would be absolved from "the guilt of innocent blood," and thereby, it was to be hoped, spared any future tangible expression of YHWH's disfavor.

A similar rationale for the death penalty is repeated in both D and RDC laws with respect to a number of capital offenses: "So shall you purge the evil from your midst" or "from Israel."[171] This rationale appears in explanation for the death penalty in the following instances: prophets or "dreamers" who urge Israelites to go and serve other gods (Deut. 13:5 RSV); urban persons who have gone, served, and worshiped other gods (Deut. 17:7); persons who fail to obey judicial verdicts (Deut. 17:12); malicious witnesses who falsely charge others with capital offenses (Deut. 19:19); ungovernable sons (Deut. 21:21); adulterers (Deut. 22:22); betrothed virgins found lying with another man inside city limits (Deut. 22:24); and certain kinds of kidnapers (Deut. 24:7). Here the evident intent is to remove persons who have committed serious offenses from the community. In effect, capital punishment would permanently *disable* the offenders, who would thus never recommit these offenses. It also seems to have been understood that doing so would somehow remove or cancel out the evil deeds they had done as well.[172] Implicitly, of course, executing such offenders could have a deterrent effect on others contemplating similar illicit activities.

### c. Deterrence

Several laws in D and the RDC explicitly include a statement of intent to *deter* others from committing similar offenses in future. Thus with respect to executing (by stoning) close family members or friends who promote allotheism it is said: "And all Israel shall hear, and fear, and never again do any such wickedness as this among you" (Deut. 13:11 RSV). So also in

---

[171] Compare Lev. 20:14, which justifies application of the death penalty in the case of a man who "takes a wife and her mother also" as a way of purifying the community: "That there may be no wickedness among you" (RSV).

[172] On "purging evil" as a biblical rationale for capital punishment, see also Bailey, *Capital Punishment* (cited above in note 6), pp. 32–35.

the case of persons executed for acting "presumptuously" by disobeying court orders: "And all the people shall hear, and fear, and not act presumptuously again" (Deut. 17:13 RSV). And again in the case of those punished under the *lex talionis* for maliciously offering false, incriminating testimony: "And the rest shall hear, and fear, and shall never again commit any such evil among you" (Deut. 19:20 RSV). Finally, as to the execution of an ungovernable son: "And all Israel shall hear, and fear" (Deut. 21:21 RSV).[173] Deuteronomy 21:22-23 refers to the practice of hanging on a tree a person who has been put to death for committing a capital crime. Given its context, following immediately after a statement regarding deterrence in Deuteronomy 21:21, it may be inferred that executed criminals were sometimes hung on trees in order to deter others from committing capital offenses.[174]

Clearly, biblical laws provided for the execution of persons who had committed a number of what were deemed serious offenses against other persons or against YHWH. What is striking is the extent to which persons accused of capital crimes were accorded what, in modern jurisprudential terms, could be characterized as due process protections.

Such protections are described in the following chapter.

---

[173] On deterrence as a biblical rationale, see also Bailey, *Capital Punishment* (cited above in note 6), pp. 31–32.

[174] Thus Spitz, "Jewish Tradition" (cited above in note 29), p. 345.

## Chapter 6

# Due Process Protections

*Then Moses and the elders of Israel charged all the people as follows: Keep the entire commandment that I am commanding you today. On the day that you cross over the Jordan into the land that YHWH your God is giving you, you shall set up large stones and cover them with plaster. You shall write on them all the words of this law when you have crossed over, to enter the land that YHWH your God is giving you, a land flowing with milk and honey . . . You shall write on the stones all the words of this law very clearly.*

*Deuteronomy 27:1-3, 8*

*Keep far from a false charge, and do not kill the innocent and those in the right, for I will not acquit the guilty.*

*Exodus 23:7*

Biblical law contains no due process clause as such. And, of course, the precise meaning of due process is ever subject to interpretation. Nevertheless, the relatively modern concept "due process" serves as an apt characterization of a number of biblical laws that served to protect the innocent accused, and thus also the larger society from miscarriage of justice. These laws are considered here.

One basic aspect of modern due process is the requirement that in order for a person to be convicted of a crime, that person should have been "on notice" that the conduct in question was a punishable offense prior to engaging in such conduct. To satisfy this requirement, the person charged should either have known, because "the law" had already announced or "published," or because he or she had been personally warned that such conduct was unlawful and subject to penalty. To the extent that biblical law was periodically read or recited in public, written down, or otherwise made known to those subject to its terms,[1] the

---

[1] Several other biblical texts describe periodic occasions when arrangements were made to read or otherwise bring the substance of the law formally to the attention of all Israelites

*notice* element of due process would have been satisfied.² For example, Deuteronomy 31:9-13:

> Then Moses wrote down this law, and gave it to the priests, the sons of Levi, who carried the ark of the covenant of YHWH, and to all the elders of Israel. Moses commanded them: "Every seventh year, in the scheduled year of remission, during the festival of booths, when all Israel comes to appear before YHWH your God at the place that he will choose, you shall read this law before all Israel in their hearing. Assemble the people—men, women, and children, as well as the aliens residing in your towns—so that they may hear and learn to fear YHWH your God and to observe diligently all the words of this law, and so that their children, who have not known it, may hear and learn to fear YHWH your God, as long as you live in the land that your are crossing over the Jordan to possess."

Thus there should have been little room for doubt as to the kinds of unlawful conduct that would be subject to the death penalty or other forms of punishment. Biblical laws also provide several other features of due process protection.

Many biblical "due process" provisions give implicit expression to the fundamental concerns that only those who actually committed capital offenses with the requisite elements of malicious intent or willful and harmful conduct should be executed, and that those who were innocent should be spared.

A number of laws provide, in effect, for equal protection, or perhaps more aptly, the equal standing of certain classes of persons before the law. In effect, these laws call for impartiality in judgment, a basic due process concern, lest the accused be convicted or punished because of who they are, rather than what they had done.³

Several other laws provide that persons who had committed homicide might seek protection from self-help justice by finding refuge in certain

---

or Jews. See, e.g., Exod. 24:3-4; 34:27-32; Deut. 4:1-40; 6:1-25; 27:1-3; Josh. 8:30-35; 24:1-28; Neh. 8:1-8. See Cohn, *Human Rights* (cited in Chapter Five, note 29), p. 225. See generally, Martin Noth, *The History of Israel* (New York: Harper & Bros., 1958), pp. 100–101. Exodus 21:29 presents another instance of notice: the goring ex's owner must have been warned. See Chapter Five, Section B.1.b.ii.(b).

² In some instances, however, the terms of certain biblical laws appear overbroad. Those prosecuted under such laws might well have complained that they did not receive adequate notice, or were being prosecuted under laws promulgated *ex post facto*. See most notably the case of the man charged with picking up sticks on the sabbath. See Chapter Five, Section B.1.f.i.(b). See also the case of the blasphemer, Chapter Five, Section B.1.d.i.(c).

³ See Chapter Four.

sanctuaries or "cities of refuge," pending further inquiry or trial. Here, concern was to protect the innocent from the fate deserved only by the guilty. Biblical tradition records a few trial scenes that illustrate various features of criminal procedure, including some that might aptly be described as due process protections.[4]

Many biblical laws could be read as expressing what has come to be known in modern law as concern for "fundamental fairness." In this connection, it is noteworthy that many laws (and some reported cases) emphasize the importance of investigating the facts or examining evidence. Some provisions evidently were intended to assure truthful testimony by witnesses in order to protect the rights or interests of the innocent accused. It is uncertain whether unanimous verdicts were required in order to convict the accused of capital or other criminal charges. In the sentencing phase, several laws mandate that punishments, including the death penalty, be narrowly tailored, applied impartially, and only to those persons found guilty of the offense charged. Moreover, punishments or penalties must not exceed what was deemed proportionate to the offense.

## A. Places or Cities of Refuge: Interim Protection for Offenders Awaiting Trial

Laws distinguishing between manslaughter and murder already have been considered.[5] These laws regularly provided protection against "avengers of blood" or others seeking self-help justice, by calling for the establishment of sanctuaries where persons who had committed homicide might seek refuge pending some sort of judicial proceedings. Though the nature of such proceedings is not spelled out, some of the laws provide clues.

### 1. Exodus 21:12-14: A "Place" of Asylum

The earliest such law is found in the CC, Exodus 21:12-14. Both the willful murderer and the man who fatally injures another but without "lying in wait" (RSV) in order to do so may escape to "a place" which YHWH would "appoint" (Exod. 21:13-14). The willful murderer must

---

[4] See Chapter Three.
[5] See Chapter Five, Sections B.1.e.i. and B.1.f.ii.

be taken from YHWH's altar and put to death. No fact-finding procedures are indicated, but some kind of evidentiary hearing may be implicit.[6] Or it may have been presumed that everyone involved would know whether or not the attack had been premeditated.

This law refers to "a place" to which homicide perpetrators might flee, but does not specifically mention Jerusalem, Shechem, or any other particular location. Reference to God's "altar" (Exod. 21:14) suggests that the place of refuge was a religious sanctuary or cult shrine. Prior to the Deuteronomic Reform, there probably had been many such sanctuaries throughout the land of Judah.[7] Perhaps all such sanctuaries could have served as places of refuge.[8]

### 2. 1 Kings 1:49-53; 2:28-29: "The Horns of the Altar"

Two instances when a religious altar functioned or was sought as a place of refuge are found early in 1 Kings. Both may be part of the "J" or Yahwist "court history" dating back to the 10th century BCE.[9] The first, 1 Kings 1:49-53, describes how Adonijah, David's oldest surviving son, whose expectation to succeed him as king was thwarted by his much younger brother, Solomon's sudden enthronement, "went and caught hold of the horns of the altar" (RSV) presumably a sanctuary in Jerusalem.[10] By doing so, Adonijah hoped to be spared Solomon's purge of possible rivals to the throne.[11] Soon afterwards, Joab, David's faithful head officer and friend, also fled to "the tent of YHWH and caught hold of the horns of the altar" (1 Kings 2:28-29 RSV), hoping to escape Solomon's purge of Adonijah's erstwhile supporters.[12] Nevertheless, Solomon ordered Joab's

---

[6] See Phillips, *Criminal Law* (cited in Chapter Five, note 36), p. 100: "[I]f the elders judged that the killing was premeditated, they were to take the murderer from the altar and execute him" (Exod. 21:14). See also *id.*, pp. 100–101 (reconstructing "the procedures which would have been adopted following an alleged accidental killing").

[7] See Chapter Five, Section B.1.e.

[8] See de Vaux (cited in Chapter Five, note 30), p. 160: "The 'place' thus denoted . . . a sanctuary, where there is an altar, apparently any lawful sanctuary of Yahweh . . ." But see Barmash, *Homicide* (cited in Chapter Four, note 6), pp. 71–93.

[9] See B. Davie Napier, *The Song of the Vineyard: A Guide Through the Old Testament*, rev. edn. (Philadelphia: Fortress Press, 1981), pp. 128–37.

[10] Solomon had not yet had the Temple built in Jerusalem. Previously, David had an altar erected there. According to 2 Sam. 7:2, the ark of the covenant was placed in a tent. Earlier, the ark had been located in the Temple at Shiloh (1 Sam. 3:2-3, 21).

[11] Solomon later had Adonijah put to death on a minor pretext. See below note 13.

[12] Joab had supported Adonijah prior to the palace revolution that placed Solomon on the throne.

execution, on the ground that he (Joab) had previously shed blood "without cause" (1 Kgs 2:28-34).[13] Even though in these circumstances this rationale probably was pretextual, Solomon's order could have been permissible under Exodus 21:14, since Joab had willfully murdered others.[14]

### 3. Deuteronomy 19:1-13: Cities of Refuge—"lest innocent blood be shed in your land"

No biblical texts explicitly state that other ancient cult shrines ever served as places of refuge for persons who had committed homicide. However, certain provisions that were part of the Deuteronomic Reform program prompt the inference that prior to that Reform, such shrines had so functioned. Once all shrines other than the Jerusalem Temple were closed down pursuant to the Deuteronomic Reform, it would have been a *long* way to Jerusalem for any manslayer seeking to escape would-be avengers. Consequently, the Revised Deuteronomic Code provided for the establishment of six cities[15] to which a manslayer might "flee . . . and save his life; lest the avenger of blood in hot anger pursue . . . and overtake him, because the way is long, and wound him mortally, though the man did not deserve to die" (Deut. 19:5-6 RSV).

It may reasonably be inferred that these six cities of refuge were meant to replace some (or possibly all) of the cult shrines that, prior to the Deuteronomic Reform, had served a similar function. The RDC provided initially for three cities of refuge, one it seems, in each of three regions (Deut. 19:1-3); but then goes on to call for the establishment of three additional such cities when the territory of Israel expanded (Deut. 19: 8-10). Experience may have shown that three such cities were not enough to replace the numerous cult shrines that had so served in earlier times. The provision in Deuteronomy 19:6 calling for the establishment of three additional cities of refuge emphatically underscores the funda-

---

[13] Another text (possibly added later in order to present Solomon's actions in a more favorable light) states that on his deathbed, David had instructed Solomon to kill Joab and Shimei. 1 Kings 2:5-6. Solomon also sent an assassin to kill Adonijah, his own brother, on the pretext that Adonijah had dared to ask to have Abishag, David's former nurse (if not also concubine) as his wife. 1 Kgs 2:13:25. First Kings 1:1-31 can be read to mean that Solomon had usurped the throne which rightfully should have passed to Adonijah, as David's oldest surviving son.

[14] See 2 Sam. 3:26-30; 18:9-15; 20:8-13.

[15] Deut. 19:1-10.

mental principle implicit in many other biblical laws: Innocent persons must not be put to death. The innocent accused might seek protection in such additional sanctuaries *"lest innocent blood be shed in your land . . . , and so the guilt of bloodshed be upon you."*[16] Applying the death penalty to an innocent person not only wrongs that person, but also brings "the guilt of bloodshed" upon the entire community that allowed the execution to go forward.

The Jerusalem Temple also may have continued to function as a place of refuge.[17] If so, by the late 7th century BCE, there would have been seven such places. The Revised Deuteronomic Code does not identify the six cities. Somewhat later biblical texts provide for and name several such cities of refuge or sanctuaries.

### 4. Deuteronomy 4:41-43; Joshua 20–21—More Such Provisions

A text attributable to the Deuteronomic Historian (DH) names three such cities, all "in the east beyond the Jordan": "Bezer . . . for the Reubenites, . . . Ramoth . . . for the Gadites, and Golan . . . for the Manassites" (Deut. 4:41-43 RSV). Possibly DH thought of these as three *more* cities of refuge, bringing the total to nine, apart from Jerusalem. Or DH may have assumed that each "tribe" of Israel, like these three in the trans-Jordan, had its own city of refuge, in which case there would have been twelve or thirteen. The Deuteronomic Historian probably was writing and editing earlier traditions *c.* 550 BCE, well after the closing of the numerous local altars, sanctuaries or cult shrines mandated by the Deuteronomic Reform nearly a century earlier.

Another tradition, also, perhaps, attributable to DH, names a total of six cities of refuge: the same three in Trans-Jordan, Bezer, Ramoth, and Golan, together with "Kedesh in Galilee in the hill country of Naphtali," "Shechem in the hill country of Ephraim," and "Kiriath-arba (that is, Hebron) in the hill country of Judah" (Josh. 20:1-9 RSV). The text in Joshua includes

---

[16] Deut. 19:10 (RSV). As will be seen, numerous other biblical due process laws likewise were intended to protect innocent persons from wrongful or mistaken execution for capital offenses. See Sections B, C, and D of this chapter. See Craig A. Stern, "Torah and Murder: The Cities of Refuge and Anglo American Law," 35 *Valparaiso Univ. L. Rev.* 461 (2001), suggesting ways Anglo-American law may have been influenced by biblical laws regarding cities of refuge.

[17] Compare Jeremiah chapters 7 and 26, where the prophet warns his contemporaries that they will not be spared YHWH's judgment by seeking sanctuary or safety in the Jerusalem Temple, for it too would be destroyed. See Chapter Three, Section F.

specific procedures for hearing cases involving manslayers who killed people "without intent or by mistake."[18] Five of these cities are identified generically in Joshua 21 as "the city of refuge for the slayer": Hebron, Shechem, Golan, Kedesh, and Ramoth.[19] Here Hebron is said to have been given to the descendents of Aaron, and the other cities of refuge to various "families of the Levites," the Kohathites, Gershonites, and Merarites. These texts may contain vestiges of tradition or recollection that priests or Levites once officiated at shrines in those cities that later became secular cities of refuge following the Deuteronomic Reform.[20]

### 5. Numbers 35; 1 Chronicles 6—More Such Cities

Numbers chapter 35, which is part of the PC, provides the most extended description of provisions concerning cities of refuge. The cities are not named, but there were said to be six of them, all given to "the Levites":[21] "three . . . beyond the Jordan, and three . . . in the land of Canaan" (Num. 35:13). Here explicit mention is made of a trial or hearing "before the congregation."[22] On the other hand, 1 Chronicles reports that "the sons of Aaron" were given eleven "cities of refuge": Hebron, Libnah, Jaffir, Eshtemoa, Hilen, Debir, Ashan, Beth-shemesh, Geba, Alemeth, and Anathoth (1 Chron. 6:57-60), while the sons of Kohath (one of the Levitical families according to 1 Chron. 6:1, 16)[23] were given eight cities of refuge: Shechem, Gezer, Jokmeam, Beth-horon, Aijalon, Gath-rimmon, Aner, and Bileam (1 Chron. 6:66-70). On this count, there would have been nineteen cities of refuge, apart from Jerusalem. Possibly the Chronicler should not be considered a reliable historian,[24] but here

---

[18] See Section B.2., of this chapter.
[19] Josh. 21:13, 21, 27, 32, and 38. Bezer is mentioned, but not characterized here as a city of refuge (Josh. 21:36). Chapter 21 distinguishes between priests (descendents of Aaron) and Levites; the latter are divided into various Levitical families. These distinctions are characteristic of P tradition, and suggest that Joshua 21 may have been edited under Priestly auspices. Much of chapter 21 substantively resembles P provisions in Numbers chapter 35.
[20] On cities of refuge, see generally de Vaux (cited in Chapter Five, note 30), pp. 160–62.
[21] Num. 35:6. Compare Josh. 21:13, according to which one of the six cities, Hebron, was to be given to the sons of Aaron.
[22] Num. 35:12, 24-25. All "the people" were said to have taken part in judging Jeremiah and Susanna. See Chapter Three, Sections F and I.
[23] The Chronicler, writing possibly as late as 350 BCE, like the PC and P, distinguishes between priests ("the sons of Aaron") and Levites.
[24] See Wellhausen (cited in Chapter Five, note 32), p. 215: "One might as well try to hear the grass growing as to derive from such a source as this a historical knowledge of the conditions of ancient Israel."

again we may see hints of recollection or acknowledgment that priests or Levites had once officiated at locations that later became secular cities of refuge. We may also see that at least in theory, if not also practice, increasing numbers of such cities were required in the course of time, from the days of the Deuternomic Reform and the RDC, through those of DH, to those of the Chronicler in the early or mid-4th Century BCE.

## B. "Diligent Inquiry": Investigation, Hearings, Evidence, and Cross Examination

Some of the trial scenes reviewed earlier in Chapter Three mention certain instances of "courtroom" inquiry or fact-finding.[25] However, relatively few biblical laws, capital or otherwise, explicitly indicate what sort of investigation or fact-finding procedures are to be followed prior to or at trial. Yet some such determination is implicit in connection with many if not all of the statutory capital offenses. Implicit procedures are considered here first.

### 1. Implicit Procedures

Biblical legislation often indicates that inquiry as to relevant facts is necessary. Such inquiry varies with the nature of the offense. For instance, in the CC, the law applying the *lex talionis* when a pregnant woman suffers miscarriage and injury resulting from contact with brawling males (Exod. 21:22-25), some procedure would have been needed in order to ascertain whether all elements of the offense had been met: (a) that the woman had been injured, and in what way (b) by brawling males, and (c) which male was responsible for the injury. Or in a case where an ox gores someone to death, certain elements must be determined: (a) whether the ox had "been accustomed to gore in the past," (b) whether its owner had "been warned," and (c) whether its owner, notwithstanding such warning, had failed to keep the animal penned in; or whether, for example, someone else had let the ox out of its pen (Exod. 21:28-32). Likewise some sort of evidentiary hearing is implicit in the laws set out in Numbers 35:16-18, where the critical issue is what type of weapon was used in commission of

---

[25] See, e.g., Chapter Three, regarding the case of Tamar, her presentation of evidence identifying Judah; witness testimony in several of the other cases; and representation and cross-examination by counsel in the case of Susanna.

the homicide. In this kind of case, it is likely that physical evidence, namely, the alleged weapon itself, would have been introduced for examination. In later biblical codes, if not in earlier common law, conviction on a capital offense required testimony of at least two witnesses.[26] Thus some sort of hearing would have had to take place at which such witnesses could submit their testimony to persons having judicial authority.

A number of laws and other traditions insist that persons responsible for holding trials distinguish between the guilty and the innocent.[27] The provisions set out in Deuteronomy 25:1-2 clearly states that judges were to determine which party is "in the right" and which one "in the wrong," and whether the one found guilty "deserves to be flogged." In order to so determine, it is implicit that some kind of fact-finding procedure would have to be carried out. Exodus 23:7a (RSV) cautions against executing "the innocent and righteous . . ."[28] If in doubt, it seems that innocence was to be presumed, leaving it to YHWH to deal with any who were acquitted though guilty.[29] Determining guilt or innocence necessarily required careful fact-finding procedures. Several capital laws expressly call for some kind of fact-finding inquiry.

## 2. Explicit Requirements

Certain capital laws mandate inquiry or investigation as to relevant facts. Such inquiry is called for in two versions of the law establishing secular cities of refuge for "the manslayer." The version in Joshua chapter 20 provides that the manslayer would be given some sort of hearing where he could "explain his case" to the elders of the city of refuge "at the entrance to the gate of the city." Assuming his explanation is found adequate, the manslayer then would be granted protection from any avenging kinsman of the deceased "until he has stood before the congregation for judgment" (RSV).[30] The term *'edah*, here translated as "congregation," may also be rendered as "people" or "assembly": in effect, the jury. Presumably the manslayer would then have opportunity to repeat his explanation or defense before this assembly which would also hear any

---

[26] See Deut. 17:6; Num. 35:30. See Section C.1., of this chapter.
[27] See Chapter Four, Chapter Five, Section B.1.f.ii, and Section A.3. of this chapter.
[28] See Chapter Four, Section A. See also Jer. 22:3 and 17, where Jeremiah warns the king of Judah and his officials not to "shed innocent blood" in their judicial capacities.
[29] Exod. 23:7b: ". . . for I will not acquit the guilty."
[30] Josh. 20:6; see also Josh. 20:9.

charges brought against him. The version in Numbers 35 lists a series of fact questions that function as indicia of intent, evidently for the purpose of determining whether the accused had committed manslaughter or murder.[31] Likewise, the Numbers law, in language virtually identical to that of Joshua 20, provides that the manslayer will be protected from any avenger "until he stands before the *'edah* for judgment" (Num. 35:12). Additionally, Numbers 35:24 indicates that there would be an adversarial proceeding at which "the *'edah*" was to "judge between the manslayer and the avenger of blood." The implication is that any avenging kinsman would also have opportunity to state his case. Though the context is not entirely clear, it seems likely that the issue to be decided is whether the homicide was intentional, performed without malicious intent, or only accidental.[32] Presumably, in order to make his case for capital punishment, the avenger would also have to produce relevant evidence including adverse testimony from at least two witnesses (Num. 35:30).

Possibly the earliest law incorporating specific provisions for an evidentiary hearing is that concerning "tokens of virginity" (RSV) found only in D (Deut. 22:13-21).[33] This law details procedures to be followed when a man charges his new bride with having had previous sexual experience. Both the man and the woman's father are to offer evidence before "the elders at the gate" (Deuteronomy 22:15),[34] functioning as a trial court, and her father then speaks in her defense. The main focus of the proceeding is presentation of "the tokens of virginity" in evidence. The garment in question (presumably bed clothing) is to be "spread before the elders of the city" for their examination. Evidently the elders had discretion to decide what would constitute sufficient "tokens" or evidence. If "the tokens" were not found, the men (or people) of the city were to stone the woman to death. Although the husband was to initiate the charge by claiming not to have found his new bride's "tokens of virginity," the woman's father and mother are assigned the task of producing these "tokens" in or on "the garment" that was to be presented in

---

[31] Num. 35:16-18, 20-23: the type of weapon used, the accused's motive, whether the accused had lain in wait, whether the fatal act was done suddenly or whether the act was merely negligent.
[32] See Chapter Five, Section B.1.b.i.
[33] A few other biblical narratives also describe procedures where physical evidence was produced or introduced as evidence. See Chapter Three, Sections A and I.
[34] It is not clear whether the statements by the parties set out in Deuteronomy. 22:14 and 16-17 were to be recited as written ("boiler-plate" language) or whether they were meant to illustrate the kinds of testimony appropriate in such cases.

evidence before the elders. These procedures suggest that the newlyweds were expected to spend their first wedding night together in the bride's parents' home.[35] The bride's parents thus would have opportunity to discover or produce exculpatory evidence.[36]

The RDC provides for some sort of inquiry (if not also hearing) in connection with several other alleged capital offenses. Most of these provisions relate to themes associated with the Deuteronomic Reform, and may have been new law rather than part of the original Deuteronomic Code. Four such texts are summarized as follows.

Deuteronomy 13:12-17 calls for the destruction of any city whose inhabitants have been induced by "scoundrels" from among the Israelites to go and serve other gods. First, however, the law stipulates: "[Y]ou shall inquire and make search and ask diligently" in order to determine "if it be true and certain that such an abominable thing has been done among you" (Deut. 13:14 RSV). Exact investigative procedures are not indicated, but the importance of diligent inquiry as to the facts is certainly emphasized. Presumably—as required by Deuteronomy 17:6—the testimony of at least two witnesses would be required as part of such a proceeding.

Deuteronomy 17:2-7 makes it a capital offense for a man or woman in any Israelite town to go, serve, and worship other gods, the sun, the moon, "or any of the host of heaven." Before condemning anyone to death under this law on mere hearsay, however, diligent fact-finding inquiry must likewise be undertaken.

> If . . . it is told you and you hear of it; then you shall inquire diligently, and [ascertain] if it is true and certain that such an abominable thing has been done in Israel. (Deut. 17:4 RSV)

This law specifically requires corroborating testimony of at least two or three witnesses if the alleged offender is to be put to death (Deut. 17:6 RSV). Moreover, it requires that "the hand of [these] witnesses shall be first against [the accused] to put him to death" (Deut. 17:7). Thus the accusing

---

[35] See Tobit chapters 7–8.
[36] Absent modern methods for analyzing blood, blood-like stains could derive from many sources. The familiar story of Joseph and his brothers (Gen. 37:29-33) might have suggested to anxious parents the possibility of substituting animal blood for human. Modern gynecologists might well question the presumption that intercourse with a virgin inevitably produces such "tokens." Requiring "tokens of virginity" the morning after the wedding night also could have had a chilling effect on a woman's willingness to engage in premarital intercourse even with her affianced, in the event he might later wish to "spurn" her for other reasons.

witnesses must throw the first stone—a sobering consideration if the witnesses were persons of conscience and at all in doubt as to the facts.

Deuteronomy 17:8-9 assigns the task of deciding difficult cases to the "Levitical priests" and "the judge who is in office" in Jerusalem.

> If any case arises requiring decision between one kind of homicide and another, one kind of legal right and another, or one kind of assault and another, any case within your towns which is too difficult for you, then you shall arise and go up to the place which YHWH your God will choose, and coming to the Levitical priests, and to the judge who is in office in those days, you shall consult them, and they shall declare to you the decision. (RSV)

The text does not indicate what sort of testimony or other evidence would be considered by the panel of priests and the judge. Presumably they would attempt to determine material facts as well as apply appropriate law. Possibly these "difficult" cases could involve adversarial proceedings and/or cross examination, as intimated in Proverbs 18:17 (RSV): "He who states his case first seems right, until the other comes and examines him." Perhaps when conflicting evidence and testimony left the court in doubt, difficult cases may have been decided by "lot" or the sacred ephod.[37]

Deuteronomy 19:16-21, the law regarding malicious witnesses, provides specifically for a hearing and diligent inquiry as to the facts:

> If a malicious witness rises against any man to accuse him of wrongdoing, then both parties to the dispute shall appear before YHWH, before the priests and the judges who are in office in those days; the judges shall inquire diligently [whether] the witness is a false witness and has accused his brother falsely . . . (Deut. 19:16-18 RSV)

Nothing is said here as to testimony by witnesses for the defense, but, presumably, hearing their testimony, as well as considering any tangible evidence, would be part of the judges' diligent inquiry.[38]

---

[37] See Prov. 18:18 (RSV): "The lot puts an end to disputes and decides between powerful contenders." Here we see an early counterpart to the purported value of "finality" if not also that of "judicial economy." Presumably, it was believed that, through divine providence, casting the lot (possibly *Urim* and *Thummim*) would reveal the truth and result in a just outcome. See Prov. 16:33.

[38] See Jer. 26:12-19 where Jeremiah himself, and then others speak in his defense. See Chapter Three, Section F.

One law in H also provides for "an inquiry." This is the law concerning what is to be done if or when a man has sexual intercourse with a woman who is a slave and betrothed to another man (Lev. 19:20-22). In such circumstances, "an inquiry shall be held" (19:20), evidently in order to ascertain relevant facts, such as whether the woman actually was a slave, or whether she had been freed. In the latter event, evidently, she would be considered responsible for her role in the affair, and, therefore, possibly culpable under Deuteronomy 22:22-27, if that was still considered good law when H was codified.

The most developed depiction of fact-finding at trial, of course, is in the story of Susanna.[39] There we see witness testimony, albeit false (*Sus.* vv. 34-40), a defense attorney's demand for examination and determination of "the facts" (*Sus.* v. 48), separation and sequestration of the witnesses (*Sus.* vv. 51-52), and their subsequent cross-examination by counsel as to the alleged offenders' exact location at the time of the alleged offense (*Sus.* vv. 52-58).

## C. Witnesses

Although some capital laws as formulated suggest that circumstantial evidence might suffice for conviction,[40] most, at least by implication, require the testimony of witnesses. The critical question in such cases would be the veracity of the testimony. At least one of the "Ten Commandments" is concerned with such veracity: "You shall not bear false witness against your neighbor" (Exod. 20:16; Deut. 5:20). This "commandment" may pertain to defamation[41] as well as testimony in court. The commandment against taking the name of YHWH in vain (Exod. 20:7; Deut. 5:11) also probably referred to perjury or false testimony under oath in court.[42] Earlier, the CC had warned against testifying falsely or maliciously, whether suborned on behalf of conspiracy with another, or to please some crowd or popular majority:

> You shall not utter a false report. You shall not join hands with a wicked man, to be a malicious witness. You shall not follow a multitude to do

---

[39] See Chapter Three, Section I.
[40] See, e.g., Deut. 22:25-27.
[41] See also Lev. 19:16.
[42] See Lev. 19:12 (RSV): "And you shall not swear by my name falsely, and so profane the name of our God: I am YHWH." See also Jer. 7:9 and Zech. 5:3, condemning those who swear falsely.

evil; nor shall you bear witness in a suit, turning aside after a multitude, so as to pervert justice. (Exod. 23:1-2 RSV)[43]

## 1. Minimum of Two Adverse Witnesses

Possibly early common law, and at any rate, later statutory law required testimony of at least two witnesses in order to convict a person of a capital crime. The earliest narrative instance is the account of Jezebel's arranging to have Naboth accused of a capital offense by two perjuring witnesses.[44] The earliest statutory provision requiring two (or three) witnesses is found in the Revised Deuteronomic Code. Deuteronomy 17:6 required testimony of at least two witnesses to sustain capital punishment in cases of alleged allotheism. As broadly phrased, this requirement may have been meant to be applicable in all kinds of death penalty cases:

> On the evidence of two witnesses or of three witnesses he that is to die shall be put to death; a person shall not be put to death on the evidence of [only] one witness. (Deut. 17:6 RSV)[45]

---

[43] As to witnesses in biblical and talmudic tradition, see David Daube, *Witnesses in Bible and Talmud* (Oxford Centre for Postgraduate Hebrew Studies, 1986), pp. 2–20. Daube collected and discussed a large number of relevant texts from these and also from extra-biblical sources. This study has been republished in Calum M. Carmichael, ed., *Collected works of David Daube* (Berkeley: Univ. of Calif. Press, 1992), vol. 1, pp. 401–23. Subsequent citations in this chapter are to the earlier (1986) publication. See also Dale S. Recinella, *The Biblical Truth About America's Death Penalty* (Boston: Northeastern Univ. Press, 2004), pp. 119–59, contrasting biblical laws with instances of current practice in America.

[44] 1 Kgs 21:8-13. See Chapter Three, Section E. Schreiber, *Jewish Law* (cited in Chapter Five, note 163), points out that the U.S. Constitution, Art. III, sect. 3, provides: "No person shall be convicted of treason unless on the testimony of two witnesses to the same overt act."

[45] According to Deuteronomy 19:15, also perhaps part of the RDC, the multiple witness requirement was extended to any crime or offense, not only those punishable by death:

> A single witness shall not prevail against a man for any crime or for any wrong in connection with any offense that he has committed; only on the evidence of two witnesses, or of three witnesses, shall a charge be sustained. (RSV)

In the New Testament, Paul applied the multiple witness requirement to alleged wrongdoing by church members: "Any charge must be sustained by the evidence of two or three witnesses" (2 Cor. 13:1). Reference here, evidently, is to noncapital offenses. See also Mt. 18:16 (two or three witnesses to be present for attempted dispute resolution). In reversing a lower court's decision in a treason case, the U.S. Supreme Court quoted both Mt. 18:16 and Deut. 19:15. Cramer v. United States, 325 U.S. 24, nn. 36 & 37 (1945).

A century or two later, Numbers 35:30, part of the Priestly Code, evidently required two or more witnesses not only in trials for murder, but for conviction on any capital charge:

> If anyone kills a person, the murderer shall be put to death on the evidence of witnesses; but no person shall be put to death on the testimony of [just] one witness. (RSV)

The requirement of two adverse witnesses may have been implicit in the D law regulating ungovernable sons: there both parents were required to bring charges and testify (Deut. 21:18-20).[46] This sort of requirement was still operative as late as the story of Susanna, where two false witnesses testify against her. Here, as a further precaution in the interest of truthful fact-finding, the witnesses are sequestered and subjected to cross-examination separately (*Sus.* vv. 51-59).[47]

Requiring more than one witness no doubt was meant to assure factually accurate as well as honest testimony. Such requirement, of course, could not guarantee the truth, since witnesses might, nevertheless, testify falsely and maliciously, as in the Naboth and Susanna stories. However, testimony by two or more witnesses could reasonably be considered more reliable than that of only one witness.[48] The basic underlying concern here, obviously, is to try to prevent the execution of innocent persons.

---

[46] In this instance, clearly, a woman's testimony was to be credited. Compare Falk, *Law and Religion* 80 (quoted in Chapter Five, note 68), referring only to the father's testimony.

[47] Later rabbinic law required witnesses to recall detailed particulars in identifying offenders, and barred admission of confessions by the accused. See Spitz (cited in Chapter Five, note 29), at p. 346. See generally Daube, *Witnesses* (cited above in note 43), pp. 16–17. In particular, see Irene Merker Rosenberg and Yale L. Rosenberg, "In the Beginning: The Talmudic Rule against Self-Incrimination," 63 *New York L. Rev.* 955, 980, 1028 (1988).

[48] See West, "Scripture" (cited in Chapter Five, note 4), p. 11, suggesting that the biblical two-witness rule "required a high degree of certainty, more than, perhaps, the [beyond] reasonable doubt standard" of contemporary American criminal jurisprudence. For contemporary discussions of concerns about eyewitness testimony, see, e.g., Nicholas A. Kahn-Fogel, "Beyond *Manson* and *Lukelongo*: A critique of American and Zambian Eyewitness Law with Recommendations for Reform in the Developing World," 20 *Fla. J. of Internat'l Law* 278–327 (2008); and Monika Jain, Comment, "Mitigating the Dangers of Capital Convictions Based on Eyewitness Testimony Through Treason's Two-Witness Rule," 91 *J. Crim. L. & Criminology* 761 (2001).

## 2. Promoting True Testimony

Truthful testimony was mandated by the Ninth of the Ten Commandments: "You shall not bear false witness against your neighbor."[49] It may also be implicit in the Third Commandment: "You shall not take the name of YHWH your God in vain" (RSV).[50] Neither of these commandments, however, provided sanctions.

The Revised Deuteronomic Code adds a potent legal provision aimed at deterring *malicious* false testimony. If a person is found to have so testified:

> [T]hen you shall do to him as he had meant to do to his brother; so shall you purge the evil from the midst of you. And the rest shall hear, and fear, and shall never again commit any such evil among you. Your eye shall not pity; it shall be life for life, eye for eye, tooth for tooth, hand for hand, foot for foot. (Deut. 19:19-21 RSV)

The denouement of the story of Susanna instances an application of this law: "And they did to [the two elders] as they had wickedly planned to do to their neighbor; acting in accordance with the law of Moses, they put them to death" (RSV).[51] The Book of Proverbs offers a series of sayings commending true, and condemning false witnesses, appealing, in effect to the conscience or moral judgment of readers. For example:

> He who speaks the truth gives honest evidence,
>   but a false witness utters deceit. (Prov. 12:17 RSV)
>
> A truthful witness saves lives,
>   but one who utters lies is a betrayer. (Prov. 14:25 RSV)[52]

Moreover, Proverbs also invokes the further sanction of self-interest against those who would offer false testimony:

---

[49] Exod. 20:16; Deut. 5:20. This commandment may also have applied more broadly to slander or defamation.

[50] Exod. 20:7; Deut. 5:11, which may have referred to testimony given under oath. See also Exod. 23:7 (RSV): "Keep away from a false charge, and do not slay the innocent and righteous . . ."

[51] Susanna v. 62. Here Deuteronomy 19:19-21 is construed to apply gender-inclusively against men who maliciously accuse a *woman* of wrong-doing.

[52] See also Prov. 14:5; 19:28; 25:18. On false witnessing or testimony in biblical tradition, see generally, Phillips, *Criminal Law* (cited in Chapter Five, note 36), pp. 142–48.

> A false witness will not go unpunished,
> and he who utters lies will not escape. (Prov. 19:5 RSV)

Indeed, testifying falsely could prove fatal: "A false witness will perish" (Prov. 21:28 RSV).[53] These sayings clearly imply that even if false witnesses might get away with perjury in the courtroom, they would nonetheless come to grief at the hand of divine providence or justice.[54]

Another new law found in the RDC requires witnesses to throw the first stones when the persons against whom they testified are condemned to die: "The hand of the witness shall be first against him to put him to death, and afterward the hand of all the people" (Deut. 17:7 RSV). This provision may have been intended to apply only in connection with the law condemning Israelites who practiced allotheism for which the penalty was death by stoning.[55] Or it may have been intended to apply in all cases where the penalty was capital punishment.[56] This law, too, seems to have been intended to encourage true testimony. If one was going to testify that a person had committed a capital offense, one would, presumably, wish to be certain that what one said was true since one might later have to play a leading role in the actual execution.[57]

### 3. The Duty to Testify

Another type of law has to do with encouraging reluctant witnesses to come forward:

> If any one sins in that he hears a public adjuration to testify and though he is a witness, whether he has seen or come to know the matter, yet does not speak, he shall bear his iniquity. (Lev. 5:1 RSV)

---

[53] See also Prov. 19:9 (RSV): "A false witness will not go unpunished, and he who utters lies will perish."

[54] This meaning probably is expressed also in the Third Commandment: "... for YHWH will not hold him guiltless who takes his name in vain" (RSV) (Exod. 20:7 and Deut. 5:11, referring to the consequences of swearing falsely under oath). Possibly that prospect remains implicit in the continuing Western court room practice of "swearing in" witnesses. Modern witnesses who testify falsely, whether in criminal or civil trials, may be subject to heavy sanctions. See Donald A. Blackwell, "The Big Lie—Contrary to What You May Have Heard on the Evening News, False and Misleading Testimony by a Civil Litigant Can and Does Have Serious Consequences," 73 *Florida Bar Journal*, no. 7 (July/August 1999), pp. 20–26.

[55] See also Deut. 13:6-11, which requires witnesses to throw the first stones when their dearest family members or friends have committed allotheism.

[56] The preceding verse, Deut. 17:6, appears to apply in this broader sense.

[57] Cohn, *Human Rights* (cited in Chapter Five, note 29), p. 39: "[T]his provision [was] probably intended to impress potential witnesses with the gravity of the responsibility they are taking upon themselves."

This provision, like Numbers 35:30, probably was part of the Priestly Code. No explicit penalty is attached to this law; however, the idea seems to be that those who failed to testify when they should have done so would know who they were. To clear their iniquity—which otherwise could result in indeterminate deleterious consequences—such persons were to confess their sins—probably to a priest—and bring their guilt or sin offerings to YHWH.[58]

## D. The Punishment Phase: Sentencing Guidelines

Punishments, particularly in earlier portions of biblical tradition, were not always narrowly tailored. Not only the offender, but also others, including the offender's whole family, might be put to death. And punishments may have been excessive or inordinate compared to the offense. One type of biblical law evidently was intended to limit punishments to guilty parties. Another was meant to limit punishments according to the nature of the offense, that is, to let the punishment more nearly fit the crime.

### 1. Fathers, Sons, and Families; or Only the Offender?

In early biblical times, it was not uncommon for both the perpetrator of an offense and some or all of his family to be punished, whether officially or by avenging kinsmen. In some traditions, God or YHWH himself was expected to wreak such vengeance. Both later biblical law and prophetic pronouncements on behalf of YHWH limited punishment to the offender alone.

The principle or practice of extended (if not completely unlimited) vengeance is indicated in Lamech's boast to his wives (Gen. 4:23-24). YHWH had "marked" Cain "lest any who came upon him should kill him" (RSV). The mark was to signify that if any one killed Cain, "vengeance" would "be taken upon him sevenfold" (Gen. 4:15). If Lamech, a descendent of Cain, can be believed, someone nevertheless had killed Cain, and "sevenfold" vengeance had been inflicted on his killer—meaning, probably, that seven, or at least several, members of the killer's family had been killed in retaliation (Gen. 4:24). Later, when a male Israelite

---

[58] Lev. 5:5-6, 7-13.

stole property that had been "devoted" to YHWH,[59] not only he, but also his sons, daughters, and cattle were put to death (Josh. 7:1-25).[60]

Early tradition in the Ritual Decalogue endorsed the idea that YHWH, himself, would punish both the wicked and their descendants. YHWH was "merciful and gracious, slow to anger, and abounding in steadfast love and faithfulness," *but* would visit "the iniquity of the parents upon the children and the children's children, to the third and the fourth generation" (Exod. 34:6-7). This principle also appears in identical language in both versions of the Decalogue, specifically in the case of those who also worshiped other gods before or besides YHWH:

> You shall not make for yourself a graven image, or any likeness of anything that is in heaven above, or that is in the earth beneath, or that is in the water under the earth; you shall not bow down to them or serve them; for I, YHWH your God, am a jealous God, visiting the iniquity of the fathers upon the children to the third and fourth generation of those who hate me . . . (Exod. 20:4-5; Deut. 5:8-9 RSV)

The Deuteronomic Code, however, established a new guideline for punishment of capital offenders:

> The fathers shall not be put to death for the children, nor shall the children be put to death for the fathers; every man shall be put to death for his own sin. (Deut. 24:16 RSV)

So far as official proceedings were concerned, subsequent to promulgation of the Deuteronomic Code, only the offender might be executed. An instance of this law's application is reported in an account of events in the tumultuous days of the divided kingdoms:

> And as soon as the royal power was firmly in his hand, [Amaziah] killed his servants who had slain the king his father. But he did not put to death the children of the murderers; according to what is written in the book of the law of Moses, where YHWH commanded, "The fathers shall not be put to death for the children, or the children be put to

---

[59] The property evidently consisted of items plundered from Jericho that had been set apart for use in the future as religious implements or fixtures.

[60] See also 2 Sam. 12:13-14, where the prophet, Nathan, declared that David's son would die in punishment for David's having murdered Uriah and marrying Uriah's widow.

death for the fathers; but every man shall die for his own sin." (2 Kgs 14:5-6 RSV)

This text is repeated, nearly verbatim, in 2 Chronicles 25:3-4.

Moreover, according to the prophets Jeremiah and Ezekiel, YHWH changed his own way of dealing with offenders. Now, or at any rate, once YHWH restored the fortunes of his people after the exile, "every one shall die for his own sin" (RSV).[61] This new theology (or theodicy) correlated with and undergirded the sentencing guideline set out in Deuteronomy 24:16 and the practice remembered in 2 Kings 14:5-6.

## 2. The *lex talionis*

A number of biblical laws, particularly in the CC, required that a wrongdoer provide restitution, compensation or damages when his actions (whether intentional or negligent) caused another person's property loss.[62] But what if one person permanently injures or kills another? Biblical law generally does not require (or allow) monetary compensation for such injuries or death. Instead, under certain circumstances, pursuant to the so-called *lex talionis*, if a permanent injury resulted, the same injury was to be inflicted on the person responsible for it.[63] Similar provisions are found elsewhere in ANE law.[64] Biblical law codes include three distinct versions of the *lex talionis*: Exodus 21:23-25; Leviticus 24:19-20; and Deuteronomy 19:16-21. One modern scholar proposes that all three biblical versions of the *lex* were inserted by a late "Pentateuchal editor," and urges that this editor intended to "stress the principle of compensation"

---

[61] Jer. 31:29-30. See also Ezek. 18:1-20, 30. An early narrative tradition also implicitly repudiated the principle of collective guilt or guilt by association: the story of Abraham's reminding YHWH that it was not right to punish the guilty with the innocent. See Chapter Four, note 5.

[62] See Exod. 21:33-36; 22:1, 4, 5-15. See also Num. 5:5-10, and Lev. 6:1-5; 24:18, 21a. See Chapter One, Section B.

[63] The Latin noun, *talio*, means "retaliation." The genitive singular form is *talionis*. Thus *lex talionis* means, literally "law of retaliation" or "law of retribution in kind." The expression is a term of art used by interpreters of biblical and other laws. The term is not found in the biblical text. As to the biblical *lex talionis*, see generally, Daube, *Studies* (cited in Chapter Five, note 32), pp. 102–53; Westbrook, *Studies* (cited in Chapter Five, note 31), pp. 39–88; Rosenberg & Rosenberg, "Lone Star Musings" (cited in Chapter Five, note 28), pp. 505–41; and Barmash, *Homicide* (cited in Chapter Four, note 6), pp. 154–77 (examining biblical and ancient Near Eastern law, and arguing that in biblical law, the *lex talionis* is understood as a principle expressing "equivalence" (id., p. 175).

[64] See, e.g. the Code of Hammurabi, CH 196, 197 and 200. See generally Westbrook, *Studies* (cited in Chapter Five, note 31), pp. 47–49.

rather than "a retaliatory theory of punishment."[65] Modern jurisprudential sensibilities might prefer that such was the intent, but indications to that effect are largely absent from the biblical texts in question.[66]

The earliest version of the *lex talionis* is found in the CC and there, in its terms, refers only to the narrowly defined circumstance where a married, pregnant woman is injured by brawling males, has a miscarriage, and sustains some permanent, disfiguring or debilitating injury, or dies as a result:

> If any harm follows, then you shall give life for life, eye for eye, tooth for tooth, hand for hand, foot for foot, burn for burn, wound for wound, stripe for stripe. (Exod. 21:23-25)[67]

Conceivably a pregnant woman could suffer a burn injury, for instance, if pushed against an oven or into a fire, or even "stripes," if one of the

---

[65] Phillips, *Criminal Law* (cited in Chapter Five, note 36), pp. 96–99. So also Edward McG. Gaffney, Jr., "Biblical Law and the First Year Curriculum of American Legal Education," 4 *J. of L. & Religion* 63, 85–86 (1986); Bernard S. Jackson, "Models in Legal History: The Case of Biblical Law," 18 *J. of L. & Religion* 1, 6–55 (2002–03); and Rosenberg & Rosenberg, "Lone Star Musings" (cited in Chapter Five, note 28), pp. 525–28. Later rabbinic law did construe the *lex talionis* to provide for compensatory damages rather than retaliation in kind, though retaining the death penalty for certain types of cases, at least in theory. See Spitz (cited in Chapter Five, note 29), p. 345. See also Louis E. Newman, "Covenant and Contract: A Framework for the Analysis of Jewish Ethics," 9 *J. of L. & Religion* 89, 106 (1991): "The rabbis effectively eliminated capital punishment (though, of course, the Bible mandates it) by introducing extraordinarily stringent conditions which had to be met before a person could be convicted of a capital offense."

[66] The only laws expressly providing for ransom or monetary compensation for homicide are found in Exodus 21:28-32 (when an ox gores a person). See Chapter Five, Section B.1.b.ii.(b). Exodus 21:22 provides for a *fine* (arguably compensation payable to the husband) when his wife has a miscarriage resulting from injury inflicted by brawling males, but there is no provision for ransom or monetary compensation in the event of her death. See Chapter Five, Section B.1.b.ii(a). Second Samuel 21:1-9 can be read to imply that ransom may have been an alternative to capital punishment when a former King had wrongfully ordered the execution or murder of persons contrary to treaty. See Westbrook, *Studies* (cited in Chapter Five, note 31), p. 51. Neither Exod. 21:28-32 nor 2 Sam. 21:1-9 refers to the *lex talionis*. Westbrook possibly overgeneralizes when, on the basis of the Samuel text, he concludes that in "the biblical system," "premeditated murder gives the right to revenge by the victim's relatives, with the choice of accepting ransom." *Id.*, p. 77. Westbrook urges that provisions for ransom in other ANE laws are implicit in various biblical texts that specifically call for the death penalty, on the theory that absent explicit statement to the contrary, it would have been assumed that ransom was available. See *id.*, pp. 78–83.

[67] See Chapter Five, Section B.1.b.ii.(a). From the context in Exod. 21:22, it appears that "harm" here refers to an injury to the woman, rather than to the fetus. Perhaps it was understood that a pregnant woman would be especially vulnerable to harm under these circumstances. Compare Dale Patrick, *Old Testament Law* (John Knox Press, 1985), p. 76: "Although this commandment, known as the *lex talionis*, is attached to this one case, it really applies to all cases of death and injury." There is no textual basis for so assuming.

brawling males was wielding a whip or stick. Alternatively, the list of possible harms and punishments may have been added to the text to reconcile it with later versions of the *lex talionis*. In any case, if the woman dies, the man who caused the fatal injury is to be put to death.

Unlike many of the other laws found in Deuteronomy 12–19, the law providing punishment for malicious, false witnesses (Deut. 19:16-21) is not directly associated with themes or institutional changes characteristic of the Deuteronomic Reform. This law may, therefore, date back to an earlier if not the original version of D. In any case, we see here another limited context in which the *lex talionis* was to apply. If it was determined (pursuant to diligent inquiry) that a person had maliciously and falsely accused someone of a crime, the accuser was to suffer the same penalty that would have been imposed on the accused had the latter been found guilty:

> [T]hen you shall do to him as he had meant to do to his brother. . . Your eye shall not pity; it shall be life for life, eye for eye, tooth for tooth, hand for hand, foot for foot. (Deut. 19:19-21 RSV)[68]

It has been said that Deuteronomy 19:21 is the "most popular" biblical text quoted by prosecutors to jurors in modern capital murder trials.[69] If so, such prosecutors (or others arguing from this text) should also point out that as read in context, it refers explicitly and solely to the punishment of malicious, false witnesses.[70]

The *lex talionis* is applied in another limited context, in Leviticus 24: 19-20, the only other biblical text where it is found. Here it relates specifically to those who commit mayhem,[71] that is, cause another person some permanent, disfiguring injury:

---

[68] Reference to eye, tooth, hand, and foot, among the provisions for punishing malicious, false witnesses, might suggest that under biblical common law, punishment for some offenses may have included dismemberment. Interpreters sometimes cite Deut. 25:11-12 as an additional instance of the *lex talionis*. That text requires cutting off a wife's hand if she assists her husband while he is fighting, by seizing his opponent's "private parts." The text, however, does not call for retaliation in kind, since the antagonists's *hand* would not have been injured. See below, note 81. There are no reported instances of this law's application, and it is not repeated in the later law codes.

[69] Mark Costanzo, Just Revenge: *Costs and Consequences of the Death Penalty* (New York: St. Martin's Press, 1997), p. 130.

[70] See Recinella, *The Biblical Truth* (cited above in note 43), pp. 185–209, contrasting the standard set out in this text with instances of prosecutorial misconduct in various U.S. jurisdictions.

[71] As to mayhem, see Chapter Five, note 89 and accompanying text.

When a man causes a disfigurement in his neighbor, as he has done it shall be done to him, fracture for fracture, eye for eye, tooth for tooth; as he has disfigured a man, he shall be disfigured. (RSV)[72]

This text adds, "fracture for fracture," but unlike Exodus 21:23-25, makes no mention of "hand for hand" or "foot for foot." Here, as in Exodus 21:22-25, it seems to make no difference whether the harm or here, disfigurement, resulted from intentional, reckless, or merely negligent conduct by the offending party. As stated, this version of the *lex talionis* does not call for capital punishment, "life for life." Homicide, of course, goes beyond mayhem or disfigurement. However, Leviticus 24:17 and 21b add, "He who kills a man shall be put to death" (RSV).[73] It is not clear whether these verses were intended to be part of the *lex talionis*, or to constitute a separate requirement.[74] As in the case of Genesis 9:5-6, Leviticus 24:17 and 21b make no special provision for negligent or accidental homicide.

How and when the provisions distinguishing murderers from manslaughterers and establishing certain due process protections for the latter would have interfaced with the life-for-life element of the *lex talionis* is unclear. Perhaps the earlier version of that *lex* at Exodus 21:22-25 would have been subsumed into or superseded by the more general mayhem law in Leviticus 24, part of the Holiness Code. The Holiness Code makes no provision for cities of refuge where a negligent manslayer might find sanctuary pending further proceedings.[75] It may be

---

[72] An implicit exception to this version of the *lex talionis* appears in Exodus 21:26-27, where it does not apply in the case of permanently disfiguring injuries to slaves. On the other hand, slaves are not here treated as mere "property." Instead, slaves who are disfigured are to be compensated by being given their freedom: "for the eye's" or "for the tooth's sake."

[73] See Michael Davis, *Justice in the Shadow of Death: Rethinking Capital and Lesser Punishments* (New York/London: Rowman & Littlefield, 1996), p. 234: "The general principle of the *lex talionis* (as traditionally understood) is *equivalence* between harm done and punishment imposed. The punishment is not for an act as such, for what was intended or risked, but for what was done ('an eye for an eye,' as the Bible says). So, for example, to kill someone, even 'by accident,' would justify the same penalty . . . as would killing deliberately." But see Chapter Five, Section B.1.b.ii and iii., discussing texts where punishment clearly does vary according to the perpetrator's intent and other factors.

[74] Both verses are separated from the language of the *lex talionis* (Lev. 24:19-20) by the quite different tort law requirement, "He who kills a beast should make it good" (Lev. 24:18, 21a). The entire block of laws found in Lev. 24:17-21 (if not also v. 22) appears to have been inserted somewhat carelessly into the story about the man of mixed ancestry who blasphemed the Name (Lev. 24:10-16, 23).

[75] See Section A.1., of this chapter. Special cities of refuge would have been unnecessary if H is correctly dated prior to the Deuteronomic Reform, since prior to that Reform, local

that the detailed procedures set out still later in Deuteronomy 19 and Numbers 35 were intended to qualify the overbroad language of Leviticus 24:17 and 21b.

As has been seen, the laws set out in Deuteronomy 19 and Numbers 35 distinguish between manslaughter and other degrees of homicide, provide cities of refuge where perpetrators may be safe while awaiting trial, require two or more witnesses, call for both parties to appear at trial, and for judges to "inquire diligently," and apply the *lex talionis* to any who offer false, malicious testimony. Read in this context, the *lex talionis* was not a general rule of life for life in any and all circumstances. Instead, in its terms, it was to apply only in cases where brawling males injured or caused the death of a married, pregnant woman; where someone gave false and malicious testimony in court; or in a case where someone had committed mayhem. Even if Leviticus 24:17 and 21b are read as extensions of, or additions to the *lex talionis* as stated in Leviticus 24:19 and 20, the requirement "He who kills a man shall be put to death," is substantially narrowed and qualified by due process provisions set out in the later codes RDC (as in Deuteronomy chapter 19) and the Priestly Code (as in Numbers chapter 35).[76]

In any event, the *lex talionis* set limits to retribution: the perpetrator's punishment was to equal but not exceed the injury inflicted on the victim.[77] It is not clear whether the victim or her representative was expected to execute such punishment himself, or whether such punishment would be carried out by a judge or other representative of the community.[78]

---

religious shrines would have been available as places of refuge.

[76] See also earlier and other due process protections for the accused described above in Sections A, B, and C of this chapter.

[77] See Mendenhall, *Law and Covenant* (cited in Chapter Five, note 39), pp. 16–17. See also Howard Zehr, "Restoring Justice," in Stassen, ed., *Capital Punishment* (cited in Chapter Five, note 3), p. 29: "'An eye for an eye' is not what it seems. In a society unused to the rule of law, it was intended as a limit on, rather than a command to do, violence. It established a rule of proportion which laid the basis for retribution." And see Hans Jochen Boecker, *Law and the Administration of Justice in the Old Testament and the Ancient East* (Minneapolis: Augsburg, 1980), pp. 174–75. Compare, e.g., the pattern of unlimited retribution illustrated in the ancient story of seven-fold revenge in the case of Cain (Gen. 4:15, 24); the legendary feud between the Hatfields and McCoys, or ongoing retaliatory killings by modern Israelis and Palestinians.

[78] None of the biblical *lex talionis* texts identifies "the government" or the Israelite or Jewish state—let alone any modern state—as the agency divinely authorized to punish malefactors. Compare Millar Burrows, "Old Testament Ethics and the Ethics of Jesus," in James L. Crenshaw and John T. Wilson, eds., *Essays in Old Testament Ethics*, J. Philip Hyatt, In Memoriam (New York: KTAV, 1974), p. 235: "Against a primitive background of blood revenge and unlimited retaliation (Gen. 4:5, 24), Hebrew law had sought to regulate the

Conceivably, as in Exodus 21:30, the victim could choose to receive compensation rather than insist on the offender's corporal or capital punishment.[79] But no biblical texts relating to the *lex* contain any indication of that alternative.

Biblical tradition reports only one case when the *lex talionis* was carried out in the form of capital punishment.[80] And there are no reported instances of mutilation as punishment for loss of or injury to a victim's bodily member.[81] It may be, of course, that there were unreported instances. In practice, the *lex talionis* provisions may have been mitigated. Two texts suggest that victims' relatives might exact ransom (damages or compensation in tort) rather than require the offender's execution: Exodus 21:30 and Numbers 35:31-32. The Exodus law applies only when the offender's ox has a known propensity for goring, and, after the owner has received due warning and failed to pen the animal in. The Numbers text, which bars ransom for the life of a murderer, could be read to imply that ransom or compensation might be acceptable for other categories of capital offenders. However, the late Ze'ev Falk probably overstated the case for such compensation in stating: "[I]n practice the principle [of the *lex talionis*] was not realized as such, but was commuted by the payment of ransom."[82]

---

age-old customs, . . . restricting the execution of the *lex talionis* to the established civil authorities (Exod. 21:23ff.; Lev. 24:19f.; Deut. 19:15-21)." It is not clear, however, that the "you" referred to in these texts stands for either local or national "established authorities."

[79] Thus Mendenhall, *Law and Covenant* (cited in Chapter Five, note 39), p. 17. See also above, note 66 and Chapter Five, Section B.1.b.ii(b).

[80] Susanna vv. 61-62, referring to Deut. 19:16-21 (malicious false witnesses). See Chapter Three, Section I. There are a few other narrative instances when murderers were executed, e.g., 2 Sam. 4:5-12; and 1 Kgs 2:31-35, but there is no reference to the *lex talionis* in those accounts.

[81] Deuteronomy 25:11-12 requires that if a woman rescues her husband from a brawl by seizing his opponent's "private parts," her hand is to be cut off. This is not, obviously, a case of a "hand for a hand," and is the only biblical law, other than what may be implicit in the *lex talionis*, calling for mutilation. Calum Carmichael, on the other hand, insists that both Exod. 21:22-25 and Deut. 19:16-21 call for capital punishment "to be followed by the systematic mutilation of the offender's corpse." Calum M. Carmichael, *The Spirit of Biblical Law* (Athens, GA: 1996), p. 107. But biblical evidence supporting this conclusion is lacking. Judges 1:6-7 refers to treatment of prisoners of war. The execution and subsequent mutilation of assassins described in 2 Sam. 4:12, while possibly illustrating Carmichael's theory, is not a case of "hand for hand."

[82] Falk, *Religious Law* (cited in Chapter Four, note 6), p. 48. Westbrook, *Studies* (cited in Chapter Five, note 31), pp. 122–23, discusses Middle Assyrian laws that allow the deceased's avenger either to kill the offender or to accept ransom—and also the offender's inheritance.

### 3. Punishment Proportional to the Offense

The *lex talionis* clearly was intended to limit the extent to which offenders might be punished—in effect, to establish the principle of equivalency. The punishment was not to be excessive; instead, it should "fit the crime." This principle is illuminated in a law that may have applied to certain types of tortuous, as well as to criminal wrong-doing:[83]

> Suppose two persons have a dispute and enter into litigation, and the judges decide between them, declaring one to be in the right and the other to be in the wrong. If the one in the wrong deserves to be flogged, the judge shall make that person lie down and be beaten in his presence with the number of lashes proportionate to the offense. (Deuteronomy 25:1-2)

This law explicitly requires that the number of lashes must be "proportionate to the offense." There is, moreover, a further limitation, this time reflecting a measure of compassionate concern for the well-being of the offender:

> Forty lashes may be given but not more; if more lashes than these are given, your neighbor will be degraded in your sight. (Deuteronomy 25:3)

More than 40 lashes were considered excessive. Implicitly, they would have caused greater pain and injury. Explicitly, any additional lashes would have been degrading. Even though subject to such punishment, when deemed appropriate to the offense, the guilty offender was nevertheless still regarded as "your neighbor."

---

[83] Compare the situation described in Exod. 21:22-25, which calls for civil damages (fine) and, in certain circumstances, criminal penalties as well. See above, note 67 and accompanying text.

## Chapter 7

# Criminal Law in the Bible and Contemporary Application

*Then Abraham came near and said, "Wilt thou indeed destroy the righteous with the wicked? Suppose there are fifty righteous within the city . . ."*
Genesis 18:23 (RSV)

*But as for me, here I am in your hands. Do with me as seems good and right to you. Only know for certain that if you put me to death, you will be bringing innocent blood upon yourselves, and upon this city and its inhabitants, for in truth YHWH sent me to you to speak all these words in your ears.*
Jeremiah 26:14-15

Although the point may be obvious, it should not be overlooked that according to biblical tradition, biblical law was given to, and intended for, the guidance or direction of Israel, Judah, and the Jewish people. It was not regarded as the law of the land for other nations, peoples, or jurisdictions. There is, therefore, no biblical warrant for supposing—or proposing—that biblical laws pertaining to the death penalty—or to any other matters of importance in biblical times—were meant to apply to criminal justice proceedings in the United States of America. Nevertheless, it is suggested here that much of biblical tradition highlights certain fundamental concerns which may be extremely important and relevant in the present era.

First, however, it should be pointed out that, when read in their contexts, several biblical laws (and other biblical texts) do not clearly stand for the propositions for which they are often cited, whether by modern proponents or by opponents of capital punishment.

## A. Modern Interpretation of Biblical Texts

For one thing, most texts purportedly opposing the death penalty do not so state clearly or categorically. For instance, the account of YHWH's marking Cain (Gen. 4:15) does not *forbid* capital punishment.[1] It is unlikely that the Sixth Commandment, "Thou shall not kill," was intended to prohibit use of the death penalty.[2] Nor is it apparent that the *lex talionis* was understood to allow capital offenders to pay damages or ransom in lieu of being put to death.[3] Nor is there any evidence that elders might undertake to reform or rehabilitate ungovernable sons before, or instead of, inflicting the death penalty.[4]

Conversely, many biblical texts commonly said to justify applying the death penalty in modern times do not say what those citing them contend. For instance, Genesis 9:5-6 (probably part of P narrative tradition) says that God told Noah, "Whoever sheds the blood of man, by man shall his blood be shed; for God made man in his own image" (RSV). Yet the broad (if not overbroad) scope of this instruction is significantly qualified by specific Mosaic laws that distinguish various types of homicide depending on circumstances and the perpetrators' intent.[5] James Megivern points out that latter-day death penalty advocates generally read Genesis 9:5-6 through the lenses of these qualifying laws, as if this Genesis text referred only to first degree murder.[6] Read literally, however, the text is not so narrowly tailored or focused. Many other texts cited by modern death penalty proponents do not, in fact, say what such proponents claim, either.[7]

The most notable example is the often-cited *lex talionis* or "law of retaliation." This law sometimes is said to authorize use of the death penalty

---

[1] See Stassen, "Biblical Teaching" (quoted in Chapter Five, note 9). The same commentator also may exaggerate when proposing that capital punishment was gradually abandoned in biblical times, quoted in Chapter Five, note 22.

[2] See Chapter Five, notes 5 and 6 and accompanying text.

[3] See Phillips, Gaffney, Westbrook, Rosenberg and Rosenberg, and Falk, cited in Chapter Six, note 65, 66, 82 and accompanying texts.

[4] See Levine, "Capital Punishment," cited in Chapter Five, note 68.

[5] See Chapter Five, Sections B.1.b.ii and iii; B.1.e.i.; and B.1.f.ii. But see Lev. 24:17, 21b, discussed in Chapter Five, Section B.1.d.ii(a) and Chapter Six, Section D.2. These Leviticus texts, like Gen. 9:5-6, do not distinguish among different categories of homicide.

[6] See Megivern, *Death Penalty*, cited in Chapter Five, note 129. The "image of God" rationale is somewhat problematic, since it could be applied to the life of the accused offender. See Schreiber, *Jewish Law*, cited in Chapter Five, note 163. To be sure, Gen. 9:5-6, as read, does not suggest such application.

[7] See, e.g., Vellenga, "Capital Punishment" (cited in Chapter Five, note 22).

in all homicide cases—at least in all cases of first degree murder.[8] As has been seen, however, the biblical *lex talionis* was not set out as a broad or general rule, but rather as providing sentencing guidelines in three quite specific circumstances: (1) when a married, pregnant woman is injured by brawling men (Exod. 21:22-25);[9] (2) in mayhem cases (Lev. 24: 19-20);[10] and (3) as punishment for malicious, false witnesses (Deut. 19:16-21).[11] It has been said that prosecutors often quote the Deuteronomic version to jurors in capital murder trials.[12] So doing would constitute prosecutorial misconduct unless such prosecutors also point out that this text refers specifically and solely to the punishment of malicious false witnesses.[13] Likewise, those who quote the Exodus version as authority for capital punishment, if truthful, should add that it applies only to fatal injuries inflicted on pregnant married women by brawling males.[14]

It appears to be the case that neither death penalty proponents nor opponents read or propose to apply all biblical death penalty texts literally. For example, death penalty opponents are not known to advocate allowing estates of negligent homicide victims to demand and receive unlimited compensatory damages when (or only when) the victim was gored by an ox.[15] Nor do such opponents propose establishing cities of refuge in Israel where persons found to have committed manslaughter may find shelter pending the death of a high priest.[16] Modern death penalty proponents do not generally call for capital punishment for such offenses as sorcery (Exod. 22:18; Lev. 20:6, 27),[17] kidnapping (Exod. 21:16;

---

[8] As with Gen. 9:5-6 and Lev. 24:17, 21b, modern death penalty advocates generally read some qualifying language such as "only in cases of first degree murder" into these texts. See Megivern, *Death Penalty* (cited in Chapter Five, note 129).
[9] See Chapter Five, Section B.1.b.ii.(a).
[10] See Chapter Six, text accompanying notes 71–74.
[11] See Chapter Five, Section B.1.e.ii.(b) and Chapter Six, Section C.2.
[12] See Chapter Six, note 69 and accompanying text.
[13] Arguably, prosecutors who quote this version of the *lex talionis* without such qualification thereby, themselves, act as malicious, false witnesses. See generally, Recinella, *Biblical Truth* (cited in Chapter Six, note 43), pp. 185–209; Welsh White, "Curbing Prosecutorial Misconduct in Capital Cases: Imposing Prohibitions on Improper Penalty Trial Argument," 39 *Am. Crim. L. Rev.* 1147, 1177–79 (2002); Elizabeth A. Brooks, Note, "Thou Shalt Not Quote the Bible: Determining the Propriety of Attorney Use of Religious Philosophy and Themes in Oral Arguments," 33 *Ga. L. Rev.* 1113, 1119–39 (1999); and Brian C. Duffy, Note, "Barring Foul Blows: An Argument for a Per Se Reversible Error Rule for Prosecutors' Use of Religious Arguments in the Sentencing Phase of Capital Cases," 50 *Vand. L. Rev.* 1335 (1997).
[14] The Leviticus version, applies only to *mayhem*, which was not a capital offense.
[15] Exodus 21:28-32. See Chapter Five, Section B.1.b.ii.(b).
[16] Deut. 19:4-13; Num. 35:6-34. See Chapter Six, Sections A.3. and A.5.
[17] See Chapter Five, Sections B.1.b.vi.(a) and B.1.d.i.(a).

Deut. 24:7),[18] worship of other gods or inciting other persons to so do (Exod. 22:20; Deut. 13:1-18; 17:2-7),[19] incest (Lev. 20:11-12, 14, 17),[20] striking or cursing parents (Exod. 21:15, 17, Lev. 20:9),[21] adultery (Deut. 22:13-27; Lev. 20:10,[22] ungovernable sons (Deut. 21:18-21),[23] violating the sabbath (Exod. 31:12-17; 35:2-3)[24], blaspheming the Name (Lev. 24:10-16),[25] buggery or bestiality (Exod. 22:19; Lev. 20:15-16),[26] false prophecy (Deut. 18:20),[27] male homosexual intercourse (Lev. 20:13),[28] refusal to accept court rulings,[29] or malicious, false testimony (Deut. 19:16-21).[30]

Nor do biblically oriented death penalty proponents generally advocate adherence to the methods of execution commonly mandated in biblical law, notably stoning or burning the offender to death.[31] Neither do purportedly biblical literalists insist upon execution by the entire local populace or by a private individual acting in the role of "the avenger of blood."[32] Nor do those who cite with approval the *lex talionis* often (or ever) commend punishing offenders by dismemberment or otherwise inflicting injuries in kind (eyes, teeth, hands, feet, burns, wounds, stripes or fractures). For that matter, few if any so-called biblical literalists propose enslaving grandsons whose fathers happen to see their grandfather naked in the course of a drunken stupor (Gen. 9:20-25), or selling daughters into slavery (Exod. 21:7-11). Nor do they propose to prohibit daughters from inheriting property if they have brothers (Num. 27:1-8), or to require men to marry their deceased brothers' childless widows (Deut. 25:5-10), or require owners of fields, orchards, and vineyards to allow the poor, widows, orphans or aliens to enter their lands in order to glean or pick fruit and produce (Deut. 24:19-22; Lev. 19:9-10; 23:22). Nor do modern biblical "literalists" mandate tithing all crops

---

[18] See Chapter Five, Sections B.1.b.v. and B.1.c.i.
[19] See Chapter Five, Sections B.1.b.vi(c) and B.1.e.ii.(a).
[20] See Chapter Five, Section B.1.d.ii.(b).
[21] See Chapter Five, Sections B.1.b.iv, and B.1.d.ii.(a).
[22] See Chapter Five, Sections B.1.c.ii.(b) and B.1.d.ii.(a).
[23] See Chapter Five, Section B.1.c.ii.(a).
[24] See Chapter Five, Section B. 1.f.i.(b).
[25] See Chapter Five, Section B.1.d.i.(c).
[26] See Chapter Five, Sections B.1.b.vi.(b) and B.1.d.ii.(a).
[27] See Chapter Five, Section B.1.e.ii.(a).
[28] See Chapter Five, Section B.1.d.ii.(b).
[29] See Chapter Five, Section B.1.e.ii.(b).
[30] *Id.*
[31] Methods of execution described in biblical tradition are discussed in the present author's article, "The Death Penalty and Due Process in Biblical Law," 81 *Univ. of Detroit Mercy Law Review* 791–93 (2004).
[32] Texts identifying executioners are examined in the same article, pp. 793–97.

every third year and the establishment of a national system of food banks to provide for the needs of orphans, widows, aliens and Levites (Deut. 14:28-29).[33]

As has been suggested, biblical death penalty laws do not appear to have been written in order to function as the basis for statutory enactments or judicial decisions in these United States. Nor do many, if any, modern biblically-oriented moralists, social philosophers or jurisprudes actually propose to apply biblical laws literally in our time. Nevertheless, many people in our time do quite plausibly consider biblical law—and other biblical texts—instructive and important, even in regard to such problematic matters as capital punishment.

## B. The Basic Value of Human Life

Certain underlying concerns, values or objectives have been identified in Part II of this book. First and foundational, is consistently high regard for human life. This value comes to expression both in the creation story, which affirms that God created human beings, both male and female, "in his own image" (Gen. 1:26-27 RSV),[34] and also in the P account of God's instructions to Noah following the flood: "Whoever sheds the

---

[33] It has been suggested that biblical "literalists," sometimes characterized as "fundamentalists," often are unfamiliar with the contents of the Bible or the findings of biblical scholarship, but instead attribute biblical authority to secular beliefs and values shared by others in their cultural settings. See generally, Charles Hudson, "The Structure of a Fundamentalist Christian Belief-System," in Samuel S. Hill, Jr. et al., eds., *Religion and the Solid South* (Nashville: Abingdon Press, 1972), pp. 122–142. See also Recinella, Biblical Truth (cited in Chapter Six, note 43), pp. 6–16. This pattern has been examined in connection with white Southern Protestant attitudes toward racial segregation. See, e.g., Everett Tilson, *Segregation and the Bible* (Nashville: Abingdon Press, 1958). Christian beliefs and values frequently have been merged or confused with secular ideologies in many other cultural settings as well. See generally, H. Richard Niebuhr, *Christ and Culture* (New York: Harper & Bros, 1951), pp. 83–115. As to white fundamentalist and biblical literalist views regarding the death penalty, see Robert L. Young, "Religious Orientation, Race, and Support for the Death Penalty," in Stassen (cited in Chapter Five, note 3). Proclivity toward violence as a means for resolving perceived concerns has been long recognized as an aspect of American society, particularly in the "old" or "deep" South. See Sheldon Hackney, "Southern Violence," in Hugh Davis Graham & Ted Robert Gurr, *The History of Violence in America: A Report to the National Commission on the Causes and Prevention of Violence* (New York: Bantam Books, 1969), pp. 505–527; and W. J. Cash's classic volume, *The Mind of the South* (New York: Vintage, 1969).

[34] Biblical Hebrew expresses emphasis by repetition of key terms. That God made human beings in his own "image" is stated three times in these two verses. Whether that "image" was conceived in terms of physical appearance or otherwise need not be determined for present purposes.

blood of man, by man shall his blood be shed; for God made man in his own image" (Gen. 9:6 RSV).[35] The basic value of human life[36] is also implicit in all other laws that make homicide a capital offense, both those laws expressed in general terms (notably Lev. 24:17, 21b)[37] and those referring to particular circumstances, such as premeditated murder (Exod. 21:12-14),[38] the death of a pregnant woman (Exod. 21:22-24),[39] death caused by a goring ox (Exod.21:28-32),[40] sacrificing children to a foreign god (Lev. 20:1-5),[41] and giving malicious and false testimony which could result in the execution of an innocent person (Deut. 19:16-21).[42]

Laws making the worship of other gods a capital offense correlate with the recurrent biblical affirmation of God (or YHWH) as the Source and Valuer of all that is,[43] and in particular, as the one and only God to whom Israel owed its existence and allegiance. With this, also, is the understanding, expressed both in numerous biblical laws and by many of the prophets, that this God, YHWH, would bring judgment upon his people in the form of catastrophe if not total destruction, should they turn away from him and instead worship other deities.[44] Thus, biblical laws making worship of other gods a capital offense also are grounded in concern to preserve the well-being, indeed, the lives of YHWH's people.[45]

Several other capital laws, though not concerned with homicide, likewise express concern for the bodily or moral integrity of persons.

---

[35] See Chapter Five, note 129.
[36] Notwithstanding assumptions and claims by many proponents and opponents of environmental exploitation, a great deal of biblical tradition underscores the positive value of all kinds of living beings. See generally Richard Hiers, "Reverence for Life and Environmental Ethics in Biblical Law and Covenant," *Forum on Religion and Ecology*, revised version available online at http://fore.research.yale.edu/religion/christianity/essays/chris_hiers_index.html Click on "PDF of Full Article" for text and endnotes.
[37] See Chapter Five, Section B.1.d.ii.(a).
[38] See Chapter Five, Section B.1.b.i.
[39] See Chapter Five, Section B.1.b.ii.(a).
[40] See Chapter Five, Section B.1.b.ii.(b).
[41] See Chapter Five, Section B.1.d.i.(b).
[42] See Chapter Five, Section B.1.e.ii.(b) and Chapter Six, Section C.2.
[43] See generally, H. Richard Niebuhr, *Radical Monotheism and Western Culture* (Louisville: Westminster/John Knox Press, 1993).
[44] See, e.g., Deut. 6:14-15; 8:11-20; 11:16-17; Jer. 7:1-15, 30-34; 11:9-17; Hos. 11:1-7 & 13:1-16.
[45] See, e.g., Exod. 22:20, considered in Chapter Five, Section B.1.b.vi.(c), and Deut. 13; 1-18; 17:2-7; & 18:20, Chapter Five, Section B.1.e.ii.(a). So, likewise, laws calling for the death of sorceresses, mediums and wizards (Exod. 22:18; Lev. 20:27), Chapter Five, Sections B.1.b.vi.(a) and B.1.d.i.(a), and the law against blaspheming the Name (Lev. 24:10-16, 23), Chapter Five, B.1.d.i.(c). The law prohibiting work on the sabbath may also have been prompted by such concern, to the extent that sabbath observance was intended to honor YHWH. See especially Exod. 20:8-11 (indicating this purpose).

For instance, laws penalizing kidnapping (Exod. 21:16; Deut. 24:7),[46] "buggery" (Exod. 22:19; Lev. 20:15-16),[47] adultery (Deut. 22:22-27; Lev. 20:10),[48] and incest (Lev. 20:2-21).[49] Some of these laws also evidently were intended to preserve family and community social structures, notably those prohibiting various types of extra-familial sexual activity. So also, laws against cursing or striking parents (Exod. 21:15, 17; Lev. 20:9),[50] and the ungovernable (or delinquent) son law (Deut. 21:18-21).[51] The law penalizing refusal to obey court rulings (Deut. 17:8-12)[52] obviously was intended to promote a just social order. Such concern likewise is implicit in the many biblical laws establishing due process protections for the accused.

## C. The Critical Importance of Not Executing Innocent Persons

Closely related to concern for the value of human life, biblical laws implicitly, and often explicitly, insist that only those persons who deserve to die should be put to death.[53] In this connection, attention is often directed to the alleged offender's intent. Moreover, several laws are designed to assure that only those who actually committed a capital offense are executed. And some of these laws caution in particular against biased or preferential treatment of the accused on the basis of their economic and social or ethnic status.

The alleged offender's intent is the focal inquiry mandated in most of the homicide statutes.[54] What may have been the earliest biblical capital law clearly articulates such inquiry: "Whoever strikes a man so that he dies shall be put to death," but only in those cases when "a man willfully

---

[46] See Chapter Five, Sections B.1.b.v. and B.1.c.i.
[47] See Chapter Five, Sections B.1.b.vi.(b), and B.1.d.ii.(a).
[48] See Chapter Five, Sections B.1.c.ii.(b) and B.1.d.ii.(a).
[49] See Chapter Five, Section B.1.d.ii.(b).
[50] See Chapter Five, Sections B.1b.iv., and B.1.d.ii.(a).
[51] See Chapter Five, Section B.1.c.ii(a). See also Good, "Capital Punishment" (cited in Chapter Three, note 13), p. 976: "It would seem . . . that the solidarity and integrity of the family was a quite central value for the Hebrews . . . . Further, the authority of and the honor and respect owed to parents are especially noticeable, and the mother in this regard stands equal to the father."
[52] See Chapter Six, Section C.2.
[53] See generally, Recinella, *The Biblical Truth* (cited in Chapter Six, note 43), contrasting biblical concerns with current American practices.
[54] As noted elsewhere, Lev. 24:17, 21b, are apparent exceptions. See Chapter Five, Section B.1.d.ii.(a).

attacks another to kill him treacherously" (Exod. 21:12-14 RSV).⁵⁵ The owner of an ox that fatally gores someone is to be executed only if his conduct constitutes gross negligence or reckless endangerment and then, only after he has been warned to take corrective action (Exod. 21:28-32).⁵⁶ Laws in the RDC (Deut. 19:4-13) and the PC (Num. 35:6-34) specifically distinguish between capital murder and manslaughter on the basis of the offender's intent or lack of same.⁵⁷ The Deuteronomic law explicitly observes that the accidental or merely negligent manslayer does "not deserve to die" and cautions against allowing "innocent blood" to be shed by those carrying out executions. Cities of refuge—places where those who had committed homicide could find sanctuary pending trial—were to be established specifically "lest innocent blood be shed . . . and so the guilt of bloodshed be upon you" (Deut. 19:4-10). Intent to commit the prohibited act is an implicit element in virtually all other capital offenses, for example, striking or cursing parents (Exod. 21:15, 17; Lev. 20:9), buggery or bestiality (Exod. 22:19; Lev. 20:15-16), kidnapping (Exod. 21:16; Deut. 24:7), adultery (Deut. 22:13-27; Lev. 20:10), incest (Lev. 20:11-21); and inciting to allotheism or the worship of other gods (Deut. 13:1-18; 17:2-7).⁵⁸

In biblical jurisprudence, it was critically important that only those found guilty of a capital offense should be punished accordingly. This concern is stated explicitly in the CC: "Keep far from false charges, and do not slay the innocent and righteous . . ." (Exod. 23:7 RSV). The Deuteronomic Code applies this principle to intergenerational punishment: "The fathers shall not be put to death for the children, nor shall

---

⁵⁵ See Chapter Five, Section B.1.b.i. Biblical law does not, however, address the questions whether minors, mentally retarded persons, or persons with mental illnesses were to be deemed capable of acting with culpable intent. As to these questions, see generally, "Beyond Atkins: A Symposium on the Implications of *Atkins v. Virginia*. 33 *U New Mexico L. Rev.* no. 2 (Spring, 2003), and Jeffrey A. Fager and Valerie West, "The Decline of the Juvenile Death Penalty: Scientific Evidence of Evolving Norms," in *Criminal Law Working Papers*, Nellco Legal Scholarship Repository, http://lsr.nellco.org/columbia/pllt/papers/0476 (2004). See Recinella, *Biblical Truth* (cited in Chapter Six, note 43), pp. 220–27, on "levels of capacity and diminished capacity: age, mental illness, and mental retardation" as factors in determining guilt and appropriateness of the death penalty.

⁵⁶ See Chapter Five, Section B.1.b.ii.(b). Gross negligence or reckless endangerment also may have been imputed when the *lex talionis* applied if pregnant wives were harmed by brawling males. See Chapter Five, Section B.1.b.ii.(b).

⁵⁷ See Chapter Five, Sections B.1.e.i., and B.1.f.ii.

⁵⁸ Notable exceptions are the cases of the man who blasphemed the Name (Lev. 24:10-16, 23) and the man who gathered sticks on the sabbath (Num. 15:32-36), both P traditions, where the offenders had no previous specific notice as to the offenses, both being cases of first impression where capital sentences were applied *ex post facto*.

the children be put to death for the fathers; every man shall be put to death for his own sin" (Deut. 24:16 RSV).[59] This fundamental principle comes to expression also in the early narrative account of Abraham's negotiation with YHWH over the fate of Sodom (Gen. 18:16-33).[60] The core issue there is whether it would be right for YHWH to kill any innocent persons along with the wicked. At the outset, Abraham addresses YHWH in the following strong language:

> Will you indeed sweep away the righteous with the wicked? Suppose there are fifty righteous within the city; will you then sweep away the place and not forgive it for the fifty righteous who are in it? Far be it from you to do such a thing, to slay the righteous with the wicked, so that the righteous fare as the wicked! Far be that from you! Shall not the Judge of all the earth do what is just? (Gen. 18:23b-25)

Eventually, as the story is told, YHWH agrees to spare the city if as few as ten innocent persons could be found there. That the innocent might wrongly be put to death was clearly a matter of great concern. Executing persons who were innocent or did "not deserve to die" would bring "the guilt of bloodshed" upon the entire community.[61] It might be suggested that the same would be particularly true in a democratic society, where the criminal justice system has been established by its citizens.[62]

---

[59] See Chapter Six, Section D.1.

[60] See Chapter Four, note 5. The story probably is part of the J narrative that may be dated c. 950 BCE. See generally, Timothy D. Lytton, "'Shall Not the Judge of the Earth Deal Justly?': Accountability, Compassion, and Judicial Authority in the Biblical Story of Sodom and Gomorrah," 18 *J. of L. & Relig.* 31 (2002-03). Lytton suggests that the story illustrates God's "accountability and compassion" in judging, norms which human judges would do well to emulate. Id. at p. 51.

[61] Deut. 19:4-10.

[62] As to execution of innocent persons in U.S. jurisdictions, see, Ursula Bentele, "Does the Death Penalty, by Risking Execution of the Innocent, Violate Substantive Due Process?," 40 Houston L. Rev. 1359 (2004); Hugo Adam Bedau, Michael L. Radelet, and Constance E. Putnam, "Convicting the Innocent in Capital Cases: Criteria, Evidence, and Inference," 32 *Drake L. Rev.* 587 (2004); R Bedau and Radelet, "Miscarriages of Justice," and Radelet, Bedau & Putnam, *In Spite of Innocence* (cited in Chapter Five, note 3); Samuel R. Gross, "Lost Lives: Miscarriages of Justice in Capital Cases," 42 *U Mich. L. Quad. Notes* 82 Spring, 1999; and frequently appearing newspaper items, e.g.: "High Court Shuns Death-row Appeal," (Knight-Ridder), *The Tampa Tribune*, Dec. 3, 1991, p. 5; "Execution and Inconsistency," (editorial), *The Washington Post*, Jan. 4, 1995, p. A14; Susan Greenbaum, "Mistakes Land Too Many on Death Row," *The Tampa Tribune*, Feb. 28, 2000, p. 6; William Raspberry, "Bush Needs to Stop Texas Executions," *The Register Guard* (Eugene, Oregon), June 26, 2000, p. 9A; Toni Lacy, "Push to Reform Death Penalty Growing," in *USA Today*, Feb. 20, 2001, page 5A; and "Study Finds Flaws in Death Penalty" (AP), *Gainesville Sun*, Feb. 12, 2002, p. 2B. See also Elizabeth Mannion,

Several biblical "due process" laws apparently were intended to assure that only those who had committed capital offenses would be put to death.[63] These laws evidently were meant both to identify the actual offenders, and also to make certain that all the elements of the charged offense had been met. Thus various laws call for evidentiary hearings or diligent inquiry as to relevant facts.[64] Several biblical trial scenes illustrate both explicit and implicit due process procedures intended to determine relevant facts in capital cases.[65]

Perhaps the most significant such due process law was the two- (or more-) witness requirement first found in the RDC (Deut. 17:6), and later extended in the PC (Num. 35:30). As stated broadly in both versions, this law apparently was intended or understood to apply in all capital cases.[66] Thus circumstantial evidence would no longer suffice for conviction as it may have done in earlier times.[67] In modern United States jurisprudence, convictions may be, and often are based solely on circumstantial evidence,[68] so long as the trier of fact is persuaded of the accused' guilt "beyond reasonable doubt." This book does not advocate adoption of a two-witness requirement for capital convictions in contemporary law. However, the biblical rule clearly was intended to assure that convictions in capital cases were based upon the best evidence available. Those who find biblical norms instructive for later social policy might wish to implement standards and practices that offer similar assurance.[69]

---

"Death Penalty Moritorium," *The Florida Voter: News and Views from the League of Women Voters* (Winter, 1994), p. 1.

[63] Lloyd R. Bailey concludes his study, *Capital Punishment: What the Bible Says* (Nashville: Abingdon Press, 1987), p. 91, urging that in modern times there should be a "strenuous demand" for "certainty as to guilt." Bailey's book does not, however, discuss biblical due process laws intended to enhance such certainty.

[64] See Chapter Six, Section B.2. Other laws implicitly require evidence or testimony in order to identify offenders or establish the elements of the offenses in question. See Chapter Six, Section B.1. Laws providing for cities of refuge were intended to provide sanctuary for offenders pending subsequent hearings or trials in homicide cases. See Chapter Six, Section A.

[65] See Chapter Three.

[66] See Chapter Six, Section C.1.

[67] See, e.g., the case of Tamar, discussed in Chapter Three, Section I.; the adultery laws in D and H, Chapter Five, Sections B.1.c.ii.(b) and B.1.d.ii.(a); and the homicide laws in the CC and H, Chapter Five, Sections B.1.b. and B.1.d.

[68] See Chapter Six, note 48 and accompanying text.

[69] In modern times, such evidence likely would include fingerprint, hair, blood type, and DNA analysis. See Jain, "Mitigating" (cited in Chapter Six, note 48), p. 783. Jain notes that Connecticut law provides: "No person shall be convicted of any crime punishable by death without the testimony of at least two witnesses, or that which is equivalent thereto." Conn. Gen. Stat., sects. 54–83 (1960, Id., note 119). See also, Joshua Hillel Hubner, Note, "Blinded by Science: Does the General Acceptance of Forensic DNA Evidence

The two-witness rule was buttressed in P tradition by a new law, requiring eye- or otherwise knowledgeable witnesses to testify (Lev. 5:1).[70] The RDC also set out one other new, though related law evidently intended to promote truthful testimony: the *lex talionis* provision for punishing false, malicious witnesses (Deut. 19:16-21).[71] In addition, still another new RDC law required witnesses in capital cases to throw the first stone if the accused was found guilty (Deut. 17:7).[72] All these provisions clearly were intended to enhance the likelihood that no innocent person would be put to death on a capital charge.

A related matter of great concern in biblical law was fair and equal treatment of persons without regard to their social-economic or alien status. Laws specifically admonish persons judging suits involving the poor to be impartial are found both in the CC (Exod. 23:3, 6) and H (Lev. 19:15).[73] Biblical law was especially solicitous as to the rights or interests of sojourners, foreigners or aliens residing in Israel—as if Mosaic law included an Equal Protection clause. Thus laws were to be applied equally to aliens as to natives of Israel.[74] Such sojourners would have constituted what now might be called "ethnic minorities." In the

---

Warrant a More Straightforward Approach to Admissibility," 18 *U. of Fla. J. of L. and Public Policy* 93 (2007); "DNA tests help free men after 12 years" (AP), *The Gainesville Sun*, Apr. 16, 1999, p. 3A; and Jonathan Alter et al., "The Death Penalty on Trial," *Newsweek*, June 12, 2000, pp. 24–34. And see Recinella, *Biblical Truth* (cited in Chapter Six, note 43), pp. 149, 169–72, and 331–33.

[70] See Chapter Six, Section C.3.
[71] See Chapter Six, Sections C.2. and D.2.
[72] See Chapter Six, Section C.2.
[73] See Chapter Four, Sections A, and B.1. Economic or class-based discrimination in application of capital punishment remains an issue in U.S. jurisprudence. See Steffen, *Executing Justice* (cited in Chapter Five, note 3), pp. 100–01 and 125, and Hanks, *Against* (cited in Chapter Five, note 10), pp. 107–10.
[74] See, e.g., Lev. 19:33-34; 24:22; Num. 15:14-16; 35:15; see also Deut. 1:16-17. See Chapter Four, Section B.2. In the United States, the category of resident aliens could be understood to include persons who themselves, or whose ancestors, came from other nations, in brief, ethnic, and racial minorities. Racial discrimination in application of the death penalty continues to be a matter of concern. See, e.g., Recinella, *Biblical Truth* (cited in Chapter Six, note 43), pp. 247–273; Charles J. Ogletree, Jr., "Black Man's Burden: Race and the Death Penalty in America," 81 *Oregon* L. Rev. 14 (2002); Megivern, *Death Penalty* (cited in Chapter Five, note 1), pp. 399 and 402; Hanks, *Against* (cited in Chapter Five, note 10), pp. 95–100; and Friends Committee on National Legislation and FCNL Education Fund, "The Death Penalty, Information Packet," pp. 4–5 (no date). Reports regarding such discrimination appear commonly in newspapers: see, e.g., Tom Wicker, "Court Ignores Death Penalty Bias," *Gainesville Sun*, Apr. 28, 1987, p. 8A; Robin Lowenthal, "Study Says Death Given More to Killers of Whites," *The Florida Times-Union*, Nov. 14, 1991, p. 1; Elizabeth Olson, "U.N. Report Criticizes U.S. for 'Racist' Use of Death Penalty," *The New York Times*, Apr. 7, 1998, p. A15; and "Study Shows Race a Factor in Death Penalty Decisions" (AP), *The Florida Alligator*, Jan. 8, 2003.

context of capital trials, these laws were meant to ensure that guilt or innocence would be determined on the basis of relevant facts, not the economic or social status, or the race or national origin of the accused. These important considerations have not yet been factored into modern equal protection jurisprudence as applied to capital cases in the United States.

In summary, biblical law gave expression to a highly positive evaluation of human life, and affirmed the bodily and moral integrity of persons individually, in families, and as essential for sustaining an ordered and just society. Those whose conduct violated laws intended to implement these values might, therefore, be subject to the death penalty.[75] Biblical law was particularly concerned lest innocent persons be wrongly executed. Moreover, only those who had recklessly or intentionally committed capital offenses were to be put to death. Numerous due process procedures were designed to effectuate these concerns. And those who sat in judgment were strongly admonished to consider the evidence impartially, according equal protection of the laws, whether the accused were rich or poor, native born or foreigners.

All these laws clearly were intended to protect and promote the interests of both the larger community and its individual members. Biblical law was concerned with the well-being of the community and its members in other ways as well. Such concern is apparent in a series of laws which can be classified, again using modern terminology, as "biblical social legislation." These laws are examined in Part III, which immediately follows.

---

[75] Although cities of refuge and custodial arrangements provided for temporary confinement pending trial or judicial decision, see Lev. 24:12, quoted in Chapter Five, text accompanying note 85, the biblical criminal justice system did not contemplate use of prison sentences or possibilities for rehabilitation or restorative justice; nor were such conditions as insanity, mental retardation, a history of abuse, or other mitigating factors considered in making sentencing decisions. See above, note 55. Biblical law likewise, and necessarily, did not address the question whether someone who had committed homicide, been incarcerated and had been genuinely rehabilitated, so as to become, in effect, a different person, might or should on that account be spared execution. But see Ezek. 18:21-23, quoted in Chapter Five, text accompanying note 22.

# Part III

# Social Legislation

*Objectivists will often hear a question such as: "What will be done about the poor or the handicapped in a free society?" The altruist-collectivist premise, implicit in that question, is that men are "their brother's keepers" and that the misfortune of some is a mortgage on others. The questioner is ignoring or evading the basic premises of Objectivist ethics and is attempting to switch the discussion onto his own collectivist base. Observe that he does not ask: "Should anything be done?" but "What will be done?"—as if the collectivist premise had been tacitly accepted and all that remains is a discussion of the means to implement it.*[1]

*If there is among you a poor man, one of your brethren, in any of your towns within the land which YHWH your God gives you, you shall not harden your heart or shut your hand against your poor brother, but you shall open your hand to him, and lend him sufficient for his need, whatever it may be. . . . You shall give to him freely, and your heart shall not be grudging when you give to him; because for this YHWH your God will bless you in all your work and in all that you undertake. For the poor will never cease out of the land; therefore, I command you, You shall open wide your hand to your brother, to the needy and to the poor, in the land.*

Deuteronomy 15:7-11(RSV)

The land of Israel, in more idyllic biblical descriptions, was said to flow "with milk and honey,"[2] and otherwise abound with nature's (or YHWH's) plenty.[3] But not all Israelites owned land or otherwise had access to its benefits. Biblical texts frequently mention the poor. Certain classes of

---

[1] Ayn Rand, *The Virtue of Selfishness* (Signet, 1961), p. 80.
[2] See Exod. 3:7-8; Num. 13:21-27; Deut. 6:3; 11:9; 26:9, 15.
[3] See e.g., Deut. 6:10-11; 8:7-10; 11:10-12.

persons were especially vulnerable because they lacked independent means of support: resident aliens or sojourners, widows, orphans, slaves, and hired servants. A few texts also mention handicapped or disabled persons. At some point in biblical history, Levites came to need assistance, and were, in effect, added to the welfare rolls.

By contrast, concern for the welfare of the poor is not characteristic of other ancient cultures, including those of Greece and Rome.[4] In Western social policy and jurisprudence, "distributive justice" is a relatively recent concept.[5] However, there has been a long tradition of concern for the poor in this country. To some extent, that concern derives from Christian and Jewish commitment to the biblical faith and the norms implicit in biblical law.

Many of the laws of Plymouth Colony (1620–1691) mandated arrangements for the relief or maintenance of poor persons. For example, a 1642 law reads:

> It is enacted by the court that every township within this Government shall make competent provision for the maintenance of their poor according as they shall find most convenient and suitable for themselves by an order and general agreement in a public town meeting.[6]

Those signing on to the Mayflower Compact committed themselves at the outset to seek "the general good of the Colony":

> We whose names are underwriten . . . doe by these presents solemnly & mutually in the presence of God, and one another, covenant and combine

---

[4] See generally, Raphael Sealey, *The Justice of the Greeks* (U Mich Press, 1994); and Alan Watson, *The Spirit of Roman Law* (U Ga Press, 1995). As to concern for the poor in other Ancient Near Eastern laws, see Moshe Weinfeld, *Social Justice in Israel and the Ancient Near East* (Magnes Press/Fortress Press, 1995).

[5] See E. Clinton Gardner, "Justice, Virtue, and Law," 2 *J. of L. & Relig.* 393 (1983), discussing distributive justice as opposed to efforts to ground a contemporary understanding of justice on notions of virtue. Gardner gives an illuminating account of law in the context of covenantal community, drawing especially on insights developed by H. Richard Niebuhr.

[6] *Records of the Colony of New Plymouth* (William White, 1861; reprinted by AMS Press, 1968) vol. 11, pp. 111–12 (adapted to modern spelling). For other instances of such legislation see id., pp. 40–41, 193–94; and vol. 1, p. 22 (provisions for widows and orphans). Such laws gave expression to the Colony's founding ideals. See, e.g., Dec. 15, 1617 letter by John Robinson and William Brewster to Edwin Sandys, quoted in Harry M. Ward, *Statism in Plymouth Colony* (Kennikat Press, 1973), p. 6:

> We are knite togeather as a body in a most stricte and sacred bond and covenante of the Lord, . . . by vertue whereof we doe hould our selves straitly tied to all care of each others good, and of the whole by every one and so mutually.

our selves togeather into a civil body politick . . .; and by vertue hereof to enacte, constitute and frame such just & equall lawes, ordinances, acts, constitutions, & offices, from time to time, as shall be thought most meete and convenient for the generall good of the Colony . . .[7]

Many early American communities, appropriately, designated themselves "commonwealths," thereby indicating commitment to an ethos or ethics of concern for the common or general welfare of their respective populaces. Such concern is expressly articulated in the General Welfare Clause of the Constitution[8] which has been held indicative as to the Framers' Constitutional intent.[9]

By the 19th century, however, both religious and secular leaders, influenced by, as well as giving expression to the unbiblical creeds of laissez-faire individualism and social Darwinism, commonly blamed the poor for their poverty,[10] and extolled the putative virtues of the wealthy.[11]

Today many otherwise pious (or self-righteous) persons proudly proclaim their hostility to the poor, and consider "welfare" programs on their behalf anathema.[12] From the lamentable "McCarthy" era of the 1950s to

---

[7] Mayflower Compact, quoted in William Bradford, *Of Plymouth Plantation*, Harvey Wish, ed. (Capricorn Books, 1962), pp. 69–70.

[8] Constitution of the United States, Preamble. Quoted at the beginning of Chapter Nine.

[9] Ellis v. City of Grand Rapids, 257 F. Supp. 564 (D. Mich., 1966) (Developing hospitals and medical care facilities in conjunction with urban renewal projects accords with the governmental objective of promoting the general welfare).

[10] Blaming the victim, of course, functions to relieve those doing the blaming from any sense of obligation to assist. See Michael Harrington, *The New American Poverty* (Holt, Rinehart & Winston, 1984), pp. 148, 174, 202–03. Additionally, as Job—one of the great biblical psychologists—observed, blaming the victim for his plight serves to alleviate the blamers' fears that they too might sometimes share such fate. See Job 6:14-23, critiquing motives of his "friends."

[11] See generally Conrad Cherry, ed., *God's New Israel: Religious Interpretations of American Destiny* (Prentice Hall, 1971), pp. 211–270. As to the history and problematics of individualism as a recurrent source of normative confusion in American culture, see Robert N. Bellah, *Habits of the Heart: Individualism and Commitment in American Life*, updated ed. with a new introduction (HarperSanFrancisco, 1996). For many years following the New Deal and the Second World War, it was commonly assumed that poverty was no longer a problem in the United States. That illusion was punctured in the early 1960s by both the civil rights movement's spotlight on the actual conditions of minority citizens and by publication of Michael Harrington's book, *The Other America* (Macmillan, 1962), which showed that poverty in the United States was not confined to "rural pockets" or non-whites, but rather affected some quarter of the overall population.

[12] Hostility toward the poor and opposition to aiding them is not new in Anglo-American law and society. See generally Joel F. Handler, *The Poverty of Welfare Reform* (Yale Univ. Press), pp. 10–31 (reviewing the history of welfare beginning with the 1349 English Statute of Laborers). In the 19th Century, Charles Dickens clearly identified such ideology, attributing it to many of his literary characters, such as Ebenezer Scrooge (prior to his famous supernaturally induced conversion) in *The Christmas Carol*, or

the present, politicians pandering to popular prejudice have often equated social welfare with socialism, and socialism with communism, denouncing all alike.[13] Promoting such ideology, of course, provides a convenient rationalization for ignoring others' needs, while pursuing one's own interests without restraint.

In contrast, biblical law is distinctive in its consistent regard for the welfare of "the poor" and otherwise vulnerable or needy members of society.[14] Several biblical laws were intended to protect such persons from abusive treatment, whether by courts or by private action. Other biblical laws called for positive or affirmative actions by individuals and the community as a whole. In what follows, both kinds of laws are considered part of the broad category of biblical social welfare legislation.[15]

This book does not propose that biblical law is directly applicable to modern legal or social policy issues. In its terms, biblical law was intended to govern the conduct of YHWH's people in ancient Israel, not that of a modern, pluralistic, democratic society. Moreover, modern circumstances

---

Alderman Cute and Sir Joseph Bowley in The Chimes. Norman C. Amaker has spelled out the impact of social policy grounded in such hostility upon the welfare of persons during the 1980s: *Civil Rights and the Reagan Administration* (Urban Inst Press, 1988). Responding to the needs of the poor has not, typically, been part of the agenda of the religious right. See Elizabeth M. Bounds, *Welfare as a Family Value: Conflicting Notions*, in Elizabeth M. Bounds, ed., *Welfare Policy* (Pilgrim Press, 1999), pp. 157–74. See also, Marvin Olasky, "Welfare Reform, Texas Style," in *Citizen*, vol. 13, no. 7, 20–21 (July, 1999) (commending voluntary church-sponsored welfare programs, but expressing concern lest these, like "the government mistakes" might result in "welfare dependency"). See generally Peggy L. Shriver, *The Bible Vote: Religion and the New Right* (Pilgrim Press, 1981). See also Steven M. Teles, *Whose Welfare? AFDC and Elite Politics* (U Kans Press, 1998), pp. 150–52 (critiquing conservative Republican contentions that government welfare programs foster "illegitimacy"). For a somewhat pungent account of antiwelfare ideologues, see Molly Ivins, *You Got to Dance with Them What Brung You* (Vintage, 1998), pp. 17–22, 26–28, 132–38, 142–44.

[13] Fay Laney Cook and Edith J. Barrett offer a more positive review of public attitudes in their book, *Support for the American Welfare State: The Views of Congress and the Public* (Colum Univ. Press, 1992). The book was written before the 1992 Congressional election.

[14] "The fundamental moral perspective of the biblical rules is its concern to protect the most vulnerable members of the community against advantage-taking or exploitation. In a word, the interest is in justice." Paul B. Rasor, "Biblical Roots of Modern Consumer Credit Law," 10 *J. of L. & Relig.* 157, 167 (1992). See also Barend A. de Vries, *Champions of the Poor: The Economic Consequences of Judeo-Christian Values* (Georgetown Univ. Press, 1998), pp. 173–82. And see Thomas W. Ogletree, *The Use of the Bible in Christian Ethics* (Fortress Press, 1983), pp. 55–57 (on the status of vulnerable persons in biblical law).

[15] Some laws considered in this book might also be characterized as "civil rights" legislation. Persons within the indicated "protected classes" under these laws, however, are largely the same as the designated beneficiaries of laws calling for affirmative care considered in Section B of Chapter Eight. Together, these laws concern the well-being or welfare of the more vulnerable members of the community.

are considerably different from those in biblical times.[16] For instance, contemporary society, especially in the United States, enjoys a level of prosperity that makes possible a standard of living for all that could not have been imagined in ancient times. Such prosperity raises new ethical and special policy questions as to how such wealth should be distributed. In modern democratic societies, such questions necessarily become political issues. On the other hand, the human condition has not changed to the extent that contemporary interpersonal and social concerns are completely different from those of persons living in the biblical period which ended barely a hundred generations ago. There are still poor, resident aliens or refugees, widows, orphans, hired workers (and, in some parts of the world, slaves) who are especially vulnerable to oppression and often lack the basic necessities for life. It may prove instructive to see how concerns about such persons were addressed in biblical times and in biblical law. In some cases, it may even turn out that modern law depends somewhat directly on biblical law.[17] This book does not undertake to identify such possible direct connections. However, to the degree that values embedded in modern Western law and public policy derive from biblical sources, it may be important to recognize how such values come to expression in biblical tradition, particularly, in biblical law. As Reinhold Niebuhr observed long ago:

> Religious ideas and traditions may not be directly involved in the organization of a community. But they are the ultimate sources of the moral standards from which political principles are derived.[18]

This observation may be especially pertinent given the difficulty modern and postmodernist moralists and legal philosophers experience in finding any basis for making normative judgments. Partly this difficulty results from contemporary culture's credulity as to the claims of moral

---

[16] Thus Edward McGlynn Gaffney, Jr., "Biblical Religion and American Politics," 1 *J. of L. & Relig.* 171, 182 (1983): "In my view, no text from a prior period can fairly be expected to provide direct answers to questions not asked at the time that the text was written."

[17] See Rasor, "Biblical Roots" (cited in note 14), p. 58: "[M]any of our modern consumer credit laws have direct antecedents in the Biblical legal codes, and modern law contains strong moral underpinnings which reflect the moral and religious norms found in Biblical law." Biblical laws, of course, substantially inform much of the law of the modern State of Israel.

[18] Reinhold Niebuhr, *The Children of Light and the Children of Darkness* (Scribner's, 1944), p. 125. See also Robert N. Bellah, *The Broken Covenant: American Civil Religion in a Time of Trial* (Seabury Press, 1975), p. ix, quoted at the beginning of the discussion at the end of this book captioned "Concluding Observations."

relativism[19] and radical empiricism. Proponents of the latter, including various pragmatic schools, often propose "solutions" to social "problems," but are unable—without recourse to normative considerations—to explain what a social *problem* is, why anyone *should* try to "solve" it, or what a *solution* might look like.[20] Social contractarians attempt to move from self-interest—the position so consistently and passionately articulated by the late Ayn Rand—to concern for others by imagining hypothetical and presumably self-enforcing agreements made by entirely "rational" people in hazy antiquity (or behind "the veil"),[21] agreements that presumably somehow remain binding in the world of actual personal and social interactions.[22] Ronald Dworkin has recommended deriving political and legal rights, principles, or norms by stipulating, postulating, or simply assuming their existence and authoritative force, which somehow others should recognize as controlling.[23] Coherent normative discourse has been virtually abandoned in Critical Legal Studies circles, where normative concerns of one sort and another nevertheless underlie and drive critical analysis.[24]

Not surprisingly, perhaps, some legal philosophers recently have taken another look at the religious traditions which—whether secularist folk

---

[19] See Mary Midgley, *Can't We Make Moral Judgments?* (Bristol Press, 1991), analyzing and critiquing moral relativist claims.

[20] See, e.g., Richard A. Posner, *The Problems of Jurisprudence* (Harvard Univ. Press, 1990). To speak of a social (or jurisprudential) "problem" is to say that there is something wrong about the situation in question. To speak of a "solution" is to say that there is or should be a *better* way to reorder the societal interactions or arrangements. Those who are committed to the notion that only objective reality or rational statements can be valid, generally do not acknowledge the basis for their own moral judgments.

[21] See John Rawls, *A Theory of Justice* (Oxford: Clarendon Press, 1972).

[22] To espouse self-interest, of course, is to take a normative position, e.g., that it is good or right for me to pursue my self-interest, or that everyone *should* seek his or her own self-interest. Seeking one's own self-interest does not mean that a person cannot or should not be concerned with others' welfare; but self-interest does not necessarily prompt concern for others' welfare. Rand's position, belabored throughout many of her writings, argues this point consistently and correctly.

[23] Ronald M. Dworkin, *Taking Rights Seriously* (Harvard Univ. Press, 1977), e.g., pp. xv, 162, 181–82, 273.

[24] As to the problematics of normative claims in once popular "Critical Legal Studies" (CLS) circles, see, e.g., E. Dana Neacsu, "CLS Stands for Critical Legal Studies, if Anyone Remembers," 8 J L & Pol'y 415 (2000). Compare Anthony Cook's proposal that the late Dr. Martin Luther King, Jr.'s vision of "the beloved community" offers a positive model for reconstructing society following the normative vacuum left by various CLS deconstructions. See Anthony E. Cook, "Beyond Critical Legal Studies: The Reconstructive Theology of Dr. Martin Luther King, Jr.," 103 *Harv. L. Rev.* 985 (1990), and his book, *The Least of These: Race, Law, and Religion in American Culture* (Routledge, 1997).

like it or not—undergird much of Western normative reflection.[25] The recent work of Michael J. Perry is especially significant in this connection, focusing on the quest for warrants for human rights claims.[26] Human rights issues are closely related to the topic of social welfare legislation, and rights language occasionally occurs in biblical tradition. For present purposes, however, it may suffice to suggest that Perry very probably is correct in concluding that human rights claims are necessarily religious in character, inasmuch as all normative judgments inevitably are based upon trust in and loyalty or commitment to some source or locus of meaning and value which is perceived and affirmed as good.[27] The same appears to be the case with respect to concern for human

---

[25] Religion—at any rate, the "Western" religions, Judaism and Christianity—is often assumed, by the cultured among the despisers, to be irrelevant or worse. See, e.g., Weinstein, "Adjudicative Justice" (cited in Chapter Eight, note 5), pp. 412–13. See comment by Brad Stetson, *Human Dignity and Contemporary Liberalism* (Praeger Pub., 1998), p. 95:

> The most apparent consequence of the liberal elites' public disparagement of traditional religious conviction and its perspective on public policy and cultural controversies is the marginalization of its contributions to the nation's civic life historically and to our current social exigencies, for example, welfare reform.

[26] See especially, Michael J. Perry, *The Idea of Human Rights: Four Inquiries* (Oxford Univ. Press, 1998). Perry argues that an intelligible case for human rights can be made only on religious grounds. This thesis necessarily runs counter to the ideology of secular rationalist and postmodernist pundits. As one commentator has noted recently:

> In arguing his case, [Perry] challenges those who wish to [contend] that religion is not helpful or convincing, especially against the argument by secular thinkers such as the neo-Kantian Jurgen Habermas, the neo-Pragmatist Richard Rorty, the neo-Liberal Ronald Dworkin, and the neo-Classicist Martha Nusbaum, all of whom say that they want to support human rights, but cannot supply a good reason for doing so.

Max L. Stackhouse, "Reflections on 'Universal Absolutes,'" 14 *J. of L. & Relig.* 97, 98–99 (1999–2000). See generally 14 *J. of L. & Relig.* 1–163 (1999–2000), symposium articles on Perry's book cited above in this note.

[27] See generally, H. Richard Niebuhr, *Radical Monotheism and Western Culture* (Harper, 1960), and below, Chapter Nine, notes 15, 21–23, and accompanying text. And see Stetson, cited above in note 25, p. 43: "To speak of human dignity as intrinsic is to speak of human dignity in its most traditional, Judeo-Christian sense." See also *id.* at p. 33, n. 43 and accompanying text. Of course, secular humanists can and do affirm the value of human life, but they do so as a matter of faith and as a moral judgment deriving from that faith. As Richard Niebuhr observes, the proposition that all men (or persons) are created equal can be understood only as an expression of commitment to the *value* or *worthiness* of all human beings, notwithstanding obvious differences. Radical Monotheism at pp. 73–77. See below Chapter Nine, note 21 (further describing and analyzing the faith and ethics of humanism).

For further discussion of the implication of H. Richard Niebuhr's insights for social or public policy, see Richard H. Hiers, "Normative Analysis in Judicial Determinations of Public Policy," 3 *J. of L. & Relig.* 77–115 (1985) and "Normative and Ostensibly

welfare. It does not follow, however, that Judaism and Christianity are the only historical religions that support an ethics of human rights or welfare.[28] In biblical tradition, human rights—and all other normative dimensions of life—are understood to be grounded in God's or YHWH's concern for human welfare (and the well-being of all creation). That concern comes to expression particularly in biblical laws governing human conduct.

---

Norm-Neutral Conventions in Contemporary Judicial Discourse," 14 *Legal Studies Forum* 107–39 (1990).

[28] See, e.g., Azizah al-Hibri, "Islam, Law and Custom: Redefining Muslim Women's Rights," 12 *Am U J Int'l L & Pol'y* 1 (1997).

## Chapter 8

# Biblical Social Welfare Legislation

*At the end of every three years you shall bring forth all the tithe of your produce in the same year, and lay it up within your towns; and the Levite, because he has no portion or inheritance with you, and the sojourner, the fatherless, and the widow, who are within your towns, shall come and eat and be filled, that YHWH your God may bless you in all the work of your hands that you do.*
Deuteronomy 14:28-29 (RSV)

*If a member of your community, whether a Hebrew man or a Hebrew woman, is sold to you and works for you six years, in the seventh year you shall set that person free. And when you send a male slave out from you a free person, you shall not send him out empty-handed. Provide liberally out of your flock, your threshing floor, and your wine press, thus giving to him some of the bounty with which YHWH your God has blessed you. Remember that you were a slave in the land of Egypt, and YHWH your God redeemed you; for this reason I lay this command upon you. . . . You shall do the same with regard to your female slave.*
Deuteronomy 15:12-15, 17b

Strangely little attention has been given to the subject of biblical social welfare laws.[1] Modern ethicists and social ethicists have proposed turning

---

[1] Otherwise excellent biblical studies typically contain no discussion of social welfare laws as such. See, e.g., Hans Jochen Boecker, *Law and the Administration of Justice in the Old Testament and Ancient East* (Augsburg Press, 1988); Calum Carmichael, *The Spirit of Biblical Law* (U Ga Press, 1996); James L. Crenshaw and John T. Willis, eds., *Essays in Old Testament Ethics* (KTAV, 1974); Dale Patrick, *Old Testament Law* (John Knox Press, 1985); John J. Pilch and Bruce J. Malina, *Biblical Social Values and their Meaning* (Hendrickson, 1993); Raymond Westbrook, "Biblical Law," in N. S. Hecht et al., eds., *An Introduction to the History and Sources of Jewish Law* (Oxford: Clarendon Press, 1996), pp. 1–17; and Moshe Weinfeld, *Social Justice in Ancient Israel and in the Ancient Near East* (Magnes Press/Fortress Press, 1995).

But see Craig L. Blumberg, *Neither Poverty Nor Riches: A Biblical Theology of Material Possessions* (Eerdman's, 1999), pp. 39–50 (on related biblical law but not specifically on welfare); Donald E. Gowan, "Wealth and Poverty in the Old Testament: The Case of the Widow, the Orphan, and the Sojourner," 41 *Interpretation* 341–53 (1987); Jeffries

primarily to prophetic rather than to legal biblical texts.[2] And studies examining connections between biblical and Jewish law generally give little attention to this topic. It may, therefore, be somewhat surprising to discover that biblical legal texts mandated a series of provisions which, taken together, can reasonably be said to constitute a well-developed social welfare system.

---

M. Hamilton, *Social Justice and Deuteronomy: The Case of Deuteronomy 15*, Society of Biblical Literature Dissertation Series no. 136 (Scholars Press, 1992) (addressing many related issues under the rubric of "social justice"); James Limburg, *The Prophets and the Powerless* (John Knox Press, 1977), pp. 28–31; Bruce V. Malchow, *Social Justice in the Hebrew Bible* (Collegeville, MN: The Liturgical Press, 1996), pp. 20–30 (interpreting law codes as expressing concern for social justice), and Christopher J. H. Wright, *Old Testament Ethics for the People of God* (InterVarsity Press, 2004), pp. 300–01 (briefly summarizing "compassionate laws"), and pp. 312–14 (noting biblical laws prioritizing "needs" of the vulnerable over "rights" of those in relatively powerful positions within the community).

[2] See, e.g., William Sloane Coffin, *The Heart is a Little to the Left: Essays on Public Morality* ix (U Press of New England, 1999): "Above all, I believe we need to claim the kinship of all people, to recover the prophetic insight that we belong to one another..."; T. B. Maston, *Biblical Ethics* 69 (Mercer Univ. Press, 1982): "There is no portion of the Old Testament that speaks more pointedly to the needs of our own day than the prophets." See also, Reinhold Niebuhr's equation of "prophetic Christianity" with social ethics in his early book, *An Interpretation of Christian Ethics* (Harper & Row, 1987), e.g., pp. 61 & 62. Robert N. Bellah's small book, *Prophetic Religion in a Democratic Society* (Kalamazoo: Fetzer Institute, 2006), devotes brief space to certain OT prophets and sayings of Jesus in the Synoptic Gospels, but none to biblical law, other than the first of the Ten Commandments, "You shall have no other gods..." (pp. 3–4). John C. Bennett makes no reference to either biblical law or prophets in *Christian Ethics and Social Policy* (Scribner's, 1950). Others also typically give little or no attention to biblical law in their reflections on ethics and social ethics: e.g., Robert McAfee Brown, James M. Gustafson, Martin Luther King, Jr., Paul Lehmann, Liston Pope, Paul Ramsey, John A. Ryan, and Roger Shinn. Joseph Fletcher, who professed to be allergic to law of all kinds, unsurprisingly, does not draw on biblical law in his moral reflections: *Situation Ethics: The New Morality* (Westminster, 1966); *Moral Responsibility: Situation Ethics at Work* (Westminster, 1967). In *Situation Ethics*, Fletcher asserts, "The prophetic J tradition gave way to the E-D tradition, with its precepts and laws." See also, *id.*, pp. 71–75, where Fletcher dismisses the moral relevance of the Ten Commandments as "TABLETS OF STONE."

But see Daniel C. Maguire, *The Moral Core of Judaism and Christianity* (Augsburg Fortress Press, 1993), pp. 131–44 (considering several biblical welfare texts under the heading of "Justice"); same author, *A Moral Creed for All Christians* (Augsburg Fortress, 1995), especially chapter 4, "Justice Bible-Style"); National Conference of Catholic Bishops, *Economic Justice to All: Pastoral Letter on Catholic Social Teachings and the United States Economy* (United States Catholic Conference, 1986); and Stanley Carlson Thies, *Transforming American Welfare: An Evangelical Perspective on Welfare Reform*, in David D. Gushee, ed., *Toward a Just and Caring Society: Christian Responses to Poverty in America* (Baker, 1999), pp. 473–98.

Several studies of welfare issues have appeared in recent years, but these typically do not consider or even mention biblical welfare legislation. See, e.g., Elizabeth M. Bounds, ed., *Welfare Policy: Feminist Critiques* (Pilgrim Press, 1999); Joel F. Handler, *The Poverty of Welfare Reform* (Yale Univ. Press, 1995); David K. Shipler, *The Working Poor: Invisible in America* (Vintage Books, 2004, 2005); Steven M. Teles, *Whose Welfare? AFDC and Elite Politics* (U Kans Press, 1998).

Arguably, much of biblical law represents legislative visions of conditions that would constitute a good society.[3] Particular laws set forth specific ways such society was to be actualized. In biblical times, of course, there was no Social Security Administration, and there were no provisions for food stamps, Aid for Families with Dependent Children, or other commonplace, modern public assistance programs. However, many biblical laws prohibited discrimination against disadvantaged persons. And various affirmative social welfare arrangements were established by law. Laws prohibiting unjust, invidious, or oppressive treatment of certain groups will be considered first. The balance of this chapter will describe the affirmative assistance provisions or programs set out in biblical laws.

## A. Protections against Injustice and Mistreatment

Several biblical laws require that officials and others involved in legal proceedings provide for the fair and equal protection of persons within the community. Related laws caution against perverting justice due to certain groups. Some specifically condemn certain types of oppressive or invidious treatment of disadvantaged and disabled persons.

### 1. Full, Fair, and Equal Justice in the Courts

Many biblical laws insist that those responsible for the administration of justice see to it that the relatively powerless or vulnerable groups within the community be accorded the same rights and protections as others.[4] Such concerns continue to surface in contemporary jurisprudence for instance, in a recent article by George Fletcher.[5]

---

[3] See Joseph Blenkinsopp, "Biblical Law and Hermeneutics: A Reply to Professor Gaffney," 4 *J. of L. & Relig.* 97, 100 (1986) (Legal matters in the Hebrew Bible are to be understood as "the inculcation of a societal ideal to which the community is directed through the laws").

[4] Such classes of persons were vulnerable not only economically, but also because they may not have been permitted to represent themselves in legal proceedings. See Rasor, "Biblical Roots" (cited in Introduction to Part III, note 14), p. 164, n. 39. But see below note 86 and also Gowan, "Wealth and Poverty" (cited in note 1 above), p. 345, reviewing texts indicating that widows had legal standing in some situations. As to biblical emphasis on justice in the courts, see generally, John T. Noonan, Jr., *Bribes* (Macmillan, 1984), pp. 14–30.

[5] See George P. Fletcher, "In God's Image: the Religious Imperative of Equality under Law," 99 *Colum L. Rev* 1608, 1615 (1999):

> The text of Genesis [1:26-27] is, in fact, the beginning of the thread favoring equality that binds the earliest legends of creation together with Lincoln's reformulation of

Categories of persons identified in biblical laws as protected classes include the poor, sojourners, orphans and widows. Lacking independent means of support, sojourners, orphans and widows necessarily would often be poor. The ceremonial invocation of blessings and curses immediately following the Deuteronomic Code names these three particular categories of persons.

Cursed be he who perverts the justice due to the sojourner, the fatherless, and the widow." And all the people shall say "Amen. (Deut. 27:19)[6]

---

the Declaration of Independence. The foundations of equality emerge in the book of Genesis; they are restated in a secular idiom in Kant; and they come into modern political discourse as an unquestioned assumption of the liberal pursuit of justice. My view is that, if we look carefully at the text of Genesis, we will find the roots of those truths that today we hold to be "self-evident."

Fletcher proposes that U.S. courts eschew "scrutiny and interest balancing in cases that challenge caste-based inequalities," urging that "the basis of equalitarian jurisprudence should not be the state and its interests but, rather, the intrinsic equality of all persons created in God's image." *Id.*, pp. 1628–29. Fletcher might also have cited a legal text, Num. 15:15-16, which derives from the same Priestly or P circles as the first creation story's image of God language. Numbers 15:15-16 is quoted below, text accompanying note 30.

See also Jack B. Weinstein, "Adjudicative Justice in a Diverse Mass Society," 8 *J L & Pol'y* 385 (2000) (calling for equalizing the adversary and adjudicatory systems in the interest of the poor or less privileged). Weinstein mistakenly states that Fletcher's "argument [is] based on language in Genesis 2:18-23," and reject's Fletcher's proposal because: "In view of the divisiveness of religions and the tendency of adherents to want to dominate or proselytize others, the First Amendment rather than the story of creation seems a better guarantor of equality in our civil society." *Id.*, pp. 412–13, n. 65. Yet Weinstein declares that the "thesis" of his own article is "rooted in Learned Hand's command, 'Thou shalt not ration justice,' and in the Bible's, nor shall 'you distinguish between the rich and poor or pervert the justice due to your poor in his suit.'" (Exod. 23:6). *Id.*, p. 388. Weinstein cites Deut. 16:19 as further authority (*id.*, p. 406, n. 53), and concludes, quoting the "Golden Rule," which he attributes jointly to Hillel and Jesus.

[6] See also Deut. 10:18 (RSV): "[YWHW] executes justice for the fatherless and the widow, and loves the sojourner, giving him food and clothing." These concerns come to expression in the prohibitions at Deut. 24:17-19 (RSV): "You shall not pervert the justice due to the sojourner or to the fatherless, or take a widows garment in pledge; but you shall remember that you were a slave in Egypt and YHWH your God redeemed you from there; therefore I command you to do this." As to Deut. 24:17-18, see generally, Hamilton, *Social Justice* (cited in note 1), pp. 130–33. The prophet Zechariah reiterated such concerns: "Thus says YHWH of hosts, Render true judgments, show kindness and mercy each to his brother, do not oppress the widow, the fatherless, the sojourner, or the poor . . ." (Zech. 7:9-10 RSV). Similarly, Jer. 7:5-6. See also Mal. 3:5 (RSV): "Then I will draw near to you for judgment; I will be a swift witness against . . . those who oppress the hireling in his wages, the widow and the orphan, against those who thrust aside the sojourner, and do not fear me, says YHWH of hosts." And see also Ps. 94:1-7 (condemning those who kill the widow, sojourner, and the fatherless), and Ps. 146:5-9 (YHWH gives the oppressed justice, the hungry food, sets prisoners free, opens the eyes of the blind, and cares for the sojourner, widow, and fatherless).

Clearly the interests of such persons were considered important to YHWH and to the community as a matter of justice, not only of charity.

The Covenant Code warns against the failure to treat the poor fairly or accord them full justice: "You shall not pervert the justice due to your poor in his suit" (Exod. 23:6 RSV). Similar concern is to be found in Proverbs:

> Do not rob the poor because he is poor,
> Or crush the afflicted at the gate;[7]
> For YHWH will plead their cause,
> And despoil of life those who despoil them. (Prov. 22:22-23 RSV)[8]

Such texts imply that the poor were entitled to fair treatment as a matter of law, and that the poor therefore were entitled to certain *rights*.[9] Equal justice for the poor, however, precludes partiality or preferential treatment by courts or judges: "Nor shall you be partial to a poor man in his suit" (Exod. 23:3 RSV).[10]

---

[7] See also Amos 5:12: "For I know how many are your transgressions . . . you who . . . push aside the needy in the gate." "At the gate" refers to the local court. See Boecker, *Administration of Justice* (cited in note 1), p. 31.

[8] Some remembered echo of the last part of this verse may have prompted Karl Marx to formulate his famous doctrine that in due course, history, unfolding mechanistically (Marx's surrogate for divine justice) would bring about the "expropriation of the expropriators."

[9] See Prov. 29:7 (RSV) ("A righteous man knows the rights of the poor; a wicked man does not understand such knowledge"); and Prov. 31:9 (RSV) ("Open your mouth, judge righteously, maintain the rights of the poor and needy"). And see Job 29:12, 16-17. As to the concept of rights in biblical law, see Susan A. Wolfson, "Modern Liberal Rights Theory and Jewish Law," 9 *J. of L. & Relig.* 399 (1992). Wolfson notes that biblical (and Jewish) law emphasize obligations more than rights, but observes that rights concepts are also present, though not in the sense characteristic of 18th century and modern radical individualism. "Modern liberal theory almost never concerns itself with duties; nevertheless, it implicitly takes account of them. The situation in Jewish law may be a similar one. That is, that Jewish law is somehow implicitly concerned with rights. . . . [Jewish] law begins with individuals already placed in their social context; the law itself places them in this context. The picture is not of autonomous individuals standing alone in their 'moral zone,' as for example Nozickian citizens do . . ." *Id.*, p. 414. And see generally Haim Hermann Cohn, *Human Rights in Jewish Law* (KTAV, 1984).

[10] See also Lev. 19:15: "You shall do no injustice in judgment; you shall not be partial to the poor or defer to the great, but in righteousness shall you judge your neighbor." Sirach 35:12-13 characterizes "the Most High" as an impartial judge: "He will not show partiality in the case of a poor man, and he will listen to the prayer of one who is wronged" (RSV). The implication is that Israelite or Jewish judges should do likewise. On equal protection in biblical law, see generally Cohn, *Human Rights* (cited above in note 9), pp. 189–96. See also Gershon Brin, *Studies in Biblical Law: From the Hebrew Bible to the Dead*

These laws apply to the treatment of protected classes of persons at trial or before the courts.[11] Several other laws condemn oppression of such persons by private actors. A number of these laws provide special privileges or immunities for those who are poor or in special need.

## 2. Laws against Oppression or Mistreatment of Protected Classes

As has been seen, biblical law required that courts protect the rights or interests of all persons equally. The underlying normative foundation for such equal treatment is the faith-understanding that all persons are *valued* positively and equally by YHWH.[12] In addition, private persons were not to take advantage of certain protected classes. These classes included the poor, aliens or sojourners, widows and orphans, servants, and also the disabled or handicapped, notably, those who are blind or deaf. Various other biblical texts additionally urged that private persons were obligated to undertake the defense of such persons in court.[13] Here, too, the equal and positive *value of persons before YHWH* is the basis for such laws.

### a. The poor

Persons who lend to the poor should refrain from charging them interest (Exod. 22:25). Leviticus 25:35-38 adds that Israelites must sell food to the poor at cost, rather than seek to profit from such sales.[14] Such laws may have been the basis for Amos' strictures against those who "trample upon the poor and take from them exactions of wheat" (Amos 5:11 RSV).[15] Similarly, if a poor man's garment is taken in pledge (or as

---

Sea Scrolls, *Journal for the Study of the Old Testament*, Supp. no. 176, 88–89 (JSOT Press, 1994) (discussing Exod. 23:3 and 23:6). And see also Chapter Four of this book.

[11] See also Ps. 82:3-4, which may have been addressed to members of the divine or heavenly council, but also implies what human courts should do: "Give justice to the weak and the fatherless; maintain the right of the afflicted and the destitute. Rescue the weak and the needy; deliver them from the hand of the wicked" (RSV).

[12] See Section A.1 of this chapter.

[13] See below, note 35 and accompanying text.

[14] Neither of these laws precluded lending at interest to fellow Israelites who were not poor.

[15] See also Ezek. 22:12. Compare Deut. 23:19-20 (RSV), which prohibits lending money at interest to "your brother" (fellow Israelite), with no mention of economic status, but permits lending at interest to a foreigner. See Reuven Yaron, "Biblical Law: Prolegomena," in Bernard S. Jackson, ed., *Jewish Law in Legal History*, Supplement to *The Jewish Law Annual* 27, 29 (E. J. Brill, 1980): "It is not difficult to see that all these provisions share a common background: they all concern loans granted on compassionate grounds . . .,

collateral) it should be returned to him before sundown, "for that is his only covering, it is his mantle for his body; in what else is he to sleep? And if he cries to me, I will hear, for I am compassionate" (Exod. 22: 26-27 RSV).[16] The same rationale is implicit in Deut. 24:17: "You shall not take a widow's garment in pledge."[17] Again we learn from Amos that not all Israelites complied with the law. Contending against those who were practicing bogus piety, Amos charged, "They lay themselves down beside every altar on garments taken in pledge" (Amos 2:8).

Debt collection that would result in poverty is also prohibited: "No man shall take a mill or an upper millstone in pledge, for he would be taking a life in pledge" (Deut. 24:6 RSV). Loss of income or employment ("livelihood") can put a person's life at risk. Here again, the well-being of persons is considered more important than any putative "property rights."[18] Concern for the welfare of persons—not simply for abstract fairness—likewise undoubtedly informs biblical laws intended to limit corrupt commercial practices, notably use of false weights and measures.[19] We might call these consumer protection laws. Such laws would have been especially important for those living on the economic margins who would be most vulnerable to fraudulent transactions.

The poor also were to enjoy another type of exemption or privilege. Certain provisions in the Priestly Code allowed the poor to offer less expensive sacrifices in order to obtain divine favor: Leviticus 5:7-13

---

intended to help one's fellow who has fallen upon bad times. In circumstances such as these the making of a profit out of one's fellow's predicament is viewed as repugnant." And see Brin, *Studies* (cited in note 10), p. 86.

[16] That such a person is poor can be inferred from the fact that he owns only the one "garment" or coat. Deuteronomy 24:12-13 (RSV) explicitly refers to *a poor man's* garment held in pledge. See generally, Brin, *Studies* (cited in note 10), pp. 82–85. On biblical conceptions of compassion, see generally, Pilch and Malina, *Biblical Social Values* (cited in note 1), pp. 28–30.

[17] See Rasor, "Biblical Roots" (cited in Introduction to Part III, note 14), p. 190: "In modern law, the moral basis is obscured by the prevailing tendency to talk in purely legalistic and economic terms. . . . The fundamental unifying principle of both the Biblical lending rules and modern consumer credit law is the desire to ensure that the most vulnerable members of society are treated fairly and to protect them from overreaching and oppression. . . . [T]his unifying principle is to be understood as a moral norm, and not simply as an economic or legal rule."

[18] See also Deut. 23:24-25, providing that Israelites who entered their neighbors' vineyards and grain fields might eat what they wished. This arrangement would have been especially beneficial to the poor, but in its terms, applied to all classes of persons. This privilege is illustrated in the NT: see Mt. 12:1 = Mk 2:23 = Lk. 6:1.

[19] Deut. 25:13-16; Lev. 19:35-36. See Mic. 6:11 (RSV): "Shall I acquit the man with wicked scales and with a bag of deceitful weights?" See also Amos 8:4-6. And see Prov. 16:11 and 20:23.

(guilt offerings), and Leviticus 14:21-32 (offerings for curing leprosy).[20] These arrangements could be seen as precedent for later graduated income taxes or Medicare fees.[21] Such texts also could be seen as an arguable biblical basis for modern liberation theology's concept of a "preferential option for the poor."[22]

Many of these laws obviously were intended to protect the welfare of those who were poor. The prophet Amos repeatedly proclaimed YHWH's impending judgment against those who, instead of according such protection, oppressed or exploited the poor.[23] Isaiah and Jeremiah likewise condemned those who abused the poor.[24] And several proverbs anticipate that it will not go well for those who oppress the poor.[25] Instead of oppressing them, YHWH's people should be defending the rights of the needy (Jer. 5:28).

### b. Sojourners or resident aliens

Biblical laws are especially solicitous as to sojourners or resident aliens. Some may have come as refugees, others as migrant workers or as permanent immigrants.[26] Evidently Israel was open to such aliens in biblical

---

[20] As to these and a few other texts reducing or eliminating obligations of those unable to afford compliance with certain religious or cultic laws, see Brin, *Studies* (cited in note 10), pp. 74–79. But see Exod. 30:11-15: Every Israelite, whether rich or poor, was to pay the same half shekel census tax (or atonement fee), in effect, a flat tax.

[21] A wisdom saying in the book of Tobit applies the principle of proportionate giving to aiding the poor: "Give alms from your possessions to all who live uprightly, and do not let your eye begrudge the gift when you make it. . . . If you have many possessions, make your gift from them in proportion; if few, do not be afraid to give according to the little you have." Tob. 4:7-8 (RSV). Here we see that a limiting, moral test has been added: only the righteous poor are to be aided. Compare 1 Cor. 16:1-2. As to other "leniencies in the law" as to the poor, see Brin, *Studies* (cited in note 10), pp. 74–89. As to contemporary discussion of biblical texts and concepts relating to allocation of tax burdens, see Adam S. Chodorow, "Biblical Tax Systems and the Case for Progressive Taxation," 23 *J. of L. & Relig.* 51–96 (2007–2008).

[22] But see biblical texts cited above, note 10 and accompanying text, mandating that courts or judges were to be impartial in administering justice to the poor.

[23] Amos 2:6-7; 4:1; 5:11; 8:4, 6.

[24] Isa. 3:13-15; 10:1-2; Jer. 2:34.

[25] Prov. 14:31 (RSV) ("He who insults a poor man insults his Maker"); 22:16 (RSV) ("He who oppresses the poor to increase his own wealth, or gives to the rich, will only come to want"). See also Prov. 22:22-23.

[26] See Cohn, *Human Rights* (cited above in note 9), p. 77: "It is now generally assumed that most of the 'strangers,' that is migrants, who, in antiquity, left their own lands and went into foreign parts were refugees in the modern sense—if not from individual persecution and oppression, at any rate from famine (cf. Gen. 12:10; Ruth 1:1; 2 Kgs 8:1) or some other disaster; and from the biblical prescriptions relating to them it is abundantly clear

times. These persons were foreigners who were living either permanently or temporarily in Israel. Not only men, but also women and children were included in this class of persons. YHWH, himself, "loves the sojourner" (Deut. 10:18); therefore Israelites should do so as well (Deut. 10:19; Lev. 19:34). The Israelites, themselves, had been sojourners in Egypt. Therefore they should have compassion on sojourners or aliens dwelling in their own midst. When strangers sojourn with them, Israelites should do them no wrong (Lev. 19:33). Likewise, the Deuteronomic Code cautions: "You shall not deprive a resident alien . . . of justice" (Deut. 24:17). The Covenant Code earlier had also warned against wronging or oppressing strangers: "You shall not wrong a stranger or oppress him, for you were strangers in the land of Egypt" (Exod. 22:21 RSV). "You shall not oppress a stranger; you know the heart of a stranger, for you were strangers in the land of Egypt" (Exod. 23:9 RSV).[27] Perhaps for the same kind of reason, a Deuteronomic law forbids oppressing escaped slaves (Deut. 23:15-16). The Israelites had escaped from slavery in Egypt: therefore they should have compassion on others who had won their freedom. Sojourners must not be required to work on the sabbath. Rather, they were to rest, so that they (along with others, including the farm animals[28]) might "be refreshed" (Exod. 23:12).[29]

For the assembly, there shall be one statute for you and for the stranger who sojourns with you, a perpetual statute throughout your generations; as you are, so shall the sojourner be before YHWH. One law and one ordinance shall be for you and for the stranger who sojourns with you. (Num. 15:15-16 RSV)[30]

---

that they were among the poor and needy who had to be given shelter, food, and raiment (Lev. 19:10; 23:22; Deut. 10:18, etc.)." Biblical law did not bar economic refugees.

[27] On such "motive clauses," see generally Hamilton, *Social Justice* (cited above in note 1), pp. 85–91; Harry P. Nasuti, "Identity, Identification, and Imitation: The Narrative Hermeneutics of Biblical Law," 4 *J. of L. & Relig.* 9 (1986); and Rifat Sonsino, *Motive Clauses in Hebrew Law: Biblical Forms and Near Eastern Parallels*, SBL Dissertation Series, no. 45 (Scholars Press, 1980).

[28] See Richard H. Hiers, "Reverence for Life and Environmental Ethics in Biblical Law and Covenant," 13 *J. of L. & Relig.* 127, 160–62 (1996–98).

[29] See also Exod. 20:8-10; Deut. 5:12-14. Sojourners were not to work on the Day of Atonement, either. Lev. 16:29-30.

[30] See also Num. 15:29-30. Impartiality in judging between Israelite and alien evidently was also called for in Deut. 1:16. Notable exceptions to the principle of equal protection for aliens were the laws allowing Israelites to foreclose and exact interest on loans to aliens. Deut. 15:3; 23:20. Other exceptions are indicated at Exod. 21:8 (foreigners not to partake of Passover), and Deut. 17:15 (foreigner may not become king). See Cohn, *Human Rights* (cited in note 9), p. 161: "These explicit exceptions seem to indicate that

Earlier, the Holiness Code had put the point even more succinctly: "You shall have one law for the sojourner and for the native; for I am YHWH your God" (Lev. 24:22 RSV). This insistence on "one law" for both Israelites and foreigners or aliens accords with the larger biblical theme that YHWH created, cares for and generally intends the welfare of all humankind.[31]

### c. Widows and orphans

Biblical law also condemned oppressing widows[32] and orphans:

> You shall not afflict any widow or orphan. If you do afflict them, and they cry to me, I will surely hear their cry; and my wrath will burn, and I will kill you with the sword, and your wives shall become widows and your children fatherless. (Exod. 22:22-24 RSV)[33]

Here YHWH, himself, would enforce this law. Deuteronomy 24:17 adds: "You shall not deprive . . . an orphan of justice." Such laws also would have provided guidance to individual Israelites concerning right or righteous conduct, and to judges or courts in resolving disputes. The prophet Isaiah, condemned those who preyed upon widows and orphans,[34] and called on fellow Israelites to correct such oppression:

> Cease to do evil, learn to do good;
>     Seek justice, correct oppression;
> defend the fatherless, plead for the widow. (Isa. 1:16-17 RSV)[35]

---

unless expressly otherwise provided, all laws applying to Israelites apply also to foreigners."

[31] See, e.g., Gen. 1:1–10:32; Ps. 8 & 145; Isa. 49:6; and Jon. chs. 1–4.

[32] It has been suggested that in biblical times, a woman whose husband had died would not have been considered a widow if she returned to her parents' house. True "widows" lacked family ties and generally had no share in family property, according to Boecker, *Administration of Justice* (cited in note 1), p. 19. But see above, Chapter Two, section B.1.c. At all events, biblical widows, like orphans, typically lived on the economic margins of society. There is no evidence, however, that relatives ever (much less "often") sold widows into slavery, *contra* Silvia Schroer, "Toward a Feminist Reconstruction of the History of Israel," in Luise Schottroff et al., *Feminist Interpretation: The Bible in Women's Perspective* (Fortress Press, 1998), p. 123.

[33] According to Proverbs 15:25, YHWH also looks out for the interests of widows in more positive terms: "YHWH tears down the house of the proud, but maintains the widow's boundaries." See also Sir. 35:14 (RSV): "He will not ignore the supplication of the fatherless, nor the widow when she pours out her story."

[34] Isa. 10:1-2; see also Jer. 7:5-7 and Mal. 3:5.

[35] See also Isa. 1:23 (RSV), condemning those who failed to "defend the fatherless" or take up "the widow's cause," and Jer. 5:28 (RSV): ". . . they judge not with justice the cause of the fatherless, to make it prosper, and they do not defend the rights of the needy."

Widows' clothing, like that of the poor, was not to be taken "in pledge" or as security (Deut. 24:17b). Perhaps, as in the case of the poor, such garments were to be returned by sundown;[36] or perhaps it was understood that widow's garments were not to be taken in pledge at all.

Orphans' inherited property also would have been subject to exploitation by the unscrupulous. Thus a Proverbs sage cautions:

> Do not remove an ancient landmark
> or enter the fields of the fatherless;
> for their redeemer is strong;
> he will plead their cause against you. (Prov. 23:10-11)

Here, "their redeemer" probably refers to their *go'el*, a near or nearest kinsman, who would take matters to court if necessary, to defend the orphan's title to the property.

### d. Labor relations: hired servants

Servants or hired workers also were to be protected from exploitation. Here we have a glimpse into biblical labor relations law. One law pertained to the work-week; the other to wages. The sabbath was to be a day of rest not only for a family, but also for its servants.[37] Householders or others who hired servants or laborers were not to hold back their wages, but were to pay them each day for their day's work:

> You shall not withhold the wages of poor and needy laborers, whether other Israelites or aliens who reside in your land in one of your towns. You shall pay them their wages daily before sunset, because they are poor and their livelihood depends on them; otherwise they might cry to YHWH against you, and you would incur guilt. (Deut. 24:14-15)

---

See also Sir. 4:9-10 (RSV), where the sage urges readers: "Deliver him who is wronged from the hand of the wrongdoer; and do not be fainthearted in judging a case. Be like a father to orphans, and instead of a husband to their mother . . ." Similar obligations are implicit in Job's account of his previous conduct: "I was a father to the poor, and I searched out the cause of him whom I did not know. I broke the fangs of the unrighteous, and made him drop his prey from his teeth." Job 29:16-17 (RSV); see also 29:11-12 (RSV). And see Prov. 31:9 (RSV): "Open your mouth, judge righteously, maintain the rights of the poor and needy."

[36] Exod. 22:26-27; Deut. 24:12-13.

[37] Exod. 20:10; 23:12; Deut. 5:12-15. See especially Exod. 23:12 and Deut. 5:14-15. On the sabbath law, see generally Walter Harrelson, *The Ten Commandments and Human Rights* (Fortress Press, 1980), pp. 79-92.

> You shall not oppress your neighbor or rob him. The wages of a hired servant shall not remain with you all night until morning. (Lev. 19:13 RSV)[38]

Here, hired servants are regarded as neighbors and withholding their pay was considered not only oppression, but tantamount to robbery. Sirach 34:22 expresses similar concerns:

> To take away a neighbor's living is to commit murder;
> to deprive an employee of his wages is to shed blood.[39]

Jeremiah even condemned a king who had failed to pay his employees or workers: "Woe to him . . . who makes his neighbor serve him for nothing, and does not give him his wages" (Jer. 22:13 RSV).

### e. Persons with disabilities

Disabled or handicapped persons were to be treated with respect. The execration formula in Deuteronomy 27 includes the imprecation: "'Cursed be anyone who misleads a blind man on the road,' and the people shall say, 'Amen!'" (Deut. 27:18). The Holiness Code adds two other prohibitions against teasing or tormenting the disabled: "You shall not curse the deaf or put a stumbling block before the blind, but you shall fear your God: I am YHWH" (Lev. 19:14 RSV). Job provides an example of such affirmative conduct with respect to disabled persons: "I was eyes to the blind, and feet to the lame" (Job 29:15).[40] In modern terms, not putting a stumbling block before the blind, or providing feet for the lame, might be construed to include providing handicap access and eliminating artificial barriers to employment for persons with disabilities. Biblical laws not only prohibit mistreating various classes or categories of vulnerable groups of persons. Several laws also require Israelites and their descendants to act affirmatively on behalf of such persons.

---

[38] Such laws may have been the basis for one of Tobit's admonitions to his son: "Do not hold over until the next day the wages of any man who works for you, but pay him at once." (Tob. 4:14 RSV). See also Mal. 3:5: "Then I [YHWH] will draw near to you for judgment . . . against those who oppress hired workers in their wages . . ." Here the offense may be either underpayment or withholding wages.

[39] Sirach 7:20-21 not only cautions against abusing faithful and devoted servants or employees; the writer urges employers to *love* worthy servants. See also Sir. 33:30-31. Job, a model of biblical righteousness, asserts that he never "rejected the cause of [his] manservant or . . . maidservant when they brought a complaint against [him]." Job 31:13 (RSV).

[40] See also Prov. 31:8 (RSV): "Open your mouth for the dumb . . ." Prophetic texts also show solicitude for the disabled: YHWH himself would care for or heal them. See Micah 4:6-7 ("the lame"); Isa. 35:5-6 (the blind, deaf and lame). See also in the NT, Lk. 14:12-14: "[W]hen you give a banquet, invite the poor, the crippled, the lame, and the blind . . ."

## B. Laws Calling for Affirmative Actions by Private Persons

Social ethics or responsible life in community involves not only refraining from harmful conduct, but also acting affirmatively on behalf of others. Those who had property or other forms of wealth in biblical times were obliged to consider the needs of other persons in their communities, not just their own welfare. "Property rights," is an expression nowhere to be found in the Bible.[41] Ultimately, the land and everything else in the world belonged to YHWH, not to Israel or any person or group of persons.[42] Thus property was to be used in accordance with YHWH's concerns and purposes, which were understood to have been set out in the law.

Biblical laws call for several types of affirmative conduct on behalf of various classes or persons.[43] Parents are to be honored;[44] numerous

---

[41] See Millar Burrows, *An Outline of Biblical Theology* (Westminster Press, 1946), p. 302: "The use of land was subject to the welfare of the community, including provision for the poor, for widows, and for resident aliens (who had no allotment in Israel). Their support was to be secured by the laws of gleaning and the like, also the sabbatical year, and the release of debts."

[42] See e.g., Exod. 9:29b; 19:5; Deut. 10:14; and Pss. 24:1-2 and 50:10-12.

[43] This concern may be especially characteristic of laws found in the Deuteronomic Code (D) and also the Deuteronomic laws set down in connection with the Deuteronomic Reform (RDC). See Gaffney, "Biblical Religion" (cited in Introduction to Part III, note 16), pp. 180–81: "[Deuteronomy] . . . is . . . a powerful program for social reform including care for disadvantaged classes . . ." See also Boecker, *Administration of Justice* (cited in note 1), pp. 181–84 on compassionate or humanitarian concerns in Deuteronomic law. And see Ze'ev W. Falk, *Religious Law and Ethics* 70–72 (Mesharim, 1991) (on the interpenetration of law and ethics in Deuteronomy). And also see Jeffrey H. Tigay, xviii, *The JPS Commentary: Deuteronomy XIX-XXII* (Jewish Publication Society, 5756/1996):

> The Torah's humanitarianism is most fully developed in Deuteronomy's legislation and exhortations on behalf of the poor and disadvantaged: debtors, indentured servants, escaped slaves, resident aliens, orphans, widows and Levites, as well as animals and even convicted criminals.

Strangely, many commentaries on Deuteronomy do not recognize the compassionate character of Deuteronomic legislation.

Such concern can also be found in the other major biblical law codes as well: the Covenant, Holiness, and Priestly Codes. As to the Covenant Code, see Elliot N. Dorff and Arthur Rosett, *A Living Tree: The Roots and Growth of Jewish Law* 28 (SUNY Press, 1988): "Toward the end of [Exodus] 22 the tone shifts again. Now the fair and compassionate treatment of strangers, widows, orphans, and debtors is no longer based solely on the fear of Divine anger. Instead, the major appeal is to the moral quality of compassion, the memory of our own suffering that leads us not to cause others to suffer." See also Paul D. Hanson, *The People Called: The Growth of Community in the Bible* (Harper & Row, 1981), pp. 44–45 (on the quality of "compassionate justice" implicit in Exod. 20: 22-26 and 22:17–23:19).

[44] Biblical law does not specifically mandate care for the aged. The commandment to honor father and mother (Exod. 20:12; Deut. 5:16), of course, includes aging and aged parents. Again, wisdom tradition suggests what may have been common law or accepted

mandated arrangements provided food for those in need of assistance; various laws called for other ways to assist the poor; and a number of laws concerned humane or compassionate treatment of slaves and indentured servants.

## 1. Food for the Poor

Several types of biblical laws call on members of the community to provide food for those who need it.[45] To begin with, landowners must allow the poor to glean or gather food for themselves and their families in privately owned fields, vineyards, and orchards. Such persons also were to be invited to join in various festivals or celebrations and partake of the food prepared for these occasions. Certain other laws also called for making food available to those who needed it. In modern times, these laws could be categorized aptly as expressions of and vehicles for distributive justice or as social welfare legislation.

### a. Gleaning rights or privileges

Laws requiring property owners to set aside portions of their harvests for persons in need are included in both the Deuteronomic and Holiness Codes. The Deuteronomic law specifically names sojourners, orphans, and widows as the intended beneficiaries or welfare recipients.

---

practice. See Sir. 3:1-16, a series of admonitions as to honoring parents. For instance, Sir. 3:12 (RSV):

O son, help your father in his old age
   and do not grieve him as long as he lives;
even if he is lacking in understanding, show forbearance;
   in all your strength do not despise him.

See also Prov. 23:22-25; Sir. 7:27-28; 8:6.

[45] Wisdom writings express similar concern. See, e.g., Prov. 22:9 (RSV): "He who has a bountiful eye will be blessed, for he shares his bread with the poor." And see Tob. 1:17; 4:16 (RSV) ("bread to the hungry" and "clothing to the naked"). Various NT texts likewise call for feeding the hungry. See, e.g., Lk. 14:13 (RSV) ("But when you give a feast, invite the poor, the maimed, the lame, the blind . . ."); Lk. 16:19-31 (RSV) (the Parable of the Rich Man and Lazarus "who desired to be fed with what fell from the rich man's table"); Mt. 25:34-45; and 1 Jn 3:17.

Likewise, biblical prophets affirmed the obligations of those with property as to the hungry. See Isa. 58:7, 10; Ezek. 18:7, 16; see also Job 22:7; 31:16-17. Weinfeld discusses these and other texts regarding support for the poor and needy, but strangely neglects relevant biblical law. See Weinfeld, *Social Justice* (cited above, note 1), pp. 215–39.

> When you reap your harvest in your field, and have forgotten a sheaf
> . . . you shall not go back to get it; it shall be for the sojourner, the
> fatherless, and the widow; that YHWH your God may bless you in all
> the work of your hands. When you beat your olive trees, you shall not
> go over the boughs again; it shall be for the sojourner, the fatherless,
> and the widow. When you gather the grapes of your vineyard, you shall
> not glean it afterward; it shall be for the sojourner, the fatherless, and
> the widow. You shall remember that you were a slave in the land of
> Egypt; therefore I command you to do this. (Deut. 24:19-22 RSV)

Here, again, the Israelites' experience of slavery in Egypt is invoked as a basis for their having compassion on others who later suffered privation. Persons granted gleaning rights could thereby obtain certain basic necessities during harvest times: grain, olives, and grapes.[46]

Somewhat abbreviated versions of the gleaning law appear in Lev. 19: 9-10 and 23:22. In both of these H texts, the named welfare recipients are "the poor" and "the sojourner" or "stranger." The category "poor" probably was intended to encompass not only needy orphans and widows, but also all others who lacked the necessary means of support. Neither of the H laws mentions olive orchards. Leviticus 19:10, like Deut. 24:19-22, also applies to grape harvests. Leviticus 23:22 refers broadly to "the harvest of your land," and therefore may have been meant to include all kinds of harvests: from fields, orchards, and vineyards alike. The Deuteronomic version suggests, but does not expressly say that the designated crops were to be left in the fields, orchards, and vineyards, in order to be gathered by "the sojourner,[47] the fatherless, and the widow" (RSV). However, the H versions explicitly state: "You shall *leave them* for the poor and for the stranger" (RSV). As with many of the requirements set out in the Holiness Code, the reason given for doing what is called for is YHWH's identity and, implicitly, his character and concerns: "I am YHWH your God" (Lev. 19:10; 23:22). This expression not only invoked

---

[46] Since the privilege of gleaning was established by law, it could be considered also a "right" or entitlement. See above, note 9.

[47] Another Deuteronomic law, possibly deriving from the Reform legislation, provides an additional benefit for sojourners: "You shall not eat anything that dies of itself; you may give it to the alien who is within your towns, that he may eat it, or you may sell it to a foreigner; for you are a people holy to YHWH your God" (Deut. 14:21 RSV). Primary concern here is to prohibit Israelites from eating such food, and perhaps only incidentally to provide for sojourners.

divine authority for so acting, but also implies that YHWH's people should be righteous and compassionate, like YHWH himself.[48]

The story of Ruth illustrates the operation of such laws. Ruth, herself, was a stranger or sojourner from the land of Moab. Moreover, she was a widow.[49] She gleans in Boaz's fields during the barley and wheat harvests (Ruth 2:1-23). Apparently she brought home what she had gleaned, as well as what Boaz gave her, for her mother-in-law's use as well as her own. None of the gleaning laws limits the quantities that gleaners might harvest. Presumably some of the food people gleaned during harvest seasons could be set aside and stored for use throughout the rest of the year.

Gleaning, alone, however, probably would not have met all food needs of the poor. Gleaning arrangements, in a way, were like modern "workfare."[50] But not all would have been able to "work" by gleaning fields, orchards, and vineyards, for instance, young children, the aged, and infirm. Other biblical laws required property owners to take additional actions in order to assure that the needy would have enough food, whether or not they were able to work.

### b. Festivals, the third-year tithe, and the seventh and fiftieth years

Biblical law provided that persons in need were to be given food from what had been set aside or gathered for two major annual festivals. The poor also were to benefit from at least two other periodic observances, one of which was expressly designed to assure their continuing support.

### i. The "feast of weeks" and the "feast of booths"

Deuteronomy 16:9-15 calls for observance of both the "feast of weeks," seven weeks following the first of the year's grain harvest,[51] and the seven-day "feast of booths" or "ingathering" in the fall when grain was threshed

---

[48] YHWH is characterized explicitly as "compassionate" in Exodus 22:27. See also Ps. 145:9 and Sir. 18:13, which emphasize YHWH's compassion for all creation. See Chapter Two, Sections B.1.c. and B.2.

[49] Ruth may not have been completely destitute. She and Naomi, her mother-in-law, may have inherited property from their husbands. But no one would have planted her or Naomi's fields while they were in Moab. Both therefore needed assistance. See above Chapter Two, sections A.1.b, and A.2.

[50] For appraisals of contemporary "workfare," see Robert B. Stulberg et al., "Is Workfare Working?" A Panel Discussion Sponsored by the Association of the Bar of the City of New York, April 19, 1999, published in 8 *J L & Pol'y* 107–77 (1999).

[51] See also Deut. 26:1-11.

and wine pressed.[52] The latter celebration evidently was a time for giving thanks and invoking YHWH's blessing on the whole year's agricultural produce and activity (Deut. 16:15). Both festivals were to be celebrated "before YHWH," not only by the immediate family, but also by "your manservant and your maidservant, the Levite . . ., the sojourner, the fatherless and the widow" (Deut. 16:14 RSV).[53] The three latter classes, in effect, constituted "the poor."[54] Providing them food at the annual fall feast of ingathering could be seen as prototype for the latter-day "thanksgiving basket" for the poor or for modern institutional equivalents, such as the Salvation Army's thanksgiving dinner. In contrast to these latter-day, voluntary charitable arrangements, however, sharing food with the poor at these biblical festivals was mandated by law: *all* were to "rejoice" before YHWH.

These provisions reflect certain innovations introduced in connection with the Deuteronomic Reform. Under its terms, all classes of persons now were to celebrate these festivals at the central shrine in Jerusalem.[55] It is difficult to imagine the entire population of Israel actually packing up and traveling to Jerusalem (or any other one place) three times a year,[56] even in times of peace. Earlier versions of the law governing these festivals required only that Israelite *males* appear before YHWH, and said nothing

---

[52] See generally, Theodor H. Gaster, *Festivals of the Jewish Year: A Modern Interpretation and Guide* (Sloan, 1968), pp. 59–98.

[53] See generally, Edward McGlynn Gaffney, Jr., "The Interaction of Biblical Religion with American Constitutional Law," in James Turner Johnson, ed., *The Bible in American Law, Politics, and Political Rhetoric* (Fortress Press/Scholars Press, 1985), p. 93. Compare Deut. 12:10-19, mandating that various other sacrificial offerings presented at the central shrine be shared with sons, daughters, male and female servants, and "the Levite that is within your towns" (RSV). Here there is no mention of sojourners, orphans, or widows.

[54] We see a late-biblical instance of provision for the poor at the feast of weeks (or Pentecost) in Tobit 2:1-2 (RSV): "Upon seeing the abundance of food [prepared in observance of this feast] I said to my son, 'Go and bring whatever poor man of our brethren you may find who is mindful of the Lord . . .'" Here a religious test is applied as to prospective welfare recipients.

[55] Deut. 16:11, 14-15 (RSV) ("you and your son and your daughter, your manservant and your maidservant, the Levite, the sojourner, the fatherless, and the widow who are within your towns"). The formula, "the place which YHWH your God will choose, to make his name dwell there" (RSV), found throughout Deuteronomy 12–19, was intended to designate the Temple in Jerusalem. (The Temple had not yet been constructed when YHWH was giving Moses "the law" in the wilderness between Egypt and the land of Canaan.) As to the cultic, legal, and political innovations associated with the Deuteronomic Reform, see generally, Bernard M. Levinson, *Deuteronomy and the Hermeneutics of Legal Innovation* (Oxford Univ. Press, 1997).

[56] According to Deut. 16:1-9, the Passover, also, now was to be eaten "at the place that YHWH your God will choose."

about their doing so only at a central shrine.[57] Those Levites who previously served as priests at the numerous cult-shrines that had been closed as a result of the Deuteronomic Reform were now deprived of their former livelihood (Deut. 12:2-14). Such Levites, under terms of the RDC law, were free to move to the central shrine at Jerusalem and to continue serving as priests there (Deut. 18:6-8). But those Levites who remained in towns and rural areas where they had lived prior to the Reform were now at least temporarily unemployed, and consequently, often found themselves among the ranks of the needy. Thus under the new Deuteronomic laws, Levites were to be provided for along with "the sojourner, the fatherless, and the widow." Other RDC laws make explicit provisions for the needs of Levites.[58]

The feast of weeks and the feast of booths were annual festivals. In addition there was a triennial tithe which was intended specifically for the benefit of persons in need. The seventh and possibly the fiftieth year celebrations also were meant to provide food for various classes of persons in need of assistance.

### ii. The third-year tithe

The third-year, or triennial tithing law is found twice in the Revised Deuteronomic Code, but not elsewhere. Both versions indicate that the recipients of this tithe were to enjoy its benefits at their respective local towns without having to go so far as Jerusalem. These recipients included Levites, sojourners, orphans, and widows:

---

[57] See Exod. 23:14-17; 34:18-24. Prior to the Deuteronomic reform, these festivals probably had been observed at the many local shrines scattered throughout the lands of Israel and Judah. Deuteronomy 16:16-17 evidently embodies vestiges of such earlier law, but without explaining how these festivals were to be observed only by males and at the same time by all the others mentioned in Deut. 16:11 and 14. The provisions in H for these three festivals do not indicate whether males only or the whole population were to participate in them. Lev. 23:4-21, 37-41. The H law says nothing about either a central shrine, or about including sojourners, orphans, widows, Levites or other needy persons in the celebrations. The Holiness Code probably antedates the Deuteronomic Reform. Here as in several other instances, the Deuteronomic law (here, probably RDC) expresses a greater measure of compassion for those in need than appears in similar provisions found in other biblical law codes. The PC contains elaborate requirements for conducting these and other festivals. However, PC laws say nothing about including the poor, sojourners, orphans, or widows among those who were to partake of the offerings on these or other occasions. See, e.g., Num. 29–30. Nor does the Passover law, found mainly in the PC, include any provisions requiring sharing food with the poor.

[58] In addition to Deut. 16:11 and 14, see also Deut. 12:12-19; 14:27, 29; and 26:11-13.

> At the end of every three years you shall bring forth all the tithe of your produce in the same year, and lay it up within your towns; and the Levite, because he has no portion or inheritance with you, and the sojourner, the fatherless, and the widow, who are within your towns, shall come and eat and be filled, that YHWH your God may bless you in all the work of your hands that you do. (Deut. 14:28-29)

This triennial tithe would be "laid up" in each town, thereby establishing a kind of food bank for the needy. Very likely arrangements were made to store those types of produce that could be preserved and to distribute them over an extended time frame, perhaps even stretching over the entire 3-year period until the next triennial tithing.[59] Thus the poor would not be dependent wholly upon what they could glean or receive at the two annual festivals.

The third-year tithing law, is repeated in similar terms in Deuteronomy 26:12. Here the purpose is clearly stated: produce tithed every third year is to be given to "the Levite, the sojourner, the fatherless and the widow, [so] that they may eat within your towns and be filled." The following three verses required that, as a part of the triennial observance, each householder was to recite a ritual oath, or oral affidavit averring that he had in fact given the full tithe as prescribed by law. The oath concludes by invoking continued divine favor:

> I have removed the sacred portion out of my house, and moreover I have given it to the Levite, the sojourner, the fatherless, and the widow, according to all thy commandment which thou has commanded me; I have not transgressed any of thy commandments, neither have I forgotten them; I have not eaten of the tithe while I was mourning, or removed any of it while I was unclean, or offered any of it to the dead; I have obeyed the voice of YHWH my God, I have done according to all that thou hast commanded me. Look down from thy holy habitation, from heaven, and bless thy people Israel and the ground which thou hast given us, as thou didst swear to our fathers, a land flowing with milk and honey. (Deut. 26:13-15 RSV)

---

[59] In biblical times it evidently was possible to store grain for many years. Genesis 41 describes the 7-year grain storage program Joseph established in Egypt. See also Lev. 25:20-22, which contemplates storing one year's crop for two additional years.

Here, as elsewhere in Deuteronomic tradition, it was understood that YHWH's future blessings were contingent upon his people's remaining faithful to him and keeping his commandments.

*iii. The Sabbatical Year*

Laws regarding a special seventh-year celebration are found in Exodus 23:10-11 and Leviticus 25:1-7.[60] The Exodus law establishes a sabbatical year of rest not only for the land, but also and particularly for the benefit of the poor:

> For six years you shall sow your land and gather in its yield; but the seventh year you shall let it rest and lie fallow, that the poor of your people may eat; and what they leave the wild beasts may eat. You shall do likewise with your vineyard, and with your olive orchard. (Exod. 23:10-11 RSV)

Neither landowners, nor, it seems, their families or servants, were to plant, reap, or gather crops this seventh year. Not only the poor, but also wildlife were to enjoy this year's produce. Unsown fields would not be likely to yield the usual harvests; but some crops, especially grains, evidently were expected to reseed themselves, at least to some extent. Vineyards and olive orchards might yield in near normal abundance. The version of this law in Leviticus 25 is similar in substance, though it does not mention olive orchards.[61] Possibly this H law was intended to amend the Exodus version, so that those who owned olive trees might be exempt and thus free to harvest and keep their precious yield for themselves every year.

The Leviticus version explicitly bars Israelites from reaping "what grows of itself," and from gathering grapes from their "undressed vines" during the sabbatical year (Lev. 25:5 RSV); yet it also assures readers that "the sabbath of the land shall provide food" for them (Lev. 25:6 RSV). How such food would be gathered is not said. Leviticus 25:20-22 appears to be a somewhat later attempt to address this problem. Here it is proposed (or predicted) that the sixth year would yield enough produce for 3 years: the sixth, seventh, and eighth. Thus the sixth year would afford a triple harvest, so that it would be unnecessary to sow, reap, or gather

---

[60] See generally, Weinfeld, *Social Justice* (cited in note 1), pp. 152–78.
[61] In its terms, Leviticus 25:1-7 applies only to fields and vineyards.

during the seventh year. Any reduction in eighth-year yields resulting from the fallow seventh would be offset by the remaining sixth-year's surplus. It is not said how this arrangement was expected to affect gleaning provisions and celebrations of the annual harvest festivals, or how it would be integrated with the third-year tithe requirement.[62] The Holiness Code version does not mention "the poor" as such. But it does name as other recipients of the seventh-year bounty the land-owner's "male and female slaves," "hired servant," and also "the sojourner."[63]

It may be conjectured that the Deuteronomic Reform law of Deuteronomy 14:28-29 introduced the third-year tithe as a substitute for the sabbatical year. Seven years would have been a long time for the poor to wait for the next supply of essentials. Moreover, unlike the sabbatical year, the third-year tithe was to be "laid up" or stored for the benefit of the needy. It may be significant that earlier CC and H laws provide for the sabbatical year but not for the third-year tithe; while the later RDC law makes no mention of the sabbatical year, but does establish the third-year tithe program expressly for the benefit of those in need of assistance. The problematics of integrating the sabbatical year with the third-year tithe also suggests that these two institutions were not observed contemporaneously, but rather that the one was meant to replace the other.

*iv. The year of jubilee*

The Holiness Code alone provides for a fiftieth year celebration: the "year of jubilee." (Lev. 25:8-17). Like the seventh-year observance, the year of jubilee, too, was to be a time of rest for those who worked the land:

> A jubilee shall that fiftieth year be to you; in it you shall neither sow, nor reap what grows of itself, nor gather the grapes from the undressed vines. For it is a jubilee; it shall be holy to you; you shall eat what it yields out of the field. (Lev. 25:11-12 RSV)

Again, it is unclear how the people were to eat what was produced if they were not first permitted to reap or gather it. Perhaps it was understood that during the fiftieth year, slaves, servants, and sojourners also were to

---

[62] The third and seventh years would coincide every 21 years.
[63] In addition, both wildlife ("the beasts") and domestic animals ("cattle") would partake of this bounty. For them, *all* the land's yield "shall be for food" (Lev. 25:7).

enjoy the land's yield, as was provided explicitly in the Sabbatical year law at Leviticus 25:6-7. Or it may have been thought sufficient for such persons to enjoy that privilege on the forty-ninth year without doing again on the fiftieth.[64]

### 2. Assisting the Poor in Other Ways: Promoting the General Welfare

As has been seen, biblical laws establish a number of arrangements whereby the community and its members were instructed to provide food for the poor. A few other laws speak more generally of aiding or supporting the poor. Typically these laws set out affirmative duties on the part of all Israelites. Again, the "poor" would have included those unable to work because of age or disability, and, typically, widows, orphans, and sojourners who did not own property or were unemployed.

#### a. *Opening your hand to the poor*

One of these laws is found in Deuteronomy 15:7-11. The fact that its content is unrelated to the Deuteronomic Reform suggests that this provision may derive from older Deuteronomic law, possibly the original Deuteronomic Code. It also appears to antedate the Deuteronomic Historian's editing of the text. Traces of such editing appear in Deuteronomy 15:4-5, which promises that there would be no poor among the people of Israel if only they would keep the commandments. Deuteronomy 15:7-11, on the other hand, presumes that there are, and always will be, poor and needy among them:

> If there is among you a poor man, one of your brethren, in any of your towns within the land which YHWH your God gives you, you shall not

---

[64] According to Leviticus 25:8-11, the year of jubilee would follow immediately after the forty-ninth year, which would have been a sabbatical year under the provisions of Lev. 25:1-7. Thus there would be no cultivation or sowing during either the forty-ninth or the fiftieth year. It is not clear that the fiftieth-year observance was meant to provide food for the poor. Nor is it certain that the Jubilee year's provisions were ever actually carried out. See generally Raymond Westbrook, "Jubilee Laws," 6 *Israel L Rev.* 209 (1971). Westbrook suggests that the jubilee laws are found only in "a late stratum" of the Holiness Code, and notes that these laws are "not at all mentioned elsewhere in the Bible." *Id.*, p. 225. Numbers 36:4 at most is a vague and passing reference. As to other possible traces of the Jubilee year see Jeffrey A. Fager, *Land Tenure and the Biblical Jubilee*, Journal for the Study of the Old Testament, Supp. no. 155, pp. 33–36 (Sheffield Academic Press, 1993) (finding that such traces fail to show that the Jubilee year was ever actually observed). But see Weinfeld, *Social Justice* (cited in note 1), p. 178.

harden your heart or shut your hand against your poor brother, but you shall open your hand to him, and lend him sufficient for his need, whatever it may be. . . . You shall give to him freely, and your heart shall not be grudging when you give to him; because for this YHWH your God will bless you in all your work and in all that you undertake. For the poor will never cease out of the land; therefore, I command you, You shall open wide your hand to your brother, to the needy and to the poor, in the land. (Deut. 15:7-11 RSV)

This law requires that Israelites assist those among them to full the extent of their need, "whatever it may be" (v. 8). Whether such assistance was to have been in the form of a loan or a gift is not indicated. If loans were not repaid by the seventh year, they were to be forgiven (Deut. 15:1-6, 9).[65] The law here presumes that there will always be poor Israelites (or Judahites) in the land. But that prospect is no excuse for failing to respond generously. Instead, it is a further reason Israelites should be ready to "open wide [their] hand to [their] brother." Such concern is echoed in the wisdom writings.[66]

---

[65] Deuteronomy 15:9 cautions against withholding assistance to a "poor brother" just because the seventh year, when all debts would be forgiven or redeemed, was near. This seventh year release from debt, described in Deut. 15:1-2, would have benefited the poor, but was not established solely for their benefit. It applied to all Israelites, but not to foreigners (Deut. 12:3). See generally, Brin, *Studies* (cited in note 10), pp. 86–87.

[66] See, e.g., Prov. 14:21b (RSV) ("[H]appy is he who is kind to the poor"), and 19:17 (RSV) ("He who is kind to the poor lends to YHWH, and he will repay him for his deed"). And see Prov. 21:13; 28:27; 31:20. See also Job 31:16-20, where Job recites his good deeds on behalf of the poor, widows, orphans, and sojourners. See also Sir. 3:30; 4:1, 3-5, 8; 7:10, 32; 12:3; 17:22; 29:8-9, 12-13; 34:21; 35:2; 40:17, 24; and Tob. 1:16-17; 4:7-11, 16-17; 12: 8-9. A few prophetic texts likewise point to individual responsibility for sheltering the poor and clothing the naked. See, e.g., Isa. 58:7; and Ezek. 18:7, 16.

The author of the epilogue to the story of Job lampoons the practice of giving gifts *to the wealthy* (or "welfare for the rich"). Only *after* Job's colossal fortunes had been restored (and then doubled) do his friends and relations—all of whom had been conspicuous by their absence throughout his time of suffering—come to offer him sympathy and comfort, and *only then* did each of them give Job "a piece of money and a ring of gold" (Job 42:10-11). See also Prov. 22:16 ("He who . . . gives to the rich, will only come to want"). See also Prov. 14:20 and 19:4. Compare Ivins (cited in Introduction to Part III, note 12), pp. 17–19, and Michael Harrington, "Keynesianism for the Rich" (ch. 5), in his book, *The Next Left* (Henry Holt & Co., 1986).

Several NT texts also call for giving to or otherwise acting for the benefit of the poor. See, e.g., Mt. 19:21 = Mk 10:21 = Lk. 18:22; Mt. 25:31-45 (the hungry, thirsty, strangers, naked, sick, and imprisoned); Luke 6:30a ("Give to everyone who begs from you"); 12:33a ("Sell your possessions, and give alms"); Acts 2:44-45; 4:32-35; Heb. 13:16; James 2:1-6, 14-17; 1 Jn 3:17. As to Jesus' sayings in Luke, see Richard H. Hiers, "Friends by Unrighteous Mammon: The Eschatological Proletariat," 38 *JAAR* 30–36 (1970).

### b. When a "brother" becomes poor

The obligation to provide *food* for the impoverished "brother" has already been considered. In addition, Leviticus 25 groups four sets of requirements as to what must be done if or when "a brother" becomes poor, in order to provide for his other needs or interests. All these laws are part of the Holiness Code's Jubilee year legislation. In this context, "brother" seems to refer to a fellow, male Israelite, not only a genetic sibling. The "brother" who becomes poor is to be assisted, but he also has his own responsibilities and options.

The first of these laws, Leviticus 25:25-28, says what is to be done if a "brother becomes poor and sells his property." In this case, his "next of kin" (or *go'el*) "shall come and redeem what his brother has sold" (RSV).[67] But what is to be done if there is no one to "redeem," that is, buy back the property? Two possibilities are presented. If the poor brother later becomes prosperous, he, himself, may buy it back, the price being adjusted in some way (Lev. 25:26-27).[68] But even if he lacks the wherewithal to repurchase the property, it will be returned to him anyway in the year of jubilee (Lev. 25:28).[69]

What happens if the "brother" becomes poor but has neither property to sell nor other adequate source of income? In that case, supporting one's brother was not a "*mitzvah*," in the modern, popular sense of an optional good deed. It was an obligation under the law. In these circumstances, the law addressed the "brother's" relatives as follows:

> And if your brother becomes poor, and cannot maintain himself with you, you shall maintain him; as a stranger and a sojourner he shall live with you. Take no interest from him or increase, but fear your God; that your brother may live beside you. (Lev. 25:35-36 RSV)

---

[67] It has been suggested that this law is illustrated in the story of Ruth, where the *go'el* (or nearer kinsman) and Boaz are discussing which of them should redeem the property in question. But in that story, "the brother" had not become poor; he had died. Naomi and Ruth were widows, but not necessarily poor. They were planning to sell the property inherited from their husbands, but had not yet sold it. Of course, by purchasing it, the *go'el* or Boaz would have obviated the need for subsequent redemption.

[68] See generally, Raymond Westbrook, "Redemption of Land," 6 *Israel L Rev* 367 (1971).

[69] There is no indication what would happen if the "brother" were to die before the Jubilee year. Would the property be returned to his heirs, or would it remain in the hands of the buyer? The fact that such obviously critical questions are not addressed suggests that the jubilee law was more a visionary ideal than an actual practice. See above, note 64.

Here "brother" probably means fellow-Israelite, perhaps female as well as male. Other Israelites may sell food to such a "brother," but they may not make a profit from such sales (Lev. 25:36-37). Rather, such sales must be at cost. To that extent, the "brother" would be spared going into deeper debt.[70] It may be noted that this law does not distinguish any circumstances leading to poverty under which the "brother's" fault might relieve relatives of responsibility for assisting him. Moreover, there is no set limit to the period of time during which an indigent "brother" might continue to receive assistance. Evidently what was called for here was basic support or maintenance, which presumably would include food, clothing and shelter.[71] The implicit rationale for this law is that the well-being of the impoverished "brother" is more important than making money; thus it would be wrong to seek to gain from the brother's misfortune. Modern laws prohibiting profiteering from sales to disaster victims are based on a similar rationale. Leviticus 25:38 adds an explicit "motive clause": "I am YHWH your God, who brought you forth out of the land of Egypt to give you the land of Canaan, and to be your God" (RSV). Since YHWH had given his people the entire land of Canaan—thus everything they have—they should not begrudge giving something to those who were poor among them.

A "brother" who "becomes poor" might also choose to sell himself as a slave or servant (Lev. 25:39-55). Apparently in such case, the "brother's" children also would become the buyer's slaves or servants.[72] What is to be done next depends on whether "the brother" had sold himself to a fellow-Israelite, or to a "stranger" or sojourner. If the sale was to a fellow-Israelite, the buyer "shall not make him serve as a slave"; rather, he must treat the "brother" as "a hired servant and as a sojourner. . . . [The buyer] shall not rule over him with harshness, but shall fear [his] God" (Lev. 25: 39-40, 43 RSV). It is unclear whether the "brother" would receive wages for his services in addition to maintenance. Curiously, there are no provisions for redemption by kinsmen when a "brother" sells himself to another

---

[70] See above, notes 14 and 15 and accompanying text.
[71] Deuteronomy 15:1-3 requires creditors to release all "neighbor's" or "brother's" debts "at the end of seven years." The debtors in question would not necessarily be poor; in fact, Deut. 15:4 contemplates the absence of poor in the land. This law evidently applied to borrowed money or property, not to those who had sold themselves into service. Modern bankruptcy law could be compared to seventh-year debt forgiveness. Both provisions allow the debtor to make a fresh start, rather than remain forever burdened by obligations to creditors.
[72] See Lev. 25:41, 54. The status of the brother's wife is not indicated.

Israelite.[73] Moreover, there is no indication that such a "brother" might later repurchase himself or his own freedom. However, such "servants" might not be sold as slaves (Lev. 25:42). And when the Jubilee year comes, the brother/servant is to be freed to "return to the possession of his fathers" (Lev. 25:41 RSV).[74]

Somewhat different rules apply if the "brother" who has become poor sells himself to a stranger or sojourner (Lev. 25:47-55). In that case, the poor "brother" can be redeemed by one of his relatives; or if he "grows rich, he may redeem himself" (Lev. 25:48-49 RSV).[75] The redemption price varies with the number of years remaining until the year of jubilee. If the poor "brother" who has sold himself to a stranger is not redeemed before the Jubilee year, he shall then be released, as in the case of the "brother" sold to a fellow-Israelite. The sojourner/owner, in the meantime, must "not rule with harshness over him," but rather, must treat him "as a servant hired year by year."[76] To that extent, this law accords with the principle embedded in several biblical codes: the law for the sojourner shall be the same as that for the native.[77] However, the "brother" sold to a sojourner might be redeemed or might redeem himself prior to the Jubilee year. It is not said that the "brother" sold to a fellow-Israelite might do so. Consequently, if keeping such a servant until the Jubilee year was advantageous to his master, an Israelite master would be in a more favorable position than an alien or sojourner master.

Whether the jubilee laws were ever put into effect is in doubt.[78] Up to 49 years would have been a long time to wait for freedom, especially given presumably shorter life expectancies in biblical times. How did the Leviticus 25 provisions for release in the Jubilee year relate to provisions in Exodus 21:1-6 and Deuteronomy 15:12-18 that called for release of a Hebrew slave after 6 years of service? If the Leviticus 25 provisions were written after the Deuteronomic law, the shift would have been in the

---

[73] Compare Exod. 21:7-8 (redemption of a daughter sold as a slave or servant), discussed in text accompanying notes 115–122.

[74] Under terms of Lev. 25:25-28, the "brother's" property would be restored to him, debt-free, in the Jubilee year.

[75] The named relatives who might so redeem him include, in the order listed: a brother, uncle, cousin, or "a near kinsman belonging to his family."

[76] Lev. 25:53 (RSV). It is unclear whether the understanding was that the brother/servant would be paid wages. That he might somehow grow rich enough to redeem himself (Lev. 25:49) suggests either that he would have received wages—as might be expected in the case of a *hired* servant—or else that he would have had some time free for independent economic pursuits.

[77] See above, note 30 and accompanying text.

[78] See above, note 64.

direction of replacing these earlier, more liberal or humane provisions.[79] But if—as seems more likely—Deuteronomy 15:12-18 was part of the law codified in connection with the Deuteronomic Reform, its more compassionate mandates would have been meant to supersede the H jubilee law on this point.[80] Even if the Jubilee year legislation was never effectuated in biblical times, it represents an important underlying principle or ideal. As one commentator observed:

> The message is that indebtedness or ownership structures should be changed when they become an obstacle to achieving or maintaining a sane society, which must be made up of free people.[81]

In normative and relational terms,[82] the Jubilee year legislation depicted a society whose members were under obligation to respect the interests or welfare of others in the community who were relatively impoverished or otherwise disadvantaged. This obligation is grounded theocentrically, on the faith-understanding that YHWH (or God) intends the well-being of his community, regardless of the economic condition or class and national origin of its members.

### c. *Levirate marriage: caring for widows*

The law of levirate marriage (Deut. 25:5-10) was expressly intended to preserve the name of a man who died without having a son. The widow's brother-in-law (*levir*, Latin) was to marry her, and their first son would "succeed to the name" of the deceased in order "that his name may not be blotted out of Israel" (Deut. 25:6).[83] This son probably would eventually inherit the deceased's property, though this arrangement is

---

[79] See Westbrook, "Jubilee Law" (cited in note 64), pp. 221–24. Patrick speculates that the H legislation (Lev. 25:35-43) was later than both the Exodus and Deuteronomic laws, that "slave owners were not abiding by this older law and that H was attempting to work out a compromise," Patrick, *Old Testament Law* (cited in note 1), p. 184.

[80] See Section B.3.b.i. of this chapter.

[81] de Vries, *Champions* (cited in Introduction to Part III, note 14), p. 174. "Sane" is a crypto-normative expression, that is, a normative judgment in the guise of naturalistic, and in this instance, psychological, language. Here "sane" functions as surrogate for "good." See generally, article cited below in note 82.

[82] See Richard H. Hiers, "Normative and Ostensibly Norm-Neutral Conventions in Contemporary Judicial Discourse," 14 *Legal Stud. Forum* 107 (1990).

[83] See also Ruth 4:10. And see above, Chapter Two, Sections B.1.c. and B.2.

not specified in the law or clearly indicated in relevant narrative traditions.[84]

Additionally, levirate marriage functioned, and may well have been intended to provide for the widow's welfare. Not only would she again have a husband to look after her needs; she would also have a son, who in time would assist her should she survive the *levir*-husband.[85] Several indications of this purpose or function appear in the law and the narratives.

The legal text refers to the *duty* which the decedent's brother owes *the widow*. The provision is clearly for the widow's benefit: the *levir* is obliged to "take her as his wife." As such, she would regain her status as a married person. The new husband presumably would care for all her needs in addition to fathering a son for her who would, among other things, carry on the family name. Moreover, if the *levir* fails to make her his wife, the widow may bring the matter before the "elders at the gate," and testify as to his refusal.[86] The elders must then undertake to persuade the *levir* to perform his duty. If they fail to do so, the widow herself is permitted—if not required—to humiliate the recalcitrant *levir* by spitting in his face "in the presence of the elders" (Deut. 25:9).[87] These provisions suggest that levirate marriage was intended to benefit not only the deceased by perpetuating his name, but also the widow, who was hereby authorized to apply such extraordinary social pressure in order to protect her own interest in being once more married. In the story of Judah and Tamar (Genesis 38), the widow, Tamar, acting in her own interests, initiates a different course of action in order to obtain a husband and offspring after Judah, her father-in-law, failed to give her his surviving son in marriage.[88]

---

[84] Some interpreters have suggested that in the story of Ruth, the nearer kinsman or *go'el* declined to purchase his deceased relative's property because, if thereby also compelled to marry the Ruth, a son from this marriage would eventually inherit that property and the *go'el* or his estate would lose the price of its purchase. See above, Chapter Two.

[85] See Ruth 4:15. Here it is said of the levirate *son*: "He shall be to you a restorer of life and a nourisher of your old age."

[86] Here, under biblical law, a woman has legal standing to testify in or before a court. See also Deut. 21:18-21 (both parents to testify to "the elders . . . at the gate" against an ungovernable son); and Deut. 22:13-21 (both parents of a new bride charged with prior promiscuity to present evidence to "the elders" in "the gate"). See also Tob. 7:14 (both Raguel and his wife, Edna, set their seals to a marriage contract). The question of women's legal competence in biblical times is discussed briefly by Silvia Schroer, "Feminist Reconstruction," cited above in note 32, pp. 122-23.

[87] She also was to pull the sandal from his foot and, after spitting in his face, declare, "so shall it be done to the man who does not build up his brother's house." Deut. 25:9 (RSV); see also Deut. 25:10.

[88] Disguising herself as a prostitute, Tamar easily seduced Judah, who thereby unwittingly substituted for his sons in the role of *levir*.

Judah's acknowledgment that Tamar had acted properly, given his own failure to do so, likewise suggests that levirate marriage was meant to provide for the widow's welfare.

The story of Ruth provides further clues suggesting that the purpose, as well as the function, of levirate marriage was to provide for the widow. For some time, Ruth had been gleaning in the fields of Boaz, a kinsman of Naomi's deceased husband, Elimelech. Ruth had married one of Elimelech's and Naomi's two sons, and had been widowed subsequently by that son's death. The other son also had died, so there was no surviving brother-in-law to marry her. Naomi, concerned for Ruth's welfare, now advises her how to proceed in order to prompt Boaz to "do the part of the next of kin" (Ruth 3:3-4, 13 RSV). She begins her advice as follows: "My daughter, should I not seek a home for you, that it may be well with you?" (Ruth 3.1 RSV). Clearly Naomi understood that the levirate arrangement—here in the form of marriage to a near kinsman—would benefit Ruth. Among other things, it would provide her "a home."[89]

In Ruth, the law of levirate marriage may be combined or blended with an instance of surrogate parenthood. Naomi, the older of the widowed women in the story, possibly is too old to have children, yet, arguably, she is the first in line for levirate marriage.[90] As the story unfolds, however, Boaz marries Ruth, the younger widow, who is definitely of child-bearing

---

[89] Some scholars urge that the procedures described in Ruth 3–4 are not properly characterized as levirate marriage, since, for one thing, here the decedent's nearest kinsman rather than brother has the duty to marry the widow. The practice described in Ruth probably should be regarded as either an early version or a later extension of the law of levirate marriage set out in Deut. 25:5-10. As in the story of Judah and Tamar, in Genesis 38, since no *levir* was available, the family responsibility fell upon the deceased's nearest male kinsman. In the case of Tamar, the deceased's father (unknowingly) filled that role. In Ruth's case, her late husband's father also was dead, so the duty devolved upon the deceased husband's nearest, surviving, adult kinsman. The plot in the story of Ruth is complicated by the fact that Boaz is not the nearest kinsman. Boaz—who wishes to marry Ruth—undertakes, before the elders at the gate, to induce this nearest kinsman, commonly designated "the *go'el*" to waive his claim by hinting that no one would want to marry "*the widow*." See generally, Daube (cited below in note 90), and Donald A. Leggett, *The Levirate and Goel Institutions in the Old Testament: With Special Attention to the Book of Ruth* (Mack Pub, 1974). See Chapter Two, Section B.2.

[90] See Ruth 1:11-13. Curiously, it is not a question here of Naomi's marrying her brother-in-law or her deceased husband's nearest kinsman. Instead, when Naomi contemplates the unlikely prospect of remarriage in order to produce sons whom her widowed daughters-in-law might eventually take as husbands, she refers simply to "a husband," as if the critical matter would be for her daughters-in-law to marry—were it possible—*her* sons. For the suggestion that in the story, the widow first expected to marry a *levir*, kinsman, or *go'el* was *Naomi*, see David Daube, *Ancient Jewish Law* (Brill: 1981), pp. 37–43.

age. Later, Naomi's friends, on learning that Ruth has borne a son, say to Naomi:

> Blessed be YHWH, who has not left *you* this day without next of kin; and may his name be renowned in Israel! He shall be to *you* a restorer of life and a nourisher of *your* old age; for your daughter-in-law who loves you, who is more to you than seven sons, has borne him. (Ruth 4:14-15)[91]

Here it is not Boaz who is Naomi's *go'el* (redeeming kinsman), but Ruth's and Boaz's son. Levirate marriage thus provided Ruth with a husband and a home; it also provided Naomi with a "next of kin," a "restorer of life" and a "nourisher" of her "old age." It reasonably may be inferred that under the law and practice of levirate marriage, the levirate son was expected to look after the welfare of his mother, should she again be widowed, and also for any widowed grandmother.[92]

### 3. Provisions for Slaves

The Holiness Code stipulates that when a "brother" sells himself either to a fellow Israelite or to a sojourner, he is to be treated as a hired servant or sojourner, not as a slave. Moreover, he must be released in the year of jubilee, if not earlier.[93] On the other hand, non-Israelite slaves along with any of their children born on the slave-owner's land, are treated as property, and may be bequeathed as such to heirs (Lev. 25:44-46).[94] Non-Israelite slaves are the only persons characterized as "property" in biblical law.[95] Even so, non-Israelite slaves enjoyed some consideration as persons

---

[91] Emphasis supplied. See also Ruth 4:17a: "And the women of the neighborhood gave him a name, saying 'A son has been born to *Naomi*'" (Emphasis added).

[92] The law and practice of levirate marriage apparently had been abandoned by the time of early Christianity. (But see Mt. 22:23-33 = Mk 12:18-23 = Lk. 20:27-40, which report a question that hypothetically recalls the practice of levirate marriage.) However, children, grandchildren, and other relatives still were expected to care for widows. See 1 Tim. 5:3-8, 16. The church also would provide assistance (Acts 6:1-6; 1 Tim. 5:16), at any rate to righteous and elderly widows. 1 Tim. 5:9-10. Younger widows were encouraged to remarry. 1 Tim. 5:11-15.

[93] Lev. 25:39-43, 47-55. See Section B.2.b. of this chapter.

[94] As an example, see Jdt. 8:7: Her deceased husband had "left her . . . men and women slaves." Possibly non-Israelite slaves might also pass to heiresses under the law of intestate succession in Numbers 27. See Chapter Two, Sections A and B.

[95] Exodus 21:21 probably refers to non-Israelite slaves. Hebrew slaves are distinguished in Exod. 21:1-6 and 21:7-11, where they clearly are recognized as having certain rights or

with interests or rights. Most of the legislation mandating special protections for slaves, however, concerned Hebrew slaves. General provisions with respect to slaves are considered first.

### a. Humane treatment of slaves generally

Sabbath day observance was ordained not only to honor YHWH, but also to provide rest for the human (and animal) members of the community. This community evidently included servants or slaves.[96] The term translated sometimes as "servant" (Heb. *'ebed*) can also mean bondman or slave. It is likely, though not certain, that slaves, like hired servants and sojourners, were meant to enjoy the weekly sabbath day of rest (and refreshment, Exod. 23:12), along with others.

Slaves, both male and female, were among those who were to have the benefit of the land's yield during the sabbatical year (Lev. 25:6). Here, slaves are mentioned along with hired servants. Nothing in this text suggests that the provision was meant to apply only to Hebrew slaves.

One other law in its terms applied to all slaves.[97] This was the biblical fugitive slave law:

> You shall not give up to his master a slave who has escaped from his master to you; he shall dwell with you, in your midst, in the place which he shall choose within one of your towns, where it pleases him best; you shall not oppress him. (Deut. 23:15-16 RSV)[98]

As the Exodus story is told, the Israelites themselves were descended from escaped slaves—a story so familiar, perhaps, that there was no need to include a "motive clause" by way of reminder or rationale for allowing escaped slaves to remain free. This provision differs significantly from its counterpart in the Code of Hammurabi, under which sheltering

---

interests as persons. Boecker speculates that the majority of slaves—presumably meaning non-Israelite slaves—"were recruited from the ranks of prisoners of war," Boecker, *Administration of Justice* (cited in note 1), p. 157. Burrows, *Outline* (cited in note 41), p. 303, nn. 39 and 40, lists biblical texts indicating that foreign slaves were acquired both by capture (Deut. 20:10-18; Josh. 9:3-27; Judg. 1:28, 30, 33, 35) and by purchase (Gen. 17:12; Exod. 12:44; Lev. 25:44-46).

[96] Exod. 20:8-11; 23:12; Deut. 5:12-15.

[97] So also Patrick, *Old Testament Law* (cited in note 1), p. 133.

[98] Under this law, arguably, Paul ought not have returned Onesimus to Philemon. See Phm. vv. 10-21. Perhaps Paul felt the law no longer binding. However, there is no clear evidence that Onesimus actually was a "runaway slave," though commentators often so assert. At any rate, Paul called on Philemon to give Onesimus his freedom.

runaway slaves was a serious and possibly capital offense (CH 15, 16, 19). Under the biblical law, the escaped slave is entitled not only to freedom; he also may live "in your midst," wherever he wishes.[99] There was to be no segregated ghetto for ex-slaves. Deuteronomy 23:16 expressly mandates open housing: the former slave may live "wherever it pleases him best." If originally from another country, such a former slave would, in effect, become a sojourner. Additionally, like other sojourners, he is to be free from "oppression," which, without further qualification, probably meant any kind of harassment or invidious treatment.

Slaves, of course, might be set free if their owner chose to release them. Judith freed her maid-slave shortly before her own death—an action clearly regarded as further evidence of her high character (Jdt. 16:23). Whether her slave was an Israelite or a foreigner is not indicated. There are no other biblical instances of voluntary manumission. However, manumission was mandatory if masters abused their slaves in certain ways. As a matter of law, a slave—male or female—*must* be set free if his or her master strikes the slave thereby causing loss of an eye or a tooth (Exod. 21:26-27).[100] Thus even non-Israelite slaves were considered more than mere physical "property." Provision for freeing a slave under such circumstances is unique, in the ancient Near East, to biblical law.[101] Additionally, as will be seen, Hebrew (or Israelite) slaves were entitled to release after specified periods of service.

### b. Special protections for "Hebrew" slaves

Laws governing the rights of Israelites who become poor and sell themselves as slaves or servants (Lev. 25:39-55) already have been

---

[99] See generally, Hamilton, *Social Justice* (cited in note 1), pp. 117–21. Hamilton suggests that the biblical fugitive slave law, which allows a slave, whether Israelite or foreigner, to "escape with impunity . . . calls into question the legitimacy of slavery everywhere, even within Israel." *Id.*, pp. 119–20.

[100] See Yaron, "Biblical Law" (cited in note 15), p. 36: "As further examples of biblical rules as yet without parallel in the ancient Near East, we may point to a series of provisions concerning slaves . . . [in Exodus and Deuteronomy]. They all display a markedly humane tendency." Exodus 21:20 imposes "liability upon a master who beats his slave or maid-servant to death." Another instance Yaron cites is Exod. 21:26-27.

[101] See Boecker, *Administration of Justice* (cited in note 1), pp. 162–63: "There is no prescription in the CH corresponding with Exod. 21:26-27. In fact, no other ancient eastern code discusses an injury to his own slave by the slave's master. They all regard the slave essentially as a possession, damage to which [only] reduces its value for the slave owner . . . There is practically no trace [in the biblical law] of the idea that the slave is property of his owner. He has rights of his own, particularly, the right to bodily integrity."

considered.¹⁰² Two other laws also were intended to protect the interests of Hebrew slaves. The first of these evidently was meant to apply when Hebrew slaves were sold involuntarily, though under their terms these laws could also apply when persons sold themselves as slaves. The second, found only in the CC, provides certain protections for Israelite women sold as slaves by their fathers.

*i. Six years of service, then free*

In his illuminating article on biblical consumer credit law, Paul Rasor notes that biblical law "does not expressly authorize or establish debt slavery," but rather assumes the existence of that custom or practice.¹⁰³ Biblical law then proceeds to provide certain protections for those affected. It is likely that many if not most Hebrew slaves were debt slaves.¹⁰⁴

According to Exodus 21:1-6, and also Deuteronomy 15:12-18, Hebrew slaves were entitled to their freedom after they had served 6 years.¹⁰⁵ These two versions of the law contain several important differences, and it may well be that provisions in the later Deuteronomic Code were meant to replace those in Exodus.¹⁰⁶ The earlier, Covenant Code, version

---

¹⁰² See Section B.2.b. of this chapter.
¹⁰³ See Rasor, "Biblical Roots" (cited in Introduction to Part III, note 14), p. 177.
¹⁰⁴ *Id.* See also Cohn, *Human Rights* (cited in note 9), p. 56: "A 'Hebrew' . . . could become a slave either by order of the court on conviction of theft, if he was unable to make restitution (Exod. 22:2), or by giving himself into bondage because of his inability to pay his debts (Lev. 25:39) . . . . It was against the law to acquire a Hebrew slave in any other way (Lev. 25:42)." But see Jer. 34:13-14 (referring to the sale of Hebrew slaves). Cohn notes related texts at Prov. 22:7; Isa. 50:1; and Amos 2:6 and 8:6 (condemning those who would buy or sell the poor and needy for silver or a pair of shoes or sandals). Burrows, *Outline* (cited in note 41), p. 303, n. 38, identifies other texts indicating voluntary or involuntary enslavement for debt: Lev. 25:47-55; 2 Kgs 4:1; and Neh. 5:5-8.
¹⁰⁵ Since neither law addresses the question, it apparently made no difference whether the slave's owner was an Israelite or a sojourning foreigner. But see Jer. 34:14, which could be read to mean that a Hebrew might be owned by a non-Israelite, and that only Israelite slave owners were obliged to free Hebrew slaves after 6 years. It could be imagined that slave owners might have tried to evade this law by selling their slaves just short of their 6 years' service. In that case, would the slave have to serve her new master for 6 more years before she could be freed? Or would service be limited to a total of 6 years, regardless of the number of owners during that time? Biblical law is silent as to this issue, but the latter prospect seems more probable. Jeremiah 34:8-17 indicates that Israelites (or Judahites) sometimes abused this law and their slaves by taking back those who had been set free.
¹⁰⁶ See Blenkinsopp, "Biblical Laws" (cited in note 3), pp. 100–01 (comparing Exod. 21: 2-11 and Deut. 15:12-18). "In general, there is so much overlap between the laws in Exod. 20–23 and those in Deut. 12–26 that it is difficult to avoid the conclusion that the latter were intended to replace the former. In the final stages of the formation of the Pentateuch, however, the decision was made to bring together all traditional legal material, irrespective of overlap or differences." *Id.*, p. 100.

deals directly with questions relating to a slave's family, notably, his wife and children:

> When you buy a Hebrew slave, he shall serve six years, and in the seventh he shall go out free, for nothing. If he comes in single, he shall go out single; if he comes in married, then his wife shall go out with him. If his master gives him a wife and she bears him sons or daughters, the wife and her children shall be her master's and he shall go out alone. But if the slave plainly says, "I love my master, my wife, and my children; I will not go out free," then his master shall bring him to God, and he shall bring him to the door or the doorpost; and his master shall bore his ear through with an awl; and he shall serve him for life. (Exod. 21:2-6 RSV)

Several alternative scenarios are covered explicitly or by implication. An unmarried male Hebrew slave, who remains unmarried, is to be set free at the end of 6 years' service. If he was already married before being bought, his wife would also be free to go with him after 6 years, as would any children born of that marriage. Presumably, the wife also would have been a slave during that time.[107] If the male slave enters servitude unmarried, but his master or lord (Heb. *'adon*) provides him with a wife—almost certainly meaning a woman who was already a slave—*and* she bears him children during the 6 years of servitude, the wife and children would continue to be slaves after his 6 years had been completed.[108] In that case, the male Hebrew slave then must make a "Hobson's choice" between taking his freedom but leaving his family, or remaining with his family but as a slave for the rest of his life. The recitation and ceremony described in Exodus 21:5-6 institutionalize procedures to be observed if he makes the latter choice. Significantly, the slave's statement is to be made "plainly." It is unclear whether the ear-piercing ceremony was to take place at a religious shrine or at the master's house. In effect, God is witness to the transaction. Possibly the pierced ear would serve as a reminder, and, should later controversy

---

[107] It would be possible, but unlikely, that a slave might be married to a free person. But if the wife was free, there would have been no need for the law to stipulate that when the male slave was freed, "his wife shall go out with him."

[108] As this law stands, there is no suggestion that a female slave, even if given a male slave as her husband, would be freed after she served her master (or mistress) for 6 years.

arise, as legal evidence showing that the slave had knowingly waived his right to freedom and so remained bound to his master.

Under terms of the Exodus (CC) law, the slave's wife and children belonged to the master only if he had given this wife to the slave, and if the children subsequently were born by her. If the slave was already married to another woman, her children apparently would not belong to the master, even if born during the 6-year period of servitude. The same, presumably, would be the case if the slave married someone other than a woman given to him during his servitude. There is no indication whether a male slave might choose a wife for himself during his time of servitude, or whether, if he did so, she would also become a slave for the duration. As the law reads, it also is unclear what would happen if the master gave the slave a wife who did not then bear him children. In such a case, *perhaps*, the wife also would go free at the end of the 6 years.

The Deuteronomic version (Deut. 15:12-18) introduces a number of changes, several of which manifest a greater degree of compassion for the affected persons.

First of all, the newer law is gender-inclusive: a female Hebrew slave or servant (Heb. *'amah*) who has been purchased shall also be free to go after 6 years of service, just like a male Hebrew slave [*'ebed*] (Deut. 15:12). Under the earlier law, a female Hebrew slave apparently could have been required to continue in servitude all her life. The newer law was also more liberal in that it provided explicitly that if *she* chooses to remain with her master at the end of that time, a female Hebrew slave, too, might do so, after waiving her right to freedom by going through a similar ceremony (Deut. 15:16-17).

A second major difference here is that the man's or woman's employer is never described as his or her "master" (*'adon*). Instead, the law simply addresses the purchaser in the second person ("you") without further characterization. Here, rather more clearly than in Exodus 21:1-6, the arrangement parallels the early American institution of indentured servitude. The change in nomenclature suggests greater sensitivity to the dignity and integrity of those experiencing a time of such service.

Another significant difference in the newer law is that, when the owner frees his slave or "bondservant," he is admonished to contribute generous provisions for the former servant's new life of freedom:

> And when you let him go free from you, you shall not let him go empty-handed; you shall furnish him liberally out of your flock, out of your

> threshing floor, and out of your wine press; as YHWH your God has blessed you, you shall give to him. (Deut. 15:13-14 RSV)[109]

Here the basis and perhaps also the measure of giving is gratitude for what YHWH has provided the former owner. As often elsewhere in Deuteronomic law, such generosity or compassion also is grounded in the Israelites' remembered experience of servitude in Egypt and of their redemption from it: "You shall remember that you were a slave in the land of Egypt, and YHWH your God redeemed you; therefore I command you this today" (Deut. 15:15 RSV).[110] Moreover, the Deuteronomic law offers certain pragmatic consolations to owners for the loss of their bondspersons, and also, perhaps, for the cost of furnishing them liberally when they go:[111]

> It shall not seem hard to you, when you let him go free from you; for at half the cost of a hired servant he has served you six years. So YHWH your God will bless you in all that you do. (Deut. 15:18 RSV)[112]

The bondsperson's services were obtained at bargain rate; and YHWH, himself, will see to it that obedient owners continue to prosper.

The most notable difference between this Deuteronomic and the earlier Covenant Code provision is that here nothing at all is said about the Hebrew bondsperson's spouse or children. Implicitly, they would remain free throughout the term of servitude, and be free to go with the "bondman" or "bondwoman" when his or her term of service was completed. Silence on this point suggests that any spouses married or children born during the period of servitude would not themselves thereby become slaves or servants. Thus, at the end of the 6 years, the "bond" or indentured servant would not have to face the Hobson's choice between freedom and family. Here, the only reasons mentioned why he or she might choose to remain

---

[109] It is clear from the context (Deut. 15:12, 17) that references to the "bondservant" as "him" were meant to be gender-inclusive.

[110] See Hamilton, *Social Justice*, Nasuti, "Identity," and Sonsino, "Motive Clauses," cited in note 27 as to "motive clauses."

[111] Deuteronomy 15:18 picks up from vv. 13-14 where the Hebrew bondsperson decides to opt for freedom, and the owner is instructed to provide generously for him or her.

[112] See Yair Zakovitch, "Some Remnants of Ancient Laws in the Deuteronomic Code," 9 *Israel L Rev* 346, 349–51 (1974), suggesting that the customary period of hired servitude in early Israel was 3 years, as may be intimated in Isaiah 16:14 and in the Code of Hammurabi.

as bondservant are love for the owner and the owner's household, and the prospect of continuing a good life under servitude (Deut. 15:16).[113]

The ultimate effect of the Deuteronomic revision of the law was to provide freedom for all Hebrew slaves, both male and female—at least those who had been sold to other Hebrews—who wished to be free, by eliminating their need to choose between freedom and family.[114] After 6 years of service, they were free to go unless they really preferred to stay and continue to serve their erstwhile owner and his household. Evidently their wives or husbands and any children born during the time of servitude remained free both then and afterward.

*ii. When a father sells his daughter as a slave*

One other law provides certain protections and benefits for Hebrew slaves. This is an old law found only in the Covenant Code (Exod. 21: 7-11). It sets out limitations on a master's conduct with respect to a female slave sold to him by her father.[115] Presumably both seller and buyer were understood to be Hebrews or Israelites. Neither text nor context indicates under what circumstances a man might decide to sell his daughter as a slave or maidservant (Heb. *'amah*). There are no narrative instances of men selling daughters,[116] nor is the existence of such practice intimated

---

[113] Other differences between the two versions of the law include the fact that in Deuteronomy, the ear-piercing ceremony calls for thrusting an awl through the servant's ear and "into the door." The Exodus version does not include this last feature. Perhaps the Deuteronomic version only specifies what was implicit or understood in connection with the Exodus ceremony. Or the meaning may have shifted so as to symbolize the relation of bondage between servant and the owner's house. In Deuteronomy, "the door" seems to be that of the householder, and there is no mention that the ceremony was to take place "before God." Possibly this alteration was one of the several accommodations or institutional adjustments to the closure of the local cult shrines that were incorporated into the laws found in Deut. chs. 12–19. Thus Levinson, *Deuteronomy* (cited in note 55), pp. 111–12. On differences between the CC and Deuteronomic laws, see generally, Patrick, *Old Testament Law* (cited in note 1), pp. 111–13 (concluding, "overall, servitude has been reduced to ownership of a person's labor, not of the person"). *Id.*, p. 113.

[114] Cf. Lev. 25:39-43, 47-55. Possibly the Deuteronomic law was intended to override the provision in Lev. 25:39-43 concerning Israelites who sold themselves as slaves to other Israelites. Under the H laws, those slaves (and their children) would not be freed until the Jubilee year. Alternatively, the Deuteronomic law may have been meant to apply only in cases where Hebrews who already had become slaves were sold to Israelites. As to Jeremiah's report concerning King Zedekiah's mandatory manumission of Hebrew slaves and the Judahites' failure to do so (Jer. 34:8-22), see Weinfeld, *Social Justice* (cited in note 1), pp. 152–56.

[115] See generally, Patrick, *Old Testament Law* (cited in note 1), p. 71.

[116] But see 2 Kgs 4:1, where a creditor comes to take a widow's children as slaves. Compare Ruth 4:5, 10, which refer to "buying" Ruth as wife in order to perpetuate the name of

in prophetic or wisdom literature.[117] Leviticus 25:39-43 and 47-55 concern the situation when a man becomes poor and sells *himself* into slavery.

The text of Exodus 21:7-11 suggests rather clearly that if a man sold his daughter, she would have the status of a concubine or wife, rather than that of a menial servant. Moreover, the buyer was obliged, under the law, to treat the woman with respect. His options were limited in three ways. The apparent sense of Exodus 21:8 is that if the buyer is displeased with her as wife, he must let her "be redeemed." Possibly the procedure for redemption in this case would be like that spelled out later in the Holiness Code at Leviticus 25:47-55.[118] The redeemer or *go'el*, presumably, would be one of her kinsmen.[119]

Alternatively, the buyer might "designate" the woman as a wife (or concubine) for his son. But in that case, the buyer must also treat her as he would treat his own daughter (Exod. 21:9). Such treatment, presumably, would be marked by affection and kindness. Biblical tradition has little to say about men's attitudes toward their daughters, but it need not be supposed that Judges 11:34-40 represented standard or common practice.[120] Finally, if the buyer keeps the woman as his wife, but then marries someone else, he still must continue to support her at the same standard of living and must continue to honor her "marital" or conjugal *rights*.[121]

---

her deceased husband (and/or father-in-law). It is unclear to whom payment would have been made; in fact, there is no indication that any payment was made. Boaz may have been speaking in metaphor, in effect, saying to the *go'el*, "If you buy the property, you also must marry the widow as part of the deal." Thus Leggett, *Levirate and Goel* (cited in note 89), pp. 216–17. In any event, Ruth was not sold by her father—or by anyone else.

[117] Hosea says that he bought (or bought back) a wife or concubine who was already an adulteress, but the text gives no further particulars as to the transaction. Hos. 3:1-3.

[118] The Leviticus law, in its terms, however, applies only when a man sells himself as a slave to a stranger or sojourner.

[119] If no one redeemed her, the owner might, perhaps, sell her to another Israelite. If the practice embodied as law in Deut. 15:12-18 were already in effect, the woman could then gain her freedom after 6 years of service. In any event, the master may not sell her to a "foreign people." (Exod. 21:8). A sale to a foreigner might result in the woman being taken from the land of Israel to another land where she would no longer be protected by Israelite law. This provision may also reflect concern to protect the woman from being married to a man who worshiped other gods. Inheritance issues also may be implicated here; see Num. 36, and Chapter Two, Section B.1.b.

[120] In that story, *anyone* who came out of Jephthah's tent could have been sacrificed as a result of his rash and tragic vow. Compare Phyllis Trible, *Texts of Terror*, pp. 92–116. Positive attitudes and acts as to daughters are indicated elsewhere, e.g., in Gen. 31:43-50; 2 Sam. 12:3; and Job 42:15. "Daughter" is clearly a term of endearment in Ruth 1:11-13; 2:8; and 3:10-11. See also Mt. 9:22; Mk. 5:34; and Lk. 8:48.

[121] Reference in these circumstances to a *purchased* wife's rights is noteworthy. "If he takes another wife to himself, he shall not diminish her food, her clothing, or her marital rights." Exod. 21:10 (RSV). It could be inferred that free married women likewise were

In summary, the buyer's three alternative duties were: (1) to allow the woman to be redeemed if he does not wish to marry her himself; or (2) if he does not marry her, he may designate her as wife for one of his sons but then must treat her as a daughter (or daughter-in-law); (3) if he does marry her, and then also marries some other woman, he is to continue her support undiminished. If he fails to meet these obligations, the woman "shall go out for nothing, without payment of money" (Exod. 21:11 RSV).[122]

The Exodus 21 law about a man's selling his daughter as a slave is not repeated or alluded to in later biblical law or other tradition. It may represent an attempt before or at the time the Covenant Code was completed to mitigate earlier if not ancient ways of treating women who had been sold as slaves by their fathers. It is significant that Exod. 21:7 does not authorize or mandate, but rather presumes the existence of such practice. The biblical law then proceeds to establish safeguards for the benefit of the woman so sold. The fact that this law is not repeated in the more recent codes may mean that in later times men no longer sold their daughters as slaves. Once such practice had been abandoned, these protective laws no longer would have been needed.

---

understood to enjoy such rights. That a man might have two wives was recognized also in Deut. 21:15-17. There it is required that even if he dislikes one of them, he must treat her, or more particularly, her son, fairly.

[122] This text makes no explicit provision for divorce either in conjunction with any of the three alternative obligations, or as part of the final arrangement if the woman "goes out," that is, regains her freedom. These requirements are somewhat like those set out in Deut. 21:10-14 concerning a man's obligation to a woman taken captive in war. In due course, the captor may make her his wife. But if he has "no delight in her," he must free her. He must not sell her or treat her as a slave, for he has "humiliated her." Here, too, there is no specific provision for divorce. In both cases, however, it may have been understood that freeing the woman also included granting her divorce. So also Carmichael, *Spirit* (cited in note 1), p. 135 as to the captive woman law.

## Chapter 9

# Biblical Social Welfare Laws and Modern Social Welfare Policy

*[Y]ou shall love your neighbor as yourself. I am YHWH.*

*Leviticus 19:18b*

*WE THE PEOPLE of the United States, in Order to form a more perfect Union, establish Justice, insure domestic Tranquility, provide for the common defense, promote the general Welfare, and secure the Blessings of Liberty to ourselves and our Posterity, do ordain and establish this CONSTITUTION for the United States of America.*

*Constitution of the United States, Preamble*

Biblical law has been of little or no interest to most proponents of Western religious social ethics. Jewish tradition has, for the most part, grounded ethics on the Talmud and subsequent interpretation, giving relatively slight attention to substantive biblical law as such. Early 20th century Social Gospel advocates focused mainly on the "teachings of Jesus," especially those found in the first three gospels.[1] More recently, proponents of Christian social ethics occasionally refer to Old Testament prophets, but hardly ever to biblical law.[2] Particularly in Protestant—and not only in Lutheran or dispensationalist—circles, the whole notion of "law" has been suspect, and many have come to believe as a matter of theological principle that biblical law has been superseded by "gospel."[3]

---

[1] See, e.g., Walter Rauschenbusch, *A Theology for the Social Gospel* (Macmillan, 1917); Shailer Mathews, *Jesus on Social Institutions* (Macmillan, 1928).

[2] See Chapter Eight, note 2.

[3] Protestant, or perhaps modernist, aversion to law is epitomized in the late Joseph Fletcher's writings on "situation ethics" (cited in Chapter Eight, note 2). See also Rudolf Bultmann's characterization of Jewish and biblical law as relating only to external matters, in contrast to the "radical obedience" preached by Jesus. On Bultmann's position, see Richard H. Hiers, *Jesus and Ethics* (Westminster Press, 1968), pp. 79–114.

Yet as been seen in this study, biblical law related to a great many social issues, in particular, to situations involving people's welfare. Numerous biblical laws were intended to insure that particularly vulnerable persons would not be subjected to oppression or discrimination. Other biblical laws called for establishing a variety of institutions or programs to assure that persons living on the socio-economic margins would enjoy at least some measure of freedom from hunger, as well as other types of support or care. Strangely, studies of biblical law hardly ever focus on its social welfare provisions.[4]

It may be significant that many of the specific humane or compassionate "welfare" laws reviewed here have close counterparts in texts attributed to one or more of the classical prophets.[5] Since both the Covenant Code (CC) and the original Deuteronomic Code (D) probably antedate the classical prophets, it appears likely that these prophets based their condemnations of contemporary practice on the standards of just and compassionate conduct articulated in these laws.[6] In turn, the classical prophetic tradition may have influenced the development of later law, such as that embodied in the Holiness Code (H) and the Deuteronomic Reform (RDC) laws.[7] At any rate, it appears that biblical law may provide an important resource or point of reference for those in our time who have similar concerns as to societal conditions and their effects on the well-being of persons. To the extent that such concerns also surface in wisdom writings, these much neglected sources of insight as to the human situation may also prove worth reexamination. There may be

---

[4] See Chapter Eight, note 1.
[5] See Chapter Eight, notes 6, 7, 15, 19, 23, 24, 34–35, 38, 40, 45, 104 and 105 and accompanying texts. In Jesus' Parable of the Rich Man and Lazarus, the rich man too late realizes his obligation to the poor and needy, but wishes Father Abraham to send someone from the dead to warn his brothers of their like obligation. Abraham denies this request: "If they do not hear Moses and the prophets, neither will they be convinced if some one should rise from the dead." (Lk. 16:11 RSV). "Moses," of course, represents biblical law.
[6] See generally, Edward McGlynn Gaffney, Jr. "Of Covenants Ancient and New: the Influence of Secular Law on Biblical Religion," 2 *J. of L. & Relig.* 117, 134–37 (1984). "[I]t can now be concluded that the major function of the later prophets was not to repudiate the law, but to refer back to the covenant tradition and to call the people repeatedly back to the terms of its covenant with YHWH." See also E. Clinton Gardner, *Justice and Ethics* (Cambridge Univ. Press, 1995), pp. 29–44 (on relations between biblical law and prophets). Various classic biblical texts derived both justice and compassion from YHWH's own nature or demands. Thus, e.g., Ps. 33:5; Isa. 30:18; and Micah 6:8. See generally, Christopher J. H. Wright, *Old Testament Ethics for the People of God* (InterVarsity Press, 2004), pp. 253–80.
[7] See Gaffney, "Covenants" (cited in note 6 above), at p. 137: "Because the prophetical concerns for social justice clearly influenced the legal tradition, it must be assumed that Israelite law was not antithetical to prophetic religion."

greater congruence between biblical law and biblical wisdom than has commonly been supposed by either legal or biblical scholars.[8]

It may be noted here only briefly that contemporary secular theorists typically try to evade normative questions by grounding their propositions upon purportedly norm-neutral "objective" considerations. Thus law and economics theorists profess to believe that the supposedly free market—the latter-day counterpart of Adam Smith's "invisible hand of Providence"—will resolve all important legal or policy questions.[9] This happy outcome is expected to take place without benefit of normative reflection on the part of those involved; such reflection on the part of the public's constitutionally and democratically elected representatives, also known as "the government," is particularly unwelcome in such circles.

Still others undertake the problematic task of trying to extrapolate societal norms from individual self-interest, as if the latter were simply objective reality and could somehow justify concern for others.[10] Among these attempts, of course, are Locke's and Hobbes's social contract theories, utilitarian philosophy, and Rawls's theory of justice. That such theories typically rely on imagined fictive scenarios is one clue to their proponents' desperation.[11] Whatever else may be said of the sharp pen wielded by the late Ayn Rand, she made it rather clear that those who pursue self-interest "rationally," that is, without importing (or smuggling) normative criteria into their analysis, will have no basis for being concerned about the welfare of other persons, especially those on the margins. Implicit in all of Rand's thought is the notion that what persons on the margins should do is to perish, preferably quietly and off-stage, so as not to disturb the equanimity of the propertied classes. Susan Wolfson's comments on the problematics of rights theory based on

---

[8] See, e.g., Chapter Eight, notes 7–10, 19, 21, 25, 33, 35, 38–40, 44, 45, 54, 66, and 104 and accompanying texts. See Joseph Blenkinsopp, *Wisdom and Law in the Old Testament: The Ordering of Life in Israel and Early Judaism* (Oxford Press, 1983) (examining close connections and parallels), and the brief survey of social welfare proverbs by James Limburg, *The Prophets and the Powerless* (John Knox Press, 1977), pp. 33–35.

[9] See, e.g., the writings of Judge Richard Posner. Posner's position is thoughtfully critiqued by Laura Carrier, "Making Moral Theory Work for Law," 99 *Colum L Rev* 1018 (1999).

[10] See Introduction to Part III, notes 21 and 22 and accompanying text.

[11] Of course self-interested persons can enter into actual agreements, contracts, or covenants in order the better to promote their own as well as their common welfare. See e.g., Introduction to Part III, notes 6–9 and accompanying text.

individualism could be applied to all jurisprudential systems founded on individual self-interest:

> [B]y having the exclusive focus of the model on the individual and his autonomous initiative in exercising his rights, a blindly inaccurate and immoral egocentricity of the individual is actually a central component of the model itself. . . . Each individual's autonomy becomes a virtual law unto itself unaccountable to anyone else, except in so far as in or out of court with the other individual's conduct.[12]

The self may, of course, be regarded as the center of value, and a person may be committed to the advancement of his or her own interests. In that case, however, one is concerned for others only incidentally or instrumentally, to the extent that what is good for the other is also good for oneself.[13] Some utilitarians, for instance, have urged that the poor should be provided a safety net lest they revolt and overthrow the privileged classes.[14] Or a group of persons may regard their collective self-interest as a matter of ultimate concern or importance. From this standpoint, what is good is what is good for the group; what is bad is what affects the group adversely. H. Richard Niebuhr characterizes this kind of faith-grounded ethics as the ethics of "henotheism."[15] Biblical social welfare law turns out to be rather more inclusive. As has been seen, biblical

---

[12] Wolfson, "Liberal Rights Theory" (cited in Chapter Eight, note 9), pp. 410–11. See also Douglas Sturm, *Community and Alienation: Essays on Process Thought and Public Life* (Univ. of Notre Dame Press, 1988), critiquing individualism in American culture. Robert N. Bellah, et al., *Habits of the Heart: Individualism and Commitment in American Life* (Univ. of Notre Dame Press, 1985) report the peculiar difficulties that Americans who are committed—in theory—to self-interest experience when attempting to articulate reasons for their undertaking to promote the well-being of others.

[13] See Erich Fromm, *The Heart of Man: Its Genius for Good and Evil* (Harper & Row, 1968), pp. 62–77 characterizing "benign" and "malignant narcissism."

[14] Proponents of this argument are unable to explain why, conditions permitting, it would not be better simply to let the poor die in misery—the outcome implicit in Ayn Rand's position—or more actively seek to bring about their demise. Unable, that is, without recourse to some further implicit norm, such as the value of human life. Philosophers often define "rational" so as to include this norm, which actually derives from humanistic commitment or faith. See below, note 21. Rationality and humanistic faith may be confused in modern (or modernist) thought because both at least indirectly derive from 18th century culture which celebrated not only reason, but human worth and dignity. To what extent 18th century humanistic faith and ethics rested upon Judeo-Christian tradition is not of concern here. No doubt there were also classical antecedents.

[15] See H. R. Niebuhr, *Radical Monotheism* (cited in Introduction to Part III, note 27), pp. 24–31. Niebuhr also characterizes this kind of faith as "social" or "tribal" faith. Its adherents derive their sense of value from their membership in the group, and are loyal to it as their "center of value." He cites nationalism as an example.

laws insist on equitable and compassionate regard for and treatment of aliens, servants, slaves, and the poor, and, perhaps more often than might be expected, women.[16]

This book does not propose that going "back to the Bible" is the answer to the quandaries of contemporary jurisprudence or public policy.[17] Biblical law was part of a covenantal relationship between Israel and YHWH, its officially acknowledged God. Nevertheless, the biblical understanding of covenant may be relevant to contemporary reflections on the relations between law and ethics.[18]

Biblical law had as its normative center or *Grundnorm* the belief that YHWH, who had brought all being into existence, affirmed that all existence was good and intended that his people, Israel, for whom he cared especially, should order their interpersonal and societal relationships on his own pattern of justice and mercy in dealing with them and others. Rights and duties enacted and implicit in biblical law all derive from this faith-understanding.[19] Biblical tradition remembers and celebrates this

---

Nationalism shows its character as a faith whenever national welfare or survival is regarded as the supreme end of life; whenever right and wrong are made dependent on the sovereign will of the nation, however determined; whenever religion and science, education and art, are valued by the measure of their contribution to national existence. *Id.*, p. 27.

See also Fromm, *Heart of Man* (cited in note 13 above), pp. 78–94, on the character and perils of "social narcissism."

[16] As to women, see Chapter Eight, notes 6, 17, 26–36, 44, 45–55, 59–63, 83–92, 96–101, 109–114, 115–122 and accompanying text.

[17] "Certainly the Chinese government is not likely to be persuaded to embrace human rights by references to the Bible." Eric Blumenson, "Who Counts Morally?," 14 *J. of L. & Relig.* 1, 39 (1999–2000), reviewing, but in this instance caricaturing and significantly misrepresenting Michael Perry's position as set out in Perry, *Idea of Human Rights*, cited in Introduction to Part III, note 26.

[18] Hamilton offers a number of constructive comments in this connection, Hamilton (cited in Chapter Eight, note 1), pp. 139–58. See also Gowan, "Wealth and Poverty" (cited in Chapter Eight, note 1), p. 353, and Fager, *Land Tenure* (cited in Chapter Eight, note 64), p. 122 (suggesting potential commonality between biblical and modern "community's moral and imperative toward its economically vulnerable members"). Without focusing directly on biblical law or covenant, Eric Mount, Jr., offers an insightful critique of a number of current issues in his recent book, *Covenant, Community, and the Common Good: An Interpretation of Christian Ethics* (Pilgrim Press, 1999). See esp. ch. 4, "Covenants of Work, Family, and Welfare," id., pp. 80–106.

[19] See generally, Louis E. Newman, "Covenant and Contract: A Framework for the Analysis of Jewish Ethics," 9 *J. of L. & Relig.* 89 (1991). "Doing God's will, then is a way, perhaps the only adequate way, for Israelites to demonstrate their gratitude." *Id.*, p. 95. "The moral duty to express gratitude to one's benefactor would appear to be the basis for all legal duties under the covenant." Gratitude is certainly one aspect of the biblical understanding of the proper relationship between God or YHWH and his people, as is indicated in several of the "motive clauses." See Chapter Eight, note 27 and accompanying text. Other aspects of that relationship include trust or confidence, loyalty or devotion to him, and caring attitudes and responsive actions—as expressed in particular

care as it was embodied historically in YHWH's delivering his people from bondage in Egypt and afterwards making his covenant with them.

Rights[20] do not evidently inhere in humanity as such, nor has it been shown that duties derive from thought experiments, however ingenious. H. Richard Niebuhr has observed that people make moral judgments and act accordingly on the basis of their trust or confidence in, and loyalty or devotion to some more or less inclusive and transcendent center of meaning and value.[21] Biblical faith, and also Judaism, Christianity, and some other world religions are committed to the "One beyond the many" who is affirmed as source and valuer of all being. Such faith Niebuhr characterized as "radical monotheism."[22] To a remarkable degree, biblical social welfare legislation accords with this faith which is fundamental to the worldview expressed in nonlegal biblical texts.[23]

---

biblical laws—as to other persons. See also Wolfson, "Liberal Rights Theory" (cited in Chapter Eight, note 9), at pp. 417, 421, 423, and 426. See also Gardner, "Justice" (cited in Introduction to Part III, note 5), pp. 409–10.

[20] As to rights as a feature of biblical tradition, see Chapter Eight, notes 9, 35, 46, 95, 101, 121, and accompanying texts.

[21] See generally, H. R. Niebuhr, *Radical Monotheism* (cited in Introduction to Part III, note 27), pp. 101–26. For persons who place their confidence or trust in humankind and devote themselves to human well-being, humanity constitutes such a transcendent center of value. All humanity, of course, transcends the self. Such *humanism*—even when labeled "secular"—functions as religion. Much of classical, modern, and postmodern thought reflects this kind of confidence and devotion, though the religious character of such faith and ethics is generally unacknowledged or denied. Humanism is, obviously, more inclusive than tribal faith/ethics systems, such as racism or nationalism. But humanism is less inclusive than the faith and ethics of reverence-for-life. See generally, Hiers, "Reverence for Life," cited in Chapter Eight, note 28. The limits of humanistic faith and ethics pose many problems: for instance, do only those now alive count, or those who may be born in future generations? Those just conceived, or still in utero? The comatose? It is also a question whether humanistic faith and ethics can be self-sustaining, that is without a transcendent, theistic grounding. And clearly humanism, like theistic religions, can be corrupted when its avowed adherents seek above all what is good for their particular groups or communities, e.g., their own nation, race, or class.

Such issues need not be addressed here. It may be enough to observe that human beings are not, as such, committed humanists. Not everyone cares about their own family or neighbors, let alone human welfare more inclusively. But humanistic faith and ethics is implicated when people of whatever philosophical or jurisprudential school affirm that what is good is what is good for human beings.

[22] *Id.*, pp. 24–63.

[23] Thus in the first creation narrative, God is said to have affirmed that all he had made is "very good" (Gen. 1:31). As the story is told, YHWH's covenant with Noah—the first and most comprehensive of biblical covenants—was also made not only with humankind, but also with every kind of living creature for all future generations. Gen. 9:8-17. See Hiers, "Reverence for Life" (cited in Chapter Eight, note 28), pp. 134–138. Many of the psalms celebrate YHWH as the creator of all that is, and praise him for his care for all creation. See, e.g., Pss. 136, 145, 147 & 148. Such "radical monotheism" also comes to expression in such classical texts as Isa. 40:12-31; 45:18-23; and 46:1-11; and the book of Jonah. See also Chapter Eight, note 31 and accompanying text.

To be sure, historical adherents to these faiths also are in constant conflict with devotions to lesser "gods" or value centers: the perennial "gods" of race, nation, caste, and class, among others.[24] This book was not written as a call for conversion to radical monotheism. The underlying thesis, rather, is that all law necessarily involves making value judgments; and that all value judgments derive from commitment to some center and sometimes overlapping or conflicting multiple centers of value.

Contemporary religious communities that share the underlying faith and ethics of radical monotheism can and do evaluate societal conditions and existing laws accordingly. Are the legitimate interests of all adequately protected or provided for under existing social arrangements? To what extent does our society provide a genuine "safety net" for those who are vulnerable or at risk? Are some left out of the benefits enjoyed by others, or unfairly disadvantaged by bearing more than their share of societal burdens? Adherents of inclusive, secular humanistic faith and ethics ask similar questions.

Biblical law, of course, does not tell us how to resolve modern social problems. But biblical law may have contemporary relevance in at least two ways. It can provide some basis for evaluating the kinds of arrangements and programs for aiding the poor and other disadvantaged individuals and classes of persons that obtain in contemporary society. And, even though particular biblical laws may have little or no direct application in the modern world, the ideal or model community toward which they point can inspire contemporary efforts to achieve a society—if not a world—in which the basic welfare interests of all, even those of low degree, are protected and affirmed through appropriate public policies and legislation.

---

[24] Such tendencies also appear in many biblical texts, necessarily in conflict or tension with more inclusive expressions of faith and ethics. See, e.g., Deut. 20:10-18; Ps. 137:7-9; and Isa. 13:1-20.

# Concluding Observations

*Now this is the commandment— the statutes and the ordinances— that YHWH your God charged me to teach you to observe in the land that you are about to cross into and occupy, so that you and your children and your children's children may fear YHWH your God all the days of your life, and keep all his decrees and his commandments that I am commanding you, so that your days may be long. Hear, therefore, O Israel, and observe them diligently, so that it may go well with you, and so that you may multiply greatly in a land flowing with milk and honey, as YHWH the God of your ancestors, has promised you. Hear, O Israel: YHWH is our God, YHWH alone. You shall love YHWH your God with all your heart, and with all your soul, and with all your might. Keep these words that I am commanding you today in your heart.*

*Deuteronomy 6:1-6*

*It is one of the oldest sociological generalizations that any coherent and viable society rests on a common set of moral understandings about good and bad, right and wrong, in the realm of individual and social action. It is almost as widely held that these common moral understandings must also in turn rest upon a common set of religious understandings that provide a picture of the universe in terms of which the moral understandings make sense.*[1]

This chapter does not attempt to summarize the particular, substantive finding reported in the preceding chapters. Chapters One and Two already include such summaries,[2] and Parts II and III both conclude with chapters reflecting upon the possible relevance of biblical laws for con-

---

[1] Robert N. Bellah, *The Broken Covenant: American Civil Religion in a Time of Trial* (Seabury Press, 1975), p. ix.
[2] See Chapter One, Section C and Chapter Two, Section D.

temporary law and social policy.[3] Readers, of course, will draw their own conclusions as to the meaning and relevance of biblical law. A few concluding observations, however, may be appropriate.

It is surprising how many biblical laws can aptly be described by terms familiar in contemporary Anglo-American jurisprudence. Several of these laws fall within the framework of what now would be called civil law. Thus we find biblical laws relating to contracts, torts and remedies, and the disposition of property, both by inheritance and by bequest. Many other laws fit more into the category of criminal laws. Most, though not all of these laws, define what would now be designated as capital crimes or offenses. And a great many laws can best be characterized as social legislation.

A number of laws and narratives refer to contractual agreements between persons (or "parties") in biblical times. These agreements include several features similar to those familiar in modern contract jurisprudence, such as "consideration" and offer and acceptance or "meeting of the minds." Many more biblical texts describe or set out a variety of "tort" laws. The collection of tort laws found in the Covenant Code in the Book of Exodus turns out to have been organized largely along lines quite similar to modern legal concepts, such as injuries to persons, damages to property, and negligent as well as reckless or intentional torts. As in modern tort theory, intentionally tortuous conduct was subject to multiple or punitive or damages.

Although no biblical laws provide for making wills with the kinds of formalities required in modern jurisdictions, such as written documents, signed by testators and certain numbers of witnesses in their presence and in the presence of each other, certain biblical narratives describe procedures that clearly are in the nature of bequests or testamentary disposition of property. And several laws provide specifically for what now is called intestate succession.

The Bible contains many criminal laws. Some of these are illustrated in a series of what may be called trial scenes. Concern for both justice and compassion are implicit in numerous laws and admonitions calling for judges to exercise impartial judgment, and assure the equal protection of the laws, without regard to the standing or status of the persons before their courts. Although modern opponents and proponents of capital punishment both often invoke the authority of certain biblical texts,

---

[3] See Chapters Seven and Nine.

these texts seldom stand for the exact propositions they are cited to prove. Clearly many biblical texts do call for the execution of persons who have committed certain types of offenses. However, a significant number of biblical laws provide what can aptly be described as due process protections for the accused. These laws implicitly, and often explicitly, affirm the value of human life, and reflect very serious concern to prevent the execution of innocent persons.

Biblical laws often have to do with providing for the well-being of both the larger community and those individuals who in one way or another may be at risk or vulnerable. Such laws can appropriately be characterized as social or social welfare legislation. Many of these laws have to do with protecting such persons from oppression or mistreatment by those with wealth or other forms of power. Several protected classes can be identified. Many other laws call for affirmative actions: that is, persons in the larger community who could do so, were required to assist others who were unable to provide for their own needs, such as the poor, resident aliens, orphans, widows, and slaves.

Biblical scholars are generally unfamiliar with such modern legal concepts and categories as contracts, torts, wills, intestate succession, equal protection, due process, affirmative action, and social legislation. These categories are not identified by such terms in the biblical texts; however, they appear to be useful and accurate ways of describing what is to be found in much of biblical law. That this is the case suggests that those involved in developing the law in biblical times did so with understandings and concerns that often resembled those of legislators and judges in later and modern times.

As has been suggested throughout this book, it is not feasible (nor would it likely be desirable) to invoke or apply biblical laws directly in modern contexts or cases. Yet biblical law may be more relevant for contemporary reflections on law and social policy than has been generally assumed.

Three distinguishable types of biblical law have been examined here: civil law, criminal law, and social legislation. Each type of law, implicitly, and often explicitly, affirms the value of individual interests as well as the well-being of the larger community. Particular laws attempt to adjust competing or conflicting interests in ways that are both fair and also compassionate: for instance, by remedying the consequences of wrong-doing, deterring would-be offenders, protecting the innocent accused, and providing for the basic needs of those unable to do so for themselves. These laws— with certain notable exceptions— assume or assert the equal and valued status of persons before God and, therefore, also their value and equality before the law. In biblical times, as in our own time, these standards and goals were never fully achieved. Yet they can and should continue to serve as guidelines for both legislatures and courts.

Such guidelines are much needed in our time, given the normative confusion which characterizes contemporary Western culture. Currently prevailing ideologies of moral relativism (whether modern or "postmodern") and self-interest (whether individualistic or some genre of collectivist)[4] underscore the absence of understandings of, and commitments to, more transcendent and inclusive beliefs and values.[5] Biblical law may offer important insights as to such matters in our time.

---

[4] See present author's articles: "Normative and Ostensibly Norm-Neutral Conventions in Contemporary Judicial Discourse," 14 *Legal Studies Forum* 107–39 (1990), and "Normative Analysis in Judicial Determination of Public Policy," 3 *J. of L. & Relig.* 77–115 (1985).

[5] See Introduction to Part III, and Chapter Nine.

# Index of Biblical Quotations and Citations

Only those quoted or discussed in the main text or in footnotes are included in this index.

## Old Testament or Hebrew Scriptures

*Genesis*

| | |
|---|---|
| 1:26-27 | 157 |
| 4:14 | 83 |
| 4:15 | 83, 144, 154 |
| 4:17 | 83 |
| 4:23-24 | 144 |
| Chapters 6–9 | 84 |
| 6:5 | 84 n.17, 149, 154 |
| 9:5-6 | 113–14 & n.129, 122–3, 124 n.168, 158 |
| 9:8-17 | 219 n.23 |
| 15:2-4 | 32 & n.20, 56 |
| 16:1-3 | 30 |
| 16:4-6 | 31 |
| 16:11 | 31 |
| 16:15-16 | 31 |
| 18:16-33 | 161 |
| 18:16–19:25 | 84 |
| 18:23 | 153 |
| 18:23-25 | 74 n.5, 161 |
| 18:32 | 74 n.5 |
| 19:4-11 | 105 |
| 21:9-14 | 31 |
| 24:36 | 52 |
| 25:5-6 | 52, 55 |
| 25:29-34 | 7, 11, 22, 49 |
| 29:15-30 | 12 |
| 29:21-30 | 22 |
| 30:3-13 | 30 |
| 30:25-36 | 12 |
| 30:25-43 | 22 |
| 31:14-16 | 33 |
| 35:23-26 | 30 |
| 37:29-33 | 65 n.5, 137 n.56 |
| Chapter 38 | 40, 200 |
| 38:8 | 40 |
| 38:24-25 | 63 |
| 38:24-26 | 64–5 |
| 38:28 | 64 |
| 39:11-18 | 65 n.5 |
| 48:5-6 | 30 |
| 48:21-22 | 53 |
| 49:1-33 | 30 |

*Exodus*

| | |
|---|---|
| 20:1–23:33 | 2, 15, 23, 89-95 |
| 20:4-5 | 145 |
| 20:7 | 139 |
| 20:12 | 93 |
| 20:14 | 97, 103 |
| 20:16 | 139 |
| 20:24–23:19 | 15 n.24 |
| Chapters 21–22 | 3 |
| 21:1-6 | 10, 198, 206–7 |
| 21:1-11 | 10, 22 |
| 21:7 | 211 |
| 21:7-11 | 10, 209–10 |
| 21:8-9 | 210 |
| 21:10 | 210 n.121 |
| 21:11 | 211 |
| 21:12–22:15 | 15, 23 |
| 21:12 | 16, 24, 102, 123 |

| | | | |
|---|---|---|---|
| 21:12-13 | 116, 129 | 22:7-11 | 13–14 |
| 21:12-14 | 23, 89–90, 118, 129, 158, 160 | 22:7-13 | 15, 24 |
| | | 22:8 | 19, 24 |
| 21:12-32 | 15-16, 23 | 22:8-15 | 19 |
| 21:12–22:27 | 15 | 22:9 | 19, 24 |
| 21:13 | 107 | 22:10-11 | 20, 24 |
| 21:13-14 | 108, 123 | 22:12 | 18, 20 |
| 21:14 | 16, 108, 130–1 | 22:13 | 20, 24 |
| 21:14-17 | 24 | 22:14 | 18 |
| 21:15 | 16, 120, 160 | 22:14-15 | 15, 20, 24 |
| 21:15-17 | 23, 78, 93 | 22: 15 | 24 |
| 21:16 | 16, 93. 96, 118, 155. 160 | 22:16-17 | 24 n.30 |
| | | 22:18 | 78, 94–5, 100, 119, 155 |
| 21:17 | 16, 103, 119 | | |
| 21:18–22:15 | 15, 24 | 22:18-20 | 24 |
| 21:18-19 | 7, 16 | 22:19 | 94–5, 103, 119, 160 |
| 21:18-20 | 93–4 | | |
| 21:18-25 | 15 n.25, 23 | 22:20 | 94, 109, 119, 121 |
| 21:18-32 | 15, 17 | 22:21 | 181 |
| 21:20 | 79 | 22:21-24 | 94 |
| 21:20-21 | 16-17, 78–9 | 22:21-28 | 39 |
| 21:22 | 15 | 22:22-24 | 182 |
| 21:22-24 | 158 | 22:25 | 11, 178 |
| 21:22-25 | 17, 23, 78, 90–1, 102, 120, 134, 149, 155 | 22:25-27 | 10, 22 |
| | | 22:26-27 | 179 |
| | | 22:28 | 101 n.84 |
| 21:23 | 24, 103 | 23:1-2 | 140 |
| 21:23-25 | 17 n.31, 146–9 | 23:3 | 76, 163, 177 |
| 21:26-27 | 15, 17, 204 | 23:4-5 | 21 |
| 21:28-32 | 14, 17, 78, 91–2, 120, 134, 158, 160 | 23:6 | 163, 177 |
| | | 23:6-8 | 76 |
| 21:29 | 91 | 23:7 | 74, 127, 135 n.29, 160 |
| 21:29-32 | 23–4 | | |
| 21:30 | 17, 92, 151 | 23:9 | 181 |
| 21:32 | 18, 79 | 23:10-11 | 192 |
| 21:33–22:15 | 15, 18, 24 | 23:12 | 181, 203 |
| 21:33-34 | 15, 18, 23 | 34:6-7 | 145 |
| 21:33-36 | 15, 18 | 34:17-25 | 2 |
| 22:1-15 | 15 | 34:17-28 | 88–9 |
| 22:1 | 15, 19, 24, 66, 94 | 35:2 | 70 |
| 22:2-3 | 15 n.25, 19 n.40, 92 | 35:2-3 | 122 |
| 22:4 | 15, 19, 24, 94 | 35:3 | 115 n.135 |
| 22:5 | 9, 15 | | |
| 22:5-6 | 18, 24 | *Leviticus* | |
| 22:5-17 | 94 | | |
| 22:6 | 15-23 | 5:1 | 143, 163 |
| 22:7 | 19, 24, 135 | 5:7-13 | 179–80 |

*Index of Biblical Quotations and Citations* 225

| | | | |
|---|---|---|---|
| 6:1-7 | 21 | 24:22 | 76, 182 |
| 14:21-32 | 180 | Chapter 25 | 42 n.66, 44–5, 192, 196, 198 |
| Chapters 18–26 | 2, 99–106 | | |
| 18:6-18 | 104 | 25:1-7 | 192 |
| 18:21 | 100 | 25:5 | 192 |
| 18:26-30 | 77 n.9 | 25:6 | 192, 203 |
| 19:9-10 | 187 | 25:6-7 | 194 |
| 19:12 | 139 n.42 | 25:8-11 | 194 n.64 |
| 19:13 | 11, 22, 184 | 25:8-17 | 193 |
| 19:14 | 184 | 25:11-12 | 193 |
| 19:15 | 76, 163 | 25:15-16 | 44 |
| 19:18 | 84 n.15, 212 | 25:20-22 | 192 |
| 19:20 | 139 | 25:23 | 44 |
| 19:20-22 | 104, 120, 139 | 25:25-28 | 45, 196 |
| 19:31 | 100–1 | 25:35-37 | 11, 178, 196–7 |
| 19:33 | 181 | 25:38 | 178, 197 |
| 19:33-34 | 76 | 25:39-40 | 197 |
| 19:34 | 181 | 25:39-43 | 210 |
| Chapter 20 | 104 | 25:39-55 | 197, 204 |
| 20:1-5 | 100–1, 120-1, 158 | 25:41-42 | 198 |
| | | 25:43 | 197 |
| 20:2 | 77 | 25:44-46 | 202 |
| 20:6 | 100 | 25:47-55 | 198, 210 |
| 20:9-10 | 78, 103, 119, 160 | 27:16-25 | 45 |
| 20:10-12 | 104 | 27:20 | 45 n.80 |
| 20:11-12 | 121, 160 | 27:28 | 45, 46 n.82 |
| 20:12 | 105 | | |
| 20:13 | 105, 121 | *Numbers* | |
| 20:14 | 104–5, 121, 125 n.171 | 3:38 | 114, 122 |
| 20:15-16 | 78, 103, 119, 160 | 5:5-10 | 21 |
| 20:27 | 78, 100, 119 | 5:11-31 | 78 n.14 |
| 21:6-7 | 106 | 15:14 | 77 |
| 21:9 | 105, 121 | 15:15-16 | 77, 181 |
| 23:22 | 187 | 15:32-36 | 70, 122 |
| 24:10-11 | 69, 101 | 15:34 | 70, 115 |
| 24:10-16 | 101–2 | 15:35-36 | 115 |
| 24:10-23 | 69–70, 121 | Chapter 16 | 114 |
| 24:12 | 69, 100 | 16:1-49 | 122 |
| 24:16 | 70, 77, 101 | 18:1-7 | 114 |
| 24:17 | 102–3, 123, 149–50 | 18:7 | 122 |
| | | 18:21-22 | 114 n.131 |
| 24:18 | 20, 149 n.74 | 18:22 | 122 |
| 24:19-20 | 102, 146, 148–9, 155 | Chapters 22–24 | 12, 22 |
| | | 22:17 | 12 |
| 24:21 | 20, 102–3, 123, 149–50 | 24:10-11 | 12 |
| | | 24:12-13 | 12 n.14 |

# 226 Index of Biblical Quotations and Citations

| | | | |
|---|---|---|---|
| Chapter 27 | 28, 34–5, 39, 55–7, 59 | 13:6-11 | 109–10, 121 |
| | | 13:11 | 125 |
| 27:1-7 | 33 | 13:12-17 | 137 |
| 27:1-11 | 29 | 13:12-18 | 110–11, 121 |
| 27:8 | 33 | 13:13 | 111 |
| 27:8-11 | 25, 29, 34 n.29, 55, 57 | 13:14 | 137 |
| | | 13:17 | 110 |
| 27:9 | 41 | 14:21 | 187 n.47 |
| Chapter 35 | 115, 123, 133–4, 136, 150 | 14:28-29 | 173, 191, 193 |
| | | 15:1-6 | 195 |
| 35:6-34 | 115, 118, 160 | 15:4-5 | 194 |
| 35:9-34 | 123 | 15:7-11 | 165, 194–5 |
| 35:12 | 136 | 15:8-9 | 195 |
| 35:13 | 133 | 15:12 | 207 |
| 35:15 | 77 | 15:12-15 | 173 |
| 35:16-18 | 115–16, 134 | 15:12-18 | 198–9, 207 |
| 35:20-23 | 116 | 15:13-14 | 207–8 |
| 35:24 | 136 | 15:15 | 208 |
| 35:26-28 | 117 | 15:16 | 209 |
| 35:30 | 136, 141, 144, 162 | 15:16-17 | 207 |
| 35:31-32 | 123, 124 n.168, 151 | 15:17 | 173 |
| | | 15:18 | 208 |
| 35:33-34 | 124 | 16:9-15 | 188–90 |
| Chapter 36 | 33–5, 59 | 16:14-5 | 189 |
| 36:1-4 | 46 | 16:18-20 | 74 |
| 36:6 | 35 | 17:2-5 | 78 |
| 36:8-9 | 34 | 17:2-7 | 111, 119, 121, 137, 160 |
| | | 17:4 | 137 |
| *Deuteronomy* | | 17:4-6 | 111 |
| 1:16-17 | 73 | 17:6 | 137, 140, 162 |
| 4:41-43 | 132–3 | 17:7 | 125, 137, 143, 163 |
| Chapter 5 | 2, 95–9 | 17:8-9 | 138 |
| 5:8-9 | 145 | 17:8-12 | 112 |
| 5:11 | 139 | 17:12 | 112, 121, 125 |
| 5:17 | 80, 82–3 | 17:13 | 126 |
| 5:18 | 97 | 18:6-8 | 190 |
| 5:20 | 139, 142 | 18:20-22 | 111, 121 |
| 6:1-6 | 219 | Chapter 19 | 150 |
| 10:17-18 | 75 | 19:1-3 | 131 |
| 10:18-19 | 181 | 19:1-13 | 131–2 |
| Chapters 12–19 | 2, 95, 106–12 | 19:4 | 107 |
| 12:2-24 | 190 | 19:4-10 | 160 |
| 13:1-5 | 109, 111 n.124, 121 | 19:4-13 | 107–8, 115, 118, 160 |
| 13:1-18 | 160 | 19:5 | 107 |
| 13:5 | 125 | 19:5-6 | 131 |

# Index of Biblical Quotations and Citations

| | | | |
|---|---|---|---|
| 19:6 | 108, 131 | 25:1-2 | 135, 152 |
| 19:10-11 | 108 | 25:2-3 | 20 |
| 19:13 | 124 | 25:3 | 152 |
| 19:15 | 140 n.45 | 25:5 | 40 |
| 19:16-18 | 138 | 25:5-10 | 40, 199, 201 n.89 |
| 19:16-21 | 72, 78, 112, 121, 138, 146, 148, 155, 158, 163 | 25:6 | 34 n.28, 40 n.54, 41 n.58, 199 |
| | | 25:7-9 | 40 |
| 19:19 | 112 | 25:9 | 210 |
| 19:19-21 | 142, 148 | 25:11-12 | 151 n.81 |
| 19:20 | 126 | 25:12-18 | 205 |
| Chapters 20-25 | 2, 95–9 | Chapter 26 | 2, 106–12 |
| 21:1-9 | 124 | 26:12 | 191 |
| 21:7-9 | 125 | 26:13-15 | 191 |
| 21:15-16 | 52 | 27:1-3 | 127 |
| 21:15-17 | 47–51, 59, 97 | 27:8 | 127 |
| 21:18-19 | 78 | 27:18 | 184 |
| 21:18-20 | 141 | 27:19 | 176 |
| 21:18-21 | 96–7, 120 | 28:1-14 | 109 |
| 21:21 | 125–6 | 28:15-68 | 110 |
| 22:1-3 | 20 | 31:9-13 | 128 |
| 22:8 | 21, 23 | 32:35 | 84 |
| 22:13-21 | 78, 97–8, 112 n.125, 120, 136 | | |
| | | *Joshua* | |
| 22:13-27 | 97–9, 160 | | |
| 22:15 | 136 | 7:1-25 | 145 |
| 22:22 | 98, 119, 125 | 11:23 | 25 |
| 22:22-23 | 126 | 13:1–19:51 | 25 |
| 22:22-27 | 78, 139 | 13:24-28 | 30 |
| 22:23-24 | 104, 120 | 17:3-6 | 28, 33 |
| 22:23-27 | 98–9, 119–20 | 19:24-31 | 30 |
| 22:24 | 125 | Chapter 20 | 132, 135–6 |
| 22:25 | 98 | 20:1-9 | 132 |
| 22:25-27 | 104 | 20:6 & 9 | 135 n.30 |
| 22:26 | 99 | Chapters 21 | 132–3 |
| 23:15-16 | 181, 203 | | |
| 23:16 | 204 | *Judges* | |
| 23:24-25 | 179 n.18 | | |
| 24:6 | 11, 179 | 4:4-5 | 73 |
| 24:7 | 95–6, 118–9, 125, 160, 181 | 11:1-2 | 29, 31 |
| | | 11:34-40 | 210 |
| 24:10-13 | 10, 22 | 17:1-4 | 39 n.47 |
| 24:14-15 | 11, 22, 183 | | |
| 24:16 | 145, 160–1 | *Ruth* | |
| 24:17 | 179, 182, 185 | | |
| 24:19-22 | 187 | 1:12-13 | 43 |
| 25:1 | 20 | 1:22 | 37 |

| | | | |
|---|---|---|---|
| 2:1-23 | 188 | 8:1-6 | 38 |
| 2:23 | 38 | 14:5-6 | 145–6 |
| Chapter 3 | 43 | | |
| 3:1, 3-4 | 201 | *1 Chronicles* | |
| 3:13 | 201 | | |
| 4:3 | 36–7, 41 | 2:34-41 | 32 |
| 4:4-6 | 41 | 5:1 | 50 |
| 4:5 | 36 nn.35 & 36, 37 | 6:1 | 133 |
| 4:9 | 36 nn. 35 & 36, 37 | 6:16 | 133 |
| 4:14-15 | 202 | 6:57-60 | 133 |
| 4:15 | 43, 200 n.85 | 6:66-70 | 133 |
| 4:17 | 43 | | |
| | | *2 Chronicles* | |
| *1 Samuel* | | 21:1-3 | 29 |
| | | 21:2-3 | 53 |
| 25:14-35 | 13 | 25:3-4 | 146 |
| 28:3 | 94 | | |
| 28:9 | 94 | *Nehemiah* | |
| 28:3-25 | 94, 119 n.152 | | |
| | | 5:1-15 | 46 n.85 |
| *2 Samuel* | | *Job* | |
| 12:1-6 | 19 | | |
| 12:1-15 | 65–6 | 29:15 | 184 |
| 12:7-9 | 19 n.41 | 29:16-17 | 183 n.35 |
| 12:13-14 | 145 n.60 | 31:13 | 184 n.39 |
| 13:23-29 | 66 | 42:10-11 | 195 n.66 |
| 13:34-38 | 66 | 42:15-16 | 54 |
| 14:1-11 | 66–7, 83 | | |
| 14:12-24 | 66 | *Psalms* | |
| 14:28-33 | 66 | | |
| | | 25:13 | 34 n.28 |
| *1 Kings* | | *Proverbs* | |
| 1:1-4 | 27 | | |
| 1:1-31 | 131 n.13 | 12:17 | 142 |
| 1:49-53 | 130–1 | 13:8 | 92 n.49 |
| 2:5-6 | 131 n.13 | 13:22 | 55 |
| 2:13-25 | 27, 131 n.13 | 14:21 | 195 n.66 |
| 2:28-29 | 130–1 | 14:25 | 142 |
| 2:28-34 | 131 | 14:31 | 180 n.25 |
| 3:16-28 | 67 | 15:25 | 38–9, 182 n.33 |
| 11:7 | 100 | 17:2 | 29, 32 n.20, 56 |
| 21:1-16 | 67–8 | 18:5 | 61, 74 n.4 |
| | | 18:17 | 138 |
| *2 Kings* | | 18:18 | 138 n.57 |
| | | 19:5 | 143 |
| Chapter 4 | 57 | 19:9 | 143 n.53 |
| 4:1-37 | 38 | 19:14 | 28, 34 n.28 |
| Chapter 8 | 57 | 19:17 | 195 n.66 |

## Index of Biblical Quotations and Citations

| | | | |
|---|---|---|---|
| 19:26 | 120 | *Amos* | |
| 20:20 | 119 n.149 | 2:8 | 179 |
| 20:22 | 84 n.15 | Chapter 5 | 111 |
| 21:28 | 143 | 5:11 | 178 |
| 22:9 | 186 n.45 | 5:14-15 | 83–4 |
| 22:16 | 180 n.25, 195 n.66 | | |
| 22:22-23 | 177 | *Jonah* | |
| 23:10 | 34 n.28 | 3:10 | 111 |
| 23:10-11 | 183 | | |
| 28:17 | 83 | *Micah* | |
| 29:7 | 76 n.7, 177 n.6 | 2:1-2 | 39 |
| 29:14 | 76 n.7 | 2:9 | 39 |
| 29:21 | 32 n.20 | 6:8 | v |
| 31:9 | 177 n.6, 183 n.35 | 6:11: | 179 n.19 |
| | | *Malachi* | |
| *Ecclesiastes* | | 3:5 | 184 n.38 |
| 6:3-5 | 17 n.30 | | |

### Old Testament Apocrypha or Deutero-Canonical

| | | | |
|---|---|---|---|
| *Isaiah* | | *Tobit* | |
| 1:16-17 | 182 | 4:7-8 | 180 n.21 |
| 1:23 | 182 n.35 | 4:14 | 184 n.38 |
| | | 5:3-15 | 12 |
| *Jeremiah* | | 5:14-15 | 9, 12 |
| 5:1 | 74 n.5 | 5:14-16 | 22 |
| 5:28 | 180, 182 n.35 | 6:10-11 | 34–5 |
| Chapter 7 | 68 | 6:11 | 46 n.83 |
| 22:13 | 184 | 6:12 | 35 |
| 22:16 | 76 n.7 | 7:12-14 | 13 |
| Chapter 26 | 68 | 7:14 | 35 n.34 |
| 26:7-24 | 68–9 | 8:20-21 | 35 n.34, 38 |
| 26:11 | 68 | 14:13 | 46 n.83 |
| 26:12-15 | 69 | 14:13-14 | 34 |
| 26:14-15 | 153 | | |
| 26:16-19 | 69 | *Judith* | |
| 26:20-24 | 69 | 8:2-3 | 55 |
| 32:11-14 | 44 | 8:7 | 35, 55–6 |
| | | 16:21 | 56 |
| *Ezekiel* | | 16:23 | 204 |
| 18:21-23 | 85 | 16:24 | 25, 55–6 |
| 22:30 | 74 n.5 | | |
| 44:5–46:18 | 46 | *Wisdom of Solomon* | |
| 46:16-18 | 46–7 | | |
| 47:13–48:29 | 25 | 1:16–5:23 | 85 n.21 |

## Sirach (Ecclesiasticus)

| | |
|---|---|
| 3:12 | 186 n.44 |
| 4:9-10 | 185 n.35 |
| 27:30-28:7 | 85 |
| 28:1 | 84 n.15 |
| 33:20 | 53 |
| 33:24 | 7, 153 |
| 34:22 | 184 |
| 35:14 | 182 n.33 |

## Susanna

| | |
|---|---|
| 20-21 | 71 |
| 28-62 | 70–2 |
| 34-40 | 63, 139 |
| 41 | 71 |
| 48 | 139 |
| 48-50 | 71 |
| 51-52 | 139 |
| 51-59 | 141 |
| 52-58 | 139 |
| 52-62 | 112 n.125 |
| 60-62 | 71–2 |
| 62 | 142 |

## Bel and the Dragon

| | |
|---|---|
| 8 & 21-22 | 121 n.158 |

# New Testament

## Matthew

| | |
|---|---|
| 1:18-19 | 120 n.153 |
| 5:21-22 | 85 |
| 6:14 | 85 |
| 7:1-2 | 85 |
| 18:35 | 85 |
| 20:1-16 | 11, 13 |
| 20:1-2 | 13 |
| 20:8 | 11 |
| 20:13 | 13 |

## Mark

| | |
|---|---|
| 11:25-26 | 85 |
| 12:38-40 | 39 |

## Luke

| | |
|---|---|
| 6:30 | 195 n.66 |
| 6:37 | 85 |
| 12:13 | 29, 50 |
| 12:33 | 195 n.66 |
| 14:12-14 | 184 n.40 |
| 14:13 | 186 n.45 |
| 15:11-32 | 50, 54 |
| 15:12 | 50 |
| 16:11 | 213 n.5 |
| 16:19-31 | 186 n.45 |
| 19:8 | 19 |
| 20:46-47 | 39 |

## John

| | |
|---|---|
| 8:3-11 | 119 |
| 8:5 | 86 |
| 8:7 | 86 |

## Romans

| | |
|---|---|
| 1:26-27 | 105 n.106 |
| 12:19 | 84 |

## 2 Corinthians

| | |
|---|---|
| 13:1 | 140 n.45 |

## Philemon

| | |
|---|---|
| 10-21 | 203 n.98 |

# Index of Names

Names listed here include those found in footnotes on the pages indicated.

Names of Biblical persons are in italics.

*Aaron* 106, 114
*Abel* 83, 123
*Abigail* 13
*Abishag* 27, 131
*Abraham, Abram* 27, 31–2, 52, 74, 161, 213
*Absalom* 65–7, 83, 105
*Adonijah* 130–1
*Ahab* 61
Ahroni, Reuben 50–1
al-Hibri, Azizah 172
Alt, Albrecht 88
Alter, Jonathan 81, 163
Amaker, Norman C. 168
*Amos* 178–80
Appu 49
Atkinson, Thomas E. 52
*Azarias* 12, 35

Baab, Otto J. 31, 34
Bailey, Lloyd R. 82–3, 86, 125–6, 162
*Balaam* 12, 22
*Balak* 12, 22
*Barabbas* 86
Barmash, Pamela 75, 124, 130, 146
Barrett, Edith J. 168
*Bathsheba* 19, 65, 98
Beattie, D. R. G. 37, 41, 43
Bedau, Hugo Adam 81, 161
Bellah, Robert N. 167, 169, 174, 215, 219
Ben-Barak, Zafrira 34, 55
Benjamin, Don C. 68

Bennett, John C. 174
Bentele, Ursula 161
Berkowitz, Beth A. 87
*Bilhah* 30, 50, 105
Blackstone, William 32
Blackwell, Donald A. 143
Blenkinsopp, Joseph 123, 175, 205, 214
Blidstein, Gerald J. 82, 123
Block, Arnold 29
Blumberg, Craig L. 173
Blumenson, Eric 216
Bohm, Robert M. 88
Bounds, Elizabeth M. 168
Bradford, William 167
Brewster, William 166
Brin, Gershon 177–8, 180
Brooks, Elizabeth A. 155
Brown, A.M. 33
Bultmann, Rudolf 212
Burrows, Millar 27, 33, 36, 38–9, 185, 203, 205

Cabana, Donald A. 81
*Cain* 83, 123, 144, 154
Campbell, Edward F., Jr. 32, 36–7, 42
Carmichael, Calum M. 48, 88, 90, 109, 140, 151, 211
Carrier, Laura 214
Carrington, Frank O. 81
Boecker, Hans Jochen 63, 150, 177, 185, 203–4

Cash, W. J.  157
Charlesworth, James H.  53
Cherry, Conrad  167
Chodorow, Adam S.  180
Clark, Ramsey  82
Coffin, William Sloane  174
Cohn, Haim Heymann  87, 128, 143, 177, 180–2, 205
Collins, J. J.  25
Conrad, John P.  81
Coogan, Michael D.  ix
Cook, Anthony E.  170
Cook, Fay Laney  168
Corbin, Arthur Linton  9–13
Costanzo, Mark  88, 148
Cranfield, C. E. B.  26
Crenshaw, James L.  150

Dake, Norman P.  123
*Daniel*  71
Daube, David  26, 33, 36, 41–4, 88, 104, 140–1, 146, 201
*David*  13, 19, 65–7, 83, 98, 105, 131, 145
Davies, Eryl W.  39–42, 48
Davis, Michael  149
*Deborah*  73
de Vaux, Roland  27, 37, 51–3, 87, 110, 130, 133
de Vries, Barend A.  168, 199
Dickens, Charles  167
Dorff, Elliot N.  87, 185
Draper, Thomas  81
Duffy, Brian C.  155
Dworkin, Ronald M.  170

*Edna*  13
*Eliezer*  21
*Elimelech*  36–7, 41, 43
*Elisha*  38
*Esau*  11, 22, 49
*Ezekiel*  46–7, 85, 121, 146

Fager, Jeffrey A.  160, 194, 216
Falk, Ze'ev W.  75, 77, 90, 92, 97, 116, 141, 151, 185
Fensham, F. Charles  27, 39

Fletcher, George P.  175–6
Fletcher, Joseph  174, 212
Floyd, Timothy W.  86
Frazer, James G.  47, 49
Freedman, David Noel  32
Freedman, H.  115
Fromm, Erich  215–16

Gaffney, Edward McG.  86, 147, 169, 185, 189, 213
Gardner, E. Clinton  166, 213, 217
Garvey, Stephen P.  86
Gaster, Theodor H.  49, 91, 113, 189
Gervitz, Stanley  50
Goldin, Judah  50
Golding, Martin P.  87
Good, Edwin M.  68, 81, 89, 91, 93–4, 97, 103, 105, 110, 112, 114, 159
Gordon, Cyrus H.  27, 32–3, 51
Gould, John M.  47
Gowan, Donald E.  173, 175, 216
Graham, Hugh Davis  159
Greenbaum, Susan  161
Gross, Samuel R.  81, 161
Grunfeld, Dayan I.  29, 39
Gurr, Ted Robert  157
Gushee, David D.  174

Haas, Kenneth C.  81
Hackney, Sheldon  157
*Hagar*  30–1
Hamilton, Jeffries M.  173–4, 176, 181, 204, 216
Handler, Joel F.  167
Hanks, Gardner C.  83, 86–8, 163
Hanson, Paul D.  185
Harrelson, Walter  82, 89, 183
Harrington, Michael  167, 195
Hart, John  44
Hawthorne, Nathaniel  83
Hecht, N. S.  173
Herzog, Isaac  52
Hill, Samuel S., Jr.  157
Hillel  176
*Hiram*  11
Hoffman, R. Joseph  68

*Hosea* 210
Hubner, Joshua Hillel 162–3
Hudson, Charles 157

Inciard, James A. 81
*Isaiah* 180
*Ishamael* 30–1
Ivins, Molly 168, 195

Jackson, Bernard S. 147, 178
*Jacob* 11, 22, 33, 49, 53
Jain, Monika 141, 162
*Jehoshaphat* 53
*Jephthah* 31, 210
*Jeremiah* 68–9, 121, 135, 138, 146, 180
*Jesus* 11, 13, 39, 50, 85–6, 176, 212–13
*Jezebel* 67–8, 140
*Joab* 66, 130–1
*Joakim* 70–1
*Job* 53–5, 167, 184, 195
Johnson, James Turner 189
Jonathan 105
*Joseph* (OT) 49, 53, 64–5, 191
*Joseph* (NT) 120
*Judah* 40, 64, 200
Judd, Daniel K. 80, 96
*Judith* 55–6, 204

Kahn-Fogel, Nicholas A. 141
Kastely, Amy Hilsman 9–12
Keeton, W. Page 9, 13–14, 18, 22, 64
Kent, James 47
King, Martin Luther, Jr. 170
Kirschenbaum, Aaron 87
Klein, Hyman 29
Koch, Klaus 88–9

*Laban* 12, 22, 33
Lacy, Toni 161
LaFave, Wayne R. 89–90, 92, 103, 107, 116
*Lamech* 83, 144
*Leah* 30, 33
Leggett, Donald A. 33, 36–7, 40–1, 43, 64, 201, 210
Levi, Gershon 89

Levine, Baruch A. 40, 44, 68, 79, 86, 91–3, 97
Levinson, Barnard M. 189
Limburg, James 174, 214
Lind, Millard 82, 114
Lipinski, E. 43
Lowenthal, Robin 163
Lytton, Timothy D. 161

Maguire, Daniel C. 174
*Mahlon* 37, 43
Maine, Henry Sumner 51–2
Malchow, Bruce V. 174
Malina, Bruce J. 173, 179
*Manasseh* 106
Mannion, Elizabeth 161–2
Marshall, Christopher D. 54
Marx, Karl 177
Maston, T. B. 74, 174
Mathews, Shailer 212
Matthews, Victor H. 68
May, G. Herbert ix
Mays, James L. 16
McCarter, P. Kyle 16
Medina, Michael 80
Meek, Theophile James 88, 91, 99
Megivern, James J. 80, 86, 113, 154–5
Mendelsohn, Isaac 49
Mendenhall, George E. 89, 150–1
Metzger, Bruce M. ix
*Micah* 69
*Michal* 98
Midgley, Mary 170
Molech 100–1, 120
Moses 29, 46, 69–70, 83, 101, 128, 213
Mount, Eric, J. 216
Muffs, Yochanan 38–9
Muntingh, L. M. 56

*Naboth* 67–8, 140
*Naomi* 36–8, 42–3, 57, 196, 201–2
Napier, B. Davie 47
Nasuti, Harry P. 181
*Nathan* 19, 65–6, 145
Neascu, E. Dana 170
Neuman, Abraham A. 52

## Index of Names

Newman, Louis E. 11, 87, 147, 216
Niebuhr, H. Richard 157–8, 171, 215, 217
Niebuhr, Reinhold 169, 174
Nissim, Joseph 29
*Noah* 122–3, 154, 157
Noonan, John T. Jr. 175
Noth, Martin 128

*Obed* 42–3
Ogletree, Charles J. 163
Ogletree, Thomas W. 168
Olasky, Marvin 168
Olson, Elizabeth 163
*Onan* 40
*Onesimus* 203

Patrick, Dale 14, 41, 48, 199, 209
*Paul* 84, 105, 140, 203
Perillo, Joseph M. 10
Perry, Michael J. 171, 216
*Philemon* 203
Phillips, Anthony 89, 93, 96–7, 113, 142, 147
Pilch, John P. 173, 179
Pope, Marvin 54
Porten, Bezalel 25, 52–3, 55–6
Posner, Richard A. 170, 214
Powers, David S. 29
Pressler, Carolyn 96, 98
Primovatz, Igor 123
Pritchard, James B. 31, 39
Putnam, Constance E. 81, 161

*Rachel* 30, 33
Rackman, Emanuel 52
Radelet, Michael L. 81, 161
*Raguel* 12–13, 35, 38
Rand, Ayn 165, 170, 214–15
*Raphael* 12, 35
Rasor, Paul 11, 168–9, 175, 179, 205
Raspberry, William 161
Rauschenbusch, Walter 212
Rawls, John 170
Recinella, Dale S. 74, 80, 83, 140, 148, 155, 159–60, 163
Redekop, Vernon W. 88

*Reuben* 50, 105
Richardson, Alan 26, 47
Robinson, John 166
Rosenberg, Merker 86–7, 141, 146–7
Rosenberg, Yale L. 86–7, 141, 146–7
Rosett, Arthur 185
Rowley, H. H. 55
Russell, Gregory D. 81
*Ruth* 36–8, 41–3, 196, 201–2, 210–11

Safrai, Shmuel 39
*Sarah, Sarai* 31
*Sarah* (Apoc.) 12, 34–5
Sasson, Jack S. 36, 38, 42
*Saul* 94, 119
Schottroff, Luise 182
Schreiber, Aaron M. 123, 140
Schroer, Silvia 182, 200
Scott, Austin W. 92
Sealey, Raphael 166
Segal, Ben-Zion 89
*Sheshan* 32–3
Shipler, David K. 174
Shriver, Peggy L. 168
Simson, Gary T. 86
Smith, Adam 214
Smith, Morton 68
Snaith, Norman H. 46
*Solomon* 11, 27, 67, 83, 130–1
Sonsino, Rifat 181
Spitz, Elie 87, 126, 141, 147
Stackhouse, Max L. 171
Stassen, Glen H. 80–1, 83, 85, 154
Steffen, Lloyd 81, 163
Stern, Craig A. 132
Stetson, Brad 171
Stone, Michael E. 26
Stulberg, Robert B. 188
Sturm, Douglas 215
*Susanna* 70, 72, 112
Szubin, H.Z. 25, 52–3, 55–6

*Tamar* 40, 64–5, 200–1
Teles, Steven M. 168, 174
Thies, Stanley Carlson 174
Thomas, D. Winton 30, 47, 49
Thompson, Dorothy 32, 40–1, 56

Thompson, Thomas 32, 40–1, 56
Tigay, Jeffrey H. 105
Tilson, Everett 157
*Tobias* 12, 22, 34–5, 38
*Tobit* 22, 34–5, 38
Trible, Phyllis 210

*Uriah* 19, 65, 145

Van den Haag, Ernest 81
Van Selms, A. 55
Van Seters, John 28, 30–1, 39
Vellenga. Jacob J. 80, 85–6
von Rad, Gerhard 30, 32, 41, 99

Ward, Harry M. 166
Watson, Alan 166
Weinfeld, Moshe 166, 186, 209
Weingreen, J. 29, 47, 68
Weinstein, Jack B. 171, 176, 194
Weir, C. J. Mullo 47, 53
Wellhausen, Julius 88, 133
West, Steven A. 81, 141
West, Valerie 160

Westbrook, Raymond 27–8, 34–7, 40, 42, 44–7, 50, 52, 59, 68, 79, 87, 89, 91–2, 98, 104, 117, 121, 146–7, 151, 194, 199
White, Welsh 155
White, William 166
Wicker, Tom 163
Willis, John T. 173
Wilson, John T. 150
Wolfson, Susan A. 177, 215, 217
Wright, Christopher J. H. 14, 59, 174
Wright, Julian H., Jr. 83

Yaron, Reuven 29, 178, 204
Young, Robert L. 157

*Zachaeus* 19
Zakovitch, Yair 208
*Zechariah* 176
*Zedekiah* 209
Zehr, Howard 150
Zeitlin, Solomon 52
*Zelophehad*, daughters 29, 33–5, 46
*Zilpah* 30

# Index of Subjects

adultery 65, 78, 86, 97–9, 103, 121 n.156, 125, 159
  betrothed slave 104, 120, 139
  betrothed virgin 98–9, 120, 125
  married woman 71, 98, 119
  pre-nuptual 97–8
affidavit *see* oaths
affirmative actions and duties 185–218
  care, duty of or to *see under* tort laws
  Levites *see* Levites
  orphans *see* orphans
  persons with disabilities *see* persons with disabilities
  poor *see* poor
  rescue, duty to *see under* tort laws
  sojourners *see* sojourners
allotheism 78, 94, 99–100, 107–11, 119, 121, 125, 137, 158
  *see also under* sacrificial offerings
alternative sentencing 66–7
Ancient Near Eastern laws
  Code of Hammurabi 30 n.14, 39, 49 n.95, 56, 90 n.43, 96 n.65, 146 n.64, 203–4, 208 n.112
  common law 28 n.8, 67–8 & n.13, 87 n.31, 105
  Hittite 49, 94 n.60, 96 n.65, 99 n.74
  Lipit-Ishtar law code 31 nn.16 &17, 49 n.95
  Nuzi 32, 48 n.89, 53 n.112, 56
  Ugaritic 55–6
Anglo-American law 14, 20–1, 26, 116 n.137, 132 n.16, 141 n.48

apostasy 108–9, 121
  *see also* allotheism *and* sacrificial offerings
asylum, place of 129–30
  *see also* cities of refuge *and* horns of the altar
avenger of blood 66, 108, 117 & n.144, 124, 129, 131
avenging kinsman 117, 136
  *see also* avenger of blood *and* kinsman/redeemer

bankruptcy 197 n.71
banishment *see under* criminal penalties
bequests *see* wills
bestiality *see* buggery
biblical law codes 2, 87–8
birthright 26–7, 47–51, 59
blaming the victim 167 & n.10
blasphemy 67 n.11, 69–70, 77, 101–2, 121
blood guilt 117 n.144
  *see also* guilt offering *and* innocent blood
bribes 74, 76
buggery 78, 94, 103, 119
burglary 19 n.40, 92

CC *see* Covenant Code
capital offenses 80–126
  adultery *see* adultery
  allotheism *see* allotheism
  blasphemy *see* blasphemy
  buggery *see* buggery

## Index of Subjects

contempt of court *see under* courts
cursing parents *see under* parents
defenses 92 n.54
excuses 92
homicide *see* homicide *and* murder
homosexual intercourse 104–5, 121
incest *see* incest
intent element *see* intent
kidnapping *see* kidnapping
malicious false testimony *see under* testimony *and* witnesses
mediums *see* mediums
murder *see* murder
sorcery *see* sorcery
striking parents *see under* parents
wizardry *see* wizards
working on the sabbath 76
worship of other gods *see* allotheism *and* sacrificial offerings
capital punishment *see* death penalty
case law *see* precedent
children 10, 100–1, 158
   as slaves 209–11
   *see also* daughters, parents, *and* sons
Christian ethics 1, 212
cities of refuge 108, 117, 128–33, 135, 149–50, 160
civil law 3, 7–59
   *see* contract law
   *see* inheritance *and* wills
   *see* tort law
civil rights 168 n.15
collateral 10–11, 178–9, 183
commercial practices 179
commonwealth 167
community 102–6, 111–12, 199, 216 n.18
compassion 4–5, 10–11, 16, 21, 110, 179, 181, 185 n.43, 186, 208, 216
compensation *see under* tort law
concubines 30 n.13, 50, 55, 105 n.101, 210
conspiracy 139–40
Constitution, U.S. 73, 140 n.44, 212
   General Welfare Clause 167
consumer protection 179

contempt of court *see under* courts
contract law 9–14, 21–2
   agreement 9, 12, 13, 21–2
   bailment 14, 19
   breach 12–14, 19
   consideration 11
   creditors 10–11
   damages 9
   duress 12
   fraud 11–12
   labor 11–13, 22
   marriage 13
   misrepresentation 12
   offer and acceptance 12
   pledges 10
   seals 13
   unconscionable 10 n.3, 22
courts 70–2
   contempt of *see* court orders
   court orders, refusal to obey 112, 125, 159
   the "gate" 96, 135, 200
   *see also* judges
covenant
   horizontal dimension 96, 102–6
   vertical dimension 99–102
   with Noah 217 n.23
Covenant Code (CC) 2, 74, 89–95
   organization of laws 15–20
criminal law 61–4
criminal offenses 61–2
criminal penalties
   banishment 83, 100 n.81, 119 n.152
   fine 98, 143 n.66
   flogging 152
   *lex talionis* 146–51
      intentional false testimony 148, 158
      mayhem 148–9
      pregnant married women, injury to 147–8, 158
   mitigation of 66–7, 83, 94
   offender only 144–6
   proportionate to offense 149 n.78, 152
   whipping 78, 98

criminal penalties (*Cont'd*)
   see also alternative sentencing, death penalty, *and* sentencing guidelines
Critical Legal Studies 170 & n.24
cross examination 67, 70–1 n.139, 138–9
cult shrines 102, 106–7, 112, 130
custody 69–70, 101, 115

D *see* Deuteronomic Code
daughters 54–5, 97, 105–6, 209–11
   see also inheritance by
   priest's daughters 105–6, 121
death penalty 69, 80–126
   see also capital offenses
   biblical rationales for 122–6
   opponents 86, 153–7
   proponents 80–2, 86–7, 153–7
debtors 10, 22, 197 n.71
Decalogue *see* Ten Commandments
defamation 139, 142 n.49
deterrence 125–6
Deuteronomic Code 2, 95–9, 194
Deuteronomic Historian 84, 106, 132, 194
Deuteronomic Reform 99, 100 n.80, 102, 106–7, 110, 113, 121, 131, 189–90, 194
development of laws 87, 88 n.34, 207–9
   see also modification of laws
discrimination *see* impartial judgment
distributive justice *see under* justice
divorce 120 n.153, 211 n.122
due process 127–52
   cities of refuge *see* cities of refuge, asylum, *and* horns of the altar
   diligent inquiry as to facts 134–9, 159–60, 162
      explicit procedures 135–9
      implicit procedures 134–5
   equal protection *see* equal protection
   evidence *see* evidence
   fundamental fairness 129
   hearing 129–30, 134–9
   notice 127–8
   witnesses *see* witnesses
   see also protecting innocent accused

elders *see under* judges
*Elohim* 4
ephod *see* lot
equal justice 175–84
   see also equal protection
equal protection 73–9, 159, 163
   equal liability 77
   *lex talionis see lex talionis*
   protected classes 75–9, 168 n.15
      the poor 75–6, 163, 176–80
      resident aliens *or* sojourners 76–8, 163–4, 176, 180–2
      servants 183–4
      slaves 79
      widows *and* orphans 176, 182–3
      women 78
   see also women, legal status of
   see also affirmative actions/duties
evidence
   circumstantial 139, 162
   physical 64–5 & n.5, 115–16, 134–7, 206–7
   presentation at trial 64–5n.5, 134–5
   virginity, tokens of 78 n.15, 120, 136–7
execution
   innocent persons 159–64
   methods of 68, 70, 86, 115, 125, 156 n.31
   only the guilty 159–64
exile 66
   see also banishment and fugitive
exploitation 11, 178–9, 196
   see also profiteering
*ex post facto* 70, 160 n.58

false charges 74, 160
   see also under testimony *and* witnesses
false prophecy *see under* prophecy
feast of booths 188–90
feast of weeks 188–90
Fifth Commandment 93

*Index of Subjects* 239

*Fiftieth Year see* Jubilee year
finality *see* lot
food banks 193
foreseeable harm. *see under* tort laws
forgiveness 82, 85, 197 n.71
fraud *see under* contract law
freedom of speech 69, 110
fugitive 82–3
fugitive slave law 203–4

general welfare 167, 194, 202
gleaning 186–8, 201
*ger, gerim see* sojourners
*go'el see* kinsman/redeemer
goring ox 91–2, 120, 147 n.66, 158
guilt of bloodshed 108

H *see* Holiness Code
handicap access 184
harlotry *see* prostitution
henotheism 215
*herem* 46 n.82, 110–11
hired workers *see* servants
Holiness Code 2, 99–106
holy 106
homicide 89–90, 102–3, 107–8
  culpable negligence 91, 107 n.111
  intentional 89, 108
  negligent 90–2 *see also*
    manslaughter
  premeditated 89, 158
  reckless 90–2, 107–8, 160
  self-defense defense 92 n.52
  *see also* murder
homosexual intercourse 104–5, 121
horns of the altar 130–1
  *see also* asylum *and* cities of refuge
human life, value of 157–9, 164
  image of God 122–3, 154, 157–8

idolatry *see* allotheism *and* sacrificial
    offerings
impartial judgment 73–9
  *see also* equal protection
incest 104–5, 121, 159
indentured servitude 207–8

individualism 167
inheritance 26–51, 57
  birthright *see* birthright
  by daughters 33–5, 59
    daughters of Zelophehad 28, 33, 35
  by slaves 32–3, 56
  by sons 28–33
  by sons-in-law 34–5, 38, 57
  by widows 26–9, 35–40, 57–8
  disinheritance 31 & n.16
  distribution by "the prince" 46–7
  houses and land 37–9
  inheritable property 27–8, 35–9
  and levirate marriage *see* levirate
    marriage
innocent blood 72, 108, 131–2, 135 n.28, 160
  guilt of 124–5, 132
innocent until proven guilty 72
intent 116, 128, 159–60, 164
inter-vivos gifts 51–6, 58
intestate succession 29, 33–4
  *see also* inheritance
Islamic law 29 n.12, 49 n.91, 172 n.28
Israel *see* Northern Kingdom

Jerusalem Temple 68–9, 106–7, 113–14, 131–2, 189–90
  *see also* Deuteronomic Reform
Jewish ethics 1, 87 n.29, 212
Jewish law 29 n.12, 52 nn. 107 & 108, 75 n.6, 87 n.29, 115 n.134, 141 n.47, 174, 177 n.9, 185 n.43
Jubilee year 44–7, 59, 193–4, 196, 198–9
Judah *see* Southern Kingdom
Judah and Tamar, trial scene 64–5
judges 138
  David as judge 65–7
  Deborah as 73 n.1
  discretion of 92
  elders as judges 69–72, 96 n.66, 136, 200
  priests as judges 45 n.81, 138
  Solomon as judge 67

judges (*Cont'd*)
  YHWH or God as judge 74–5, 84–5, 94 n.61, 100–1, 121, 143, 158, 161, 182
juries 68–9, 71, 133 n.22, 135–6
jurisprudence
  biblical 160–1
  modern 69, 116 n.137, 214–16
justice 4, 21, 74, 175–8
  distributive 166
  divine 74–5 *see also* under judges
  impartial *see* impartial judgment *and* equal protection

kidnapping 93, 95–6, 118–19, 125, 159
kinsman/redeemer 40–4, 183, 196–8, 201–2, 210

laissez-faire 167
law and economics theory 214
*levir see* levirate marriage
levirate marriage 40–3, 57 n.136, 58, 64, 199–202
Levites 113–14, 122, 133, 166, 189–91
Levitical priests 138
*llex talionis* 17, 77–8, 90–1, 112, 135, 154–5
loans 11
  interest on 11, 178 n.15
LORD, the 4
lot 101 n.86, 138 n.37

malicious false testimony *see under* testimony
malicious false witnesses *see under* witnesses
malicious prosecution 67–8
manslaughter 107–8, 115–18, 160
manslayer 102, 124 n.168
marriage 42 n.63
  contracts 13
  daughters of Zelophehad 46
  inheritance 42–3
  levirate *see* levirate marriage
Mayflower Compact 166–7
mayhem 102 n.89

mediums 78, 94, 100, 119
  *see also* sorceresses and wizards
mercy 85, 110
  *see also* compassion
migrant workers *see* sojourners
miscarriage 17, 91, 147 n.66
modification of laws 102–4, 117–22
  *see also* development of laws
Moloch 77, 100
  *see also* sacrificial offerings
moral relativism 169–70
mothers 67, 96, 136
  surrogate motherhood 30–1, 43
motive clauses 181, 187 & n.27, 197
  as to slaves 187
  as to sojourners 181–2
  supporting indigent "brother" 197
murder 108, 118, 156
  attempted 108
  first degree 89 n.38, 154–5
  second degree 89–90 & n,39, 116 n.140
  *see also* homicide

Ninth Commandment 142
normative language 199
Northern Kingdom (Israel) 2, 106, 110 n.118, 113

oaths 19–20, 139, 143 n.54, 191
open housing 204
oppression, laws against 178–84, 204
  *see also* exploitation
orphans 182–3, 186–7, 189–92

P *see* priestly tradition
PC ee Priestly Code
parables 11, 13, 19 n.41, 47 n.87, 50, 54
parents
  authority of 96–7
  cursing 78, 93, 103, 119, 159
  honor due to 93, 185
  striking 78, 93, 120, 159
  surrogate 30–2, 58, 201–2
  testimony by 96–7, 136, 141
perjury 112 n.125, 139–40, 143

## Index of Subjects

Persian Empire 113
persons with disabilities 184
Plymouth Colony 166–7
poor 166–79, 186–99
  exemptions or privileges 179–80
  hostility to 167–8 n.12
  impartial judgment for *see* equal protection
  provisions for needs of 166–8
    food 186–94
    other 194–9
precedent 68–70
presumptions 20, 98–9, 120, 137 n.36
  innocence of accused 72, 104, 135
  irrebuttable 91, 98–9, 115–16
Priestly Code (PC) 2, 77, 112–17, 133
Priestly tradition (P) 2
priests 113
  Aaron as father of 114
  High Priest, death of 117, 124
  as judges *see* judges
  prerogatives of 114, 122
primogeniture 51
profiteering 197
  *see also* exploitation
progressive taxes or fees 180
property
  *see* contracts
  damage to (*see* tort law)
  Jubilee laws 44–7
    *see also* Jubilee Year
  kinsman or redeemer of
    *see* kinsman/redeemer
  land or "real" property 44
    not sold in perpetuity 44
  slaves as 79, 149 n.72, 202
  transfer of 25–59
    *see also* inheritance *and* wills
  women as owners of 37–40
    *see also* women, legal status
prophecy
  false 108–9, 111, 121
  in name of other gods 111, 121
prophets 1, 69, 76, 83, 109, 180, 213
prosecutorial misconduct 148 n.70, 155

prostitution 64–5, 105–6, 121
protected classes *see* under equal protection
protecting innocent accused 72, 75, 128, 135
  *see also* due process
punishment
  entire families 144–5
  limited to offending persons 145–6
  subsequent generations 145–6
  *see also* criminal penalties, death penalty, execution, *lex talionis*, sentencing guidelines, and vengeance
purging or purifying the land 123–5

RD *see* Ritual Decalogue
RDC *see* Revised Deuteronomic Code
radical empiricism 170
radical monotheism 217–18
ransom 17, 91–2 & n.49, 117 n.144, 123–4, 117 n.144, 147 n.66, 151
rape 64–5 n.5, 71, 98, 105
*rechem* 19 n.12
  *see also* compassion *and* mercy
refugees *see* sojourners
relational value theory 199
religious shrines *see* cult shrines
repentance 85
resident aliens *see* Sojourners
restitution *see under* tort laws
revenge *see* vengeance
Revised Deuteronomic Code (RDC) 2, 100–12, 131
rights
  conjugal 210–11 & n.121
  gleaning *see* gleaning
  human 171–2
  of the poor 76 n.7, 177
  property 179, 185
  of slaves 204–5
Ritual Decalogue (RD) 2, 88–9

sabbath
  observance of 70
  rest for sojourners 181, 203

sabbath (*Cont'd*)
  rest for workers or servants  183, 203
  violations of  70, 115
Sabbatical year  59 n.142, 192–3, 203
sacrificial offerings
  to other gods  94, 95 n.62, 119, 121, 158
  guilt offerings  21, 104
    Canaanite  106–7
    Moloch  100–1, 120–1
  to YHWH  95, 106–7
  *see also* allotheism
safety laws  21, 23
"safety net"  215, 218
sanctuaries  102, 130
  *see also* asylum, cities of refuge, cult shrines *and* horns of the altar
self-defense  92 n.152
self-interest as basis for ethics  142, 170, 214–15
sentencing guidelines  144, 160–1
servants  183–4
  indentured *see* indentured servants
  wages  183–4
  *see also* under protected classes
Seventh Commandment  97
  *see also* adultery
sexual assault *see* rape
Shiloh  69
Sixth Commandment  82–3, 154
slaves  79, 104, 139, 149 n.72
  "brother" sells self as  197, 202
  daughters sold as  209–11
  debt slaves  205
  escaped slaves  181, 203–4
  fugitive *see* escaped slaves
  Hebrew  202–11
  humane treatment of  203–4
  manumission  204, 209 n.114
  as property  79, 202
  providing for when freed  208
  time or term of servitude  205, 210
  wives and children  202, 206–8
social contract theory  170, 214
social Darwinism  167
social ethics  1, 173–4, 185, 211–13
social legislation  164, 165–218

*see also* social welfare laws *and* welfare legislation
social welfare laws  173–211
sojourners  76–8, 163, 180–2, 186–92
sons
  inheritance by *see under* inheritance
  ungovernable  96–7, 120, 125, 159
sorceresses  78
sorcery  94
Southern Kingdom (Judah)  2, 13, 106, 110 n.118
strangers *see* sojourners
Susanna, trial scene  70–2

tabernacle *see* tent of meeting
Talmud  39 n.37, 115 n.134, 140 n.43, 141 n.47, 212
Temple *see* Jerusalem Temple
Ten Commandments  82, 89, 103, 139
tent of meeting  114 n.131
testation *see* wills
testimony
  by parents  136, 141
  defendant  68, 136
  malicious false  111, 142
  *see also* under witnesses
  *see also* oaths
Third Commandment  142, 143 n.54
Third Year tithe  190–3
tort laws  14–21, 22–4
  bailees  24
  Book of Exodus  15–21, 23
  breach of trust  19, 23
  burglary  92
  conversion  19, 23
  damage to property  14–15, 18–21, 24
  damages *see under* Remedies
  duty of care  22
  duty to rescue  20–1
  embezzlement *see* conversion
  foreseeable harm  18, 20–3, 91
  injuries to animals  18–20
  injuries to persons  14–18, 21, 23
  intentional torts  14, 19, 23
  negligence  18, 20, 23
    culpable  18
  proximate cause  22

## Index of Subjects

reckless endangerment 14, 17, 23–4, 116
remedies 14, 17, 23
  compensation 14, 16–18, 20, 22–3, 91–2, 146, 147 n.65
  multiple damages 14, 19, 23
  no fault 18, 24
  punitive 14, 21, 23–4
  restitution 14, 18–21, 23–4
  theft 19, 23
treason 47 n.87, 67–8, 140 n.45
trials 63–72

ungovernable sons *see under* sons
utilitarian theory 215

vengeance 83–4, 144
violence 157 n.33
vulnerable persons 92 n.52, 165–6, 168–9, 175-84, 199, 216 n.18, 218

wages 12, 183–4
welfare for the wealthy 195 n.66
welfare legislation 165–218
widows 35–40, 182–3, 186–92
  inheritance by *see under* inheritance
  levirate marriage *see* levirate marriage
wildlife 192
wills 25–6, 51–9
  Abraham's 52
  devisees or beneficiaries 55–6
  double portions 48–51, 53
  first-born sons 49
  Jacob's 49, 53
  Jehoshaphat's 53
  Job's 53–5
  Judith's 55–6
  son of the disliked wife 48–9
wisdom writings 85
  *see also Proverbs and Sirach in biblical citations index*
witnesses 139–44
  cross examination 71
  duty to testify 143–4
  first to throw stones 86, 137, 143, 163
  malicious false 67–8, 71–2, 111–12, 121–2, 125, 138–9, 142, 155, 163
  minimum number required 68–9, 71–2, 140–1, 162–3
  sequestration 71, 139, 141
wizards 78, 100, 119
  penalty for consulting 100
women, legal status of 55, 64–5, 67, 71, 78, 96 & n.67, 99, 136, 141, 200 & n.86, 207, 210–11 & n.121
"workfare" 180
worship of other gods *see* allotheism *and* sacrificial offerings

Yahwist court history 130
YHWH 4

Zelophehad, daughters *see under* inheritance *and* marriage